Money in Britain

Money in Britain

Monetary Policy, Innovation and Europe

Michael J. Artis
University of Manchester

Mervyn K. Lewis
University of Nottingham

Philip Allan
New York · London · Toronto · Sydney · Tokyo · Singapore

First published 1991 by
Philip Allan
66 Wood Lane End, Hemel Hempstead
Hertfordshire HP2 4RG
A division of
Simon & Schuster International Group

Typeset in 10/12 pt Times
by Keyset Composition, Colchester, UK

Printed and bound in Great Britain
BPCC Wheatons Ltd, Exeter.

British Library Cataloguing in Publication Data

Artis, M. J.
 Money in Britain: monetary policy, innovation and
 Europe.
 I. Title   II. Lewis, M. K.
 336.3

 ISBN 0-8600-3073-3
 ISBN 0-8600-3176-4 pbk

---

1 2 3 4 5   95 94 93 92 91

Contents

Preface   **xi**

1   Background to monetary policy   **1**
   1.1   The new environment of monetary policy   1
   1.2   Changes in British banking   7

2   Monetary systems   **22**
   2.1   Monetary standards   22
   2.2   The gold standard   27
   2.3   Bretton Woods   38
   2.4   The international non-system?   45

3   Inflation in the United Kingdom   **51**
   3.1   The era of 'inflation first'   51
   3.2   Non-monetary studies of inflation   58
   3.3   Money and prices   72

4   The demand for money   **78**
   4.1   Theories of the demand for money   79
   4.2   Estimating money demand   83
   4.3   Principal research findings   90
   4.4   Monetary disequilibrium and buffer stock models   102

5   The transmission mechanism of monetary policy   **112**
   5.1   The theory of economic policy   112
   5.2   Transmission mechanisms   116
   5.3   Intermediate target variables   127

6   Controlling the monetary aggregates   **135**
   6.1   Bank intermediation   138
   6.2   Direct methods of monetary control   148
   6.3   Money supply identity approaches   154
   6.4   The monetary base debate revisited   164

7   Control of interest rates   **173**
   7.1   The Bank and the money market   175
   7.2   Funding and overfunding   184
   7.3   The effects of interest rate policy   188

8   Exchange rate management and the EMS   **197**
   8.1   The exchange rate in the transmission mechanism 198
   8.2   The exchange rate as an intermediate target   202
   8.3   UK exchange rate policies in the 1980s   207
   8.4   The European Monetary System   216
   8.5   The United Kingdom and the EMS   232

9   Change in the financial sector   **239**
   9.1   International banking and financial integration 241
   9.2   Securitization   247
   9.3   Currency substitution and policy coordination   253
   9.4   Banking, deregulation and monetary policy   258
   9.5   Monetary policy and the balance of payments   263

10   The future of money in Britain   **270**
   10.1   Monetary systems and inflation control   270
   10.2   The external discipline of the EMS   277
   10.3   European Monetary Union   283
   10.4   From EMS to EMU   290
   10.5   Alternative monetary standards?   295

References   **305**
Subject index   **323**
Author index   **331**

List of figures

1.1   Liabilities of banking groups, 1955–79   13
1.2   The offshore/onshore differential (3-month Eurosterling–
      3-month local authority loans)   19

2.1   Prices in Britain: the historical record, 1290–1988   31

3.1   Inflation (CPI, GDP deflator), 1970–89   59
3.2   The Phillips Curve (1971–89)   60
3.3   Relative producer prices, 1970–89   65
3.4   Annual rates of change in prices and wages   67
3.5   Partial hysteresis in the natural rate   70
3.6   Inflation and monetary growth, 1971–89   74

4.1   A buffer stock model   81
4.2   Interest rates and the demand for money, 1920–83   92
4.3   M3 velocity, 1963–88   100

5.1   Two models of the transmission mechanism   120
5.2   The transmission of monetary policy   126

6.1   Relationships among monetary aggregates and their
      components   137
6.2   Increases in £M3, bank lending and the PSBR, 1979–88   162

7.1   Interest rate determination in the money market under
      different reserves regimes   177
7.2   United Kingdom: money market interest rates   180

7.3   Funding the PSBR   186

8.1   The open economy under global monetarism   201
8.2   Exchange rate and monetary targets   203
8.3   The sterling/DM exchange rate   215
8.4   Sterling's effective limits in the ERM 22 October 1990   220
8.5   Exchange rate realignments   225
8.6   Competitiveness 1979–88: normalized unit labour costs   229

9.1   Comparison of on- and off-balance sheet banking   251
9.2   Models of currency substitution   255
9.3   Ratio of foreign currency deposits held by residents to M3,
       1975 Q1 – 1988 Q3   257
9.4   Internal and external balance under international financial
       laissez-faire   267

10.1   Inflation in the UK and the ERM   278

List of tables

1.1 Retail prices and wages in Britain, 1300–1990   3
1.2 UK balance sheet of British deposit banks, 1880–1988   9

2.1 Classification of monetary systems   25

3.1 Proximate accounting for inflation in the UK, 1970/1–1987/8   61
3.2 Price–cost interrelationships, 1980   64
3.3 Wage inflation 1978–89   71
3.4 Money to prices: a direct relationship   75

4.1 Summary of selected studies of the long-run demand for money in the UK   91
4.2 Summary of selected studies of the short-run demand for money in the UK   94

6.1 Monetary targets, indicative ranges and out-turns for the MTFSI   136
6.2 Maturity analysis of British non-retail banks in sterling and foreign currencies by class of business, as at February 1980   144
6.3 Maturity analysis of sterling and foreign currency business with non-bank customers of retail and wholesale banks in Britain, as at end-January, 1987   145
6.4 Various aspects of sterling business of UK banks, February 1980   149
6.5 A simplified flow-of-funds account   157
6.6 Counterparts to the increase in £M3, 1979–89, £ million   161

7.1 Comparative model responses to a temporary 2-point cut in
short-term interest rates   192
7.2 Effects of a temporary (2-year) interest rate increase (+2
points) in NIESR model 11   193

8.1 The exchange rate–price–wage pass through in NI Model 11:
a 10% depreciation   209
8.2 Design of the MTFS: extracts from the Financial Statement
and Budget Report   212
8.3 Content of the MTFS   213
8.4 ECU valuation (EEC calculation) at 15 October 1990   217
8.5 Central rates and intervention margins (as of 8 October 1990) 219
8.6 ERM parity realignments   224

9.1 Measures of international bank lending and the Eurocurrency
market as at end of year, 1977–89   242
9.2 Private and government sector imbalances and the current
account, 1989   264

10.1 Comparison of different monetary systems   273

Preface

This book was conceived as a new edition of our earlier book *Monetary Control in the United Kingdom*, which was written with the 1981 reforms of the monetary system much in mind. Developments since that time have proved so momentous, however, that despite the fact that *Monetary Control* was as up to date as we could make it at the time of writing, and took account of the 1981 watershed, a completely new treatment seemed called for. This is what we have tried to provide in the current volume, whose wider scope is reflected in the title. Obviously we have to leave it to our readers to judge the success of our efforts.

The book has been in gestation for several years and draws to some extent upon our (separate) writings. Thus we have inevitably incurred numerous debts of gratitude. One of us (Michael Artis) held a Houblon–Norman Fellowship at the Bank of England and officials there were most generous with their time in commenting upon drafts of many of the chapters. Among them we particularly acknowledge Bill Allen, Roger Clews, Phil Davis, Bill Easton, Don Eggington, Stephen Hall, Brian Henry and Joe Wilcox. Michael Foot assisted with Chapter 7. They cannot, of course – nor can the Bank of England – be held responsible for anything we say. Kevin Dowd in Nottingham, Phil Lawler in Manchester and Robert Wallace in Adelaide (Flinders) were also generous with their time in commenting upon particular chapters, though again they cannot be held responsible for the final results.

As the scene of production moved between Manchester, the Bank of England and Nottingham, we incurred additional debts of gratitude to an army of patient secretaries – including Jill Brown at Nottingham and Lisa McDonald at the Bank of England; in Manchester, Hilary Thornton and Chantay Cole bore the brunt of the work, with additional assistance from Sue Massey, Kay Sanders, Janet Edgar and Anna Espley.

Finally, we thank our publishers in the persons of Philip Allan and Peter Johns for their encouragement and patience.

1

Background to monetary policy

1.1 The new environment of monetary policy

Some remarkable changes have taken place in the British banking system, in its regulatory framework and in the conduct of monetary policy in recent times. It is possible, also, to insist that there is much that is of a continuing nature. Control of interest rates in the 'money market' – described by the Governor of the Bank of England in 1987 as 'the single instrument of monetary policy'[1] – has been central to British monetary policy for over 150 years: *plus ça change, plus c'est la même chose*. But while it is true that some aspects of monetary policy have changed only to be changed back again (such as policy towards fixed exchange rates), there have been a number of changes which seem more permanent in their nature – in particular, the globalization of financial services, the development of the European Community (EC) and the array of innovations introduced into the financial sector through the impact of new financial technologies.

Admittedly, it is in the nature of things for each generation to suppose that it is passing through a unique period of change and tackling unique problems. There is one respect in which the supposition is justified for the past twenty years, and that is in the nature of the international monetary system. The distinctive characteristics of the present system and the implications which they carry for the prosecution of national monetary policies have not received the attention that they deserve.

The outstanding feature of present monetary arrangements concerns the determination of the value of money. In the past, the value of the internal currency was intrinsic or was maintained in a fixed or nearly fixed relationship to a monetary substance or some other external standard of value. For example, in the issue of William the Conqueror, a 'pound' referred to a pound of silver, so that its purchasing power was governed by the price of silver. Later, in 1816 and again in 1925, the value of the pound sterling was laid down as a specific weight of fine gold (113 grains) to which the value of sterling was to be kept equal. After the Second World War, national currencies were maintained at a fixed rate of exchange relative to the US dollar, itself backed by a gold commitment. That all changed in 1971.

The significance of that change has been characterized by Milton Friedman (1986):

> The world's current monetary system is, I believe, unprecedented. No major currency has any link to a commodity. What economists call outside money consists entirely of government fiat in the form of paper currency, minor coin, and book keeping entries such as deposits at US Federal Reserve Banks. The major earlier episodes in which governments departed from a specie standard and issued irredeemable paper money were expected to be temporary, and most of them were. The others ended in disaster, as in the hyperinflations after World Wars I and II. They were followed by monetary reforms that restored some relation between the currency and a commodity. Only since President Nixon ended Bretton Woods by closing the gold window on August 15, 1971, have the United States and all other major countries explicitly adopted monetary systems in which there is no link to a commodity and no commitment to restoring such a link. (p. 643)

The period since 1971 is by no means the first time that the link between major national currencies and a commodity base has been severed. And not all such periods have been inflationary. During the 1930s much of the world employed money which had no commodity value, was not convertible into a monetary substance or into a currency which was convertible, and which had no immediate prospect of convertibility; yet the money of many countries did maintain its value as successfully as when it had been based on a commodity. Moreover, it can be argued that the closing of the US 'gold window' in 1971 was simply part of the same evolution that was already giving rise to a gathering inflationary momentum in the late 1960s and would result in the explosion of the 1970s – that the departure from gold was symptomatic of these inflationary tendencies rather than the reverse. But there can be little doubt of the symbolic significance of the break as the culmination of a long evolution and because the years since 1971 are the first, as Friedman says, in which there has been no solid prospect or serious political intention of restoring convertibility.

It is a matter of record that, worldwide, the years since 1971 have been ones of high inflation, and that is especially the case for Britain. Maintenance of the value of money is not the only referent for British monetary policy at present: the state of the balance of payments and output growth and unemployment can scarcely be ignored. Nevertheless, the figures in Table 1.1 do underscore the argument of some economists that it is simply not sufficient to give central banks a mandate to 'do good'; some new monetary standard or monetary constitution may be needed to substitute for the long-run price stability which commodity-based money provided.

What should be the standard for monetary policy? When Sir Dennis Robertson asked this question in 1928 he conceded that the question had little immediacy, because people were attached to the 'mythology' of gold and monetary orthodoxy. By 1945 the mystique of gold had still not gone and was carried through into the Bretton Woods system, which required members to define their currency in terms of a fixed weight of gold or to adhere to a stable exchange rate with the US dollar, which was convertible into gold. Since 1971 circumstances have been such that the question is a meaningful one at least for the leading industrial countries. Domestic interest rates, incomes and prices in the countries, or groups of countries, issuing inconvertible paper money need no longer be subjected

Table 1.1   Retail prices and wages in Britain, 1300–1990 (compounded annual growth rates)

	Retail prices (per cent p.a.)	Money wages (per cent p.a.)
1300–1400	0.16	0.35
1400–1500	−0.09	0.18
1500–1600	1.59	0.70
1600–1700	0.27	0.46
1700–1800	0.68	0.64
1800–1900	−0.28	0.63
1900–1910	0.94	0.27
1910–1920	10.15	11.61
1920–1930	−4.46	−4.48
1930–1940	1.53	1.84
1940–1950	2.33	4.94
1950–1960	4.05	5.41
1960–1970	4.06	5.06
1970–1980	13.68	15.56
1980–1990	6.55	8.84

Sources:

Phelps-Brown and Hopkins, 'Seven centuries of building wages', *Economica*, August 1955.
Phelps-Brown and Hopkins, 'Seven centuries of the prices of consumables, compared with builders' wage rates', *Economica*, November 1956.
Mitchell and Deane, *Abstract of British Historical Statistics*, Cambridge University Press, 1962.
CSO, *Economic Trends*, Annual Supplement, 1982 edition and February 1991.

to pressures calculated to make them conform to a predetermined exchange rate relationship or gold parity. A fiduciary or fiat monetary system makes an independent policy possible; however, that independence does not in itself indicate what policy ought to be pursued.

The purely fiduciary character of national moneys is most readily apparent in the case of two major currencies, the US dollar and the Japanese yen, and for other leading currencies such as the Swiss franc, the Canadian dollar, and the Australian dollar (until October 1990 the pound sterling belonged in this grouping). The currencies have no fixed external reference point and the central banks of these countries do not exchange the domestic money at a fixed price in terms of some other currency or grouping of currencies. If such countries are to achieve price stability then they do so by means of *internal stabilization*. Internal stabilization of the value of money requires that monetary policies are used to keep the purchasing power of a country's money reasonably stable in terms of goods and services on domestic markets. This was the policy pursued by Britain, with only limited success, during the 1980s. Where the desired path for domestic prices differs from that of other major countries, exchange rate flexibility is needed to separate domestic from international prices.

Matters are different for those numerous smaller countries which have chosen to peg their currencies to one of the major industrial countries, mostly to the US dollar, or to a basket of the currencies of the leading countries, so choosing *external stabilization*. External stabilization involves fixing the value of money in terms of foreign moneys (or some other external object); there is a direct link between the macroeconomic behaviour of the domestic economy and that of the country to which it is pegged which precludes the taking of independent, national policies for internal stabilization of prices. By opting for external stabilization, a country forgoes its monetary autonomy and effectively delegates to the major country the responsibility for its inflation performance.

For the member countries of the European Monetary System (EMS) adherence to the Exchange Rate Mechanism (ERM), whereby the currencies are aligned to each other within predetermined bands (either 4.5 or 12 per cent wide), a different result ensues. Viewed as a semi-fixed exchange rate system, countries retain some ability to pursue internal stabilization of incomes and prices differently from other members of the Community. As realignments within the system become less frequent and countries move from broad to narrow parity bands, inflation rates can be expected to converge to the Community average as monetary policies within the Community are harmonized. If the system operates symmetrically, that inflation performance will depend jointly on the monetary policies of the member countries. If, however, countries take the monetary policies of Germany as their norm, there will be convergence to the German rate of inflation. Such convergence is tantamount to a policy of external stabilization by the other Community countries, but this means that Germany itself must practise internal stabilization by maintaining policies which keep the internal purchasing power of the Deutschmark stable.

When the members of the European Community proceed on to monetary union, the inflation rate in the Community countries will be governed by the policies followed by the money-issuing authority, the European central bank. It must presumably follow a policy of internal stabilization for the Community as a whole. Conceivably, the European central bank could, as an alternative, link the single European currency to the US dollar or yen or could adopt some other external link (such as to a commodity base); however, these options seem unlikely.

Thus the question of the appropriate monetary standard remains an issue for the member countries of the European Community. A monetary constitution for an integrated Europe has yet to be devised. And while the rate of inflation in Germany (at an average 3 per cent per annum during the 1980s) has been low in comparison with the inflation rate of many other countries, it has not been long-run price stability of the sort which existed under earlier international monetary systems.

Chapter 2 explores the nature of the present international monetary system of fiduciary moneys, examines how it differs from earlier arrangements, and considers the issues involved in the choice of a monetary standard. The terms monetary system, monetary standard and monetary mechanism need to be clarified. A monetary system embraces a number of different types of money. Even within a particular country there has rarely if ever been only one form of money used. In the past gold, silver and bank notes and deposits have coexisted; at present coinage, paper money, central bank money and credit money of banks and other institutions are involved. Use of the word system to describe this complex implies that there are definite relations of value between various moneys. A 'monetary system' refers to this organic whole: that is, as the set of policies and/or arrangements carried out by and through the monetary institutions which constitute the whole. An examination of different monetary systems, then, compares the alternative arrangements for monetary management. By a 'monetary standard' we mean the criterion or reference point guiding these social arrangements. A study of the 'monetary mechanism' deals with the ways in which the various elements of the system interact and operate, and hence with the processes which can enable achievement of the standard.

Chapter 3 focuses specifically upon the determination of prices, for a fiat money system has important implications for the process of inflation.

Milton Friedman's statement 'inflation is always and everywhere a monetary phenomenon' is so often quoted and is now so well known that it is easy to overlook that inflation need not be a monetary phenomenon and has the potential to be so only in a fiat money system. When money either is a commodity or has a value tied to a commodity, inflation is ultimately a story of fluctuations in the prices of goods in general relative to that other commodity. In that sense, inflation under a commodity standard might be seen to be a *real* matter, not a monetary one. With the universal adoption of independent paper money since 1971, there is at least the precondition for inflation to be a monetary phenomenon. Yet in the standard explanations of inflation in the United Kingdom, money is often almost, and sometimes entirely, absent. That apparent paradox is considered in the chapter.

The remaining chapters of the book are concerned broadly with the monetary mechanisms: in particular, with the way monetary policies influence the economy. Successive chapters examine the demand for money (Chapter 4), alternative views of the transmission mechanism of monetary policy (Chapter 5), the control of the money supply aggregates (Chapter 6), and the institutional processes by which the Bank of England seeks control over interest rates (Chapter 7). Our emphasis in these chapters is upon policy processes in the present environment and upon current policy issues, not so much upon providing an episodal account of monetary policy. Nevertheless, we trace over the decade of the 1980s a clear switch from the monetary aggregates to the exchange rate as a target of policy which eventually culminated in Britain's decision in October 1990 to join the Exchange Rate Mechanism of the European Monetary System and, by implication, to participate more fully in the process of European integration. Chapter 8 examines the elevation of the exchange rate in British monetary policy and the workings of the EMS.

A switch of this kind from internal stabilization to external stabilization does limit the ability of the adherent to undertake independently monetary policies for internal stability, but need necessitate no major alterations to existing institutions. However, institutions have changed in response to other developments – financial technology, integration of markets, securitization and deregulation – and Chapter 9 explores these changes and the implications for monetary policy. We argue that in the new environment the long-standing dichotomy in policy circles between internal balance and external balance may no longer provide a useful framework for policy formulation. A further theme – which runs through several chapters of the book – is that the previously clear-cut dividing lines between banks and other financial institutions and markets are blurred and that in consequence what can be thought of as the 'control core' of the monetary system has shrunk. Our argument here is a simple one, yet to our knowledge it has not been made elsewhere and it is at some variance with received theory and monetarist policy prescriptions (as reflected in Friedman's writings). Furthermore, it offers a ready rationale for the authorities' present market operations.

While Britain's full entry into the European Monetary System does not require major institutional change, progression to European Monetary Union (EMU) would transform monetary arrangements in Britain. Chapter 10 focuses upon these issues and compares the inflation control associated with alternative monetary systems, so linking up with the question of the monetary standard posed at the beginning of this chapter.

What follows in the rest of this chapter is a background briefing on changes in the British monetary system, some of which covers ground treated in the precursor to this volume, *Monetary Control in the United Kingdom*, published in 1981.

1.2 Changes in British banking

Monetary policy is not independent of institutional arrangements; it both influences and is influenced by the evolution of the banking and financial system. As the financial sector evolves and the financial environment in which monetary policy must operate changes, so perhaps monetary policy may need to adapt and change with it. This seems especially likely if, as we suggested earlier, change has been particularly rapid as in the 1970s and 1980s.

In seeking to convey how much change has occurred, we are aided by our own recollections as students of money in the 1950s and 1960s. Like many other economists at that time, we were introduced to banking and monetary analysis through a reading of Richard Sayers' book *Modern Banking*, the seventh and last edition of which came out in 1967. A comparison of Sayers' description of banking in the mid 1960s with the structure of banking today is instructive. Sayers made two major observations about the structure of banking and we must remember that he was writing generally and referring to banking worldwide, as well as in Britain. He observed that the domain of banking was national and was becoming increasingly so. In his words, 'banking organisation does not easily straddle national frontiers' so that 'the business of banking of the world is organised in the main on national lines' (p. 16). Sayers also recorded that 'the ordinary business of banking' had been practised in its then form for generations and that the shape of British banking had been settled for a century (p. 21).

Table 1.2 shows the aggregate balance sheet of the UK retail or 'deposit' banks from 1880 through to 1988 (after 1966 this group comprises the four London clearing banks, the two Scottish clearing banks, TSB and Standard Chartered), and the allocation of sterling assets into the main categories of cash balances, money at call, bills discounted, securities and investments and finally loans and advances. On Sayers' second point it is interesting to note that the distribution of assets of the UK deposit banks into those categories in 1966 differed little from the distribution in 1880.

Since then three major developments have transformed the shape of banking in Britain and many other countries. First, there has been the internationalization of banking and the growth of currency business, which is part of the wider provision of private sector financing across national borders. For the banks in Table 1.2, foreign currency assets (not shown) in 1988 amounted to about 32 per cent of sterling assets. For the British banking system as a whole (including the merchant banks and other wholesale banking financiers, and the overseas banks) the position is reversed, and assets in sterling are about 70 per cent of foreign currency assets. Second, there has been the creation of techniques of risk spreading and the collective division among the banks of funding needs, by means of interbank arrangements. Reflecting the growth of these markets, assets held as cash balances have fallen to minuscule levels in comparison with earlier years. Loans and advances, relative to total banking assets, have risen to levels far in excess of anything seen previously among British banks. Such balance sheet comparisons leave out of the reckoning the rapid expansion of 'off-balance sheet financing' or 'invisible banking' activities, which for some banks are a multiple of their on-balance sheet business. Finally, the holding company organization has been employed and, through it, the major banks have evolved into financial services conglomerates. They now produce intermediary services in a variety of markets in a variety of ways.

It has been a remarkable twenty years of adjustment, and one has to go back to the mid nineteenth century to find a similar period of change. Structural change then lasted for nearly fifty years and saw the full flowering of the gold standard, a decline in the use of notes and the rise of cheque deposits, and the formation of limited liability banking which led to the transformation of banks from small regional county partnerships to national and international organizations. It would seem that structural change in banking and financial markets is once again a major force, which continues to reshape the nature of banking and finance.

Of course, change is rarely absent from the financial system; yet the period under examination has been marked by two major occasions of conscious institutional restructuring – Competition and Credit Control (CCC) in 1971 and, a decade later, the reforms of 1981. Both sets of reforms can be seen as embodying a combination of a desire for greater freedom from regulation in the monetary system and a desire to set an

Table 1.2 UK balance sheet of British deposit banks, 1880–1988 (per cent of total assets)

	Liabilities			Assets[3]				
	Paid-up[1] capital	Other[2] liabilities	Deposits	Cash balances	Money at call	Bills discounted	Securities and investments	Loans and advances
1880	16.8	4.0	79.2	8.9	8.2	12.8	17.0	50.6
1890	15.2	3.1	81.6	9.6	9.1	10.7	21.1	47.4
1900	12.0	3.2	84.8	10.5	10.3	7.3	21.3	48.4
1910	10.6	2.5	86.9	11.8	11.4	8.1	19.6	47.0
1920	5.9	2.4	91.6	14.5	6.6	14.4	20.6	42.5
1930	7.2	1.5	91.3	14.2	7.6	14.1	19.3	42.9
1940	5.2	1.4	93.4	14.7	6.0	7.7	32.1	28.7
1950	2.7	1.7	95.4	9.0	9.0	18.4	28.4	24.0
1960	3.7	1.4	94.8	9.7	8.7	14.5	18.3	39.9
1966	5.3	1.2	93.5	9.9	12.4	11.2	13.3	46.4
1978	7.1	7.1	85.8	4.6	23.1	3.2	7.4	49.7
1988	6.0	8.3	85.7	1.2	19.7	3.2	3.9	64.8

Notes:

1. For 1978 and 1988, calculated from annual reports as Shareholders Funds as per cent of All Assets.
2. Calculated for 1978 and 1988 from monthly series.
3. Distribution of all assets for 1880–1966, and of sterling assets only for 1978 and 1988.

Sources:

1880–1966: D. K. Sheppard, *The Growth and Role of U.K. Financial Institutions 1888–1962*, Methuen, 1971.
1978–1988: Committee of London Clearing Banks, *Abstract of Banking Statistics*, May 1988.

effective framework for the operation of monetary policy in the new conditions of competition and deregulation. In both cases actual progress has disappointed the more ambitious initial projections of what could be achieved, and ten years on from the latter revolution the ambiguities are obvious and numerous.

Pressures for change

The years of the 1960s provide a clear illustration of the relationship between the structure of the monetary system and the nature of monetary policy. Prior to CCC, there was an obvious complementarity between the cartelized structure of the banking industry and the Bank of England's exercise of direct controls over bank advances (administered through what were euphemistically called 'requests') and its price leadership of interest rates through its setting of Bank rate.

This kind of structure had existed since the turn of the century and was by no means confined to banking. Provision of financial services was compartmentalized into institutional groupings, such as the clearing banks, stockbrokers, discount houses, building societies and insurance companies, each carrying out distinctive functions rooted in long-standing attitudes as to 'proper' activities. All of these institutional groups formed themselves into associations which provided self-regulation of member institutions. Like other clubs,[2] these associations typically established codes of conduct governing acceptable practices and behaviour, and instituted entry qualifications which determined those deemed fit to join. With membership limited to those who were believed on the basis of personal knowledge and direct evidence to be trustworthy, entry to the group itself became a seal of approval which lowered the search and information costs of other market participants. This principle of practitioner-based self-regulation survives today, for it is the central feature of the 'new' regulatory system for financial services introduced in 1986, albeit underpinned by a legislative framework in the form of the Financial Services Act.

Not surprisingly, the traditional system embodied a degree of self-interest on the part of the members themselves, for the setting of minimum commissions and the fixing of interest rates and various charges enabled the association to act also as a price-fixing cartel. In addition, it reflected two further characteristics of the British financial system which persist today. One is the dominance of the City of London. Banking, insurance, money markets, stockbroking, commodities and futures trading, accounting and legal services are all based in the City. In the case of banking, by 1920 commercial banking was dominated by five clearing banks which held four-fifths of deposits. The City and British banking generally revolved around a small, cohesive group of bankers who recognized their fiduciary responsibilities and emphasized the importance of trust and confidence to the system.

A second aspect is the authority of the Bank of England: an authority which historically preceded its legal status. As banker to government, custodian of overseas reserves, manager of the national debt and bankers' banker, the Bank is involved in most of the major markets, and the transactions which it carries out put it in daily contact with the major institutions. This enables it to establish contacts and acquire information to which few others are privy.

The significance of the Bank of England's position came from it favouring an informal gentlemen's club approach to supervision rather than any reliance upon laws and statutes.[3] From its viewpoint the club approach had a number of benefits. Many of the administrative chores of supervision could be entrusted to the club, while the ability to deal with a limited number of institutions facilitated the use of moral suasion as a tool of monetary policy. Moral suasion can be described as an exchange of cooperation by banks in return for a flow of information from the central bank, and information is more easily transferred via informal meetings with a small, homogeneous group of banking officials. Setting of interest rates by the cartel in line with Bank rate transmitted policy changes in interest rates to bank loan rates in a predictable way and prevented a competitive bidding up of deposit rates in 'rate wars' which could imperil bank safety. Banks, in turn, were able to maintain low capitalization: as Table 1.2 shows, in 1950 UK deposit banks held equity capital equal to only 2.7 per cent of total assets.

This was the regulatory and institutional framework which continued largely unchanged through to the end of the 1960s. Since then the framework has been subject to considerable pressure from a number of sources. Improvements in technology have been important, especially in recent years, in broadening the product range which individual institutions can profitably distribute to their customer base and allowing tie-ups between geographically separated institutions. In the case of the banks, the barriers which separated them from other financial service groupings were largely 'internal' ones rather then externally imposed. Attitudes are often capable of changing more rapidly than laws, and in the 1960s that happened with the British banks as they entered into a variety of other financial activities such as credit cards, unit trusts, insurance, leasing, factoring, merchant banking and so on. In view of the continuance of price fixing and credit directives over 'banking' business, there were strong commercial incentives for the banks to divert the new ventures away from their own balance sheets to those of subsidiaries.

Deregulation represents another proximate cause of change. A basic distinction is made in the literature on regulation between the idea that regulation is motivated by the 'public interest', i.e. to promote macroeconomic efficiency, and the notion that regulation really acts so as to serve 'private interests' including the self-interest of the regulators themselves.[4] Somewhere in between these two is the political support maximizing model of Keeler (1984), which emphasizes the social consensus upon which regulation in the public interest relies. All of these models make clear that regulation cannot remain static but must vary over time in response to changes in technology and market conditions, shifts in the distribution of benefits and gains from regulation, and public perceptions as to the benefits and costs of regulatory interference. Each, however, offers a different perspective on the factors which may lead to deregulation.

One of the major strands of the 'private interest' view of regulation is the capture of the gains by producer interests, tolerated by the regulators in return for their cooperation. Financial regulation in the United Kingdom and many other countries built upon – and officially sanctioned – an interest rate cartel operated by a small number of private banks. It can be argued that tight regulation initially served the bankers' interests. In the aftermath of the 1930s, caution was uppermost in their minds and competition subdued. Close cooperation with the authorities enabled banks to run capital reserves down to historically low levels. Only later, as memories of the crisis faded and a new generation of bankers came to the fore, would the erosion of market shares and the benefits of enhanced competition be stressed.

Development of the Eurocurrency markets in the United Kingdom brought an influx of foreign banking firms to the City and the formation of parallel markets for banking and finance. In a very real sense there were two Cities – the domestic City and the international City. The former, dominated by the best of British financial 'clubs', namely the clearing banks and The Stock Exchange, was inward-looking, concentrating on traditional operations and with officially sanctioned price fixing, at least for traditional business. The international City was based around the Euromarkets and inhabited by US bankers and securities houses, along with European universal banks, competing globally for banking and securities business.

Pressure to deregulate both banking and securities markets came from the contrast between the heady growth of the second City and the relative stagnation of the first, with the immediate focus upon banking. The clearing banks were singled out for the application of portfolio controls and interest rate regulations. They alone were subject to the Special Deposits scheme, a cash reserve ratio and a liquid assets ratio, and adhered to interest rate ceilings upon deposits and loan rates. Sustained application of these controls saw them fall behind the other banks (accepting houses, discount houses, foreign banks and other UK banks). Figure 1.1 shows the liabilities of the two groups of banks, and those of the building societies as at 1955, 1960, 1970 and 1979.

In any case, the control system began to appear to suffer from substantial leakages as markets innovated ways to avoid the impact of quantitative controls over bank advances and the other restrictions upon banks. Under the public interest theory, deregulation results from environmental or technological developments which erode industry boundaries and reduce the pay-off from inherited regulatory techniques: an acknowledgement that existing controls have outlived their usefulness.

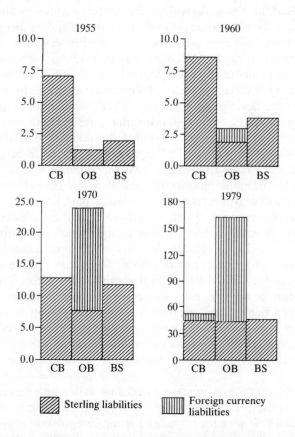

Figure 1.1   Liabilities of banking groups, 1955–79, £ million. CB: London clearing banks; OB: other banks (accepting houses, discount houses, foreign banks, other British banks); BS: building societies.

When financial services are involved, there is an extra dimension. For most industries, the choices open to the regulator usually do not include the ability to alter market prices across the whole economy as a means of influencing output. Regulators must use taxes, quotas, embargoes and 'voluntary' restraints. Monetary authorities do have general instruments at their disposal. They can enter the bond market or the foreign exchange market like any other transactor and buy or sell domestic and foreign assets. These 'market' actions can be distinguished from the 'regulatory' ones. For example, constraint upon the reserve base of the banks for a *money supply policy*, as under monetary base control, can be effected by using money market operations to lever excess reserves from the banks or by the interaction of Special Deposits (a variable cash reserve ratio) against required minimum cash reserve and liquid assets ratios, the tools of the 1960s. A *credit policy* can be operated by altering the cost of credit, the present-day policy, or by using lending directives and direct controls over hire purchase, both used in earlier years to restrict the quantity of credit. Attempts may be made to influence the foreign exchanges in an *exchange rate policy*, by conducting open market purchases and sales of foreign securities for domestic securities (normally given the pejorative description 'intervention') or by means of exchange controls and special taxes on foreign investment, used in earlier years.

Much deregulation consists of a switch from regulatory to market actions and, within the category of regulatory actions, from credit controls to protective measures. In this way, the authorities seek in the public interest to strengthen monetary controls in an altered environment. An element of self-interest on the regulators' part, however, might be seen in the alacrity with which they have moved to replace the dismantled controls with prudential forms of supervision – self-interest here being power and employment. But it must be remembered that controls can perform a number of functions. Secondary reserve ratios which operated in the United Kingdom through to 1980 can be seen to protect depositors as well as assist monetary control, while the close direct regulation which existed over bank lending and, through the cartel, interest rates acted as a substitute for bankers' own prudence. In the new framework, capital adequacy ratios ostensibly reinforce bankers' caution, but also act as gearing constraints upon banks' balance sheet expansion.

Attitudes in the community too began to change in line with the temper and mood of the times, and across a number of countries and in a number of activities which have seen the privatization and deregulation of airlines and transport as well as that of financial services. In the aftermath of the 1930s, some limitation upon competition seemed, at least to many people, to be a not unreasonable price to pay to ensure the safety and soundness of the banking system. After the Second World War, community expectations were high about the economic and social benefits which might come from government intervention and control, and a concentrated and regulated financial structure seemed consistent with the ability to implement monetary policy. As thinking on these matters changed, so more emphasis was given to fostering competition as a means of achieving efficiency in the allocation of resources (see for example the 1967 National Board for Prices and Incomes Report on *Bank Charges* (No. 34), while progress in changing the structure of the system was eased by the assurance seemingly provided in the early studies of the demand for money that an alternative form of monetary control compatible with freer markets was feasible. Those studies raised the possibility of effecting changes in the quantity of money by using interest rates to slide up and down a relatively stable aggregate demand for money function.

Competition and Credit Control

Competition and Credit Control in 1971 began the process of deregulation. It represented the first attempt to bring the two Cities closer together by enabling the primary banking system to engage in Eurocurrency banking and liability management practices. Both the quantitative controls and the cartel agreements about interest rates were swept away, while the regulatory balance sheet ratios were tidied up, lightened and made less discriminatory by extension to other institutions. The minimum 8 per cent cash reserve ratio became a 1.5 per cent cash requirement involving just bankers' balances at the Bank of England. The liquid assets ratio was cut from 28 to 12.5 per cent and redefined as a reserve assets ratio embracing bankers' balances, call money, bills and very short-term bonds. The power to call to Special Deposit was retained but like the new reserve assets ratio was extended to all banks, not just the clearing banks (the reserve assets ratio was also extended, at a lower level, to the finance houses). In place of direct controls over bank advances the reforms held out the promise of a market-based solution to the control problem: 'Importance was now attached to the monetary aggregates; their rate of growth was to be controlled by the market instrument of interest rates' (Bank of England, 1978).

Operation of the system belied this hope in some degree. After an initial period in which the new system was run in under conditions of recession, where the rise in bank advances and the money supply could be seen as an appropriate response, concern grew that the monetary expansion was excessive. Demand for money equations of the type which had provided the backbone of the argument that the new system could be controlled through interest rates 'broke down' (see Chapter 4). Successive calls to Special Deposits and increases in interest rates were insufficient to stem the tide. Interest rate adjustments by the banks themselves were too sluggish to prevent a peculiar form of arbitrage – borrowing from banks at or near base rate and redepositing with them in certificates of deposit (CDs) – a phenomenon which came to be known as 'round-tripping'.

By the end of 1973 the authorities felt obliged to resort to a new policy instrument – the Supplementary Special Deposit or 'corset'. Supplementary Special Deposits were levied as a progressively rising proportion of the excess of the growth of 'interest-bearing eligible liabilities' (IBELS) over a prespecified allowable base. As no interest was paid on the Deposits the corset had the aspect of a progressive tax on excessive expansion of the balance sheet.[5] The banks reacted to this primarily by rationing their customers for credit and in this way the authorities effectively reinvented in the corset a somewhat more 'market-friendly' form of advances control. Like the old advances control the corset was nominally effective and the growth in the money aggregates was slowed; but as the sobriquet implies, the belief was that, in the same way as with advances controls, the market was innovating ways around it. Because intermediation was forced off the banks' balance sheets by this process, the response to the corset was seen as one of disintermediation: financing intermediated via banks' balance sheets as deposits and loans switched to the bills and other securities markets as direct financing – often facilitated by a banker's credit-enhancing endorsement. While this was something of a problem in itself, particularly as the precise extent of the offsetting disintermediation was not easy to estimate, the repeated use of the weapon invited a problem of 'instrument instability'. Anticipation of a new call to Special Supplementary Deposit would lead to a scramble by banks to inflate their liabilities base prior to the corset's application. This, in turn, induced in the authorities a counter-response of predating the base date from which permissible growth would be allowed.

In this way the spirit of CCC was severely compromised. In the same fashion, an attempt to make the Bank's responses in the money market more 'market-based' also came to grief (see Chapter 7). By the second half of the 1970s, the impetus towards finding a market-based solution to the monetary control problem was renewed. This was simply a reflection of the high inflation of the mid-1970s and the revealed difficulties of the incomes policy solution. The 1974–9 Labour Government first found that incomes policies could not be implemented effectively until a crisis level of inflation had already been reached, and then that the sustainability of an adequate policy was beyond their grasp. Money supply targets had been an internal guide to policy within the Bank of England since 1974. Public adoption of them by the Labour Government in July 1976 was certainly less than the ideological embrace of a different approach and much more a reflection of an eclectic and pragmatic policy viewpoint. But it laid the ground for the next revolution in the monetary framework introduced by the Conservative Government in 1981.

The reforms of 1981

In the 1981 reforms the cash requirement was further reduced to 0.5 per cent (and changed from a reserve ratio requirement to an explicit revenue-raising tax) and the reserve assets ratio was abolished, along with the corset. A right to call Special Deposits was retained (but has not been subsequently used). New procedures were inaugurated for money market and subsequent gilt-edged market operations. These reforms are themselves to be understood in the context of two very important preceding events: first, the abolition of exchange controls in 1979; and second, the announcement and introduction of a 'medium-term financial strategy' (MTFS) in 1979–80.

Abolition of exchange controls was undertaken shortly after the Conservative Government assumed office, and was executed rapidly between June and October 1979. The event is significant for the restriction it implies on the capacity for British monetary regulations to be nationally differentiated and for removing a degree of freedom in interest rate (or alternatively exchange rate) policy. In the first instance, the removal of exchange controls can be seen as amounting to the removal of a form of protection for the domestic banking industry from international competition. In the presence of such controls, the price of a heavy regulation of the domestic banking industry, whether through the imposition of onerous reserve ratio requirements or through direct restrictions on advances, is some domestic disintermediation from the industry. 'Near banks', not subject to the regulations, and direct borrowing–lending operations are fostered. When exchange controls are abolished and direct controls are retained, the disintermediation process involves offshore banks as well, for financing can be diverted overseas and produced externally free of the regulatory jurisdiction of the country concerned. Not surprisingly, therefore, the corset was an immediate casualty of the abolition of exchange control in the United Kingdom (banks were, for another year, under voluntary restraint not to arrange for customers to use the loophole available).

The second important effect that the removal of exchange controls brings about is the restoration of the power of arbitrage to equalize onshore and offshore sterling interest rates. Figure 1.2 demonstrates in a striking way the closing of the offshore/onshore differential with the abolition of exchange control. Since the offshore or 'Euro' sterling rate for an *x*-months loan or deposit can be unpacked into a combination of the US rate for that period together with the depreciation or appreciation of the pound in terms of dollars as reflected in the *x*-months forward foreign exchange premium or discount (all of this can of course be worded equally in terms of any other currencies), it is implied that with abolition of exchange control, exchange rate and interest rate policy cannot be independent.

On assuming office in 1979 the Conservative Government made clear its attachment to monetary targets as the means of defeating inflation, and in 1980 it published the first version of its medium-term financial strategy (MTFS). The core of the MTFS is (or was) the projection over the medium term of a deceleration in monetary growth, flanked by a medium-term reduction in the public sector borrowing requirement (PSBR) in relation to gross domestic product (GDP), the latter implying the subjugation of budgetary policies to this 'monetary standard'.

Given the importance so obviously attached to monetary constraint as the cornerstone of economic management, it may seem strange that the government would choose this time to weaken the anti-inflationary weapon by putting aside direct monetary controls. To an extent there may have been no choice, for the 1981 reforms embodied the lesson of the abolition of exchange control. Even without the removal of exchange controls, the idea that monetary policy was weakened can be questioned. Continued reliance on direct controls, especially the corset, led the banks to find ever more ingenious ways to window-dress their balance sheet, so that the controls became increasingly irksome to all concerned, and less potent. Moreover, in terms of seeking a greater role for the market and a smaller one for the Bank in interest rate determination and in the money market generally, operating reforms could be seen as laying a foundation for moving on to monetary base control, regarded by many as a more effective control device (see Chapter 6).

Difficulties with the MTFS interrupted this progression. Interest in monetary base control withered as concern grew that it would be inappropriate to target the money supply, at least on its original £M3 expression. The exchange rate was introduced as a significant conditioning variable on the response to monetary target overruns, then – to all appearances – as a target variable in its own right. By 1988 this too had given way to what seemed like the fine-tuning of demand in the interests of the control of inflation, using the short-term interest rate as the instrument. This not only implied the downgrading of the monetary aggregates as targets and also the re-emergence of Bank of England-led

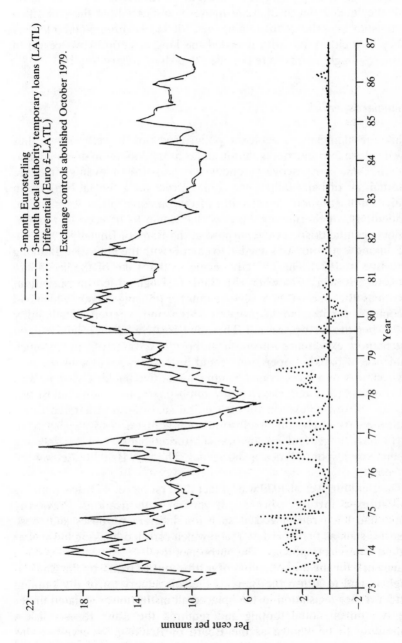

Figure 1.2 The offshore/onshore differential (3-month Eurosterling–3-month local authority loans).

Legend:
- 3-month Eurosterling
- 3-month local authority temporary loans (LATL)
- Differential (Euro £-LATL)

Exchange controls abolished October 1979.

Per cent per annum

Year

interest rate adjustments in the money markets, but seemed itself to have devolved into a 'stop-go' cycle of classic proportions exciting a fascination with the 'next balance of trade figures' reminiscent of the embattled circumstances of the 1970s. Joining the EMS in 1990 brought this phase of policy to a close, and with it ended the longest period (two years) of unrelieved high interest rate policy in British monetary history.

Financial supervision

While the 'domestic monetarism' policy aspect of the reforms was thus thwarted the theme of deregulation and competition was maintained, and with it came a rediscovery, under the pressure of events, that the externalities of bank failure can create a role for a central bank or an equivalent institution. Supervision of the banking industry (and also, incidentally, of the money markets) has come to be seen as a major defining characteristic of the purpose of the Bank of England.

Banking legislation was needed to comply with the First EEC Banking Directive of 1977. The Directive came in the wake of the secondary banking crises in 1974 when the Bank of England led an operation, known as 'the lifeboat', to cushion a number of 'fringe' banks which had become overexposed in the property market and experienced a liquidity crisis when property prices fell. Thus the Directive fell on receptive ears. The lifeboat experience forced the authorities to think of ways in which prudence in banking operations could be encouraged, for in the new environment of a more complex and competitive banking system, with many new players and a less 'clubby' atmosphere, the traditional British solution of self-regulation through moral suasion and tolerated cartel arrangements had become badly outdated. A first necessity appeared to be to have a general system for chartering banks and for locating supervisory responsibilities in one agency. The 1979 Banking Act was the outcome.

The Banking Act of 1979 was in fact the first piece of British banking legislation to involve a process of general authorizations. Previously banks had been recognized as such for different purposes and those agencies such as the Board of Trade which certified banking businesses had no supervisory powers. The purpose of the 1979 Act was to set out a framework for the authorization of institutions as banks by the Bank of England and to affirm the Bank as the sole supervisor of the banking system. Later legislation in 1987 placed all institutions regulated under the Act on an equal footing and required the Bank to establish a committee to be known as the Board of Banking Supervision: this confirmed arrangements already instituted internally by the Bank after the failure of Johnson Matthey Bank in 1984, and these included the formal establishment of a Banking Supervision Division. Consequently, unlike in some other systems overseas, the functions of prudential supervision and monetary policy control in the United Kingdom were to be combined in the central bank.

During the 1980s this authority was used by the Bank of England not only to institute a new system of monetary control but also to establish a basis for supervision within the statutory framework. In consultation with the banks it introduced guidelines for the assessment of capital adequacy and liquidity. In doing so, the Bank consciously sought to avoid adopting regimes involving hard-and-fast rules, insisting that circumstances alter cases and that a prescribed uniformity would involve insensitive and excessive regulation. Presented as the continuance of a hallowed tradition, the incentive for a low-profile supervisory code was refreshed by an evident concern to preserve and enhance the role of the City of London as a world financial centre. To this end, the more liberal regime applied to banks was carried through to The Stock Exchange with 'Big Bang' in 1986, to the building societies and to the financial system generally. To better ensure that the process would not lead, by way of overexpansion and subsequent collapse, back to a reregulation, substantial effort was expended by the Bank and the authorities in building a framework which encouraged prudent and honest behaviour and in extending guidelines for effective supervision across the financial services industry with the Financial Services Act and the Building Societies Act of 1986. The globalization of markets and parallel developments and concerns elsewhere, especially under the European Community 1992 initiatives, ensured that these efforts were given an international dimension.

Notes

1. Bank of England, 1987.
2. The theory of clubs is reviewed by Sandler and Tschirhart (1980), and their importance in banking is considered by Goodhart (1988).
3. The Bank's traditional approach is described in McMahon (1984) and Llewellyn (1985).
4. See Posner (1974) and Peltzman (1976).
5. A more complete analysis of the corset can be found in Chapter 6 and Bank of England (1984a, Ch. 6, pp. 117–27).

2

Monetary systems

2.1 Monetary standards

Since 1971, the world has been on an inconvertible paper or fiat money standard. We define a fiat money system as one based on claims such as paper money, coinage and deposits at the central bank of a country which are not convertible by law or custom into anything other than themselves, and which have no fixed value in terms of any objective standard or monetary substance. Nevertheless, despite being intrinsically useless and produced at little or no cost, fiat money usually has a monetary face value well in excess of its resource cost.

The properties and workings of a fiat money system have been extensively analyzed in economics textbooks, albeit at a highly abstract level and for an individual country. Friedman's (1969b) 'helicopter money models' and Patinkin's (1965) 'market experiments' are ones in which the monetary injections are of fiat money. In fact the historical experience of fiat money systems is limited. By far the usual arrangement has been for money to comprise, or be based upon, a certain commodity (or certain commodities). Departures from a commodity base, if not exactly unknown, were often temporary expedients in times of war or financial crisis such as the 1930s, were not expected to be permanent and proved not to be so. An international monetary system based almost entirely on fiat moneys, as now operates, is a relatively new phenomenon. Experience in the 1930s led men of affairs at the time to contemplate a continuing system of free paper currencies with considerable trepidation. For example:

> The dangers which the universal adoption of independent standards involves are that such a step would encourage the already strong tendencies toward

economic nationalism; that it would bring about perpetually fluctuating rates of exchange; and that it would at any moment of difficulty facilitate the abuse of the printing press by governments. . . . the existence of universal paper standards threatens an indefinite continuance of chaos in the monetary affairs of the world unless agreement is reached as to general price policy. But such an agreement would make an international adoption of paper unnecessary, for the same ends could then be reached under an international gold standard.
T. E. Gregory (1933)

Equally, it is easy to understand why, despite such warnings, rational thinkers have been attracted to an independent monetary standard. The appeal of commodity-based money lies in the promise of price and exchange rate stability. A well-managed fiat money system can in principle do just as well, perhaps better, in achieving these objectives. Moreover, it can do so at a much lower potential social cost by avoiding the inefficiency inherent in tying up stocks of a valuable commodity for monetary use. If supplied in a proper fashion, fiat money can be issued at near zero social cost – due to its trivial intrinsic content. When there is monetary mismanagement, however, the true cost of a fiat money system is much higher, as Milton Friedman (1986) has noted. To the cost of issue must be added the effects of unstable exchanges and higher and more variable wage and price inflation upon economic decision-making, along with resources diverted into hedging against the consequences of absolute price level uncertainty; this must include some part of the cost of establishing and operating markets for swaps, futures, options and other hedging instruments.

The successful operation of a fiat money system requires the exercise of restraint by or upon the issuing authority. The whole point of a commodity-based system is to impose such restrictions upon the monetary authority, in particular to prevent inflationary policies. A commodity-based system can be thought of as a paper money standard in which there is inbuilt monetary regulation and control. So long as the monetary structure is tied to a commodity the volume of money is limited by the supply of the commodity. Yet it is only by breaking free of these chains that an independent fiat money system can realize its potential benefits (and its actual costs). Monetary systems can be seen as institutional arrangements which, while allowing the monetary authorities to exercise responsibility for money, at the same time usually provide for, or have implicit in them, rules or conventions that constrain or limit the ability of the authorities to pursue independent national policies. In this respect, alternative sets of policies, for example relating to exchange rates, may serve to govern monetary behaviour in a non-commodity system. Indeed, the Bretton Woods system constituted one such structure and was designed as a middle way between the rigidity of a commodity-based standard and the laxity of free paper money systems.

Monetary systems, then, may be compared in terms of *ideal* character-istics or *actual* advantages and costs, in terms of whether the system is *automatic* (with stability emerging spontaneously as a consequence of market outcomes) or *managed* (with the authorities manipulating monetary conditions so that the value of money is made reasonably stable in terms of some objective standard). Within the managed category, the authorities' policies may be guided closely by specific *rules* constraining behaviour to within narrow limits or loosely with the authorities possessing *discretion* as to policies, i.e. considerable latitude in terms of decision-making powers.

Table 2.1 is based on different criteria. In Chapter 1 we defined a monetary system as a set of arrangements or policies governing the types of money constituting the structure, and we classify systems in terms of the reference point of those policies, i.e. the nature of the monetary standard. Most of the sixteen systems defined in the table can be classified under one of five heads: independent standards, single commodity-based standards, multicommodity-based standards, currency standards and index standards. Two systems – the limping gold standard and the balance of payments standard – overlap these classifications.

Fiat money is set apart from the other systems in not being linked with some external object. This linkage need not be direct. Where, for example, liabilities of 'near-banks' are convertible into bank money which in turn is redeemable in terms of central bank money, the issue is whether the value of that item to which the remaining portions adjust is itself tied to something external to the monetary system.

This is not to say that fiat money has no value. While having no intrinsic value, and thus no non-monetary demand, it is valued by individuals because of its ability to purchase other goods: the value of the monetary unit is the claim on goods and services which holders acquire when it is transferred to others. This was recognized by J. S. Mill (1940):

> After experience had shown that pieces of paper, of no intrinsic value, by
> merely bearing upon them the written profession of being equivalent to a
> certain number of francs, dollars or pounds, could be made to circulate as such,
> and to produce all the benefit to the issuers which could have been produced by
> the coins which they purported to represent; governments began to think that it
> would be a happy device if they could appropriate to themselves this benefit,
> free from the condition to which individuals issuing such paper substitutes for
> money were subject, of giving, when required, for the sign the thing signified.
> They determined to try whether they could emancipate themselves from this
> unpleasant obligation, and make a piece of paper issued by them pass for a
> pound, by merely calling it a pound, and consenting to receive it in payment of
> taxes. And such is the influence of almost all established governments, that

Table 2.1 Classification of monetary systems

			Some external value	
No external value	One commodity	Two or more commodities	One or more currencies	Index standards
Fiat money Freely issued inconvertible paper, credit or token money.	*Monometallism* A system based on one metal freely minted into coins which are exportable and meltable.	*Bimetallism* Use of a monetary unit defined as a specified weight of silver *or* a specified weight of gold, both freely minted and therefore standing in a fixed ratio in terms of one another.	*Exchange standard* The practice of fixing the value of the domestic monetary unit in terms of the value of the monetary unit of a foreign country.	*Tabular standard* The monetary unit would be defined as a specified combination of physical quantities of a selected group of commodities. Indexation would allow the definition of the monetary unit to be adjusted periodically to offset movements in the prices of the selected group relative to all commodities.
	Gold specie standard Gold coins circulate along with bank notes which can be exchanged into gold coins on demand and for the smallest coin available.	*Symmetallism* The monetary unit is defined as a specified weight of silver *plus* a specified weight of gold. The two metals are exchangeable at a fixed price in terms of the monetary unit when combined in the legally fixed proportions, but their relative price is free to vary.	*Currency basket* Fixing the value of the domestic monetary unit relative to a composite unit comprising a number of foreign currencies, often weighted according to trade.	*Goods standard* Maintaining by monetary management the value of money stable relative to an index of goods.
	Limping gold standard Convertibility into metal rather than token money is at the authorities' discretion.	*Composite commodity reserve standard* The monetary unit consists of, or is defined in terms of, warehouse receipts of a fixed weight bundle of commodities held in store or as a reserve base.	*Balance of payments standard* Use of monetary policy to maintain equilibrium in the balance of payments.	
	Gold bullion standard Gold coins no longer circulate and bank notes can be exchanged only for gold bullion and, often, only for specified groups.			*Earnings standard* Maintaining the value of money stable in terms of an index of wages (earnings).
	Gold exchange standard A country's currency is convertible into the currency of a country on the gold standard, and so indirectly into gold.			*Labour standard* Expanding money supply to accommodate full employment wage outcomes, as under an incomes policy.

they have generally succeeded in attaining this object: I believe I might say they have always succeeded for a time, and the power has only been lost to them after they had compromised it by the most flagrant abuse.

In the case supposed, the functions of money are performed by a thing which derives its power for performing them solely from convention; but convention is quite sufficient to confer the power; since nothing more is needful to make a person accept anything as money, and even at any arbitrary value, than the persuasion that it will be taken from him on the same terms by others. (p. 542)

Consequently, the linking of money to an external object – one or more commodities, another currency or some index of items – should not be looked on as giving value to money. The principal point of the linkage is instead to ensure confidence and sustain the convention by protecting against the over-issue of money and otherwise restricting the set of feasible policies which can be pursued by the authorities.

The second criterion underlying the table turns on this point. Within each category, the systems are ordered vertically from automatic to more managed systems, reflecting the method by which the linkage is brought about. Slight changes in the method of adjustment account for some different classifications. As we shall see, a gold standard of any form carries implications for exchange rate relationships. An exchange standard is distinguished from a gold standard when stable exchange rates are the criterion of monetary policies and not the result of linking money to gold. A fiat money system converts into an index system, without any necessary change in institutional mechanisms, when there is a limitation of the amount of money so as to stabilize the prices of a selected group of commodities (a goods standard) or of labour services (an earnings standard). Both standards imply the existence of a monetary mechanism which enables the required stabilization to be achieved by monetary means. When, instead, the quantity of money is passively adjusted to accommodate wage outcomes at full employment, we have a labour standard of the Hicksian sort (Hicks, 1955). Such a standard was envisaged for monetary policy in Australia in the mid 1980s under the Accord between the trade unions and the federal government, whereby an incomes policy would govern wages (and thus prices) while fiscal policy would ensure full employment, rendering the money supply endogenous (see Davis and Lewis, 1988).

While some of the systems have a long history, others such as symmetallism, tabular standards and commodity reserve currency systems exist only in economists' theorizing. They were proposed, and interest in them continues today, because none of the systems which have been in operation has provided a basis for measuring economic value comparable, in terms of uniformity and constancy, with the way that the adoption of the metre and kilogram has established them as the basis for measuring distance and weight. This was noted by Sir Roy Harrod (1969):

> It is a strange fact that after so many centuries of experience in so many countries man has not yet succeeded in providing for himself a money with stable value. (p. 4)

Commodity-based systems have been the most widely used and those involving the precious metals, gold and silver, have exhibited the greatest appeal.

2.2 The gold standard

Metallic standards (and we focus mainly on gold) are seen by some as the hallmark of probity and responsible finance and by others as rooted in mythology and legend. Keynes in particular took the latter view, describing gold as a 'barbaric relic'.[1] To his followers the gold standard is associated with the rule of bankers and the dictates of sound money over the ordinary people and their elected representatives – a system belonging to a less enlightened era which to the extent that it preserved the value of money did so only by allowing the threat of unemployment to discipline the wage demands of workers. Moreover, it can be claimed that commodity-based systems, gold included, have not passed the survivor test; they have always broken down (Fischer, 1986). Others dispute such views. They look upon the years before the First World War as an island of price stability, brought about by a smoothly operating mechanism which automatically ensured balance of payments equilibria and stable exchange rates. Far from failing the test of time, 'commodity money is the only type of money that, at the present time, can be said to have passed the test of history in market economies' (Niehans, 1978, p. 140).

That history is a long one. Coinage of gold and silver can be dated from the seventh century BC and although the precise beginnings of the use of the precious metals for storing value in bar form are lost in the mists of time, it may have been a regular custom for 'thousands of years' (Toynbee, 1954). The pound sterling dates back to the silver issue of William the Conqueror with a penny then worth 1/240 of a pound. These historical origins of the currency account for some of the present-day resistance in Britain to the idea of replacing the pound with a new single European currency; yet the change to the new penny in 1971 and the demise of the guinea, sovereign, crown, half-crown, florin, shilling and farthing suggest that nothing is immutable.

Given the long history of commodity-based money, a gold standard of the universal form that we now associate with the description was in operation for a remarkably short period of time, 1879–1914 and 1925–31, and for many of those years its workings were the subject of fierce controversy. A *gold standard* can be said to exist when a country maintains equality between the value of the domestic monetary unit and a stipulated amount of gold. *Mint parity* provides only an official valuation of the currency in terms of gold; various provisions must exist to maintain the parity. Chief among these means in a full-blown gold coin (specie) standard is *convertibility*. With free coinage and minting, it would pay an individual to have gold bars converted into coins should coins exhibit any tendency to rise in value relative to their gold content, and to reconvert the coins into bullion should coins fall in value. When there is also freedom to export or import gold in unlimited quantities, the domestic currency is kept equal in value to the specified weight of gold on world markets. Thus an *international gold standard* exists when a number of countries provide for convertibility between currency and gold and allow unrestricted export and import of gold. Such a system was not in place until 1879 and then only the United States, Britain and Germany permitted full and automatic convertibility; France, Belgium and Switzerland were effectively on 'limping standards'.[2]

Prior to 1879, Britain stood almost alone (with Portugal) in its attachment to gold. Gold suited Britain, in comparison with silver, because as the richest country a larger proportion of its monetary transactions could be conveniently carried out using gold, the higher-valued metal. Even so, the problem of ensuring adequate low-value coinage remained. In 1615 the smallest gold coin of 5 shillings (5/-), weighing barely two grams, represented more than a week's wages of a labourer. It is argued (contrary to the 'happenstance' or policy error view outlined below) that the institution of a full gold standard had to await technological innovations in the early nineteenth century which made it feasible to produce token coins which were costly to counterfeit (Redish, 1988).

Convenience of the coinage posed problems for the two monometallic standards. Under a silver standard, high-value coins would be excessively heavy. Under a gold standard, full-bodied low-value coins would be excessively tiny. As we have seen, one solution to small coin inconvenience is the issue of token coins; another is for the banking system to issue small-denomination banknotes (this was the situation in the United States after 1834). Growth of the banking system would also solve the bulkiness of silver coinage, by allowing large-denomination banknotes to circulate and enabling commercial transactions to be effected by bank deposits. More usually, however, small-denomination silver coins circulated alongside gold coins, used primarily for high-valued transactions.

This was the attraction of *bimetallism* which operated other than in Britain for the first three-quarters of the nineteenth century.

Under a bimetallic system, a country's mint was ready to convert either silver or gold into specified coins at a fixed gold–silver price ratio, set by law. Difficulties came about when countries maintained legal mint ratios between the two metals which were incompatible with each other and with market conditions. Undervaluation would see one of the metals disappear from circulation as Gresham's Law came into operation,[3] and bimetallism become *de facto* silver or gold monometallism unless the official mint ratio was readjusted in line with market equilibrium (or unless market conditions varied again).

Indeed, one such readjustment in 1717 saw gold first emerge as the dominant currency in Britain, when Sir Isaac Newton, then Master of the Mint, set a mint ratio less favourable to silver than that ruling in France. With the purchasing power of silver greater abroad than in England, silver was exported rather than minted at home, leaving in circulation only silver coins of such a poor condition that it was not profitable to melt them down and ship abroad. Thus, as Hawtrey (1947) observed:

> The virtual gold standard to which the English public had become accustomed was founded on nothing but the overvaluation of gold in the coinage system. (p. 69)

When in 1798 Napoleon I set a mint ratio which reversed that movement so that gold flowed to France and silver came to England for minting, making it likely that Britain might revert to a silver standard, England closed its mint to silver, as it had to gold the year before when convertibility was suspended under wartime pressures. Later, under the Coinage Act of 1816, gold was named as the 'standard measure of value, and equivalent for property'. This is usually taken as the date when England officially came on to a gold standard, although banknotes were not made convertible until 1821, and the legal right to have silver coined remained until the 1870s (Fetter, 1965). This is the basis of the convertibility was suspended under wartime pressures. Later, under the standard which had operated in Britain after the policy error of 1717.

However engineered, the gold standard did provide Britain with a remarkable degree of long-term price stability. The price level of consumable goods on the eve of the suspension of the gold standard in 1931 was *in absolute terms* almost exactly the same as that in 1821. Sir John Hicks recalled as a child growing up in the early 1900s being aware that letter postage, from one part of Britain to another, was one penny (still 1/240 of a pound) and had been so for more than fifty years.[4] Nevertheless, prices in general were far from stable over shorter periods of time, as shown in Figure 2.1. During the nineteenth century, for example, prices generally were on a declining path from 1813 to 1851, then had an upward path until 1873, and fell substantially until the end of the century.

For any system in which the value of the currency is tied to a commodity standard (or any other external value), we can express the pound price of goods as the product of the parity price of the standard commodity and the terms of trade between the standard commodity and other commodities,[5] i.e.:

$$\frac{\text{pound}}{\text{goods}} = \frac{\text{standard commodity}}{\text{goods}} \times \frac{\text{pound}}{\text{standard commodity}}$$

The essence of commodity-based money is to fix the relationship of the monetary unit (pound) to the standard, so leaving movements in the relative price of the standard commodity to goods in general as the sole source of fluctuations in commodity prices. It follows that if the aim is to achieve stability of prices, defined as some index of prices, the standard commodity should be one the prices of which move *pari passu* with those of the goods making up the chosen index. This requires that tastes and demands for the commodity in question move in line with other goods and that its supply be subject to much the same resource constraints and technology as those for other goods.

On these criteria gold is far from ideal. Its standard of value is likely to be upset by the discovery of new mines or technical processes in mining, by tastes in adornment such as jewellery, and by hoarding habits in traditional societies. The 'automaticity' of the gold standard proved to be slow-working at best. In response to a failure of gold production to keep pace with the growth of trade and incomes, the idea was that commodity prices would fall, so raising the relative price of gold and making extra production profitable.[6] Annual production of gold in fact declined during the long period of falling prices from the 1870s to the 1890s and did not increase substantially before 1895, after which new discoveries in the Transvaal and the Klondike, and improvements in technology, saw gold production rise.[7]

In the meantime, the process of deflation produced considerable hardship among farmers and other debtors because nominal interest rates did not fall as rapidly as did commodity prices, so that *ex post* real interest rates increased. (This behaviour has been the case in most periods of deflation, including the disinflation of the 1980s.) Many at the time argued for a return to silver, and the issue was fought out in the US presidential campaign of 1896.[8] Production of silver had expanded considerably, and with reduced demand from demonetization the price of silver halved between 1870 and 1895 (so giving the lie to the idea that the

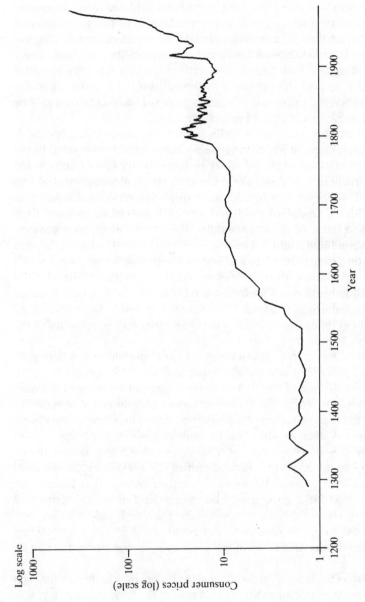

Note: Ten-yearly data until 1800; thereafter yearly observations.

Figure 2.1 Prices in Britain: the historical record, 1290–1988 (January 1974; 100).
Source: as for Table 1.1.

metal gives value to money). Edgeworth, Fisher, Marshall, Pierson and Walras all came out against gold, most favouring bimetallism. Marshall's alternative was symmetallism,[9] in which the monetary unit would be defined in terms of stipulated weights of both gold *and* silver – one can imagine, say, one ounce of gold and fifteen ounces of silver combined in one bar – rather than gold *or* silver, as under bimetallism. Broadening the base to the two metals would lessen the impact of demand and supply shifts affecting one metal alone, and thus result in a less variable price level. In this respect the system of symmetallism is a forerunner of the commodity reserve proposals in which a group of commodities would be chosen to be representative of prices in general.

Edgeworth saw that symmetallism had one major disadvantage. Unlike bimetallism, in which the money price of gold *and* silver is fixed, the relative price of gold and silver in terms of monetary units could fluctuate freely in world and domestic markets. Symmetallism could be introduced independently by countries without international agreement on a common bundle of gold and silver. If countries defined their currencies in terms of different bundles of gold and silver, the exchange rates between them could not be fixed and would need to vary. The idea of fluctuating exchange rates was out of temper with the times, which preferred the stable exchange rates provided by monometallism.

Marshall himself much preferred a tabular standard – a constructed standard – for bringing about price stability, an idea later refined by Irving Fisher (1920) and revived by the 'new Monetary economists' in the 1980s (see Chapter 10).

Practical support for alternatives to gold died down when gold production picked up and the declining path of prices gave way to an upward trend. Some of the deflationary consequences before then may have been alleviated by the transition from predominantly commodity money to the increasing use of fiduciary money of one kind or another – banknotes and debt money such as bank deposits. There was a good reason for this development. A well-known deficiency of a gold or commodity standard is the resource cost of the commodity. Growth of incomes and the demand for money over time require that labour and capital be used for digging gold from the ground in South Africa and reburying it in central bank vaults in New York or London, as Sir Roy Harrod once said.[10] These costs can be lowered by the economizing device of reducing the ratio of gold reserves to the domestic money supply.

A fractional reserve system is such a device in which at least two moneys circulate: a commodity such as gold in the form of currency, and banknotes or deposits for which banks themselves hold gold as backing. If the banks can function effectively with gold reserves that are some fraction of their outstanding obligations, so that the quantity of money is much larger than the stocks of monetary gold, society gets its monetary services at a lower cost while individuals benefit from the explicit or implicit interest (services) which banks pay on deposits.

It was a feature of the gold standard that this economizing process occurred over time without design by banks and other institutions engaging in maturity intermediation. Most savers wish to keep part of their assets readily withdrawable at no risk of nominal capital loss to meet unexpected consumption shocks. Borrowers generally prefer to go long – or, at least, that was the case before the advent of high inflation. These differences leave room for banks to borrow at call, and lend longer. But to successfully issue call obligations the bank must convince depositors that it can meet encashment demands. Once the confidence exists, no one feels it actually necessary to make the conversion and the debt can serve as 'money'. This is simply the exercise of consumer sovereignty, in that whatever is considered as good as money thereby becomes money. Such was the case historically with private paper money, government paper money, chequing facilities, savings deposits and so on.

Whether, in the circumstances of the nineteenth century, this process of financial innovation should be seen as a largely fortuitous development or as itself induced by the combination of gold shortage, secular deflation and high real interest rates remains a question which to our knowledge has not previously been posed. However, the innovations, in their turn, seem likely to have contributed to changes in the character of the gold standard which would become clearer under the gold exchange standard which operated in the interwar period and under which the pre-1913 practice of using gold-based currencies (especially sterling) to supplement gold as reserve assets became widespread. One effect of the growth of debt money was to weaken the influence of the automatic forces. While the whole superstructure of claims was still ultimately tied to gold by the redemption of bank liabilities and central banks' reserves of gold and gold-based assets, the indirect linkage meant that there could be no certainty that a country's money supply would always rise and fall automatically in line with gold movements as was expected under the 'rules of the game'. Further, the pyramiding of an increasing quantity of debt money on a limited quantity of gold held the potential for instability in times of crisis when the threat of gold conversions loomed. Monetary controls and monetary management increased. Limits were placed upon the fiduciary issues of currency: by national legislation establishing minimum ratios of the metallic (gold) reserves against the central bank's banknotes and sometimes against deposit liabilities, and by restrictions upon the covered and uncovered note issue. There was also an expansion in the number and powers of central banks. Nowhere is this more evident than in the practice of exchange rate management.

Convertibility and the free export and import of gold offered a mechanism by which foreign payments could be made. A person in England needing to make a payment in dollars could always present sterling notes for conversion into gold bars at the official gold parity, ship the gold to New York, exchange the gold for dollars at the Federal Reserve Bank and then arrange payment of the debt. Not surprisingly, most international transactions were not made in this way but rather, as now, through the foreign exchange markets. In order to buy dollar goods, Britons had to persuade someone to exchange sterling for dollars. Americans buying British goods had to persuade someone to change dollars for sterling. Either the total purchases of the two groups must balance, or members of one group must be willing to accumulate the currency of the other, with the exchange rate adjusting to help bring this about, again as occurs now. The difference was that exchange rates fluctuated only within strict limits, reflecting the existence of the indirect payments mechanism described above.

Exchange rates were anchored to the mint par of exchange, i.e. the ratio of the gold content of one currency to that of another, simply because things related to the same thing must be related to each other. In 1816, the value of the pound was set equal to 113 fine grains of pure gold, while in 1834 the gold dollar contained 23.22 fine grains of pure gold, giving a mint par to exchange of $4.8665 = £1 prior to the First World War. Sir John Hicks (1986) remembers as a schoolboy that it was simply taken for granted that one pound was equal to 4.86 US dollars, 25 French or Swiss francs, 20 German marks, a little less than 10 Japanese yen, and so on. Indeed, these exchange rates were learnt from arithmetic books.

It was possible for exchange rates to vary from mint par, but they would usually do so only up to the limit implied by the cost of transporting gold in either direction between the two gold standard countries concerned. In pre-First World War years, the cost of shipping gold across the Atlantic including freight, insurance, agency fees and interest during the time of transit was about two cents. Hence $4.846 would constitute the 'gold export point', at which rate it would be advantageous to ship gold in payment rather than use the foreign exchange market. On the other hand, $4.886 would be the 'gold import point' for the United Kingdom. These specie points would constitute, respectively, the lower and upper limits to the movement of sterling in the market without producing gold shipments.

Sir Dennis Robertson saw the mint par of exchange as simply a special case of the purchasing power parity of money, whereby exchange rates will theoretically equalize the purchasing power of currencies over goods, once allowance is made for the cost of transport and any commodity taxes levied on them. In this case, gold is the good which is most easily and readily traded. Thus:

> It will still be true that the normal rate of exchange between them depends on the relative values of their moneys in terms of traded goods. But since gold is among the goods which become most easily the subject of trade, we can simplify matters by saying that the normal rate of exchange depends on the relative values of the two moneys in terms of gold, that is, on the relative weights of gold defined in the laws of the two countries as the bases of their respective standards. And refining further, we can say that the actual rate of exchange cannot diverge from this normal level in either direction by an amount which exceeds the cost of sending gold from one country to the other. (Robertson, 1948, p. 61)

If the exchange rate moved beyond the gold specie points, reserves of gold would flow to the country with the relatively low price level from the country with the relatively high price level, expanding the monetary base in the first and contracting it in the other. Under the automatic workings of the gold standard this movement in the monetary base was expected to expand the total money supply in the low-price country and contract it in the high-price country. Presumably, this would eventually bring their price levels into line with mint parities along the lines envisaged in Hume's price-specie-flow mechanism (Hume, 1752). The actual movements of gold would normally be carried out by arbitrageurs in the foreign exchange and bullion markets by exchanging currency for gold in the two countries.

It is undisputed that the gold standard did produce what is, especially by modern standards, a remarkable degree of exchange rate stability. Whether, or to what extent, it did so by the classical mechanism envisaged above is less clear. There is still no definitive account of how the gold standard really worked. Other mechanisms which may have operated include adjustments in spending and employment, flows of capital (especially long-term lending emanating from London), trade and offsetting capital flows as predicted by the monetary theory of the balance of payments, and movements in the terms of trade between manufacturing and commodity exporting countries (see Eichengreen, 1985). It would also seem that the gold standard was, to a large degree, a managed system with central bank policy in some cases facilitating, and in other cases overriding, the 'automatic' adjustment process.

Central banks had a number of tools at their disposal such as intervention in the gold market, adjustments to the gold reserve or changes in the regulations about convertibility (although intervention in the foreign exchange market was rare until the late 1930s when countries were no longer tied firmly to gold). For the Bank of England the main instrument was Bank rate. Amendments to the usury law in 1833 enabled Bank rate to be flexible upwards. Hawtrey (1938) dates its use from 1839, Keynes (1930) from 1844.

> The efficacy of Bank-rate for the management of a managed money was a great discovery and also a most novel one – a few years earlier the Bank of England had not had the slightest understanding of any connection between Bank-rate policy and the maintenance of the standard. (Keynes, p. 17)

When sterling tended to depreciate relative to the gold export point, a rise in Bank rate would occur. In the early years, the Bank acted more as a price leader among banks and discount houses, for by increasing interest charges to its own customers it could force up other short-term rates. Later, as the Bank's share of banking business declined, increases in interest rates were made effective by open market operations, accommodating discount house borrowing at a rate in excess of bill rates. In the nature of this mechanism there is, as we shall see later, a singular extent of continuity in the Bank's operations.

Increases in interest rates had two principal consequences. One was to attract short-term capital flows which acted as a palliative for the situation by reducing or even reversing the gold flow. Walter Bagehot once remarked that '8 per cent will bring gold from the moon'. Such sensitivity of capital flows to interest rates owed much to the credible commitment to fixed exchange rates which the metallic standard offered: countries on gold were expected to be so forever, and moreover at the same parity. When countries did suspend convertibility temporarily (e.g. the United States during the Greenback era, Britain in the Napoleonic wars and after the First World War), such was the attachment to the historic parities that resumption took place at the old levels. Britain effectively had the same official metallic value from 1717 to 1931, the United States from 1834 to 1934. *This really was monetary stability* and it meant that it was possible at any time to give force to a statement that sterling was relatively high or relatively low. As people became convinced of the fixity of rates, the process became self-reinforcing and capital more responsive. In this respect, to borrow Sir Roy Harrod's (1969) description, capital movements were 'helpful' to the authorities when protecting parity.

Striking evidence on the mobility of capital in this period is provided in Bayoumi (1990). The perceived *permanence* of the arrangements, including the parities, is nowhere more eloquently described than in Keynes (1919):

> The inhabitant of London could order by telephone, sipping his morning tea in bed, the various products of the whole earth, and in such quantity as he might

see fit, and reaonably expect their early delivery upon his doorstep; he could at the same moment and by the same means adventure his wealth in the natural resources and new enterprises of any quarter of the world, and share, without exertion or even trouble, in their prospective fruits and advantages; or he could decide to couple the security of his fortunes with the good faith of the townspeople of any substantial municipality in any continent that fancy or information might recommend. He could secure forthwith, if he wished it, cheap and comfortable means of transit to any country or climate without passport or other formality, could despatch his servant to the neighbouring office of a bank for such supply of the precious metals as might seem convenient, and could then proceed abroad to foreign quarters, without knowledge of their religion, language, or customs, bearing coined wealth upon his person, and would consider himself greatly aggrieved and much surprised at the least interference. But, most important of all, he regarded this state of affairs as normal, certain, and permanent, except in the direction of further improvement, and any deviation from it as aberrant, scandalous, and avoidable. (pp. 9–10)

The other side of an increase in interest rates was to tighten credit, discourage spending on stock and fixed investment and to deflate home demand, so reinforcing or complementing the restriction of the money supply due to the decline in gold stocks and the monetary base. As debt money assumed a larger part of the money supply, and more money came to be created as a byproduct of the lending activities of banks, interest rates and conditions in the credit market came to be seen as the cornerstone of monetary policy. As capital flows induced by Bank rate increasingly offset the initial gold flows, eliminating the need for the monetary base actually to force a reduction in money, reliance was placed upon credit and not money supply policy to bring out the adjustments to incomes and prices needed for longer-term stabilization of the trade and exchange rate position.

For most gold standard countries, stable exchange rates, instead of being the result of linking monetary units to gold, became in Irving Fisher's (1934) description 'the criterion of monetary stability' (p. 1). Monetary policy was thought of primarily in terms of maintaining a constant exchange value in terms of other currencies, with foreign rather than domestic convertibility the governing objective – i.e. an *exchange standard*. Increasingly, use of interest rates, with the central discount rate raised or lowered according to whether the balance of payments was weak or strong, and the exchange rate depreciating or appreciating, constituted the 'rules of the game' and became the mechanism of monetary policy.

In this respect, also, there has been a remarkable continuity in the *modus operandi* of policy, especially in the United Kingdom. And with the tendency to elevate the exchange rate to the status of the monetary standard in place of gold, it was a short step from the gold standard to Bretton Woods.

2.3   Bretton Woods

Under the rules of the Bretton Woods (or IMF) system, member countries of the IMF were required to define the parity of their currencies in terms of gold and to maintain what amounted to indirect convertibility into gold. Indirect gold convertibility came about via the stabilization of exchange values and gold prices. A parity for a country's currency in terms of gold implied, as under the gold standard, an official exchange rate between it and other currencies, in particular the US dollar. The dollar was the primary intervention and vehicle currency and was the key currency in that it was the only country which allowed its currency to be convertible (for external purposes) into gold – moreover at the 1934 parity of $35 per ounce. Exchange rates were to be maintained within ±1 per cent of parity, creating, albeit artificially, analogues of the old gold shipping points (but wider); and there was indirect convertibility into gold much as under a gold exchange standard. In addition, intervention took place in the London gold market to ensure that the private market price of gold did not differ from $35 per ounce by much more than the cost of shipping gold from New York to London. Both features of a commodity currency standard – parity and convertibility – were present. To all appearances a gold standard of sorts was still in operation.

In some other respects the role of gold was downplayed. No country undertook to redeem money domestically into gold, and in many countries private hoarding of gold in specie form was not allowed. While IMF member countries maintained convertibility of their currencies into other currencies through the foreign exchange market (and thus indirectly into gold), that conversion was no longer at a parity meant to be immutable. Par values could be altered for any (non-dollar) currency adjudged to be in fundamental disequilibrium (although it was implicit that the dollar would not, being in effect 'as good as gold').

This fixed-but-adjustable exchange rate mechanism grew out of the interwar experiences. At the onset of the Great Depression the international gold standard broke down. Countries issued inconvertible money and pursued nationalistic policies. Currencies were devalued competitively and tariff barriers were raised – dubbed by Joan Robinson as 'beggar thy neighbour' policies – while exchange controls were introduced along with multiple exchange rates and other capital restricting devices. As a consequence, an inconvertible paper money standard was indelibly associated in the public mind with disorder in the foreign exchanges. There were in fact moves back towards some greater fixity of exchange rates in the later 1930s which in many ways were not dissimilar to those in the 1980s. A number of currency blocs formed, the largest by far being the Sterling Area which arose when the gold standard collapsed and which at one time or another comprised Britain and the Commonwealth (excluding Canada), the Scandinavian countries and Iceland, Japan, Argentina, Egypt and Turkey. Free movements of capital took place within the area, and exchange controls and trade restrictions were applied to outside countries. (Some would see here parallels with the EMS, sometimes seen as a Deutschmark currency area.) There was also the equivalent of the Plaza Agreement and the Louvre Accord of the 1980s in the Tripartite Monetary Agreement of September 26th 1936, whereby the United States, France and Britain (including the Sterling Area) agreed to support each other's currencies and bring about such substantial day-to-day stability of exchange rates that the rates of exchange between the three currencies were generally regarded as fixed. Exchange rates were subject to adjustment by agreement with the other two parties if a serious disequilibrium occurred. Belgium, the Netherlands and Switzerland later joined this arrangement which lasted until the outbreak of the Second World War.

The Bretton Woods system was established (by forty-four countries meeting in Bretton Woods, New Hampshire in 1944) as an alternative to either a gold standard or a fiat money standard, and which took what was seen as the best features from both. The gold standard provided exchange rate stability along with rules and cooperation in promoting free trade and capital movements, but was regarded as contributing to depression when countries deflated to defend fixed parities. Fiat money, it seemed, led to inflation and unstable exchanges, but did enable countries to recover from unemployment by avoiding having to force down prices to bring them into line with gold parities. What emerged was the system of rigid, but adjustable, parities. Exchange rates would normally be kept fixed, with the widened 'gold points' allowing some margin for market clearing of fluctuations in trading positions.

In terms of the four so-called 'desirables' of international monetary arrangements, namely fixed exchange rates, free trade, monetary autonomy and free capital movements, the architects of Bretton Woods were prepared to compromise on freedom of capital flows. Countries agreed to a 'code of conduct' dealing with cooperation, trade, convertibility and orderly exchange arrangements, yet continued restrictions on capital markets were envisaged and tolerated. The IMF, for its part, undertook to promote stability of exchange rates by lending out resources ('drawings') to help countries ride out minor fluctuations in the demand and supply of foreign exchange, while permitting orderly changes in parity to correct a 'fundamental disequilibrium'. Exchange rates would thus be allowed to be brought into conformity with seriously misaligned price levels – not the reverse as under the gold standard.

On this description, it would not be accurate to depict the Bretton Woods system as a gold standard. Nor could it be termed an exchange standard, for stabilization of the exchange rate was compromised by the trade-off of external for internal stability. To the extent that the authorities paid exclusive attention to stabilizing aggregate demand or providing a stable growth of employment it might be said that the countries were on an *employment standard*.[11] If the commitments to the IMF were adhered to, it might be more accurate to call the system a *balance of payments standard*.[12] Action to correct a balance of payments disequilibrium by either deflationary or inflationary policies or an adjustment to par values implied making the balance of payments the criterion of policy.

If so, the Bretton Woods system was soon transformed into an exchange standard, with maintenance of the existing parity central to policy formulation. This was not due to any unwillingness of the IMF to approve changes for it was never difficult for member countries to alter parity, and these were sometimes at the urging of the IMF itself. Instead, countries became increasingly reluctant to change parities for a mixture of reasons. Revaluations were domestically unpopular because they jeopardized the competitiveness of domestic export- and import-competing industries. Devaluation called into question the competence of economic policy-makers, and avoidance of devaluation became a sort of international 'virility test'. Countries with large external borrowings in their own currency felt under an obligation to make every possible effort to maintain the value of their currencies at much the same level as had prevailed when the debts were incurred. Finally, there was the problem of speculation and of 'unhelpful' capital movements.

Under the gold standard, capital movements were 'helpful' because exchange rate parities were credibly fixed by the existence of the gold specie points. The prescribed ±1 per cent ranges in the Bretton Woods system provided no similar assurance, because many governments were not prepared to follow through with the policies that maintenance of the exchange rate really needed. Moreover, countries liberalized the controls over capital movements that the founding fathers of Bretton Woods appear to have taken for granted. Speculators were able to bet against the ability and willingness of the authorities to sustain the parity. To make matters worse, the method of changing rates discontinuously in large discrete jumps – the adjustable peg – made obvious the direction of change, allowing speculators the luxury of anticipating change with facility and virtually no risk. A government contemplating an adjustment to parity had to take cognizance of the likelihood that a change would merely encourage speculators to expect that it would be altered again in response to future payments difficulties, so making matters worse 'next time round'. Future policy credibility and the avoidance of increasingly large and destabilizing speculation pointed to the desirability of using the adjustable peg provisions of the IMF system as seldom as possible:

> The Bretton Woods agreement provided for adjustments in par values if they turned out to be unrealistic, and this had been done in a few cases, such as the devaluation of sterling in 1949. Actually, there were rather few of these instances; during most of the 1960s there were none at all, particularly not between 1961 and 1967. Gradually tacit agreement had emerged among the central banks and finance ministers of the world that the devaluation clause of the Bretton Woods agreement should not be used because it was disruptive and would lead to speculation. Instead of the adjustable peg envisaged by the Bretton Woods agreement we should have 'fixed and immutable exchange rates,' to use the words of Robert Roosa who was Undersecretary of the Treasury during the early 1960s. In other words, the exchange rate adjustment clause of the Bretton Woods agreement had been set aside, though the 1967 devaluation of sterling could not be prevented. Houthakker (1977, pp. 10–11)

This transition highlighted the system's internal contradictions. With the exchange rate instrument unused, this left the 'adjustment' problem – the policy problem of how external balance was to be attained in an environment in which countries were unwilling to sacrifice internal balance to defend existing exchange rate parities. Here we follow analyses of the time in envisaging in Tinbergen terms a two target–two instrument framework (see Chapter 3). Those analyses assumed that an identifiable relationship existed between the pressure of aggregate demand and inflation (a Phillips Curve), so that full employment and stable prices were lumped together as a single target, internal balance, to be matched against the other target of equilibrium in the balance of payments, external balance. Where the studies differed was in the choice of instruments to resolve conflicts between internal and external balance.

In Meade's classic analysis (1951) of the conflict, four economic situations (called by Swan, 1955, 'zones of economic unhappiness') were distinguished. Countries experiencing inflation or recession can be faced with either a surplus or a deficit in the balance of payments. In two of the situations, recession-surplus and inflation-deficit, expansionary and contractionary expenditure policies respectively can at least ameliorate both problems. In the other two situations, recession-deficit and inflation-surplus, expenditure policies directed at internal balance seem likely to worsen the external position, and another policy tool is required. This might lead to a switching policy (see Johnson, 1958) whereby alterations to the exchange rate, tariffs or import restrictions switch demand between domestic and internationally traded goods.

Swan's (1955) influential model of the internal–external balance conflict made the two 'instruments' real expenditures and the cost (or competitiveness) ratio, ep^*/w, which relates international prices (p^*) via the exchange rate (e) to local wage costs (w). With exchange rates fixed, variations in the cost ratio require changes in the tariff structure or in local wages (or profits). Tariffs were ruled out by international commitments to free world trade, putting the burden onto wage adjustments as the sole means of bringing about changes in the alignment of domestic to international costs (i.e. altering competitiveness). Swan's analysis always had this alternative to exchange rate changes in mind, for the model was devised to illuminate policy problems in Australia where a wages policy could be implemented through the centralized wage-fixing machinery. It was thus readily transportable to those European countries (including Britain) where incomes policies were a viable policy option, but not to North America and other countries with more decentralized labour markets.

In Canada and the United States, analysis of the internal–external balance conflict proceeded along different lines. Swan defined external balance in terms of the current account, treating capital movements as given. This may have been a useful first approximation to the state of the world capital market in the 1950s, but it was less appropriate after full convertibility was restored in 1959. Mundell (1962, 1963b) defined external balance to include both the current account and capital flows, with the latter sensitive to domestic financial policies. He argued that by an appropriate use of the two instruments of fiscal and monetary policy it might be possible to attain internal and external balance under fixed exchange rates without recourse to commercial policies. This 'appropriate use' involved assigning fiscal policy to internal balance and monetary policy to external balance, the latter requiring that interest rates be varied inversely to the strength of the balance of payments much as under the 'rules of the game' of the classical gold standard.

For most countries Mundell's solution offered only a short-run palliative. The price of a Mundell 'solution' to an uncompetitiveness problem is a capital account surplus matching the current account deficit which, if capital markets are rather imperfect (as they were then), is unsustainable. Lurking also in the background to policy formulation was a third goal, namely economic growth. Sustained reliance upon high interest rates in deficit-prone countries was seen as inimical to the encouragement of high investment and growth. Countries were left reliant upon direct controls. Surplus countries tried to sterilize the money supply from the consequences of the accretion of international reserves, while applying, among a number of instruments, ceilings and taxes on the interest rates paid to foreigners and special reserve requirements on foreign deposits, which served to ameliorate the effects but did not correct the underlying payments position. Deficit countries applied import quotas and export subsidies, two-tiered exchange rates (a rate less favourable than parity for overseas investment by residents) and exchange controls. As the market found ways around these restrictions, policy-makers were faced with the choice of tightening existing controls and introducing ever more Draconian measures – which to them were increasingly tedious to operate – or somehow escaping from the strait-jacket of fixed parities. There was discussion of a system based on a 'crawling peg'[13] as one way of letting exchange rates be somewhat more flexible without abandoning entirely the precepts of the Bretton Woods system, but it came to nothing. (In any case, as demonstrated by those countries – e.g. Australia – which later implemented a crawling peg exchange rate system, it was bedevilled by speculation and relied upon *dirigiste* exchange controls.)[14] Floating exchange rates emerged as the only escape route.

A move to floating exchange rates solved the 'liquidity' and 'confidence' problems of the Bretton Woods system identified by Triffin (1960). The liquidity issue arose because attempts to hold exchange rates fixed in the face of massive and destabilizing speculative capital flows created a need for large international reserves – certainly much larger than those likely under floating rates or those needed when commitment to the gold standard lent a credibility to fixed parities. Yet accumulation of US dollars provided the major source of monetary reserves (which consisted of gold, dollars, sterling and other foreign exchange, and net claims in the form of the gold tranche at the IMF). Expansion of gold reserves came from newly mined gold and from gold sales of the Soviet Union. Augmenting this growth required either an increase in the price of gold – politically unacceptable because of the windfall gains which would accrue to South Africa and the Soviet Union – or a deflation of commodity prices relative to gold. Price deflation satisfied liquidity preferences for gold in the 1930s but was unwelcome in the post-war growth environment.

Reliance upon a continued growth in foreign exchange reserves relative to gold to augment liquidity gave rise to the confidence problem. To expand liquidity, the United States had to run a balance of payments deficit, but the deficit eroded confidence in the system. As external dollar liabilities grew, the world was exposed to the danger of a financial crisis if confidence in the dollar's convertibility faltered and there should be a flight from dollars into gold. In consequence:

> The United States became more and more reluctant to sell gold to other countries, and let this reluctance be known. Technically the United States was

still under an obligation to sell gold in exchange for foreign-held dollars, an obligation which we had accepted when the Bretton Woods agreement went into force shortly after World War II. We were supposed to make our gold available without limit to other countries for monetary purposes, but in fact we increasingly discouraged other countries from asking for gold. I don't believe we ever actually told any country they couldn't have it, but it was made clear to them that such requests were not welcome, to say the least, and most of them took the hint. They did not ask for gold when they had accumulated dollars as they had done previously; instead they held these dollars as an investment – perhaps an involuntary investment. And this of course was the essence of 'benign neglect'. Houthakker (1977, p. 18)

This was one of a number of steps down the path to an inconvertible dollar and the demonetization of gold. Others were the reluctance of central banks on occasions such as 1960 to intervene in the London gold bullion market, which led to the formation of the gold 'pool', and the decision in 1968 to create a two-tiered gold market with the private market price free to exceed the official price, while gold moved (not very freely it would seem from the above quotation) on a closed circuit among the central banks. In the event, the closing of the gold window – indisputably one of the most important milestones in monetary history – was tacked on almost as an afterthought to a speech by President Nixon announcing a package of domestic economic measures; the precise reasons prompting it remain shrouded in mystery:

It is one of those minor mysteries of history that, like many events I have described from my own recollections, may one day be clarified when various people write their memoirs and the relevant documents are published. But the event itself is not in doubt, namely that in early August 1971 the British inquired about the possibility of gold cover for their dollar holdings. The Bank of England held fairly sizeable dollar reserves and was obviously afraid that the dollar might be devalued. In order to prevent a capital loss the British wanted their dollars guaranteed at their gold value. To Treasury officials in Washington, one of whom told me about it a few days later, this was a low blow. The United States had gone to great lengths to defend the pound sterling especially in 1964. In 1967 this rather futile exercise could not be successfully repeated and the pound sterling was actually devalued. Still, we had always been ready to help Britain, so when the Bank of England expressed distrust of the dollar, one can readily imagine that Connally [Secretary to the Treasury] and some of his collaborators were incensed. Connally himself, at the subsequent meeting at Camp David, referred to the British request (which was at least partially agreed to) as a sign that the international monetary situation was rapidly falling apart. It may have been the last straw as far as he was concerned. After a weekend meeting at Camp David ending on August 15, 1971, the United States decided to formally sever the link between the dollar and gold, thus bringing the Bretton Woods agreement to an end. Houthakker (1977, pp. 22–3)

2.4 The international non-system?

As Goodhart (1984a) has noted, the breakdown of Bretton Woods was viewed by the leading countries as liberating them from unwelcome constraints. The French no longer had to passively accept dollars created by the US payments deficit under what President de Gaulle called the 'exorbitant privilege' which the United States possessed in having the dollar as the primary reserve currency (the seigniorage question). For its part, the United States was able to escape from the 'nth currency constraint', whereby if other countries (Germany, Japan?) maintained undervalued currencies in the pursuit of export-led growth, the dollar was necessarily overvalued and in deficit. Germany and other low inflation countries could avoid the problem of 'imported inflation', for fixed parities implied ultimate convergence of inflation in individual countries to the world (US) average. Britain felt released from stop–go and the balance of payments constraint of fixed parities which the UK governments thought held back a faster rate of growth. This liberation has in most cases proved to be illusory.

Many leading experts, notably Williamson (1976), have seized upon the absence of constraints to characterize present arrangements as a 'non-system', by which they mean the absence of an explicit set of rules. According to McMahon (1988):

> If words are to retain any meaning, an international monetary system must involve some kind of set of rules governing the monetary relationships between nations: in particular, the determination of exchange rates and the nature, convertibility, and acceptability of international assets. The rules may be of many kinds, they may be tight or loose, simple or complex, but they must exist in a form that can be clearly expressed and they must be accepted by all the nations participating in the system. And acceptance of rules must not be simply a matter of governments' signatures: it must have behavioral meaning in the sense that observance of any set of international monetary rules will at times constrain, and explicitly constrain, individual national policies. . . . (pp. 5–6)
> . . . up to 1971 or perhaps 1973, we had an international monetary system. Since then we have not. (p. 5)

This follows a long tradition in monetary economics of defining a fiat money system in negative terms – for example as 'a monetary system in which the value or purchasing power of a monetary unit is not kept equal to the value of a specific quantity of a particular commodity or of a group of commodities' (Kent, quoted in Mason, 1963, p. 183). Looked at in this way, the present system is one in which there are no agreed rules upon international behaviour. Issuers of money do not promise to exchange it for gold or any other commodity. Many countries (those which form the European Exchange Rate Mechanism excepted) do not make their money convertible at a fixed rate into another currency. Nor is any assignment of instruments to targets implied. No limits are placed upon money creation; countries can choose inflation, deflation, any fiscal–monetary policy mix, slow or fast growth; they can lend or borrow as much as they like.

However, the absence of a 'system' in the sense defined by Williamson and McMahon need not imply disorder. Order in monetary arrangements can be induced spontaneously[15] as well as by design; coordination can arise voluntarily without coercion; actions can be constrained without there being any central direction. It is these distinctions which underlie Corden's (1983) insight that present arrangements in fact have similarities with one of the oldest of systems, that of *laissez-faire* – in Corden's words, the present system is a form of 'international financial *laissez-faire*'.

Textbooks on economic principles often begin with parables about housewives going off to market each day for shopping. These actions are not managed or centrally directed, nor for that matter are they uncoordinated or unconstrained. The coordination comes through the market-place. Purchase plans are drawn up on the basis of household preferences and expected prices. When confronted by quoted selling prices, these plans are revised along with market-clearing prices.

So it is internationally. Households, firms and governments formulate plans about exports and imports, consumption and savings, holdings of money and assets. These actions are integrated, revised, constrained and coordinated through the international market-places for goods, services and assets, by exchange rates and interest rates and overall demands and supplies.

A special twist comes from the different currencies employed. Continuing the analogy, it is as if a songwriter, artist or author must sell his work before every purchase. The intrinsic value of the music sheet, canvas and oil or manuscript and ink is low, but if valued they exchange for goods in the market in excess of this value. Our author, say, might well live in the lap of luxury but if preferences change and his writings fall from favour, then he must work harder to pay his way. So it would seem is the case with countries; 'fiat money has no intrinsic value other than what the issuing government (central bank) manages to establish' (McKinnon, 1984, p. 20).

What determines the value of money? What implications follow for economic policy-making? What is the monetary standard that guides policy? Considering the first of these, the factors influencing the value of money like that of any economic substance can be proximately classified in terms of 'demand' and 'supply'. Demand here refers to monetary demand. This creates somewhat of a paradox since the existence of a monetary demand presupposes that the money has value, yet there is no non-monetary demand at all for the money. Here is the essence of Wallace's (1990) contention that nominal values in the present system are at base 'indeterminate'. On the other side, the influence of supply in determining value is readily apparent. If each monetary unit exchanged in terms of its marginal cost of production then there would be a literal paper standard – a commodity system based on paper. It follows that if each unit (i.e. pound) is able to be exchanged for goods of greater value than the cost of printing the unit, then it is due to some scarcity or artificial restriction upon supply. This puts the emphasis upon the conditions governing the issue of money and the policies followed by the monetary authorities in rendering values determinate: or, if preferred, in Wallace's terms 'legal restrictions or anticipated government interventions' (p. 13).

The 'monetary' explanation of variations in the value of money, i.e. inflation or deflation, is simply an application of the standard principles of the theory of value to the determination of the purchasing power of fiat money. Inflation means a sustained decline in the purchasing power or value of money in terms of goods and services, money being the medium in which the prices of goods and services are stated, goods are paid for and debts are discharged. If more pounds are issued, and the supply of goods is unchanged, then each pound ultimately exchanges for fewer goods. That is, prices of goods rise in terms of the *numéraire* of money. Here, in the simplest of terms, is the basis of the 'quantity approach' to prices, with inflation due to failure by governments to make money scarce.

But scarcity is a relationship between supply *and* demand. A declining value of money can be caused by a fall in demand with a given supply as well as by an increase in supply relative to a given demand. Any monetary explanation of inflation must therefore allow for variations in demand arising from variations in interest rates, the growth of incomes, expectations and other factors. Appropriately defined, such variations can remain part of a supply-side explanation. But they also allow non-monetary influences to enter the story. There is in addition a more systematic interaction between demand and supply which features in non-monetary explanations of inflation. Since the number of pounds demanded depends not only upon the number of goods being purchased, but also on the prices of those goods, any increase in prices raises the amount of money demanded and leads to pressure for money creation to occur. While not denying the proximate importance of changes in the money supply, these changes are seen as resultants of prior increases in wages and other costs. The chapters immediately following examine, respectively, the non-monetary influences upon prices (Chapter 3) and the demand for money in the UK (Chapter 4).

It is customary to draw a distinction between money's value in terms of domestic goods and services and its value in terms of foreign goods and services. External purchasing power refers to the price of the monetary unit of one country in terms of the unit of another country, with depreciation paralleling inflation. The supply story of the quantity theory also embraces the external purchasing power of money under floating exchanges. UK residents engaging in international trade must persuade foreigners to buy pounds, and vice versa for foreigners wishing to buy British goods. Ignoring 'hoarding' of foreign exchange, these trades produce exchange rates which equalize the purchasing power of the currencies over goods. That is, purchasing power parity implies that the pound–kronor exchange rate is such that a given number of pounds buys about the same amount of goods in Britain as the amount of kronor that can be acquired with those pounds buys in Sweden. If pounds become more plentiful, each one buys less foreign as well as less domestic goods, with the exchange rate adjusting to the monetary disturbance. Later chapters examine this transmission in more detail.

Here, as under the gold standard, the quantity theory visualizes exchange rates as being underpinned by purchasing power parity, but this theorem provides a much less definite anchor in the new environment. In particular, the story needs to be supplemented by an account of asset holding preferences and of the effect of expectations of future monetary policies.

Asset preferences are important, for if foreigners add to their holding of sterling assets, then Britons are receiving foreign currency without having to sell goods and services on current account, and the exchange value of the pound is relatively high. This high value is needed to induce British citizens to buy foreign goods and so have a current account deficit to match the capital inflow.

These interrelationships assume importance in view of the internationalization of the financial system noted in the previous chapter, for developments in private international finance seem likely to have altered, in a fundamental way, modes of exchange rate behaviour. When Friedman (1953), Meade (1955), Johnson (1969) and others presented the case for flexible exchange rates, they envisaged that trade flows would dominate foreign exchange markets, so that purchasing power parity would enable speculators to judge whether the exchange rate was high or low, and so stabilize its behaviour. Now trade surpluses and deficits are being balanced to a large degree by flows of private capital, as under interregional adjustment. In response to a payments deficit, members of a region must issue liabilities, that is borrow, or draw down assets, or do both, in order to finance the imbalance. Liabilities could be issued to banks by means of bank borrowing or be issued in national or international capital markets. Alternatively, members of the region can run down bank balances or sell other assets. Funds flow from the surplus to the deficit region, financing the imbalance. To that extent, the need for movements in exchange rates to bring about short-run adjustments to trade flows is largely obviated. This process can continue until national banks and lenders in other regions are unwilling to lend further or members of the region run out of assets which can be sold off or borrowed against. Exchange rates will be responding more to lenders' preferences for assets denominated in the various currencies than to the trade flows which supply the assets. Here we have the basis for the 'asset approach' to exchange rate determination (see Chapter 5).

Turning now to future monetary policies, we have said that the domestic and external purchasing power of money rests ultimately on scarcity in supply. Suppose that an increase in supply is anticipated. There is no domestic market for money as such where these expectations can be acted upon (the so-called 'money market' being really a market for bills and other short-term securities). In many respects the market for goods can be considered to be the 'other side' of the market for money, so people can write down the real value of the money supply by bidding up prices. But there is also the foreign exchange market which allows views about future policies to find expression. If market participants expect a fast rate of domestic money creation, they will tend to write down the external value of the pound in anticipation. In order to placate such expectations, and protect the value of money, governments of all persuasions have felt the need to establish the credibility of policies.

This brings us to the question of what it is that guides policies in the new environment and how credibility can be achieved. Governments welcomed the transition to international *laissez-faire* for the liberation it apparently afforded for domestic policies. Mundell (1969) accurately predicted what transpired:

> The argument [for floating exchange rates] is often put, falsely, in the Tinbergen framework, as the need to have an additional instrument, the exchange rate, to achieve a necessary target (or restraint), balance of payments equilibrium. But fixing the exchange rate implies stabilizing domestic prices in terms of international prices, while the requirement of equilibrium in the balance of payments at a given level of reserves requires a passive adjustment of the quantity of money. If, therefore, the exchange rate is freed the balance of payments is equilibrated directly, but the money supply must then be adjusted to achieve the goal of internal price stability (relative to international prices). The 'additional' instrument disappears. (p. 636)

In one form or another, and by employing various means, most of the major countries have adopted what L. G. Melville (later Sir Lesley

Melville) described in Adelaide, South Australia in 1934 during the last
era of fiat money as a *goods standard*:

> So, today, the greater part of the world rejects the gold standard and pledges its
> adherence to some kind of goods standard. By a goods standard is meant a
> monetary system under which the quantity of money would be regulated rather
> with reference to the prices of a selected group of goods than with reference to
> the quantity of gold.[16]

UK monetary arrangements during the 1980s can be readily interpreted
in this vein. That is, the government had the objective of using interest
rates to keep the internal value of money reasonably stable in terms of
(the underlying value of) the retail price index. The chapters below flesh
out how the monetary authorities sought, with varying emphasis, to
achieve this aim.

Notes

1. Keynes (1923, p. 172).
2. See Eichengreen (1985) and Robertson (1948).
3. For an explanation of Gresham's Law see Harrod (1969) and Burstein (1963).
4. Hicks (1986, p. 2).
5. See Cooper (1982).
6. The alleged automaticity is examined by Sir Roy Harrod (1965).
7. Cooper (1982).
8. William Jennings Bryan campaigned for silver and is renowned for his Cross of Gold speech ('ye shall not crucify mankind on a cross of gold'). His campaign was doomed by the rash of gold discoveries in that year which put prices on an upward path.
9. Marshall (1887).
10. Harrod (1965) p. 58.
11. Buchanan (1962, p. 165, n. 2.) He doubts whether an employment standard should be called a monetary standard at all.
12. Mason (1963, p. 99).
13. Williamson (1965).
14. Polasek and Lewis (1985).
15. Spontaneous systems are examined in Gallarotti (1989).
16. Cited in Mason (1963).

3

Inflation in the United Kingdom

3.1 The era of 'inflation first'

Whether or not inflation is, as Friedman (1987) has put it 'always and everywhere a monetary phenomenon', it is clear that the process of inflation in real economies involves much more than a costless and automatic marking-up of prices in line with a monetary expansion. The model of inflation as a reverse monetary reform in which successively 'lighter' pounds replace the earlier currency, however useful for understanding the steady state implications of monetary shocks, cannot obscure the fact that real-world inflationary processes are marked by sharp changes in relative prices, sharply changing real interest rates, unlegislated real tax changes and labour market interactions. In the same way a process of disinflation involves disruptive relative price changes and consequential quantity adjustments. As we observed in Chapter 2, falling prices under the gold standard in the second half of the nineteenth century were accompanied by high real interest rates and debtor hardship.

The experience of the 1970s following the first oil price (OPEC) shock in 1973–4 marked the end of the post-war boom and, for many countries, produced an unacceptable mixture of high inflation, rising unemployment and macroeconomic uncertainty. The second oil price rise in 1979 produced a more determined and uniform commitment among the leading industrial countries to counter-inflationary priorities. This was marked *inter alia* by a commitment to deflationary monetary policies. This background is important to the United Kingdom's own counter-inflationary policies and deserves some discussion in its own right.

The global disinflation

The global commitment to inflation first policies which took hold after 1979 both conditioned and reflected the United Kingdom's own policies. The relative effect arose because the United Kingdom was early off the mark in ushering in the policies of monetary deceleration and curbing the size of the public sector, and because it played a leading role, at meetings of the G-7 and elsewhere and in concert with the United States, in promulgating and exporting these policies.[1] The conditioning arose from the uniformity with which the G-7 (and other) countries embraced these doctrines, or their own versions of them.

The OECD's study of the disinflation of the 1980s (Coe *et al.*, 1988) concludes that in fact '[t]he principal factors accounting for the disinflation were the restrictive monetary policies adopted in OECD countries' (p. 113), and attributes some fifteen points of the disinflation (1980–7) to these policies. The OECD study deploys the Interlink model to reach this assessment; within the model non-oil commodity prices are endogenous. According to the study, one of the principal avenues by which the restrictive monetary policies worked was by way of reducing the demand for, and prices of, these goods – indeed the OECD finds that non-oil commodity price impacts other than those arising from the effect induced by restrictive monetary policies were negligible. The study thus amplifies in a vital respect the view put forward by Beckerman and Jenkinson (1987) that the disinflation depended on declining commodity price pressures rather than on unemployment, by suggesting that the decline in commodity prices and the rise in unemployment were both due to policy impacts.[2]

From the insular UK point of view, the combined OECD effect on commodity prices was in itself favourable to the reduction of inflation. The other side of the coin, of course, was the recessionary impact of the fall in world trade growth which amplified UK unemployment. There are some interesting parallels here with the workings of monetary policy under the classical gold standard. Triffin (1968) argued that because London was the major source of credit for the finance of international trade in foodstuffs and raw materials, a rise in Bank rate had a larger effect abroad than at home. The increased cost of holding stock led foreign producers to dump stocks of primary commodities onto world markets. When combined with an inelastic and leftward shifting demand curve for primary goods, the consequence was for the prices of these commodities to fall sharply relative to other goods. This improvement in Britain's terms of trade, elicited by tight money, more than compensated for the effect of tight credit upon domestic demand. Britain, it may be noted, also did relatively well during the worldwide Depression of the

1930s, particularly in comparison with primary-exporting countries such as Australia and New Zealand. While the global setting of the 1980s matched the United Kingdom's own counter-inflationary priorities, both its policies and the background of inflationary experience in the United Kingdom were distinctive in various ways.

Economists frequently employ the theory of economic policy to assess the design and execution of macroeconomic policies. The central principle of this analysis – Tinbergen's (1956) 'counting rule' – is that for every target to be attained there must be at least one effective instrument. Formally, the ultimate target variables ($y_1 . . .y_n$) are defined as those which the authorities wish to influence, and the authorities are assumed to have a desired level for each target. The instrument variables ($x_1 . . .x_m$) are those determined entirely by the authorities in order to achieve the desired levels of the targets, given that the two sets of variables are related by functions of the form

$$y_1 = f_1 (x_1 . . . x_m; z_1 . . . z_r)$$ (3.1)

$$y_n = f_n (x_1 . . . x_m; z_1 . . . z_r)$$

where $z_1 . . . z_r$ are the unchangeable exogenous variables. An economic policy is a particular set of values of the policy instruments.

When targets are enumerated (say 6 per cent unemployment, 3 per cent inflation, balance of payments equilibrium), the approach tells us that these three (mutually independent) targets can be achieved only if the authorities have at least the same number (three) of effective, independent policy instruments. Intuitively this may be seen from the above equations, by noting that for each equation, when the x's and z's are fixed, the y variable takes on a value to ensure equality. If instead the y value is fixed, one of the x variables must perform the equalizing function. Thus, if there are n y values fixed, there must be at least n x variables (instruments) free to vary. This is the 'counting rule'. But there is an important proviso. The availability of n instruments does not guarantee that as many targets can be hit: there have to be n *independent* instruments, in the sense that they are quite free to vary (e.g. taxes or government spending can be raised or lowered at will) and in the sense that they do in fact have different effects upon the targets.

With three weapons of economic policy – fiscal, monetary and external – it would seem possible to achieve the generally accepted macroeconomic targets of employment, price stability and external equilibrium. The policy problem would seem to be one of finding a satisfactory mix of the instruments and tackling *all* objectives simultaneously. In line with another general principle of policy, due to Mundell (1962), each instrument of policy would be employed in this mix according to its comparative advantage in affecting particular targets.

Macroeconomic policy formulation in Britain since 1979 would seem to have followed a markedly different approach. Rather than attack economic problems together, it has been argued that they need to be tackled *sequentially*: inflation first, then unemployment – an approach which, borrowing from Australian terminology, we call the 'inflation first' strategy. A second feature of policy formulation has been that instead of seeking to utilize the comparative advantages of the various instruments in a policy package, the emphasis has been upon the interrelatedness of the instruments – of forming them into an integrated, coherent and effective whole, and using them as if they were one (to achieve price stability in the first instance).

While it is difficult to associate these ideas with any particular school of economic thought, the second element is not inconsistent with what Tobin (1989) calls the 'common funnel theorem'. The theorem says that the consequences for a given amount of aggregate demand for output and employment (Y) on the one hand, and wages and prices (P) on the other hand, are independent of the sources and composition of that demand. Neither monetary policy nor fiscal policy affects P or Y directly, both through the same medium. In the simile employed by Tobin, demands which derive from the instruments of monetary policy (M) and the instruments of fiscal policy (which alter the velocity of money, V) are seen to be poured, along with demands from other sources (the private economy and overseas), into a common funnel.

Like all simple ideas the level of abstraction which is involved here is considerable and the list of qualifications is long. One major proviso relates to the differential effect of monetary policy upon the external account in a regime of floating exchange rates with free movement of international funds (see Chapters 5 and 8). A policy of tight money and fiscal expansion, as instituted in the United States in the early 1980s, raises interest rates, attracts funds from overseas and appreciates the local currency. This appreciation makes internationally traded goods cheaper in terms of the local currency and in domestic price indices. Whether the policy can be sustained depends on overseas reactions, since the home country has a current account deficit and overseas countries import inflationary pressures via the depreciation of their currencies; in this respect the policy is of a beggar-thy-neighbour variety.

Other qualifications come from the effect of the differential fiscal/monetary policy mix upon the supply of public and private goods, and the composition of demand, with Keynesians arguing the value of public works for employment and 'supply-siders' the advantages of tax cuts for creating work incentives. Another theme, which featured much in earlier policy discussion, was the extent to which incomes policy could sever the nexus between P and Y implied by the common funnel. However, in the context of 1979 the subject of incomes policies had become politically charged and, in the mind of the government, associated with the old order.

Thus the general message remained. High unemployment and inflation could not be fought simultaneously by macroeconomic policies. Monetary policy had no special handle upon prices other than through deflation of aggregate demand for goods and services: there was no 'free lunch' in reducing inflation. In terms of Tobin's analysis, from the viewpoint of P and Y, fiscal policy and monetary policy are collinear instruments. This tying together of the two is most clear in the government's medium-term financial strategy (MTFS), which was presented annually throughout the Thatcher administration as the 'framework for the Government's economic policy'. The main role of the MTFS has been to reduce inflation, initially by having reducing targets for the growth rate of the broad money supply (M3) while curtailing the public sector borrowing requirement (PSBR). Besides monetary aggregates and the PSBR, the MTFS has also included plans for public expenditure and taxation.

Given that the government *did* want to reduce inflation, it was clearly advantageous to emphasize in the context of the MTFS the benefits that would come from doing so and 'go quiet' about the consequences for output and employment. Nevertheless, it is possible to discern a marked alteration in government attitudes to the $P-Y$ relationship and the instruments appropriate for it. In a reversal of past practice, the UK authorities held to the view that macroeconomic policy should be devoted to combating inflation and microeconomic policies related to the structure of markets and competition at promoting employment and growth (see the sixth Mais Lecture delivered by the then Chancellor of the Exchequer, Nigel Lawson, on 18 July 1984). Combined with this rearrangement there seemed to be a conception of the economic structure in which inflation and the uncertainties it generates play a causal role in contributing to other macroeconomic problems: faster inflation depresses business investment and distorts price signals and the working of markets generally, making for a coincidence of high inflation and high unemployment, much along the lines argued by Friedman (1977) in his Nobel Prize lecture. For Britain a major distortion was seen to come from union power in labour markets, so that some short-term unemployment followed by the institution of a stable inflationary environment seemed desirable for the government's macroeconomic reforms. When these elements are put together the result is a major reordering of policy priorities in which the cure of inflation is seen as a precondition for the achievement of other economic goals, including a sustained expansion of employment.

The current MTFS, like its forerunners, reaffirms that the objective of policy is to bring down the rate of inflation, with the ultimate aim being stable prices, although exactly what this constitutes is not clear. At the beginning of the 1990s, the low-inflation countries (Germany, the Netherlands, Japan and Switzerland) seem willing to settle for an inflation rate of about 2–3 per cent per annum. This may be a reflection of the upward bias inherent in the price indices used to measure inflation,[3] or perhaps it is a recognition that prices remain sufficiently inflexible downwards that a gently rising price level is needed as a lubricant to ensure that relative price movements occur – what Hahn (1982) called the 'natural rate of inflation'.

But in other respects it is not immediately obvious why a permanently rising price level is desirable. Despite the continued emphasis in the economics literature upon the costs which inflation imposes on the holding of money balances for transactions purposes (the so-called 'shoe leather' effects), by far the greater burden seems likely to emanate from money's role as a medium of account; that is, from the accounting, information and psychic costs of having a floating standard of value. People just do not carry log tables around in their heads, and to function properly as a unit of account, money, as the measuring rod, should desirably have a constant value.

Sir John Hicks (1977) put these points incisively in his essay 'Expected inflation':

> Does it in fact make any difference to the working of an economy whether the value of money is constant or whether it is falling, so long as it is falling at a rate which is fully expected and fully allowed for?
>
> There is indeed only one reason, which has occurred to economists, why lesser inflation should be preferable to greater, even on this stringent test. I cannot, for my part, regard it as a very compelling reason, so long as the rate of inflation is moderate. It does indeed happen, in extreme inflations, that the loss of value from holding the depreciating money becomes a major consideration; when people receive money, they seek to pass it on as quickly as possible. Money loses its function as a store of value; so people are driven to satisfy their needs for 'convenience and security' in other ways, by holding their resources in what must inevitably be less convenient forms. One may grant that this would happen, in extreme inflation, even if the fall in the value of money was quite correctly foreseen. And one may grant that the loss which is imposed is a genuine loss, certainly a loss in 'welfare', and quite probably a loss that will reflect itself, to some extent, on the volume of production. If the want for 'convenience' has to be satisfied in more cumbrous ways, there will be costs of doing so; people will be spending their time in an unproductive activity, which could have been avoided.

There is no doubt that in major inflations this has happened; and that it has then been important. But it is hard to be convinced that in milder inflations, when there is no question of a 'flight from the currency', it is of much significance. It simply does not strike one as a compelling reason for preferring inflation at 3 per cent to inflation at 5 per cent per annum. Yet I believe that there is such a reason; but it is partly (at least) of a different character.

It is correct, nowadays, to take it that inflation is expected; but it is a mistake to suppose that the expectation is consistent. There is a schizophrenia about inflation. While in part of their behaviour (their investment behaviour, in particular) people show themselves to be inflation-minded, in the rest of it they go on as if they expected prices to be stable. The habits – business habits as well as personal habits – which are based on the assumption of stable prices are too strong to be easily broken. Nor is it just habits (like the division of housekeeping money within the family, one of the most intimate points at which – we have been learning – accelerated inflation hurts); it is also institutions. The accounting system, the tax system, even the general legal system, all are based on the assumption of a stable value of money; if the value of money is seriously changeable, they are twisted out of shape. The accountant's 'profits' cease to be true profits; the taxes that are imposed are different to what was intended; the fines and penalties imposed by the courts, as well as the compensations which they award, lose their proper effect. Now it is of course true that these things can be put right (for a time) by legislation; but only by re-opening issues that had been taken to be closed. There is a waste of time in re-discussing them – surely a much more serious waste of time and energy than is involved in holding 'too small' money balances. (pp. 113–14)

In not allowing for such factors, economic theorists leave a considerable gulf between the rather meagre costs of inflation formalized rigorously in theoretical models and the 'person-in-the-street' notions of the costs of inflation which would appear to have produced such a groundswell of support for anti-inflationary policies.[4]

Deflation also imposes costs. People will be as reluctant to borrow or incur debts if they expect money to increase in value as they will be to lend out funds if money is expected to depreciate in value. In this case, however, there are grounds for thinking that the adjustments which ensue may not be symmetric. In response to an expected increase/decrease in prices, bondholders will seek to shift out of/into securities *vis-à-vis* commodities and equities. But whereas bond yields can readily increase to cover the expected deflation of value, there are lower limits below which the rate of interest cannot go, and these establish the maximum rate of deflation which a society can reasonably tolerate. Quite possibly, Keynes had something like this in mind with his theory of the liquidity trap.

There is another aspect of inflation in which person-in-the-street views may differ from those of economists. Inflation is frequently defined popularly as 'too much money chasing too few goods'. Yet money rarely features in the standard 'story' of inflation in the United Kingdom. It is appropriate to begin our examination of the role of money with that non-monetary story.

3.2 Non-monetary studies of inflation

Inflation experience in the United Kingdom in the 1970s and 1980s affords a rich variety of economic pathologies. Figure 3.1 plots the time series of inflation rates over the period from 1970 to 1989, calculated for two different price indices – the GDP deflator and the consumer price index (implicit deflator of consumers' expenditure). Each tells a similar story in that inflation peaks in the mid-1970s, only to pick up again rather sharply at the end of the decade, then dying away to a new low rate in 1982 before emerging strongly again in the late 1980s. There are some differences in levels and timing between the two series. In particular the mid 1970s increase in inflation is apparent first in the CPI deflator, though the eventual peak rate is higher in terms of the GDP deflator, while the reduction in inflation through the late 1970s is somewhat more pronounced in the CPI deflator than it is in the GDP deflator. Finally, in the disinflationary phase of the 1980s and the later rebound, the CPI deflator can be seen to lead.

Very roughly, these differences seem to coincide with the outlines of an inflation story which focuses on the import price explosion of the mid 1970s, followed by an induced wage explosion, and then by a deceleration due in part to successful domestic incomes policies – pursued in turn by a rebound (assisted by a further oil price rise in 1979) and ending up with the disinflation of the Thatcher period, during which exchange rate appreciation was a significant factor, along with steeply rising unemployment, in reducing inflation. A sharp resurgence of inflation is evident in the progress of the GDP deflator after 1986, followed by a much greater rise in the CPI (which, however, itself accelerated through 1990, not shown on the graph.) Figure 3.2 plots, on an annual basis, the Phillips Curve observations for the period – discussed later in the chapter.

We now turn to a preliminary exercise in the explanation of inflation, in the form of a proximate accounting framework based on the input–output tables. The figures shown in Table 3.1 are based on weighting together rates of increase in employment costs, profit margins, import prices and indirect taxes, using as weights the coefficients given in the most recently available summary input–output tables for 1984.[5] These tables show the breakdown of the final output category consumer's expenditure in terms of income from employment, gross profits and other trading incomes

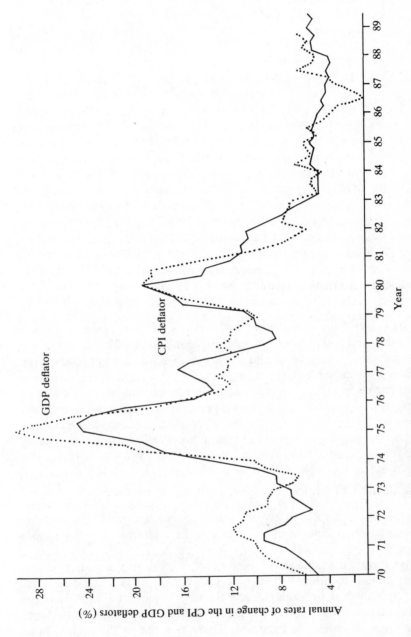

Figure 3.1 Inflation (CPI, GDP deflator), 1970–89.

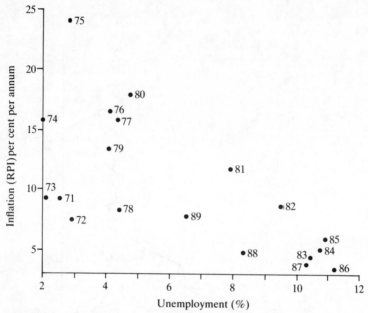

Figure 3.2 The Phillips Curve (1971–89).

('other costs'), imports of goods and services, taxes on expenditures less subsidies and a final category, sales by final demand. The weight of the last category is very small and it has been ignored for purposes of the table; price indices corresponding to the several input categories were constructed from data on factor incomes and expenditures. The former were used to yield employment costs per unit of output and, as a residual, non-employment factor costs; the latter yield the implicit deflator of imports of goods and services and an index of indirect taxes, measuring the ratio of indirect tax revenues at current prices to real output.[6] The explicand in the table is the rate of change of the implicit deflator of consumers' expenditure.

The framework used is thus not itself an identity, and although the explanation is certainly only proximate, it does not exactly exhaust the identified rate of increase in consumer prices. However, it seems close enough to merit attention.[7]

What does the table show? First of all, it confirms the outlines of the story already mentioned. The import price surge of 1972/3 and 1973/4 is clearly identified, for example, as is the wage explosion of 1974/5 and the rebound in 1979/80. A profit push seems indicated in the wake of the wage explosion, as might be expected. There is a rise in the import price contribution in the early 1980s, together with a wage push, giving way to a

Table 3.1 Proximate accounting[1] for inflation in the UK, 1970/1–1987/8 (%)

Year to	Increase in CPI[2]	Contribution from				
		Employment costs	Other production costs	Import prices	Indirect taxes	Unidentified residual
1971	8.6	3.0	2.6	0.9	0.3	1.8
1972	6.5	3.9	2.5	0.6	0.2	-0.8
1973	8.6	3.1	3.1	5.3	-0.1	-2.9
1974	16.9	8.3	3.3	9.4	-0.3	-3.7
1975	23.7	12.4	3.0	3.0	4.6	1.0
1976	15.8	4.3	4.4	4.8	3.8	-1.6
1977	14.8	3.2	3.6	3.1	4.8	0.2
1978	9.1	4.3	1.9	0.6	2.2	0.0
1979	13.6	5.5	3.7	2.0	5.2	-2.8
1980	16.2	8.3	1.6	2.2	4.7	-0.5
1981	11.2	3.9	2.0	1.8	3.4	0.1
1982	8.7	1.6	2.2	1.7	2.0	1.3
1983	5.0	1.2	2.1	1.7	0.5	-0.5
1984	5.1	1.7	1.1	2.0	0.4	-0.1
1985	5.2	1.6	1.3	0.9	1.0	0.4
1986	4.4	1.7	-0.5	-0.9	2.0	2.1
1987	3.9	1.3	1.9	0.6	1.0	-0.9
1988	5.0	2.5	1.3	-0.2	1.2	0.1

Notes:

1. For details, see text.
2. Implicit deflator of the consumers' expenditure series.

Source: CSO Public Database.

markedly more quiescent period for the rest of the decade shown in the table (which indicates only the beginning of the resurgence of inflation in 1989–90 with an expansion of wage costs in 1988).

Perhaps more surprising is the contribution to inflation identified with net indirect taxes, which is substantial in the three years 1975–7 and again in 1979 to 1981. It may be recalled that, by construction, our index of indirect taxes would demonstrate a positive contribution to inflation even if tax rates were only indexed, and on these grounds alone we would expect to see indirect taxes contributing some 17 per cent of yearly CPI inflation (this being the input–output weight of indirect taxes in consumers' expenditure). But it is evident that in many of the years in question the contribution of indirect taxes was in fact much greater: this is particularly true of 1979–81. In each of these years indirect tax rates were increased, in 1979 substantially.[8]

The evidence of a proximate accounting framework clearly should not be pushed too far: inflation, after all, is a general rise in prices (costs) and in a steady inflation all costs and prices will be rising in line with one another without implying causality. Stein (1982) has strictured Keynesians for falling into the trap of merely redescribing inflation by resorting to explanations of this type.

With this observation we turn to a consideration of wage and price equations. We would maintain that these, properly specified, are not mere accounting identities, and would argue that the procedure of accounting for inflation through such equations is not, *pace* Stein, merely a redescription, but a substantive contribution (albeit not an exhaustive one) to the explanation of inflation. However, our principal interest is not in a Tinbergen decomposition of inflation in terms of the explanatory variables of such equations – for a highly competent example of which, see Rowlatt (1988) – but rather in the way in which the modelling of wage and price behaviour has changed over the past decade or so. We begin with pricing equations.

Pricing equations

Econometric studies in the 1960s of price determination in the UK economy were not far removed from the proximate accounting framework just described. Following the lead of Klein and Ball (1961), estimated price equations were simple constant percentage mark-ups on wage costs, import costs and indirect taxes. Later modellers of price behaviour in the United Kingdom absorbed two different theoretical ideas.

One was the 'normal cost' hypothesis, first clearly set out by Neild

(1963). According to this hypothesis firms would set prices on the basis of a mark-up over the unit cost of producing a 'normal' rate of output. In the specification of the hypothesis, a good deal of care was typically expended on the measurement of normal output levels; as an alternative, coefficients might be imposed – rather in the style of the proximate accounting exercise of the previous section, on the basis of information derived from the input–output tables.

Within the normal cost paradigm the chief area of dispute was whether the size of the normal mark-up reflected demand influences or not.[9] The strong form of the hypothesis held that such influences were insignificant, and in a series of apparently exhaustive tests Godley and Nordhaus (1972) and Coutts, Godley and Nordhaus (1978) sought to show that the strong form of the hypothesis was supported. However, Smith (1982) demonstrated that these investigations had neglected crucial specifications of the hypothesis and that, when these were tested, demand influence was found to be statistically significant, though not numerically powerful.

Events in the 1970s dislodged the normal cost paradigm. The turbulence of output conditions made the projection of normal levels of operation more difficult, and modellers became more conscious of the effects of expectations and of the impact of foreign on domestic prices. Under the normal cost paradigm that influence had been confined essentially to the part which could be comprehended as a raw material input cost. The reasoning of the Law of One Price, however, was that competition in like goods would condition domestic to follow foreign prices at least so long as nothing happened to change relative real wages.

At the outset of the disinflationary 1980s, the idea of the Law of One Price was widely entertained as indicative of the dependence of the United Kingdom on foreign prices. A Bank of England paper by Brown, Enoch and Mortimer-Lee (1980) summarized the state of knowledge, as embodied in three leading econometric models at the time: Table 3.2 is drawn from their study. While the principal implication of the Law to which attention was drawn at the time was the inability of nominal devaluation to affect the real exchange rate, the authors considered the symmetry of the response of prices and wages to exchange rate changes, noting – as it turned out, prophetically – that 'wages may respond more slowly to an appreciation and the attendant slowing of inflation than to a quickening of inflation consequent upon depreciation. This. . .would suggest that, whilst the gain in cost competitiveness following depreciation might be short-lived, the deterioration in competitiveness resulting from appreciation could be painfully long' (p. 8).

Figure 3.3 captures the strong rise in UK relative export prices due to the appreciation of sterling in 1979–81. A naïve view of the Law of One

Table 3.2 Price–cost interrelationships, 1980*

Dependent variables*	Total weight of variables*		Foreign cost/price variables in equation	Domestic cost/price variables in equation	Other variables in equation (excluding dummies)	Lags	Forms of equation
	Foreign	Domestic					
Export prices							
Treasury							
UVI for exports of manufactured goods	0.52	0.48	Competitors' export prices	Wholesale price index of manufacturing (excluding food, drink and tobacco)	Adjustment for indirect tax	Two quarters on foreign and domestic prices	Linear in logs
LBS							
UVI for exports of manufactured goods	1.00	0.00	Competitors' world prices of manufactures	Unit labour costs in manufacturing	Time trend	Partial adjustment	Hendry
NIESR							
Deflator of manufacturing exports	0.48	0.49	Competitors' world prices of manufacturing	Wholesale price index of manufacturing (excluding food, drink and tobacco)	None	Lagged endogenous variable	First difference in logs
Wholesale prices							
Treasury							
Wholesale price index of home output (excluding food, drink and tobacco)	0.37	0.76	UVI for imports excluding food, drink and tobacco and finished manufactures	(1) Trend unit wage costs in manufacturing (2) Nationalized industries prices	Indirect taxes	Three quarters on domestic costs; four quarters on foreign	Linear
LBS							
Wholesale price index of manufacturing output	0.28	0.69	Index of world wholesale prices	Unit labour costs in manufacturing	None	Partial adjustment	Hendry
NIESR							
Wholesale price index of manufacturing output (excluding food, drink and tobacco)	0.50	0.43	Deflator of imports of goods and services	(1) Average earnings (2) Other employment costs (3) Manufacturing productivity	None	Lagged dependent variable	Linear in rates of change

Note: * As reported in Brown, Enoch and Mortimer-Lee (1980); the model manuals are those for 1979.

Source: Brown, Enoch and Mortimer-Lee (1980), Tables E and G.

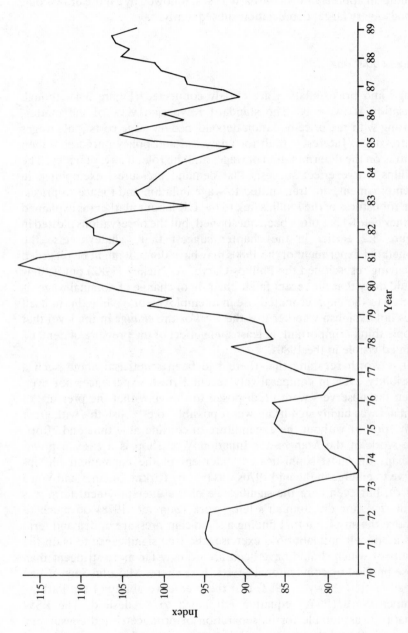

Figure 3.3 Relative producer prices, 1970–89.

Price is clearly not sustained. The real exchange rate underwent a significant appreciation in the early 1980s, followed by a more drawn-out, but also very large, depreciation subsequently.[10]

Wage equations

Wage and price inflation are closely connected (Figure 3.4), though causation is two-way. The standard Keynesian view of the matter, starting with the price equation dependence on wage costs, puts wages centre-stage. Interest – both for analytical and policy purposes – then centres on the determination of wages and the role, if any, of policy. The Phillips Curve effect suggests that demand pressures, exemplified in unemployment, are transmitted to wage inflation and thence to prices. The robustness of the Phillips link to the UK labour market (as explained further below) has often been questioned, but the observations plotted in Figure 3.2 earlier in the chapter suggest that, whatever else the monetarist experiment of the 1980s may have done, it might be regarded as having resuscitated the Phillips Curve. As Nickell (1982) put it, 'few would deny that the recent fall in the rate of change of nominal wages is related to the unprecedented rise in unemployment'. While this in itself does not establish whether it is the *level* or the *change* in the level that people think is important, at least some effect of the pressure of demand seemed visible in the 1980s.

It is worth recalling that there had been scepticism about such a possibility even in comparatively recent British experience; not even when the observers were predisposed to the view that the pressure of demand was highly significant was it possible to establish this with great conviction or without the expenditure of considerable time and effort. The work of the Manchester Inflation Workshop is a case in point. Perhaps the most sophisticated statement of the augmented Phillips Curve to emerge in the mid 1970s was that by Parkin, Sumner and Ward (1976), but even here the significance of the unemployment term was tenuous;[11] nor did Sumner's later work (Sumner, 1978) do much to remove the suspicion that finding a significant pressure of demand term was a difficult and laborious exercise, the true significance tests on the results of which should have been accordingly far more stringent than those implied by conventional t-tests. Elsewhere, Malcolm Sawyer had already noted (Sawyer, 1982) that the predictive ability of the Parkin–Sumner–Ward (PSW) equation left much to be desired. The PSW equation was notable for its separation of producers' and consumers' expectations and the operational distinction drawn between supply and

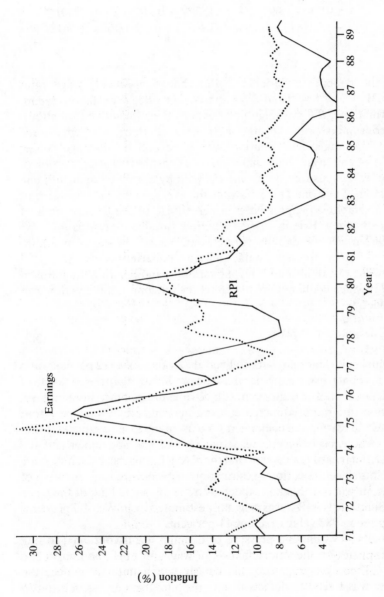

Figure 3.4 Annual rates of change in prices (RPI) and wages (earnings in manufacturing), 1971–89.

demand price versions of the real wage. The equation ran as follows (suppressing the error term):

$$w_t = 5.9108 - 1.9973u + 0.5027P^Q_E + 0.2029P^Q_F + 0.2944P^Q$$
$$-0.7056T_1 - 0.2944\,(T_2 + T_3) + 0.4607D62 - 1.0612D66$$

$$(3.2)$$

where the dependent variable is the change in weekly wage rates $w_t = \ln(W_t/W_{t-1}) \times 400$ and P^Q_E = employers' price expectations (adaptive formation); P^Q_F = foreign price expectations (adaptive formation); P^Q = consumers' price expectations (Carlson–Parkin); T_1 = employers' national insurance contribution as proportion of average wage; (T_2+T_3) = employees' national insurance contribution as proportion of average wage, plus rate of income tax paid by a married man with one child under 11 and one 11–15, earning the average wage; u = number of wholly unemployed expressed as a percentage of the total number of employees (Great Britain); $D62$ = dummy variable for pay pause, 1961 III = 1962 II; $D66$ = dummy variable for freeze and severe restraint, 1966 III = 1967 II; quarterly data, quarter on quarter (as for w).

Rounding off, omitting irrelevant variables and ignoring the terms in $T_1 \ldots T_3$ (which could not greatly affect the outcome), this equation can be reduced to

$$w = 6 - 2u + P^Q$$

$$(3.3)$$

from which it is clear that, with stylized 1982 values of u (12 per cent) and P^Q (10 per cent), wage inflation would be predicted to proceed at a rate of *minus* 8 per cent. The same point can be re-expressed in a different way, in terms of the required increase in the natural rate of unemployment (NAIRU). Treating the coefficient on u as an unbiased estimate of that on the difference between the actual rate of unemployment and the NAIRU,[12] it is easily calculated that the NAIRU must have risen by some nine points since the period of estimation to generate a wage inflation of 10 per cent when prices are expected to rise by something of the same order. Since the NAIRU was originally estimated by PSW at 1.7 per cent, this implies a 1982 value of about 11 per cent.

Difficulty in estimating pressure of demand terms continued to dog empirical work on the determination of wages through the mid to late 1970s.[13] Three reactions are particularly worth noting. In one, the difficulty was traced to defects in the mapping from excess demand to unemployment; in particular it was (and is) argued that the unemployment benefits regime exerted significant effects on unemployment, producing an unstable relationship over time. The work of Sumner (1978) and that of Minford (1981) is in this vein. But while there is no doubt about the partial derivative of u with respect to a true index of the replacement ratio (ratio of benefits to earnings), holding demand constant, there is a lot of doubt about the correct way to measure the ratio and how to model the effect. For example, the time series of the replacement ratio based on the maximum hypothetical entitlements of representative unemployed workers has little correlation with the time series of the actual replacement ratio based on benefits actually paid.[14]

Another reaction to the breakdown of the Phillips relation was work on the real wage hypothesis, which in the later 1970s came to be regarded as a rival hypothesis. It is certainly true that it is possible to derive estimating equations of the real wage hypothesis genre from a characterization of bargaining conditions which is far removed from the atomistic markets underpinning which is typically provided for the Phillips Curve. However, the hallmark of real wage hypothesis equations is the inclusion of the lagged real wage as a determining variable, not the absence of unemployment (which may, after all, play a role in bargaining models), and the pressure of this variable can alternatively be rationalized as a supplementary indicator of excess demand, or as a proportional control variable.[15] In consequence, estimation adopted a more eclectic posture in relation to the earlier phase, with both lagged real wages and unemployment variables being included. Difficulties with the use of unemployment as an excess demand indicator prompted yet a third reaction, exemplified in the work of Wren-Lewis (1985). This may be characterized as an attempt to dispense with the excess demand indicator approach, substituting for it a reduced form of supply and demand variables. In this context, output was shown to exert significant negative (but long-lagged) effects on wage inflation.

The dramatic rise in unemployment in the 1980s and the fall in inflation then, as already noted, gave room for the expression of a renewed belief in Phillips Curve effects – of a sort. A major qualification must be noted. If the data for the 1980s confirm a Phillips effect, they must also suggest – as we have already noted – that the natural rate of unemployment has risen as compared with earlier years. Indeed, there is a suspicion derived from the stubbornness of wage inflation at persistent high levels of unemployment that it is the *change* in unemployment which is the discipline on wage inflation. Once the increase stops and unemployment levels off at a higher level, inflation may resume at something like its old rate. This 'hysteresis' effect is suggested by studies which find prominent ΔU-effects in wage inflation equations (e.g. Coe and Gagliardi (1986)) or identify persistent U-effects as those associated solely with *short-term* unemployment. The long-term unemployed on this view have no influence on the labour market as their skills atrophy – they might as well have emigrated. Complete hysteresis seems a strong proposition. A partial hysteresis effect is reasonable; such an effect, if not identified, may easily lead to the impression that the natural rate of unemployment has risen, an impression that is widely shared in the United Kingdom.[16] To give this assertion more formal expression, consider the diagram in Figure 3.5. In it is drawn the Phillips Curve corresponding to the equation

$$\dot{w} = a_0 + \dot{p}^e - a_1 \Delta u - a_2 (u - u^n) + a_3 S - a_4 (w/p)_{-1} \qquad (3.4)$$

Values of $\dot{p}^e$, S (other factors) and $(w/p)_{-1}$ are taken as given since we want to abstract from these effects. The flatter line in the figure has a slope of $-a_2$, the steeper line a slope of $-(a_2 + a_1)$. Suppose we start from a point like A, where unemployment is equal to the natural rate, and from this point a recession occurs. Unemployment rises to u_0, say. The operative Phillips Curve while this is happening is the steep one, and inflation falls to the level corresponding to point B. However, at this point, unemployment stops rising. This means that the a_1 effect disappears; the operative Phillips Curve for a sustained level of unemployment is the flatter one. Inflation thus resumes at a rate corresponding to point C. Someone whose estimate of the unemployment effect does not distinguish between terms in u and Δu (which available data may not encourage) will be forced to conclude that the

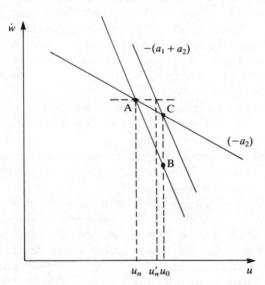

Note:
u_n 'moves' to u_n' as u goes to u_0.

Figure 3.5   Partial hysteresis in the natural rate.

natural rate has risen. For example, to sustain the point C with an estimate of a_1 which is 'falsely' raised to (a_1+a_2) because of a failure to distinguish between the two types of unemployment effect, it could be said that the natural rate of unemployment had risen to u'_n. The excess of current unemployment at u_0 over u'_n, given the slope $a_1 + a_2$, generates the small fall in inflation between A and C. The occurrence of large Δu effects, then, can give rise to the continual re-estimation of the natural rate in the direction of the current rate – a feature, it seems, of British wage inflation estimation.

Confirmation of the empirics awaits a lengthy investigation. What Table 3.3 shows, by way of illustration for the period 1978–89, is three wage inflation equations – each of which is a reconstituted Phillips Curve incorporating a lagged real wage term, the first containing terms both in the *level* and in the *change* in unemployment, the other eliminating one or other of these two terms. When both are included neither term is individually very significant, though either one when entered on its own is highly significant. In these equations the coefficient on inflation expectations (proxied by the lagged inflation term) is not large. Due to the

Table 3.3 Wage inflation 1978–89

	Dependent variable: inflation in manufacturing earnings Estimation period: 1978 Q1 – 1989 Q2		
Equation	1	2	3
Constant	0.0574 (3.02)	0.0792 (6.32)	0.0356 (5.24)
Inertia term: lagged dependent	0.2987 (2.60)	0.2723 (2.36)	0.3388 (3.06)
Lagged price inflation	0.2966 (3.91)	0.2433 (3.57)	0.3410 (5.08)
Lagged real wages	−0.1058 (3.53)	−0.0713 (3.64)	−0.1294 (5.61)
Unemployment *level*	−0.58E-5 (1.23)	−0.12E-4 (4.40)	–
Unemployment *change*	−0.16E-4 (1.50)	–	−0.19E-4 (4.52)
$\bar{R}^2$	0.934	0.932	0.939
SE	0.008	0.008	0.008

Note:
Except for unemployment (000s), variables are in logs, with inflation as a four quarter log difference. Lagged real wages are entered with a four quarter lag. Figures in parentheses are t-ratios.

presence of the lagged real wage term, this does not imply any lack of *static* homogeneity and, although at variance with some results generated in the later 1970s, is similar to those generated on earlier data sets (see Artis and Miller (1979) for a comment and rationalization).

3.3 Money and prices

The explanations of inflation we have considered so far are conventional Keynesian accounts, and monetary influences have been excluded. However, there is no contradiction *in principle* between allowing a substantial role to money in inflation and describing its determinants in the conventional way. The conventional account in essence then comprises the intermediate variables or transmission mechanism, and is not necessarily in conflict with a monetarist account. The essential requirements of the latter are that the demand for money and the real economy both be stable. But even then, of course, monetary conditions may not be the initiator of inflation. One-time changes in the price level coming from the large changes in oil prices, depreciation of the currency, variations in indirect taxes or imposts and the removal of subsidies become inflation, as monetarists define it (as a sustained rate of increase of prices generally), if accommodated by increases in the quantity of money. Only the strong version of the money-only story requires exogeneity of the money supply process as well.

Before looking at the UK evidence, there is one aspect of the doctrine that 'money matters' with which we readily concur. Upheavals in the international monetary system in the early 1970s and the ultimate breakdown of fixed exchange rates severed the nexus that had previously existed in the longer run between domestic and international prices, so removing what probably was the anchor for nominal variables and altering the character of price and wage determination. In the more 'flexi-price' world ushered in, we should assume expectations of inflation to be more volatile so that relationships forged when those expectations were tied down would, inevitably, collapse. Domestic prices are potentially more susceptible to influence via domestic policies but they are also potentially more responsive to wage shocks and influences of the type modelled in earlier sections. Regime change seems likely.

Evidence of the actual involvement of money in the process of UK inflation is of two sorts: reduced form regressions of money and inflation (for example, HM Treasury 1981) and studies of the stability of the demand for money function. It is indeed paradoxical that the inception of monetarist policies has seen both of these pieces of evidence evaporate. Just as monetary targets were introduced around the mid 1970s, evidence of the rock-solid character of the post-war demand for money function dissipated as observations for the 1970s successively slipped off the previous estimated demand curves (see Chapter 4). While policy-makers may have taken heart from the reduced form regressions, those equations also broke down following the monetarist experiment of the 1980s. What support there was from the larger econometric models, relating exchange rates to monetary movements, was lost from sight as well in the same experience.

The graphical association of money and prices (Figure 3.6) now reveals more clearly than was earlier apparent what has happened. In the first part of the period, there *does* appear to have been a relationship in which money (M3) led prices; in the second half of the period this relationship visibly crumbles.

We replicated the Treasury reduced form (due to Wren-Lewis) and extended the sample period. As can be seen (Table 3.4), the equation estimated in the period to the end of 1978 has a high degree of explanatory power; the coefficient estimates are close to those of the original and suggest homogeneity of prices in money. The Wren-Lewis equations allowed for some rough adjustments in respect of the impact of the corset on M3. Making similar allowances our replication was slightly closer to the original and slightly more robust than the estimates shown in the table. However, the basis for adjustments to M3 is very shaky and the number of special factors that might be allowed for (Topping and Bishop, 1989) very large, so we have preferred to stick to the unadjusted figures.

The figures quoted in the second column of results show the effect of extending the sample period by four quarters: as can be seen, this is quite dramatic; the residual sum of squares doubles and the standard error rises by 50 per cent. A further deterioration follows the addition of another year's data. The full period estimate is obviously quite different from the original one. Such a deterioration of M3 relationships undermined those who were still forecasting high inflation based on M3 behaviour in the early 1980s. As Figure 3.6 shows, inflation fell despite a continued high rate of M3 growth, although there were gathering doubts at the end of the 1980s concerning the permanence of the achievement. For a policy based on targeting M3, deterioration in a key relationship like this might have been fatal; however, monetary targeting was always after bigger fish.

In examining what particular contribution monetary policy can make to inflation control, we return to the idea of there being various dimensions to the role of money in inflation. The first, derived from money as the initiator, is to prevent the monetary sector from initiating inflationary pressures. To strict monetarists, this task is all that is needed. Do that, and everything else will fall into place.

The second task comes from money as the accommodator. If inflation

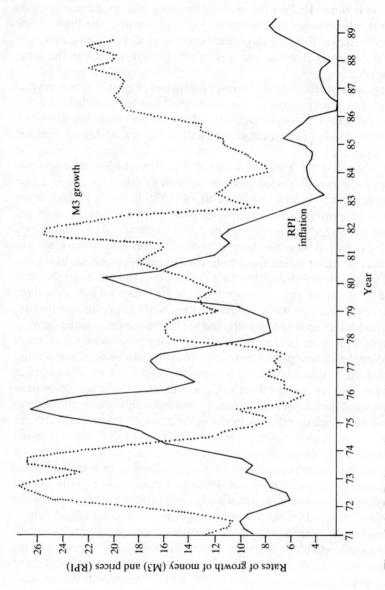

Figure 3.6 Inflation and monetary growth, 1971–89.

Table 3.4   Money to prices: a direct relationship

	Estimation period			
	1966Q3 – 1978Q4	1966Q3 – 1979Q4	1966Q3 – 1980Q4	1966Q3 – 1988Q4
Dependent variable	$\Delta \ln p$	$\Delta \ln p$	$\Delta \ln p$	$\Delta \ln p$
$\ln M_{-1}$	0.075	0.070	0.057	0.022
	(5.31)	(3.72)	(3.11)	(1.76)
$\ln M_{-14}$	0.094	0.107	0.057	−0.028
	(2.51)	(2.03)	(1.50)	(1.87)
$d \ln M_{-4}$	−0.20	−0.134	−0.099	−0.040
	(2.79)	(1.46)	(1.05)	(0.64)
$d \ln M_{-12}$	0.276	0.354	0.295	0.131
	(3.90)	(4.04)	(0.310)	(2.04)
$\ln p_{-1}$	−0.169	−0.166	−0.106	0.002
	(3.81)	(2.81)	(2.44)	(0.20)
$d \ln p_{-1}$	0.590	0.463	0.416	0.602
	(5.33)	(3.86)	(3.57)	(6.87)
$\bar{R}^2$	0.858	0.740	0.707	0.621
RSS	0.0017	0.0036	0.0044	0.0082
SE	0.0066	0.0090	0.0096	0.0102

Notes:
p is retail prices, M is M3. Constant terms and seasonals included in estimation but not reported. Figures in parentheses are t-statistics.

is initiated from the side of wages or other costs, the inflationary pressures will still finish up in the money market. This is because the number of pounds demanded depends not only upon the number of goods being purchased, but also on the prices of these goods. With a stable demand function, any increase in prices raises the amount of money demanded and leads to pressure for money creation to occur. Failure to provide this increase in the money supply may brake inflationary pressures as the diffused cost of borrowing inhibits expenditures and eventually bears down upon prices.

In the face of entrenched inflationary expectations and real wage resistance, a policy of non-accommodation runs the risk of endangering the stability of financial institutions, or of increasing unemployment, or both. The source of the difficulty is the failure of the nominal variables – wage and income aspirations, nominal rates of interest and the exchange rate – to keep in line with the chosen rate of monetary growth. That being the case, an obvious suggestion is to take inflation control one stage further back, into wage and product markets. By altering the climate surrounding wage and price determination it might be possible to prevent the inflationary pressures from ever arising. Here we are brought to a third dimension to the role of money, as setting the environment for decentralized decision-making; and something along such lines – call it a new monetary standard – would seem to be at the back of the medium-term financial strategy.

It is by no means a new idea. Much the same idea – although with the execution proposed by markedly different means – can be traced to the early post-war years, when architects of the Keynesian revolution, economists such as Kalecki, Joan Robinson and Worswick, warned that having the State underwrite full employment creates, in Joan Robinson's (1946) words, 'a chronic danger of inflation'. With wage and price determination substantially moved from the economic into the political arena, those economists saw the appropriate solution as also being political, in the form of incomes policy – advice which has been only fitfully followed in the decades since.

Interpreted in that light, recent experience represents an attempted transition back to a pre-Keynesian environment. By means of the setting of monetary targets the government tried to make it known from the outset that its policy was 'no accommodation', and in this roundabout way effectively withdrew the commitment to full employment. Monetary targets allowed this message to be slipped in without pre-announcing the likely unemployment costs, a clear statement of which might have prevented the policy from ever being implemented.

In the event, as we shall see in the following chapters, the money supply has proved difficult to keep on course. The four-year MTFS has become almost like a Soviet plan. One monetary aggregate has become many (M0, M1, sterling M3, PSL2, etc.), exchange rates have been added, and short-run monetary relationships seem unstable. But, on the interpretation given above, in the 1980s all such worries were secondary. The name of the game was the declaration of a new monetary rule book, thereby giving pre-commitment to price stability. How successfully that can be reaffirmed and carried out in the 1990s is the central issue for British monetary policy.

In order to be able to address this issue, it is necessary to look both ahead and back: ahead to how European monetary arrangements and harmonization may facilitate that task and alter the environment in which Britain is to pursue inflation control; and back to how policy worked out in the 1980s. Succeeding chapters focus upon the key monetary relations – the demand for money and the supply of money, the transmission mechanism of policy, interest rate determination and exchange rate management – and the consequences for them posed by increased financial integration. The final chapter then returns to the monetary rule book.

Notes

1. Artis and Ostry (1986) refer to the successful export of the doctrine of 'Ronald Thatcherism' in this context. Among the Anglo-Saxon countries, Australia was first in instituting inflation-first policies in January 1976.
2. Beckerman and Jenkinson (1987) do not deny this possibility, only that unemployment exerted any independent effect. As will be seen below, we suspect that unemployment or its increase did have an independent effect on inflation.
3. This upward bias comes from improvements in the quality (and price) of existing goods and from delays in introducing new goods into the 'basket' sampled by the statisticians, so that the initial period of declining prices as the good moves into mass production is excluded from the measure.
4. This gap is admitted by Driffill, Mizon and Ulph (1990). One study which does recognize the importance of 'accounting costs' is Niehans (1978).
5. CSO: *UK National Accounts*, 1988 edn.
6. This measure in effect treats all indirect taxes as if they were specific duties, so that if all indirect taxes were indexed to inflation, it would increase *pari passu* with the CPI, and thus show a constant proportionate 'contribution to inflation'.
7. In proportionate terms the residual unidentified element is biggest in 1986, with no ready explanation to hand.
8. In 1976 the national insurance surcharge was introduced, which by a quirk of British national accounting procedures is treated as an indirect tax (even though the regular national insurance contributions are not so treated).
9. Given the procyclical behaviour of productivity and thus the counter-cyclical variation in actual unit labour costs, the hypothesis already allowed for the *actual* mark-up to vary with demand.
10. The *long-run* solutions of the wage–price sectors in current (1990) versions of the main macro models of the United Kingdom show homogeneity of wages and prices in the exchange rate (see Chapter 8).
11. Unemployment was not significant in the unrestricted forms of the preferred equation, though it became so when restrictions were applied to the price and tax expectations terms.
12. This would be reasonable if the NAIRU were constant during the estimation period and if we think of the equation as $\dot{w} = \alpha + \beta(u^* - u) + X$, for then the estimated constant term contains βu^* and the coefficient on u is an estimate of β.
13. The experience caused one of the present authors to entitle a paper on the subject 'Is there a wage equation?' (Artis, 1981).
14. More generally, Atkinson (1982) has deplored the crudity of much work in this area, contrasting it unfavourably with the increasing sophistication with which measurement of the cost of capital is undertaken.
15. In this guise, the error correction model approach to econometric testing gave technical support to the appearance of the lagged real wage in wage inflation estimates.
16. Radaelli (1988) collects together estimates made over a period of time which confirm this.

4

The demand for money

Introduction

The *sine qua non* of monetary targeting policies is stability in the demand for money. Without stability such policies are, indeed, meaningless. The rise to prominence of monetary targeting owed much to a belief that stability of the demand for money could be relied upon. Two temporal definitions of stability were in question – both short- and long-run – and in both cases claims for stability were current at the end of the 1960s, though it may be questioned whether more than long-run stability is necessary; and more certainly, as we shall see, whether at best anything more than long-run stability can be supported empirically. Stability, here, is stability with respect to a set of arguments constituting the demand for money function as opposed to numerical constancy of the velocity of circulation; and the arguments of the demand for money must be such that if stability of the function is shown to exist then control of the money supply (which also has to be possible) will have a predictable effect on prices over some period of time. It is an empirical matter whether the degree of stability in the demand for money is sufficient to justify monetary targeting policies and an empirical (institutional and political) matter whether the money supply is controllable.

In this chapter we consider the state of knowledge with regard to the demand for money, leaving examination of the supply of money to later. We start by considering the principal elements in the theory of the demand for money before going on to consider the problems facing the empirical investigator and some of the main features of the research record. The outstanding feature of that research is that although there seems good evidence that the demand for money was stable over long

78

periods up to the early 1970s, the evidence thereafter offers much less reassurance. In discussing this record we find it important to ask what money supply process the estimates of the demand for money assume; the last section of the chapter offers some illustrative accounts of why this is important.

4.1 Theories of the demand for money

At the general level, two main approaches to the theory of the demand for money have developed. One looks to the functions of money to suggest various motives for holding money, specifically a transactions motive stemming from money's use as a medium of exchange and an asset or portfolio motive deriving from money acting as a store of value. While prompted by the transactions, precautionary and speculative motives for holding money suggested by Keynes in Chapters 13 and 15 of the *General Theory* – his finance motive is generally ignored[1] – the antecedents of this approach can be traced to Irving Fisher and the Cambridge School (Patinkin, 1976; Eshag, 1963). The other approach, due to Friedman (1956), dispenses with the need to identify any specific roles for money, taking a general value theory approach to the demand for money in which money is treated as a representative asset like any other in producing a flow of utility services for its holder.

Early accounts of the *transactions motive* assumed that balances held for transactions increase in proportion to money incomes and consist entirely of money which, by definition, is what is needed to complete a transaction by means of a payment. Implicitly, the costs of exchanging out of funds held in some other form into money at the point of need is prohibitive. Baumol (1952) and Tobin (1956) altered this assumption. They allowed balances set aside for transactions purposes to be invested as well in securities, and applied inventory theory to determine the amount held as money. For them, the motive for holding money is to reduce the transactions costs of realizing income-earning assets when money is required for transactions. Determinants of the demand for money are the flow of transactions, interest forgone by holding money balances instead of securities, and the costs – brokerage charges and inconvenience – of effecting transfers between the two assets. The idea is that, given the pattern of payments and payments habits, transactors choose that frequency of transfers and average level of money balances which maximizes interest income net of the transactions costs.

By making specific assumptions about the determinants it is possible to derive from these models precise hypotheses about the response of money balances to potential explanatory variables. Working balances are usually assumed to follow a regular 'sawtooth' pattern as income is received at regular intervals and expenditures occur at a steady rate. Transactions costs (in terms of pecuniary charges or the time, effort or shoe leather involved) can be fixed, i.e. equal in amount for each purchase or sale of securities, and also variable, in the form of brokerage fees and interest penalties which depend on the value of the securities encashed. The predictions are that the elasticity of money balances with respect to real income lies between 0.5 (fixed transactions costs) and 1.0 (proportionate transactions costs); that the interest rate elasticity ranges from −0.5 (fixed costs) to −2.0 (proportionate costs); and that nominal money balances will increase proportionately with prices (Niehans, 1978, ch. 3).

A number of qualifications arise. First, the existence of fixed transactions costs makes it possible for 'corner solutions' to arise. In an economy in which income is received in monetary form and payments are made only by using money – where, in effect, a form of Clower's (1967) cash-in-advance constraint applies – an individual will not hold securities at all as part of working balances unless the interest income exceeds the cost of the return trip to the securities market. This may give rise to discontinuities in the response of money holdings to alterations in interest rates and transactions costs (for example, individuals who do not find it worth while to hold securities will exhibit a zero interest rate response and a unit income response).

Second, the models rely on a lack of synchronization between receipts and payments, but do not let the payment habits which bring this about (i.e. the frequency of pay periods and the timing of payments) adapt to economic incentives. Use of credit cards, for instance, may enable a person to defer monetary payments until income is received and so economize on the holding of money balances. While payment practices are treated as exogenous in the standard models, in reality they seem likely to be a complex mix of autonomous developments arising from scientific advances in information technology and those induced by environmental factors such as high and variable interest rates.

Third, limitations come from the deterministic nature of the models in that irregularities and uncertainties in the pattern of transactions are assumed away. Whereas irregular purchases and sales seem unlikely to alter the main conclusions of the Baumol–Tobin models, allowance for a cash flow which is not known with certainty overlaps the transactions demand with the *precautionary motive*. An early, but remarkably prescient, account by Miller and Orr (1966) showed that quite different decision rules can result. Instead of regular transfers being made to bring money balances to the desired level m_t^*, there is implied a range for an individual's money holdings with adjustments occurring in a lumpy, discontinuous fashion when balances hit the upper and lower bounds.

This idea of an upper and lower threshold was explored again by Akerlof and Milbourne (1980) in a transactions demand context and underlies the *buffer stock approach*. The idea is that individuals find it costly to monitor continually the level of their money balances; they therefore tolerate limited deviations in these balances around their predicted levels, pre-setting a ceiling and a floor to the level the balance may reach before a review, and a transfer of funds out of, or into, the money balance is considered. An undue increase in their balances occurring, say, through unexpected receipts would prompt a transfer into an earning asset, taking the money balance back to its return point if the ceiling is breached, while an undue drawdown of money balances, which would threaten the likelihood of a costly overdraft, would prompt a transfer in the opposite direction if the floor is hit. These ideas are shown graphically in Figure 4.1. The level of the return point money balance would be reviewed as, over time, the individual's income and expenditure level changes in a permanent way. The theory retains the idea that a rise in money income will prompt a rise in demand for money but introduces a distinction between a probably very high short-run elasticity (when the money balance rises towards its ceiling level) and a more moderate long-run elasticity (for if the increase in income proves permanent, there will be an equilibrium adjustment of the return point level).

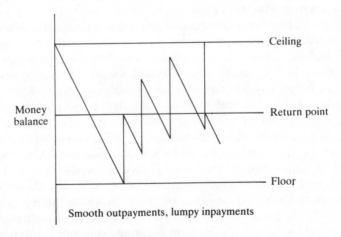

Figure 4.1 A buffer stock model.

Keynes described a *speculative motive* for holding money as an asset, which was to take advantage of expected declines in the prices of securities (i.e. anticipated future rises in interest rates). This was generalized by Tobin (1958) and Markowitz (1959) into a portfolio approach in which the motive for holding money balances is the avoidance of capital losses when there may be no definite expectation of interest rates rising or falling but simply uncertainty about the direction and extent of future interest rate changes. Each individual is confronted by a choice of holding a portion of wealth in money, offering low risk and low return, and a proportion in securities, promising a higher return but greater risk, and can hold various mixtures of the two depending on the mean and variance of expected returns and the preferences for risk-taking. This general approach yields predictions that desired holdings of money will depend on wealth, the expected return from money (including non-pecuniary benefits such as liquidity services) and the expected returns (and variances) of alternative wealth-holding forms.

In contrast to the above, in his well-known restatement of the *quantity theory* as a theory of the demand for money, Friedman (1956), in line with his methodology of positive economics (Friedman, 1953), argued that no special analytic principles were needed to study the demand for money. Rather, the general concepts of value theory could be used without an explicit description of the source of money's utility to an individual demander. Money is simply one form in which individuals choose to hold their wealth and is analytically no different from any other good that produces a flow of services to its holders. Since the service flow from the stock of money accrues over time, money is a capital good rather than a consumption good and the modelling of its demand is merely an application of capital theory.

In line with Friedman's doctrine of positive economics, the aim of the exercise is to produce a formulation which predicts much – the course of money income – from little – knowledge of the behaviour of the quantity of money (indeed ultimately high-powered money). The link comes from a demand for money function which is a simple aggregate of individual demands such that the real value of a selected monetary total bears a relatively stable relation to a limited number of measures of the aggregate budget constraint (wealth or permanent income) and opportunity cost variables (interest on bonds, dividends on equities, the anticipated inflation of commodity prices). What particular variables are selected is itself a matter for empirical investigation. In the same vein, the approach (Friedman and Schwartz, 1970) eschews a definition of money based on grounds of principle in favour of one based on grounds of usefulness; i.e. the aggregate which yields the most accurate predictions. Interest rate and income elasticities are responses which remain to be revealed by the data as would be the case if one were examining the demand for motor cars or refrigerators.

While the operational attractions of such an empirically based approach are obvious, it is clear that the separation of empirics from explicit modelling can give rise to problems. One of Friedman's own studies illustrates the point. On the strength of the decline in the velocity of money in the United States from 1869 to 1957, Friedman (1959) estimated the income elasticity of money (M2) as 1.8, much higher than the elasticity revealed by other studies, yet entirely possible if one merely concludes that money services 'must' be a luxury. But later evidence makes it apparent that Friedman attributed to a high income elasticity variations in the velocity of money due to other influences such as interest rates and the growth of banking.

Despite the fact that Friedman's programme differs from the alternative approach in eschewing the need to puzzle over the sources of utility from money holding and despite the fact that the interpretation placed on the results obtained differs between the two, the reality is that there are few substantive differences to be found among investigators about the kinds of variables which are expected to feature in statistical estimates of the demand for money. Denoting desired or long-run values with an asterisk (*), the symbolic specification (4.1) captures the very general agreement that has emerged:

$$M^* = Pf(y, r, r_M, \dot{p}^e) \qquad f_y > 0; f_{\dot{p}^e} < 0; f_r < 0; f_{r_M} > 0 \quad \textbf{(4.1)}$$

Here P, the price level, enters as a scale variable implying that the demand for money should be viewed as, at bottom, a demand for real money balances. Then income (y) appears either as a proxy for transactions or as a proxy for wealth or permanent income. Also, there is general agreement that an opportunity cost variable or vector should appear. Typically, this is implemented by choosing a single representative rate of interest (r) while allowing for the influence of the 'own' rate of interest on money itself (r_M). More controversially, the expected inflation rate $\dot{p}^e$ is a candidate component of the opportunity cost vector in some instances.

4.2 Estimating money demand

Two general issues

In moving to the stage of estimation, two general features of empirical research into the demand for money deserve mention. The first concerns the purpose of estimation. One approach is to view the role of theory as providing a structure and estimation as a way of quantifying that structure, parameterizing and confirming (not disproving) the theory. A strongly held theoretical position would fit in with this approach, which may lead the investigator to expend large amounts of effort in transforming the data and computing many alternative but similar specifications to arrive at a preferred exemplar of the theory. Perhaps curiously, given what we have described above as his empirically based approach, it is Friedman who is seen as the arch-exponent of this practice (see Hendry and Ericsson, 1983). The point is that although Friedman does not see the value of discussing motives for money-holding, he does have a strong attachment to the identification of a demand for money which is stable in a key 'few' variables. Hendry and Ericsson (1983) see his work with Schwartz (Friedman and Schwartz, 1982) as exemplifying an overdone and overly exhaustive search for ways of supporting this contention. According to the alternative general approach, time would be better spent in a more open-minded search over alternative theoretical specifications. An important part of such a procedure is to provide a list of diagnostics which *inter alia* test for stability, for forecasting ability and for the acceptability of particular restrictions if these are suggested by some theory.

While the difference between the two general approaches can be so stated, it has to be said that in practice the dividing line between one and the other must be blurred. Data quality is rarely so good that some experimentation with alternative definitions and transformations is not justified, and well-worked theory is itself a piece of information which should legitimately influence the process of data transformation and specification search. Of course, one person's 'well-worked theory' may appear to another as mere prejudice, and perhaps the point is that there is no wholly objective way of proceeding.

A second general issue concerns the long run and the short run. It is commonly argued that the relationships suggested by economic theory are long-run relationships, with that theory giving little guidance about the dynamics or short-run relationships involved. One important strand in money demand research thus concentrates on long-run relationships; traditionally by using low frequency or temporally averaged data, more recently by using 'cointegration' techniques. Another strand has tried to tackle the problem of estimating short-run money demand functions by using high frequency data and postulating some dynamic adjustment mechanism. In the first wave of such research work the partial adjustment mechanism became very popular and we comment on this in some detail below. More recently, the ECM or error correction model (e.g. Hendry and Mizon, 1978) has been seen as providing a more general adjustment framework.

Specific problems and solutions: the choice of variables

The relationship (4.1) can be restated as (4.2), making explicit the conception of the demand for money as a demand for real balances; if, in addition, the income elasticity of real balances is thought of as unity, then (4.2) can be further transformed as an inverse velocity function (4.3), with the 'Cambridge k', the ratio of money to nominal income on the LHS.

$$M^*/P = f(y, r, r_M, \dot{p}^e) \tag{4.2}$$

$$M^*/Py = f(r, r_M, \dot{p}^e) \tag{4.3}$$

All three functional relationships ((4.1) – (4.3)) have formed the basis of empirical work undertaken in Britain.

Much work has been done to find the precise empirical counterparts of these theoretical variables by transforming actual magnitudes into expected ones, experimenting with various functional forms and using different measures of the budget constraint and the opportunity cost of holding money. In terms of scale variables, the existence of both transactions and asset theories of the demand for money means that it is not immediately apparent whether it is wealth or income which should enter the demand function, but the absence until very recently of adequate wealth figures has meant that most extant studies have employed some measure of income. In some cases, a permanent income measure forms the basis for the equation, but given the lack of reliable means of estimating this subjective concept, its inclusion – on the assumption that permanent income can be adequately proxied by a backward-looking distributed lag of current and past income – can be seen (as we show below) to be achieved by appropriate transformations which yield an equation containing current income and lagged money stock values. ('News' formulations of money demand functions, in which the underlying demand is related exclusively to forward-looking variables and in which estimation proceeds by exploiting the idea that the values of these variables change only as expectations are disappointed, are rare – but see Cuthbertson and Taylor (1989) for an example.)

Portfolio approaches to the demand for money emphasize that wealth-holders have a choice of holding money or a variety of financial and real assets; i.e. bills, bonds, equities and commodities. In an open economy, foreigners hold domestic currency in the form of bank deposits and other short-term paper, while domestic residents hold foreign currency claims in equivalent forms, so that interest rates on foreign securities also influence the demand for money. However, in most instances selection of one representative rate, such as the yield on long- or short-term securities, has proved to be adequate. So far as long rates are concerned, government bond yields have been used more than corporate bond yields, at least in the United Kingdom, because information on them is readily available and they are more exogenous than private yields. Money market rates such as local authority rates (United Kingdom) and the commercial paper rate (United States) are popular because they vary more during periods of monetary disturbances.

The impact of inflation expectations upon the demand for money has never been resolved theoretically (Steindl, 1973). Friedman (1956) has money substituting for both securities and real assets, so that both nominal interest rates and the anticipated rate of change of prices ($\dot{p}^e$) enter the demand function, as in the equations above. By contrast, the theoretical Keynesian position sees the margin of substitution, given financial wealth, as that between money and bonds. In practice, it seems that inflation expectations are incorporated into nominal interest rates (but only partially in the short run), so that the cost of holding money relative to securities is the real rate of interest plus the anticipated decline in the purchasing power of money. Given this, the impact of $\dot{p}^e$ is taken up by the nominal rate of interest, and this is the approach followed in most empirical work.

Though most of the early empirical studies left out the variable r_M, the practice has less often predominated as own rates of return have – with deregulation, financial innovation and the advent of high inflation and high interest rates – become more often explicit. Since the cost of holding money depends on the difference between market rates of interest (r) and the own rate (r_M), use of r alone is predicated on the assumption that the own rate adjusts sluggishly to market forces. Such rigidity was to be expected from the cartel arrangements which marked the UK clearing banks' interest rate setting prior to the institution of Competition and Credit Control in 1971, just as it was from the regulations affecting time and savings deposits in the United States before the liberalization of bank interest rates in the 1980s.

Finally, there is the question of the appropriate definition of money itself. Here Friedman's approach affords the robust advice to use whatever data definition performs best. In the alternative approach, it is clear that different parts of the theory apply to different definitions of money. The transactions approach, for example, suggests concentrating on a narrow measure of money, where the portfolio approach suggests a broader magnitude. Generally, researchers have investigated a range of alternative definitions.

Dynamics

The second major problem has been that of modelling dynamics so that the issue of short-run stability can be investigated. Heller (1985, p. 151) and later Hamburger (1977) obtained estimates of the short-run demand for money by fitting long-run (i.e. equilibrium) equations to quarterly data, but most other studies found that sensible results depended upon introducing lags into the equations estimated. Substitution of expected for actual magnitudes into (4.1)–(4.3) is one method of doing so and Feige (1967) showed that the usual Koyck distributed lag formulation, by which expected values of income and interest rates are approximated by geometrically declining lags on present and actual past values, gives rise to an equation with lagged monetary variables. More usually, however, the hypothesis of partial adjustment was incorporated: that people will not move to their desired long-run money holding immediately, but will take time to do so, either through inertia or because it is too costly to move instantaneously. Like the demand function itself, this idea was borrowed from general value theory on the basis that individuals would adjust their actual real money balances to desired levels along much the same lines as they would bring stocks of consumer durables to their desired levels (Chow, 1966). With the addition of the partial adjustment assumption, the standard functions which featured in empirical work on the short-run demand for money can be derived. With all variables (other than perhaps r) transformed to natural logarithms, the simplified long-run demand function can be written as

$$M_t^* - P_t = a + by_t + cr_t + u_t \qquad (4.4)$$

where u_t is a random variable. Some studies (Chow, 1966; Laidler and Parkin, 1970; Goldfeld, 1973) employed what is now called the 'real adjustment hypothesis':

$$m_t - m_{t-1} = \lambda(m_t^* - m_{t-1}) \qquad (4.5)$$

where m represents real money balances $(M - P)$. In combination with (4.4) this gives

$$M_t - P_t = a\lambda + b\lambda y_t + c\lambda r_t + \lambda u_t + (1 - \lambda)(M_{t-1} - P_{t-1}) \qquad (4.6)$$

While actual real balances in any quarter are not at the desired long-run level (assuming $0 < \lambda < 1$), their movement is always towards the desired level. In that way all of the quarterly observations of real balances are capable of tracing out the long-run demand curve once allowance is made for the estimated speed of adjustment.

Two characteristics of (4.6) may be noted: first, the lag response of the demand for real money balances to the arguments of the real demand for money function is identical for every argument; second, there is an asymmetry in the response of *nominal* money balances demanded to prices and to other arguments. The first of these properties indicates that the source of the lag entertained by the partial adjustment hypothesis is the costliness of adjustment itself and not, for example, learning about the change in the value of the argument (which is to be taken account of in some transformation of the relevant explanatory variables). The second of these properties, however, seems unacceptable. The speed of adjustment is an aggregate of individual responses. Prices, interest rates and, for quarterly observations, even income must be seen as given to the individual, leaving nominal balances as the only magnitude which can be adjusted. The partial adjustment hypothesis recognizes that adjustment costs prevent individuals from speedily bringing money holdings to desired levels. Yet the formulation above carries the implication that nominal money holdings adjust fully and instantaneously to prices while responding only partially to movements in interest rates and real income. This can be seen by rewriting (4.5) as

$$M_t - M_{t-1} = \lambda(m^* - m_{t-1}) + \Delta P_t \qquad (4.7)$$

and noting that the coefficient on ΔP_t is unity.

Other studies (Goodhart and Crockett, 1970; Goldfeld, 1976) accordingly preferred the nominal adjustment hypothesis

$$M_t - M_{t-1} = \lambda(M_t^* - M_{t-1}) \qquad (4.8)$$

which when combined with (4.4) gives

$$M_t = a\lambda + b\lambda y_t + c\lambda r_t + \lambda u_t + \lambda P_t + (1-\lambda) M_{t-1} \qquad (4.9)$$

or if estimated in real terms

$$M_t - P_t = a\lambda + b\lambda y_t + c\lambda r_t + \lambda u_t + (1-\lambda)(M_{t-1} - P_t) \qquad (4.10)$$

It is apparent that (4.10) is similar to (4.6), differing only in the replacement of $(M_{t-1} - P_{t-1})$ by $(M_{t-1} - P_t)$, and most likely in practice the two formulations would yield similar results.

Some recent investigations of the demand for money have implemented a more general approach to modelling the dynamics of the demand for money, the so-called error correction model introduced by Hendry and Mizon (1978). While the reader is referred to Cuthbertson (1985, 1991) for an excellent review and exposition of this approach, a brief comment is appropriate here.

Suppose, for convenience, that the long-run demand for money – as well as being homogeneous in prices – is, as indicated in (4.2), unit elastic in real income, so that

$$M_t^* = P_t + y_t - \alpha r_t \qquad (4.11)$$

The error correction approach suggests that while the demand for money will be evolving as P, y and r evolve, it will also be responding to past disequilibria which are, in effect, errors which remain uncorrected. Thus an important component in a short-run estimating function will be a term representing an error correction mechanism (ECM). In the Hendry–Mizon (1978) study and other related papers the suggestion generally was that an appropriate representation of the ECM was a set of terms consisting of lagged values of the levels of the variables in an equation otherwise cast in difference terms. Solving such an equation for the steady state shows that an estimate of the long-run function can be recovered. An equation like (4.12) shows what is involved:

$$\Delta M_t = a_0 + a_i \Delta M_{t-i} + b_i \Delta P_{t-i} + c_i \Delta y_{t-i} + d (M - P - y)_{t-1}$$
$$+ e_i \Delta r_{t-i} + f r_{t-1} \qquad (4.12)$$

This equation allows for a lavish representation of distributed lags and may be supplemented by further orders of difference ($\Delta \Delta P_{t-i}$ might have a role for example). When solving for the stationary state, the Δs can be set to zero along with the lags so that the long-run function can be recovered from (4.12) as

$$M_t = - a_0/d + P_t + y_t - f/dr_t \qquad (4.13)$$

Of course it would be appropriate to test whether the unit restrictions on the coefficients of P and y in the ECM were supported by the data and whether other variables have a role to play at any stage (i.e. just in the short run or in both the short and long run). The dynamics of (4.12) are obviously quite complex. By allowing the data to speak freely on the issue of lags where the input of economic theory is smallest, while accommodating the estimation of the long-run function at the same time, the ECM approach has proved an attractive one for recent research. However, the criteria suggested for choosing the final dynamic specification are not always in harmony with this blueprint: in particular, a tension remains between the criterion of data-coherence and that of theory-coherence (see e.g. Taylor, 1987; Cuthbertson and Taylor, 1989).

Similar attractions have been retained in the two-step procedure recently recommended by Engle and Granger (1987). Here the long-run function (4.11) is estimated first in a cointegrating regression omitting all dynamics; then, in a second step, the lagged residuals from this function are entered as the error correction term in a dynamic ECM formulation which allows the researcher to capture the short-run dynamics. This (now standard) approach to estimation with time series has been implemented on UK monetary data by Hendry and Ericsson (1987) and by Hall *et al.* (1989).

4.3 Principal research findings

Tables 4.1 and 4.2 summarize some of the principal research findings for the United Kingdom on, respectively, the long- and short-run demand function for money.

Long-run studies

The studies by Kavanagh and Walters and Laidler, following graphical analyses of Paish (1958, 1959) and Dow (1958), suggested a much greater stability of the demand for money in the United Kingdom than many had thought existed. Moreover, as Laidler noted, the demand for money function for Britain over the long run did not look very different from that of the United States. This first generation of long-run demand studies effectively established the role of the interest rate and suggested income elasticities around unity and the homogeneity of nominal money demand in prices.

In more recent work, a similar range of presumptions seems to apply. Artis and Lewis (1984) reran the Paish–Dow graphical analysis on extended data, and Patterson's note (Patterson, 1987) on this study, while recommending (and implementing) more rigorous techniques, effectively substantiated several of the original findings including the critical price and income elasticities. In effect, as noted by Cuthbertson (1991), the Artis–Lewis equation can be viewed as the long-run cointegrating regression for a dynamic error correction formulation of the type employed by Patterson. This is a valuable insight for it enables us to represent a long-run demand for money function in terms of two variables, the ratio of money supply to nominal income (M/Y) and the rate of interest (r).

Figure 4.2 plots the data used by Artis–Lewis and Patterson, along with extra observations for 1982 and 1983 (the last available). Readily apparent is the inverse relationship between (r) and (M/Y) predicted by standard theory: indeed, the regression line (calculated incidentally using observations only for the years examined by Paish–Dow, 1920–57) looks much like the demand for money schedules drawn in textbooks. Also apparent in the figure are some substantial deviations from the line, most

Table 4.1 Summary of selected studies of the long-run demand for money in the UK

Authors	Sample period	Money variable	Income variable	Interest rate	Elasticity with respect to		Comments
					Income	Interest rate	
Kavanagh & Walters (1966)	1880–1961	M1	National income	Consol rate	1.15	−0.31	
	1926–1960	M2	National income	Consol rate	1.27	−0.46	
Laidler (1971)	1900–1965 excl. war years	M1	National income	Consol rate	0.96	−0.50	
		M2	Permanent income	Treasury bill rate	0.80	−0.57	
					0.67	−0.15	
Graves (1980)	1911–1966	M1	National income	Commercial bill rate	0.30	−0.10	Instability in standard equations; includes variable for urbanization and age distribution of populations.
Friedman & Schwartz (1982)	1874–1975	M2/M3	Net national product	Commercial bill rate less own rate	0.88	−0.19	Dummy variables for interwar and post-war shifts.
Batts & Dowling (1984)	1880–1975	M1	Net national product	Commercial bill rate	0.57	−0.07	Instability evident around war years and possibly 1970s.
		M2	Net national product	Commercial bill rate	0.47	−0.08	
Artis & Lewis (1984)	1920–1981 excl. 1973–1976	M2	GDP	Consol rate	1.00	−.59	Possible shift during war years.
Longbottom & Holly (1985)	1878–1975	M2/M3	NNP	Commercial bill less own rate	1.08	−.09	Dummy variables for shift in war years. Possible instability in 1930s. Inclusion of CDs gives instability in 1970s.
Hendry & Ericsson (1987)	1875–1970	M2/M3	NNP	Long rate	1.00	−.40	National debt/real income ratio significant.

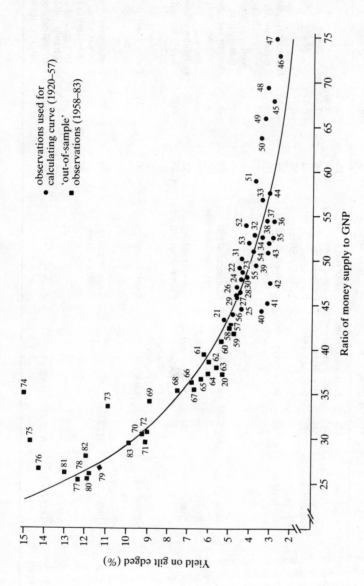

Figure 4.2   Interest rates and the demand for money, 1920–83. *Source:* Artis and Lewis (1984).

notably around the war years and the mid 1970s, which require special explanation. The latter period, embracing Competition and Credit Control and its immediate aftermath, has proved to be a troublesome one in recent examinations of the demand for money function.

Friedman and Schwartz (1982) reported long-run stability in their demand for money function and claimed similarity between it and a function estimated on US data. Some of the claims made by these authors, and many of their basic techniques, were severely criticized by Hendry and Ericsson (1983, 1991). Friedman and Schwartz (1991) have defended their work in equally vigorous fashion. A characteristic of Friedman and Schwartz's research is the use of cycle-average data, i.e. observations converted into averages of business cycle phases, so as to eliminate short-term cyclical movements (when transactors can be off their demand curves). Hendry and Ericsson note that phase-averaging results in the loss of information and in combination with the *ad hoc* use made of dummy variables effectively prejudges what is a transitory departure from equilibrium and what is a major alteration to the underlying relationship. Thus Friedman and Schwartz were charged with failing to integrate a description of steady-state behaviour with a dynamic process of adjustment to equilibrium.

From the point of view of the results established, as opposed to the methods by which they are derived, Hendry and Ericsson's critique was blunted by the later analysis of Longbottom and Holly (1985) which re-estimated Friedman and Schwartz's model for the United Kingdom using annual rather than phase-average data, and which employed Hendry-style econometric procedures yet reported very similar results to Friedman and Schwartz. Moreover, Hendry and Ericsson themselves in subsequent work (Hendry and Ericsson, 1987) establish a model which has parameter constancy over the entire period 1875–1970 (although some instability appears when the model is extended to the years 1971–5), and which supports homogeneity of money in both prices and real income, provided that allowance is made for the influence of the ratio of national debt to income – a variable not used by Friedman and Schwartz.

These long-run results point to a greater underlying stability of the demand for money function than is evident from the short-run studies considered below. That observation in itself does not say much, and it is probably too soon to seek to do so in view of the limited number of long-run studies which extend the data sample beyond 1975.

Short-run studies

Investigation of short-run studies did not get under way in the United Kingdom until the late 1960s. Notwithstanding some ambiguities, the

Table 4.2 Summary of selected studies of the short-run demand for money in the UK

Author(s)	Sample period	Money variable	Income variable	Interest rate	Elasticities with respect to		Comments
					Income	Interest rate	
Laidler & Parkin (1970)	1955–1967	M2	GDP	Treasury bill	0.59	−.02	
Goodhart & Crockett (1970)	1955Q3 – 69Q3	M1	GDP	3mo LA Consol	1.25 1.09	−1.05 −0.00	
Price (1972)	1963Q2 – 69Q3	M3	GDP	3mo LA Consol	1.41 1.54	−0.21 −0.51	
Hacche (1974)	1963Q4 – 72Q4	M1	TFE	3mo LA Consol	0.70	−0.06 −0.21	
	1963Q4 – 72Q4	M3	TFE	3mo LA	(i) * (ii)1.00	* −0.25	(ii) Inserting interest rate variable for shift after 1971.
Artis & Lewis (1976)	1963Q2 – 72Q1 1963Q2 – 73Q1	M1 M3	GDP GDP	Consol Consol	1.24 (1) 3.89 (2) 1.21	−0.66 −1.46 −0.34	Instability in 1971. (1) Standard equation. (2) Interest rate adjustment equation.

Study	Period		Scale	Interest rate			Comments
Hamburger (1977)	1963Q1 – 70Q4	M1	GDP	3mo Eurodollar	0.67	−1.07	No adjustment lags in model. Instability in 1972.
Coghlan (1978)	1964Q1 – 76Q4	M1	TFE	3mo LA	1.01	−0.30	Complex adjustment lags. No stability.
Boughton (1979)	1963Q2 – 77Q3 1963Q2 – 77Q3	M1 M3	GDP GDP	3mo LA Consol	1.32 *	−0.51 *	Instability in 1971. Instability evident.
Grice & Bennett (1984)	1963–78	M3	TFE	Return on gilts	0.32	0.00	Dynamic instability present. Dummy variable added.
Andersen (1985)	1960–83	M1	GDP	(1) Treasury bill rate (2) Treasury bill rate	0.68 0.70	−0.45 −0.49	(1) Standard equation. (2) Interest rate adjustment
Taylor (1987)	1964Q2 – 85Q4	M3	GDP	Treasury bill/ own rate differential	1.00	−0.26	Own rate = max. (7 day rate, high interest account rate). Stable through period, inflation significant.
Cuthbertson & Taylor (1989)	1963Q1 – 79Q4	M1	PDY	Local authority 3 month rate Local authority 3 month rate	(1) 1.00 (2) 1.00	−7.1 −4.5	(1) Buffer stock model, fully adjusted estimates. (2) ECM model.

results established in the first wave of these studies, through to the mid 1970s (see Table 4.2), appeared sufficiently consistent with the long-run findings to have important implications for policy. These were seen to be as follows:

1. If a stable demand function containing a limited number of explanatory variables exists, policy actions which alter the money stock can be expected eventually to have predictable effects on ultimate goal variables. Otherwise, the ultimate response will be unpredictable and there may be no reliable basis for either discretionary policy or fixed monetary growth rate rules. A fairly general form of the demand for money function – encompassing ideas drawn from major theories – seemed capable of explaining the course of monetary behaviour in the United Kingdom (as in the United States and other countries). In most cases, the variables influencing the aggregate demand function could be limited to income and one or two interest rates.

2. Knowledge of the income elasticity of the demand for money is needed by those who advocate the adoption of monetary rules aimed at a constant rate of monetary growth. A fairly clear picture emerged from the earlier studies, with the long-run income elasticities of time deposits and savings bank deposits greater than unity, that of current deposits or M1 around or slightly less than unity, and that of broad money sometimes well over unity.

3. At least one interest rate had a significant negative impact upon the demand for money. The nature of the response of money balances to interest rates is important for monetary policy. Within the IS–LM framework, this elasticity is one of the crucial parameters for assessing the relative efficacy of fiscal and monetary policy with a low elasticity signifying a greater potency of monetary policy and a lesser potency of fiscal policy. A considerable measure of agreement existed about the elasticity: in most cases, the response was found to be inelastic, and sometimes less than $(-)0.5$.

Instability in short-run functions

This unanimity began to break down in the 1970s as evidence mounted that demand functions of the type hitherto estimated – basically partial-adjustment versions of the long-run functions – proved to exhibit instability. By 'instability' we refer to three interrelated features. First, when equations estimated with data for the 1950s and 1960s were used to predict the behaviour of real or nominal money balances in the 1970s, errors of prediction occurred. Clear evidence of this was provided by Artis and Lewis (1974, 1976) and Hacche (1974), who showed that the Bank of England's demand for money functions seriously underpredicted monetary growth in the 1971–3 period. Second, when data for the 1970s were incorporated into the sample used for estimating the equations, the coefficient on the lagged dependent variable changed, usually increasing markedly, suggesting that there had been some change in the nature of the adjustment process. Indeed, in some work the coefficient on the lagged variable consistently exceeded unity, indicating an explosive time path (see studies in Table 4.2). Third, in order to accommodate the additional data from the 1970s, some studies found it necessary to add variables which previous researchers had not found it necessary to incorporate, or to include dummy variables (Thornton, 1985; Grice and Bennett, 1984; Taylor, 1987).

These difficulties were found to be much more acute for the broader money aggregates than for narrow money (see e.g. Hendry, 1979) and were not limited to a handful of aberrant observations in the first half of the 1970s – although this period was most notably stressful. It has still not proved possible to reassemble in the 1980s a consensus about the demand for money, or at least the demand for broad money, comparable with the consensus briefly enjoyed at the end of the 1960s. Significantly, £M3 was finally officially dropped from the list of monetary aggregates in the government's medium-term financial strategy in 1987.

Looking back at the short-run studies from a later vantage point it is apparent that a number of problems were present which had not been resolved. First, there was an inconsistency between the quarterly and annual studies of the demand for money. The annual studies assumed implicitly that any adjustments in the monetary sector were completed within the year. When quarterly data are used, this assumption can be tested explicitly by allowing balances to be in the process of adjusting to equilibrium. Almost invariably the speeds of adjustment which were estimated indicated that less than 50 per cent, and sometimes as little as 15 per cent, of the difference between actual and desired money balances would be eliminated in one year, and that in consequence many years elapse before the adjustment of balances is, say, 90 per cent completed. By way of example, Goodhart and Crockett (1970) reported adjustment coefficients ranging from 0.04 to 0.15. Lags of such length surprised many economists; these sluggish responses do not sit easily with preconceived notions that money markets facilitate rapid adjustment within the hour, let alone the quarter or the year.

Second, a peculiarity also existed with respect to the measured interest rate elasticities. It would seem likely that high interest elasticities would be found for assets which are the closest substitutes for money, since in this case only a slight change in yield should induce a large reshuffle of portfolios (that is, the demand for money schedule should be relatively flat). In fact the reverse is found, with higher elasticities suggesting that long-term securities are closer substitutes for money than shorter-term ones. Arithmetically, the estimates follow directly from the lower amplitude of cyclical fluctuations of long rates *vis-à-vis* short rates. Expectations of market participants about future short-term interest rates are generally thought to be the dominant influence upon the yield curve, but the authorities' practice of effecting transactions in securities at the short end of the market may have some independent effect. If so, the specification which sees interest rates as exogenously determining money balances, with a long lag, must be called into question.

Nor were the implications of the apparently different responses to income of the components of the money stock appreciated at the time. The results suggest that for long-run stability, the growth rate of more liquid assets such as current deposits should be lower than that for term, interest-bearing deposits. Unless the components of the aggregate have identical elasticities (and own rates have zero elasticities), no unique aggregate relationship can be derived from logarithmic functions. Studies using actual as opposed to logarithmic values do not so obviously violate the required aggregation conditions, but once differences in the adjustment speeds of components are allowed for, their validity is less clear, and different adjustment speeds have generally been found for the components of broad money.

Perhaps much of the growth of time and savings deposits relative to current deposits in the 1960s should be attributed to factors other than income. For many of these years, the path of income resembles an upward trend, and it could be proxying for a variety of other factors, such as improvements in the quality of interest-bearing claims, improvement in the payments mechanism, changes in the distribution of wealth, developments in cash management systems or growing accessibility of short-term credit – all of which may have reduced the demand for means of payment. Some of these factors have surfaced in recent empirical work examining the instability of the short-run demand for money – to which we now turn.

Accounting for instability

Many factors may have contributed to the poor predictive performance of the short-run models. The prior stability of the demand for money may have been exaggerated. A large number of complex and special factors can interact to generate the aggregate demand for money, and the search for a simple successfully aggregated function may be too ambitious. Econometric methods have changed: the diagnostic tests applied to present-day models are by earlier standards extensive, but so are the specification searches applied to the data. More emphasis is given now to post-sample prediction tests; rarely are these made outside the sample known to the researcher when selecting the hypothesis. One should in consequence look to the robustness of a battery of results over time and not at one or two particular equations from the set.

A useful starting-point is the model being tested. The usual approach is to treat the observations of nominal or real money balances as movements along a (short-run) demand function induced by changes in the nominated variables. This interpretation is justifiable only if we can exclude the possibilities that (a) the demand schedule itself may have shifted and/or changed unpredictably, and (b) actual real balances may have differed from the public's desired holdings. The choice between these interpretations is central to an assessment of monetary management. Consider a large expansion of money such as occurred in the United Kingdom in 1972–3 or, more recently, in the late 1980s. If some factor(s) peculiar to the period produced successive shifts of the demand function, the contribution of the money balances themselves to economic instability would seem to be minor. The increase in money balances is simply an accommodating response to a non-inflationary increase in the demand for them. On the alternative interpretation, monetary growth was presumably in excess of demand, producing subsequent pressures on asset prices, exchange rates, output, incomes and ultimately the rate of inflation.

Given the simple form of the estimated demand functions there is a real possibility that some important variables have been omitted. Transactions costs, the pattern of monetary payments and the own rate of interest on money were all assumed constant in the first generation of short-run functions, but these assumptions have been undermined by the substantial innovation and deregulation which have occurred in the financial sector since the early 1970s.

Underprediction of monetary growth occurred in 1971–3 and the money supply (M3) ran ahead of income, i.e. the velocity of money fell (see Figure 4.3). This decline in velocity coincided with the release of lending controls, alterations to required reserve ratios and the ending of the clearing banks' interest rate cartel arrangements. Reimposition of controls in 1974 saw the money supply begin to move back towards the predicted path, and the velocity of M3 rose. Underprediction again in the early 1980s and the beginning of the decline in velocity seemed to be associated with the removal of exchange controls and the remaining direct monetary controls, while the more recent growth in money

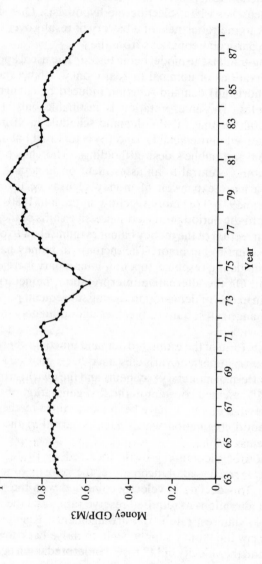

Figure 4.3   M3 velocity, 1963 Q1 – 1988 Q2, quarterly, seasonally adjusted. *Source:* Central Statistical Office/Bank of England.

coincides with a further round of competitive responses to deregulation by banks and building societies.

Factors like the own rate of interest, greater volatility of bond prices, 'roundtripping' via certificates of deposit, greater volatility of bond prices, and dummy variables to allow for policy and regulatory changes have been added to standard equations (Hacche, 1974; Artis and Lewis, 1976; Grice and Bennett, 1984; Taylor, 1987); but the explanations they provide are limited and/or open to question. Dummy variables are of course a direct confession of ignorance; gross wealth, added by Grice and Bennett, itself contains money and therefore accommodates, without explaining the phenomenon.

Measurement of the own rate on money is far from straightforward. Weighted average measures of the own rate like those employed by Artis and Lewis (1976) do not resolve the instability. Selecting particular rates (Hacche, 1974) raises the difficulty that they may in fact be acting like dummy variables and are being made to carry more weight than is properly attributable to them. Taylor's (1987) paper provides an account of the demand for money (£M3) in which the choice of own rate at least for the period before the introduction of high interest chequing accounts is relatively uncontentious (being proxied by the 7-day deposit rate), and where the period of CCC appears to need no separate explanation provided that the specification of the equation – which includes a second difference in long bond yields and an inflation term – is accepted. For the later 1980s, the equation – with the own rate now proxied more contentiously by the interest rate offered on high interest accounts – continues to perform and to forecast satisfactorily. Taylor's formulation is among the more convincing now available, yet arguably it still begs many of the questions raised by financial intermediation and may be attributing to the variables included effects which appropriately belong elsewhere.

It is clear in fact that financial innovation raises special problems for estimation. Increased competition in principle adds to non-price competitiveness as well as to measurable own rates of interest: the liquidity services of banks are more aggressively marketed and more readily accessible (with automated equipment) than used to be the case. Even where rates of return are explicit and observable the public may not incorporate perceptions of these opportunities immediately into its information set and allowance needs to be made for learning. Hall *et al.* (1989) report work along these lines.

Rather than look to new factors which might have shifted the demand function or to changes which might have altered the pecuniary or non-pecuniary returns from holding deposits in ways such as to produce a complete change in the parameters of demand, an alternative explanation within the terms of reference of the standard demand function may be sought (Atkinson and Chouraqui, 1987). Uncertainty introduced by the process of inflation and disinflation seems the most likely candidate. Klein (1977) defined the quality of money balances as the flow of monetary services yielded per real dollar (or pound) which we can assume to be positively related to the degree of price predictability as greater certainty about the future purchasing power of money enhances the usefulness of holding claims which are constant in nominal terms (see also Kent, 1985). The abandonment of fixed exchange rates and the arrival of a period of unstable exchanges, commodity price rises and activist economic policies seem likely to have led to expectations of rising and unstable inflation, so leading people to shift out of holding money balances, increasing velocity in the early 1970s. Conversely, disinflation in the 1980s should see the demand for money rise and velocity fall.

Referring again to Figure 4.3, both hypothesized movements are in the right direction to explain velocity movements in each decade, after making allowance for the special CCC velocity fall to 1974, and presumably are common to experiences in a number of countries, as observed by Atkinson and Chouraqui. If the adjustments of expectations are sufficiently abrupt and ill defined, they seem unlikely to be captured by the standard equations which ought, nevertheless, to settle down if the process of disinflation is concluded and the resurgence of inflation in the late 1980s proves to be an aberration.

Friedman (1988) reaches the same conclusions as Atkinson and Chouraqui, while starting from a quite different tack. His paper examines the impact of stock market prices upon the demand for money and finds that the response in the period 1974–85 is markedly different from that measured for the years 1886–1974. This he attributes to the transition from commodity to fiat money, ushering in an era of increased long-term uncertainty about future nominal values. As a consequence, he argues that anticipated inflation and deflation came to exert greater significance upon the demand for money.

4.4 Monetary disequilibrium and buffer stock models

So far we have focused upon the demand function and its arguments. The short-run demand for money function, however, embraces two hypotheses: one about the nature of the long-run demand function, the other about the path to equilibrium. These are jointly tested, which leaves open the possibility that the observed instability may come from the adjustment mechanism rather than from the underlying demand function.

Lagged adjustment of nominal money balances to demand, we recall, rested on the notion that due to adjustment costs, transactors are individually slow to adjust their actual holdings of money to desired levels. When these individual responses are aggregated we obtain a partial adjustment of the supply of money to the quantity demanded. There are a number of grounds on which we can query this formulation. To begin with, as emphasized by Tobin and Brainard (1968), not *all* assets can be adjusted in this fashion; if some assets are adjusted slowly, there must be at least one asset which acts as a residual, buffering the impact of the slowly moving component of the portfolios. This is merely an application of the rules of system-wide demand analysis to the financial sector (see Green, 1984 and Weale, 1986 for examples). Nor is it obvious that the process of adjustment should be the same for increases as it is for decreases in money. Inertia in consumption habits may make it easier for some people to reduce money balances by spending in excess of income than to attempt to increase them by saving. Finally, and this is our main concern, while such adjustment can occur at a micro level, it is not clear that it survives the aggregation procedure. Here we question the almost universal practice of reconciling the short-run to the long-run demand by positing a passive supply of nominal balances. One individual may augment his or her money holdings in this way but the economy as a whole cannot do so if the central bank is controlling the quantity of money: in that event, one individual's accretion of money is someone else's loss.

Although those who investigated the short-run demand for money rarely did so (though see Fisher (1968) for an honourable exception), one can of course point out circumstances in which the assumption of a passive money supply is in fact justified. One is when the central bank stabilizes interest rates and allows the quantity of money to respond to demand. Another is when the exchange rate is pegged at a fixed level, which enables money balances to be replenished via overseas transactions. With a fixed rate of exchange and interest rate pegging policies, transactors are afforded some implicit guarantees about their freedom to exchange money for bonds or foreign securities on demand; to this extent (and the account is obviously a highly stylized one) the amount of money actually in existence is determined by demand, as excess supplies can be instantaneously liquidated and excess demands satisfied without repercussions for the arguments of the demand function.

However accurate this description is of the 1960s, and we have reasons to query it, clearly different institutional arrangements operated in the 1970s. Monetary authorities moved away from interest rate setting to monetary targets, and from fixed to floating exchange rates. Activist monetary policies were followed. All of these are circumstances in which discrepancies between actual and desired money holdings might arise. The institution of Competition and Credit Control in 1971 and the release of advances controls coincided with expansionary budget deficits (the 'Barber boom') and a move to flexible exchange rates, all of which may have combined to generate unanticipated money supply shocks which forced the private sector away from its demand curve for some time. Here we have another possible explanation for the apparent disturbance to demand functions and the velocity of money in the 1970s.

By the same token, of course, monetary policies in the 1980s have seen some movement back towards previous arrangements: more attention has been paid to influencing the course of the exchange rate and to interest rate setting. Supply shocks of the magnitude of the 1970s may be less likely to be sustained. Putting to one side the question of changing policy regimes, we wish to focus upon the portfolio reallocations which result from any disequilibrium between desired and actual money holdings. How long the discrepancy exists and the means by which it is removed become the relevant questions. By assuming the nominal money stock to be demand-determined, the answers to these questions were effectively prejudged by the earlier researchers.

The essence of the disequilibrium idea can be obtained from Figure 4.1 above by considering the effects of an increase in money balances. Only when balances reach the upper threshold are actions taken by the individual to bring the quantity of money back to the desired level. These actions involve increased purchases of assets and/or goods. Conversely, sales of goods or assets are made only when money balances fall to the lower limit. By these means, an individual's actual money holdings will rise and fall, gravitating over time around an average or desired level, m_t^*. In the short run, however, an increase (or decrease) in balances can occur without provoking any immediate reaction from the individual. When considering an expansion of the aggregate money stock distributed across a number of individuals, the overall position seems likely to be muddied. Some individuals will be pushed immediately to their upper threshold and others will absorb the increase, while money spent by the first group could end up in someone else's ceiling–floor range. Yet it is apparent that some part can be willingly held – even if not demanded as part of desired holdings – at unchanged levels of expenditures and asset prices. Here we have an example of the buffer stock function of money.

Central to the buffer stock approach is the idea that a disequilibrium in the financial sector can be met by a temporary deviation of the buffer stock from its desired level. When considering the implications which then follow for modelling the demand for money, the question is not whether money serves as a buffer (for it is inherent in the role of money in straddling the means of exchange and store of value functions that money balances will temporarily rise and fall), but over what time period it acts as a buffer. If the necessary discrepancy in money balances is offset more or less instantaneously, then other assets (or even expenditure flows) serve as the main cushion preliminary to a major reshuffling of portfolios. Alternatively, the drop in money balances may, if money is held as a buffer, simply be maintained until transitory inflows of money restore cash balances to their initial (desired) level. The cost of transacting into and out of the buffer stock asset appears critical in this. If, for example, it is relatively easy to transact from narrow money to the interest-bearing component of broad money, but somewhat more difficult and costly to transact from broad money to other assets, then we might expect to find that broad rather than narrow money would be the buffer. Paradoxically, while other assets would be a poor buffer because of the costs of investment and disinvestment, narrow money would be a poor candidate because, *ex hypothesi*, it is so *easy* to transact out of this aggregate.

These possible responses indicate the various roles of money as a buffer stock. When transactors move to offset the discrepancy quickly, the buffering role of money is the same as that envisaged by Friedman and others analyzing exogenous monetary disturbances in a simple quantity theory framework, with money serving as a temporary store of value. The case in which the discrepancy is allowed to persist corresponds in broad terms with the 'shock-absorber' models of Carr and Darby (1981). Somewhere in between the taut and slack responses we have the role for money envisaged in most of the buffer stock models (see Laidler (1984), Goodhart (1984a) and Knoester (1984) for surveys of the concept, and Cuthbertson and Taylor (1987) for an examination of the empirical work which has resulted).

Dynamic effects

The implications of a buffer stock formulation for the dynamic processes by which equilibrium is secured are worth spelling out. If from an initial position of equilibrium there is a disturbance to money supply (say, an increase) then the adjustment process must require either an adjustment to the arguments of the demand function to absorb the added money, or a subsequent, negative, supply response – or some combination of both. The speed with which either or any of these adjustments is promoted in turn depends on the size of the shock and the tolerance afforded in the aggregate by the width of the ceiling–floor gap.

Adjustments within the monetary sector itself are usually ignored or downplayed. Own rates of interest on monetary assets (r_M) are assumed to be either invariant or tied to market rates of interest (r) by supposing that competition forces banks to pay deposit rates which move in harmony with market offerings (Davis and Lewis, 1982, p. 371). Impacts upon the components of the money multiplier also feature little in the empirical work. Consequently there is no direct mechanism in the money market by which a disequilibrium between the demand and supply of money is extinguished. Instead the adjustment is assumed to occur in the markets for other commodities or assets: many economists consider the market for money as the 'other side' of the market for goods and assets. This is not the complete story; monetary disturbances may have some capacity for self-extinction also. If there is an interaction between deposit holding and loan decisions, an excess supply of money could be used, in part or in full, to repay outstanding loans or advances, and this route is suggested by Davidson (1987). Buying some domestic or foreign securities from the central bank under interest rate or exchange rate targeting provides another mechanism. In these ways, the adjustment may be shared between supply and the arguments of demand. In the latter case, changes in one or more of the variables, arguments of the demand function, are required. Consider again (4.1), namely

$$M^* = Pf(y, r, r_M, \dot{p}^e)$$

If r_M is omitted, by supposing that it is either invariant or tied to r, then the demand for money adjusts to supply when one or more of $P, y, \dot{p}^e, r$ change as monetary disequilibrium $(M - M^*)$ induces price or quantity adjustments in other markets.

The scenario which fits in most readily with the quantity theory (monetarist) framework neglects supply adjustment and, with the money supply assumed to be exogenously determined, sees the burden of adjustment as falling almost immediately upon the demand for money. With the shock-absorber role of money emphasized, some lag in adjustment and slackness in responses is implied and temporary, self-reversing, shocks to the money supply may well leave little trace beyond an accommodating rise and fall in money holdings. Sustained shocks, however, will after some delay initiate a set of responses which will resolve the initial disequilibrium. Three channels exist for this process of equilibration:

1. An interest rate effect bringing money demand temporarily or permanently into line with the new supply.
2. An income effect, involving changes in real income (y) and the demand for money induced by the monetary disturbance.
3. A price change to restore real money balances to the new equilibrium level.

In asking which of these adjustments is the most likely to occur, consideration needs to be given to the period of time under examination, the size of the supply disturbance and the transmission mechanism envisaged. Most econometric models in the Keynesian tradition have visualized the adjustment proceeding in a particular way. Asset markets are typically seen to respond first. Adjustments in goods markets then follow. Variations in interest rates and output both have consequences for the balance of payments (and thus the exchange rate), but in addition feed through to prices via excess demands for goods and labour and as expectations of inflation are revised.

Second, perceptions of the transmission mechanism are influenced by what is meant by 'asset' markets. If portfolios comprise simply the money and bonds of Keynesian analysis, imbalances can initially be resolved only by a change in the price of bonds, i.e. 'the' rate of interest. Should asset portfolios be made up of many assets, ranging from money through to consumer durables and even real estate, a monetary disturbance will have direct implications for the demand for existing and newly produced goods.

Finally, a distinction needs to be drawn in a growth context between types of equilibrium. A *temporary* or *quasi-equilibrium* exists when $M = M^*$, and a long-run or full equilibrium when both $M = M^*$ and $\dot{M} = \dot{M}^*$. Assuming a new constant growth rate of the money stock of g_1, a temporary equilibrium can be achieved by one-off changes in the determinants of money demand while *full equilibrium* requires them to be continuously changing. For M^* to grow at the rate of g_1, either $\dot{P} = g_1$ (prices grow at a rate of g_1) or the other determinants are continuously changing. Considering these other variables, few would argue that monetary expansion generates significant enduring increases in the growth rate of real income (although potential income may rise to some extent). While most would contemplate some change in the level of interest rates and inflation expectations, none would suggest that they are continuously changing in long-run equilibrium.

One scenario envisaged in monetarist analyses embodying what is called super neutrality is for real income to settle down at an unchanging natural rate, for interest rates to settle back to a constant level in real terms, and for prices and price expectations to satisfy the condition

$$\dot{P} = \dot{p}^e = \dot{M} = g_1 \tag{4.14}$$

There would, however, be some transitional consequences as inflation expectations adjust. With the original growth rate of the money supply (and the demand for money) at $g_0 < g_1$, the upward revision of inflation expectations from g_0 to g_1, and of nominal interest rates via the Fisher effect, will bring about a once-for-all reduction in the demand for money.

In order that real balances fall, prices must temporarily grow faster than the new equilibrium rate g_1.

In an open economy other possible determinants, such as exchange rate expectations, enter the analysis. Where world prices are growing at the old equilibrium rate of g_0, an increase in monetary growth to g_1 in a (small) country operating flexible exchange rates necessitates a continuous depreciation of the exchange rate at the rate $(g_1 - g_0)$. Exchange rate expectations may thus undergo a change in level (since the exchange rate falls continuously), but as these expectations relate to the *rate* of exchange rate change, they do not change continuously.

Consequently, among the arguments of the demand for money, prices (P) seem the most likely element to adjust the demand for money to the supply and satisfy the requirement $\dot{M} = \dot{M}^* = g_1$ for long-run equilibrium. A reaction in terms of interest rates, as featured in Keynesian liquidity preference analysis, or in real income, seems more appropriate for examinations of temporary equilibria.

Consequences for modelling

Some problems are posed for money demand estimation by these considerations. Single equation estimation of the demand for money may still proceed with money on the left-hand side, on the understanding that this now consists of an equilibrium (or perhaps an anticipated) component and a disequilibrium (unanticipated) component. Then, the menu of variables on the right-hand side must include measures of the unexpected, disequilibrium money shock. Cuthbertson and Taylor (1989) provide an example. In their model, people are assumed to minimize a multiperiod cost-of-adjustment function which involves anticipations of the future values of the determinants of money demand; but actual money holdings also reflect, in addition to an inertia term, unanticipated values of the determinants. The money supply is demand-determined. Interpreting the monetary shock as being represented by a linear combination of these different influences, the results have a straightforward buffer stock–real balance effect interpretation (Cuthbertson, 1989). Moreover, the estimated equation fits and forecasts well. Nevertheless the achievement is not without its limitations. First, the estimate is for M1, whereas on general grounds, a broader aggregate like M3 seems a more plausible candidate for the role of buffer. Second, though providing a good fit to the data and adequate forecasting ability, the equation can be outperformed statistically by a more atheoretical ECM model (Cuthbertson and Taylor, 1989). Third, both equations imply very high interest rate elasticities, which are out of line with earlier studies.

A different estimation response is embodied in those studies which treat money as exogenous and focus directly on the response of the determinants of demand to monetary disequilibria. Generally r, y and P can be expected to share in the adjustment process, but all three cannot be put on to the left-hand side of a simple equation. A number of small-scale buffer stock models have been built (Jonson, Moses and Wymer, 1977; Coghlan, 1979; Laidler and Bentley, 1983; Davidson and Ireland, 1985; Davidson, 1987) in which an exogenous monetary disturbance will initially be absorbed in portfolios and partially removed in each period through a variety of transactions, some of which involve adjustments to the money stock itself and some of which alter the arguments of the demand function. Elements of all three adjustment mechanisms we have discussed for exogenous money are incorporated along with portfolio reallocations which directly reduce the money supply, particularly purchases of foreign assets, bond purchases from the authorities or reductions in bank advances. A demand for money function can be estimated implicitly in the process.

Use of single equation methods in this case seems justifiable only if one of the arguments of the demand for money function bears the brunt of adjusting demand to supply disturbances. In the short run, interest rates seem to be the likeliest candidate, and Artis and Lewis (1976) proposed interest rate adjustment equations for an examination of states of temporary equilibria. These equations took the form

$$M_t^* - P_t = m_t = a + by_t + cr_t + u_t \tag{4.15}$$

$$\Delta r_t = \alpha(r_t^* - r_{t-1}) \tag{4.16}$$

which allows for the actual rate of interest to adjust partially to the market clearing value r^*_t required to equilibrate the demand for money (4.15) and the current supply, i.e.

$$r^* = \frac{1}{c}(m_t - by_t - a - u_t) \tag{4.17}$$

Combining the two gives an equation for estimation

$$r_t = \beta_0 + \beta_1 y_t + \beta_2 m_t + \beta_3 r_{t-1} + w_t \tag{4.18}$$

where

$$\beta_0 = -\alpha\, a/c, \ \beta_1 = -\alpha\, b/c, \ \beta_2 = a/c, \ \beta_3 = (1 - \alpha)$$

and

$$w_t = -\alpha\, u_t/c.$$

Andersen (1985) compares the performance of equations like (4.18) with the standard equations, and finds that in four of the seven countries studied, namely the United States, Japan, the United Kingdom and Italy, the alternative procedure provides more stable estimates of the demand for money function in the 1970s and 1980s. As would be expected, relatively short lags are estimated (one to three-quarters at most). But so long as interest rates carry implications for a subsequent course of expenditures, these responses cannot measure more than quasi-equilibrium in the monetary sector.

For an analysis of the longer-run situation, analogous modelling gives a price adjustment equation

$$\Delta P_t = \gamma(P_t^* - P_{t-1}) \tag{4.19}$$

where P_t^* is the price level which brings real money balances to the desired level m_t^* as defined in (4.15). While one could then solve through to obtain an equation in which P_t appears on the left-hand side, Laidler (1982) notes that if instead M_t is added to both sides of the resulting equation, what results is:

$$M_t - P_t = \gamma a + \gamma b Y_t + \gamma c r_t + \gamma u_t + (1 - \gamma)(M_t - P_{t-1}) \tag{4.20}$$

This expression is of course very similar to the partial adjustment-augmented demand functions (4.6) and (4.10) above, except for the last term in which $M_t - P_{t-1}$ appears instead of $M_{t-1} - P_{t-1}$ (as in 4.10). Despite this apparent similarity the interpretation is quite different. Lags arise not from within the demand for money due to individuals' response to the costs of rapid adjustment, or even within the financial sector, but from production lags or institutional impediments in wage- and price-setting mechanisms in the economy as a whole. Considered in conjunction with the relatively short lags suggested by the interest rate equations – which might give an indication of sluggish adjustment due to buffer stock money and inertia in portfolio behaviour – a more plausible explanation is thereby provided for the long lags found in conventional studies.

Conclusions

The demand for money is a well-worn research field. The form and specification of the function and its stability are potentially highly significant for monetary policy, and indeed research findings have influenced policy directions in obvious ways in recent years. What is striking in this connection is that the impression of stability conveyed by the early generation of money demand functions was shattered in the mid 1970s and the image has never been restored despite considerable advances in econometric technique. Monetary economists have probably contributed to this impression by the search for single-cause explanations and their particular interest in the short-run functions. Demand for money functions do appear to have been broadly identified over long periods of time in the past and there are some reasons to think that recent history is one of exceptional turbulence, making identification of a demand function difficult. In particular, besides the obvious mixture of financial innovation and deregulation it seems clear that single equation estimation makes particular assumptions about the money supply process and monetary adjustments which are typically unexamined and which often appear heroic. When these assumptions are removed, a more complex analysis involving the markets for assets and goods as well as money is required. The interaction between these markets defines the transmission mechanism of monetary policy, to which we now turn.

Note

1. The finance motive is examined by Smith (1979). Cuthbertson (1985) provides an excellent account of the standard approaches to the demand for money.

5

The transmission mechanism of monetary policy

5.1 The theory of economic policy

The formal theory of economic policy indicates a fundamental distinction between variables which are under the direct control of the policy-makers, known as policy instruments, and variables which can claim some welfare significance and so, although not under the authorities' direct control, are variables the policy-makers wish to influence: these are ultimate target variables (see Chapter 3, section 1).

In between the instruments and the ultimate, or goal, variables it is possible to distinguish a further category of intermediate variables. These variables are heavily influenced by the authorities' policy instruments without being directly controllable, and they may therefore appear to be good indicators of the combined effect of the use the authorities make of their various policy instruments and may have a temporal lead over the ultimate variables; they may in certain cases be described as forming part of the transmission mechanism through which changes in the policy instruments affect the ultimate target variables. Schematically, the theory suggests that we can think of the sequence

$$I \rightarrow IV \rightarrow UV \tag{5.1}$$

where I is the set of policy instruments, IV the set of intermediate variables and UV the set of ultimate variables. The useful properties of intermediate variables may well lead to a case being made out that a particular intermediate or indicator variable should become a target itself. The selection and assignment of variables to these various classes depend on institutional data and on the transmission mechanism assumed by the analyst.

An example from standard Keynesian fiscal policy analysis clarifies the categorization. In a Keynesian transmission mechanism for fiscal policy, it would be conventional to select as ultimate objectives at least the rate of capacity utilization and the rate of inflation; tax rates of various kinds and rates of government expenditure are the policy instruments which are used to realize desired values for these variables. In view of the multiplicity of instruments, the task of describing or 'indicating' fiscal policy stance would be eased by nominating an intermediate variable. The budget deficit is an obvious candidate; here the policy effects are scaled in net revenue terms, and a thoroughgoing Keynesian analysis would suggest that a demand-weighted version of the deficit would be even better – for not all taxes have the same demand impact.

Further, because the deficit varies not only as a result of variations in the policy instruments but also to an important degree because of non-policy influences, it may be desired to purge the deficit of these influences by normalizing the deficit measurement at full employment. Thus we arrive at the demand-weighted full employment or 'structural' budget surplus measure. This is a coherent example of application of the theory: the nomination of ultimate variables and policy instruments seems relatively unequivocal; at the same time the theory of the transmission mechanism assumed indicates a consistent way of transforming an intermediate variable into an indicator. While this is something of a second-best to using all the information available, say in the form of simulations of an econometric model, it seems likely that there would be communication advantages in using the indicator. Indeed, it would not be difficult to imagine circumstances in which the indicator might be turned into an intermediate target variable.

The true situation is rather more complicated than this example suggests. For a start, views about the transmission mechanism differ. Second, how fine the distinction should be between instrument and intermediate variable in a particular case is a matter of convenience for the purpose in hand, but judgement on this differs from one observer to another and often produces confusion as a result. Third, nominating indicator variables as intermediate targets may give rise to a change in behaviour with the result that the indicator value of the variable becomes compromised.

When we turn to monetary policy, the position is more complex still. Treasury fiscal actions impinge, albeit through various fiscal and budgetary agencies, directly upon ultimate spending units lying outside the control of the authorities. Monetary policy is implemented through a network of financial intermediaries and markets. In a complex financial system, the thrust of monetary policy instruments proceeds towards the policy objectives by a transmission process which successively incorpo-

rates a number of financial influences as the effects span out from the
Bank of England to the discount houses and the money market, the
banking system and other financial intermediaries, and the bond,
mortgage and stock markets. The precise way in which policy actions feed
through the financial and economic system is called the *transmission
mechanism*, and the various influences represent the *channels* of policy.
Actions by the authorities in terms of the instruments, such as the
discounting of bills, open market operations in bills and gilt-edged
securities and interventions in foreign exchange markets, lack in themselves a common scale upon which they can be aggregated. An
intermediate variable is intended to solve this index number problem and
to indicate how well the financial system is responding to the policy
instruments. At the same time, the appropriateness of the authorities'
response to the (mis)behaviour of the ultimate objectives can more
readily be judged by this *indicator*.

A classical elision

It seems quite obvious that if for the purpose in hand a particular
indicator variable can be taken to be exclusively determined by the policy
instruments available, then it will save some unnecessary explanation if
that variable is treated in effect as an instrument. This is the classical
elision that economists – including, as Flemming (1988) has recently
reminded us, Keynes himself – have perpetrated in the case of the money
supply. On a strict reading, the money supply – which after all includes
the deposit liabilities of commercial banks – is certainly not a policy
instrument. It is an intermediate variable. Nevertheless, Keynes and
many other economists elide the distinction between the authorities'
control of the interest rate instrument and their influence over the
intermediate variable, the money supply, simply treating the money
supply as if it were an instrument. Expositions of the standard
macroeconomic IS/LM model routinely do this. This would appear in
principle to be perfectly straightforward if we wish to abstract from the
control problem in order to focus on other issues. Clearly, treating a
variable 'as if' it were a policy instrument does not imply that it actually is
one. Nevertheless, the practice can create confusion in the minds of those
who do not incorporate the 'as if' clause into what they are reading, for
the control problem is a major issue in policy practice. As Mr Robin
Leigh-Pemberton, Governor of the Bank of England, has remarked,
there is no switch on the wall in his office which turns the money supply on
and off; it only works the light.

So far we have been considering definitions of the money supply that incorporate the liabilities (deposits) of commercial banks. For a definition of the money supply as the monetary base, the question of which is the instrument – the base itself or the terms (the rate of interest) on which the authorities will decide to meet the excess demand for monetary base – is arguably more a matter of convention. British economists historically have preferred to treat the (money market) rate of interest as the instrument, stressing that the Bank of England has always closely monitored this rate of interest and has often intervened vigorously to enforce a particular value for it. American economists historically have taken the opposite line, stressing that the monetary base is the instrument.[1] It can of course always be argued that it is only due to the authorities' position in the market for base money that they are *able* to set 'the' interest rate; the interest rate is just the price at which they are prepared as monopoly supplier to meet the excess demand for base money. This argument perhaps squares the circle; it is certainly quite different from asserting that the authorities *as a matter of fact* simply set the quantity of base money independently of interest rate considerations. That base money *should* be targeted is a separate issue (one that we take up in Chapter 6).

Distorting the indicator signal

Another puzzle arises from the identification of an indicator variable with an intermediate target variable. Two (possibly interacting) problems are involved. First, the authorities, having announced a target for the intermediate variable in question, may proceed to use instruments to hit the target in combinations not previously encountered in historical experience. Formally, then, given a suitable model, it will certainly be possible to show for example that the effects of bringing about a given change in the money supply will depend on the instruments used to do so: see Richardson (1981) for an illustration using the Treasury's macroeconometric model. The authorities may even invent a new instrument to control the indicator: for example, a tax on banking would undoubtedly assist the control of the size of the banking industry and thus the money supply but at the cost, it is easy to see, of changing the relationship between the size of the banking industry and the rest of the economy. The 'corset' was a tax on (incremental) banking with this type of effect and from this point of view was most aptly named. Not only did it restrict the banking industry; it also disguised the true situation.

A more subtle problem arises if the selection of an indicator variable as a target *ipso facto* provides an incentive to the private sector to change its behaviour. This would be an example of the well-known Lucas critique

(1976), and may explain Goodhart's Law. Lucas argued that it is incorrect to evaluate economic policies by the traditional method of extrapolating econometric equations forward by feeding new values of the explanatory variables into the estimated relationships. This is because changes in policy will themselves induce alterations in the underlying structure of the economy and estimated relationships, i.e. the structure of the economy is not invariant to economic policy. Such feedback is well understood in the physical sciences. In economics, human behaviour may pose special difficulties if well-informed and knowledgeable people change their behaviour – and economic relationships – in the face of government policy actions.

Goodhart's Law (Goodhart, 1984a) takes up this point. It states that whenever the authorities do attempt to exploit an observed regularity (e.g. the demand for money), the pattern will change. In so far as this results from a systematic adaptation of the private sector's behaviour to the perception that the authorities are treating an indicator as a target, we have indeed a Law rather than a coincident observation. A good example is perhaps the reaction of exchange rates to overshoots of monetary targets: instead of depreciating, as would be the expected reaction of the exchange rate to a monetary expansion, an appreciation is the rational (Currie, 1984) – and actually observed (Smith and Goodhart, 1985 p. 190) – response when the expansion is thought to portend a rise in the interest rate, as under a policy regime in which the authorities are pursuing a target for the money supply.

5.2 Transmission mechanisms

As already explained, ideas about the transmission mechanism of policy have a fundamental bearing on the choice of indicator or intermediate target variable. So we look first at different views about the transmission mechanism of monetary policy before focusing on the issues involved in choosing an intermediate variable targeting strategy.

From the 1960s through to the second half of the 1970s the mainstream view of the transmission mechanism of monetary policy stressed that much of what policy did was to exploit credit rationing and imperfections in the markets – either directly, by means of direct controls over the availability and terms of credit, or indirectly via the institutions' sluggish response to interest rate changes stimulated by the authorities' actions. Econometric models of the UK economy adopted an IS/LM-type framework in which monetary policy begins with short-term money market rates and proceeds to longer-term yields and thence, in some cases via the stock market, to expenditures such as fixed investments. (The history of econometric model-building in the United Kingdom from the 1950s to the end of the 1980s is surveyed in Kenway, 1989.)

While the model-builders worked assiduously to identify interest rate influences upon expenditures, the rewards were not commensurate with the effort (Savage, 1978). In part, this reflected the inadequacy of measures of the expected rate of return on new investment and of the real cost of capital. With the latter, difficulties were experienced in measuring the opportunity cost in ways which would take account of inflation expectations and the different impact of inflation and taxation upon various areas of the corporate sector. It is also the case that policy sought to shield manufacturing industry as far as possible from interest rate variations, leaving the personal sector to bear the brunt. Thus the results obtained were not indicative of the effect interest rates might have had upon investment without this cosseting. Not surprisingly, then, the earlier versions of econometric models (such as those developed at the Treasury and the National Institute) based on the 1960s data sample find that monetary policy rested almost entirely on the impact of changes in hire purchase terms and the availability of bank lending upon personal consumption, and changes in the cost and availability of building society finance upon dwelling investment.

Most of the observation sample was of fixed exchange rates and for reasons connected partly with the size of the national debt, partly with the low inflation experience, variations in the interest rate were not great either. Monetary policy, as revealed, was not rated a powerful contender in this account: Artis (1978) is a representative contemporary attempt to review the empirical evidence for the period 1960–74 which reaches the conclusion that – with the exception of 1971–3 – monetary policy 'did not do very much at all, and was not supposed to' (p. 303). The second part of this conclusion reflects the revealed preference of the authorities for alternative means of adjustment, notably fiscal and incomes policies, which of course makes sense under fixed exchange rates in terms of Mundell's (1963b) dichotomy, for the comparative advantage of monetary policy can be expected to be in stabilizing the balance of payments rather than domestic incomes. However, when balance of payments crises did occur, it was often a case of all hands to the pump.

Monetarists argued that mainstream Keynesian analysis missed the wood while looking for the trees – demonstrations of the monetarist viewpoint favoured heroic single equation reduced form exercises as contrasted with the structural model approach of the mainstream Keynesian tradition. According to the monetarist approach, the Keynesian tradition underplayed the role of the money supply in the transmission mechanism, sidelining it to a passive role as an inconsequential endogenous output and overlooking the implications of the findings of investigators of the demand for money. Monetarism also faulted the Keynesian prejudice of treating the price level as a parameter or too weakly endogenizing it. Paradoxically – since it does not concern the *monetary* mechanism as such – it was perhaps this last point which was to prove the most telling contribution.

Indeed, up to the point at which the price response is invoked there seemed very little to distinguish the monetarist account of the transmission mechanism (see e.g. Friedman and Schwartz, 1963; Friedman, 1970) from the Keynesian one as expounded by Tobin and the Yale School (Tobin, 1969, 1978), despite efforts of both groups to differentiate their products; surprisingly, much is still made of these differences in elementary textbooks. In both accounts, initial monetary disturbances unbalance portfolios and lead to a rectification process which involves an adjustment of expenditures and asset prices, promoting changes in output and eventually in prices (the Keynesian account placing less emphasis on this) until the aggregate demand for money relationship is again satisfied. Some differences of emphasis arose about the breadth and the relative role of asset price adjustments and possible direct effects of excess money (real balance effects).

Specific exhibits of the monetarist case in the United Kingdom, on the other hand, were easily dismissed; thus money did not appear to be exogenous to output or prices (Williams *et al.*, 1976), nor did a stable money multiplier connect prior changes in money to subsequent changes in nominal income on the data set for the 1950s and 1960s (Artis and Nobay, 1969). In retrospect, all this holds together. The strong version of monetarism needed three things: a stable demand for money, a steeply sloped aggregate supply curve and exogenous money. The latter was substantially denied by the fixed-exchange-rate, interest rate pegging policies of the time and monetarists were in danger of trying to prove too much in suggesting otherwise.

Conceptions of the dominant features of the transmission mechanism were further developed against the background of a number of significant events. The first of these was the 1971–3 Heath–Barber boom associated with the Competition and Credit Control (CCC) reforms; the second was the worldwide resort to floating exchange rates after 1973; the third, the experience of high and variable inflation in the 1970s; the fourth, nearer to the present, the actual experience of monetary targeting against a background of financial innovation and deregulation.

Competition and credit control

The period 1971–3 was a remarkable one in post-war British history. A reform of the monetary system (CCC) led to a large expansion of the money supply as ceilings on bank lending were removed; this was accompanied by a fiscal expansion and the floating of the exchange rate in a deliberate 'dash for growth'. These circumstances were far removed from the 'stable exchange rate, endogenous money' characterization of the earlier period. The inflationary consequences of the 1971–3 policies are hard to disentangle from those of the closely coincident world boom (1973) and the rise in oil prices in OPEC I in 1973–4, but the joint effect was very big. Some observers were led into an erroneous identification of a two-year lag in the relationships of broad money to prices by the observations arising in this period; despite the potential for error – and we showed in Chapter 3 how the univariate relationships between broad money and prices broke down in the later 1970s and 1980s – the view was influential.[2] This period was also the first occasion on which the Bank of England undertook to monitor the development of the monetary aggregates through its measured money demand functions; the exercise led, through the obvious difficulty of interpreting what was going on, to the elaboration of the buffer stock approach to the demand for money (see Chapter 4), which was to prove a point of convergence between Keynesian and monetarist ideas (Cobham, 1984).

Floating exchange rates

Friedman's monetarism was essentially a closed economy doctrine – and when applied to an open economy remains an account of what McKinnon calls 'an insular economy'. In such an economy, the exchange rate is just an output variable, with no feedback (see Figure 5.1). The floating of the exchange rate does have the merit of making an autonomous money supply policy without exchange controls *possible*, but all that this does in essence is to make the closed economy results hold fully. The relevant analysis is that of Hume's price–specie flow mechanism and purchasing power parity. Price levels in each country are tied to the money stock via the simple quantity theory, $MV = Py$. Prices in each country are brought to conformity with purchasing power parity according to the exchange rate system. Under fixed exchange rates such as implied by an international gold standard, prices in a country are subjected to pressures via the flow of international reserves (specie) calculated to bring them into line with prices ruling elsewhere, while exchange rates remain within the bounds defined by the fixed (e.g. gold) parity. Under floating rates, exchange rates conform to the price levels which result from independent monetary policies.

Friedman enunciated his view as recently as 1980 in his evidence to the House of Commons Select Committee on the Treasury and Civil Service. When asked whether the exchange rate was not the principal part of the

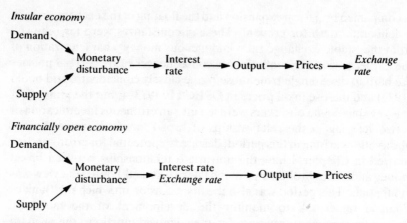

Figure 5.1 Two models of the transmission mechanism. *Source*: McKinnon, R.I. *An International Standard for Monetary Stabilization*, March, 1984.

transmission mechanism of monetary policy in the United Kingdom, he responded:

> I strongly disagree. Monetary policy actions affect asset portfolios in the first instance, spending decisions in the second, which translate into effects on output and then on prices. The changes in exchange rates are in turn mostly a response to these effects of home policy on output and prices and of similar policy abroad. The question is topsy turvy. (p. 80)

The Keynesian transmission mechanism suggested that floating rates would raise the power of monetary policy by adding devaluation to the effects of a monetary expansion, but received theory was slower to take up the inflationary consequences.

Towards the end of the 1970s much work had been done to integrate the implications of floating rates into the analysis of monetary policy. In the 'financially open economy' (McKinnon's phrase again – see Figure 5.1), the transmission mechanism has the exchange rate playing an important role from the start, along with the interest rate. The relevant analysis stresses the implications of the exchange rate for pricing decisions and the role of expectations in determining, along with interest rates, what happens to the exchange rate. This is the asset theory of exchange rates which succeeds in integrating elements of both monetarist and Keynesian views, deriving the following conclusions:

1. The exchange rate is determined in asset markets, like the rate of interest.
2. Expectations about the variables which determine asset behaviour play a crucial role.

3.   The exchange rate, like the interest rate, is an important channel whereby monetary policy is transmitted to the domestic economy.

In the asset theory with fixed exchange rates, international reserve flows are determined by stock equilibrium in the short run and adjust to a long-run flow equilibrium determined by purchasing power parity, much along lines sketched out earlier (this is also called the monetary theory of the balance of payments). Under flexible rates, reserves are fixed and in this case it is the exchange rate which adjusts to the long-run requirements of purchasing power parity. But in the short run, and this is where the model contributes new ideas, the exchange rate is determined by the requirements of asset equilibrium. Consider Tobin's (1969) general equilibrium model of a closed economy with three assets: money, securities and equity claims. It is well known that because of the adding-up constraint, market equilibrium only has to determine values of the rates on the two earning assets (i.e. bond rates and equity rates). When this model is extended to a two-country world economy under flexible exchange rates, we have a six-asset menu comprising the two moneys, securities denominated in those moneys, and equity claims on capital in the two countries. The interaction of their demands and fixed supplies now determines four rates of return and the relative price of the two moneys (that is, the exchange rate).

Values of the exchange rate and interest rates are thus simultaneously determined in the short run by asset equilibrium. If the exchange rate so determined by stock conditions is inconsistent with flow demands, then a non-zero current account balance results. With no change in the level of foreign exchange reserves, this in turn implies a non-zero capital account and changing stocks of domestic and foreign assets. These modify the short-run stock equilibrium and produce a new exchange rate which gives rise to a different current account position, and so on. Eventually the process converges to a long-run equilibrium where stock equilibrium prevails and both the current and capital accounts are balanced. In this way, the exchange rate is both the relative price of national moneys and the relative price of national outputs.

Among the determinants of the demands for the assets is either the expected behaviour of the exchange rate or the nominal rate of the interest, which in turn is influenced by exchange rate expectations. In order to determine the exchange rate it is necessary to analyse the formation of exchange rate expectations. It is popular to model expectations rationally, tying them to the behaviour of the demands and supplies of money (Dornbusch, 1976) which leads to the well-known theoretical result that exchange rates can be expected in the short run to overshoot their long-run equilibrium. Dornbusch's classic paper on overshooting paved the way for other analyses which capitalize on the overshooting phenomenon (Buiter and Miller (1981) is a well-known example). Indeed, the implication of the theory is that exchange rates respond much like asset prices in other speculative markets, such as the equity market, and there has been considerable interest more recently in the contribution of 'bandwagon', 'bubbles', and similar speculative effects to variations in exchange rates.[3]

If the exchange rate is proximately determined by asset equilibrium, monetary policy may fairly quickly involve exchange rate changes, as the prices of other currencies change in terms of the one whose quantity has altered. Since demands for domestic goods depend on both interest rates and relative prices, policy-induced changes in exchange rates can exert inflationary or deflationary impacts on domestic demand via changes in exports and imports (that is, the traded goods sector). There is a transmission mechanism which operates even if the interest rate channel is weak.

Of course, the asset model is one of how exchange rates *might* respond in unmanaged markets, not how exchange rates actually *do* behave. Yet the likelihood of strong and perhaps quite rapid relationships between the exchange rate and major domestic policy objectives means that exchange rate policy cannot be divorced from overall macroeconomic policy, while the links implied in the model between monetary policy, expectations, the exchange rate and domestic prices go some way to providing a theoretical rationale for recent policy emphases. Chapters 7 and 8 give more detail, including some current econometric evidence for the United Kingdom.

High and variable inflation

The inflation of the 1970s was important in influencing views about the transmission mechanism in several ways. It afforded evidence of powerful wealth (extended real balance) effects; it helped remove any lingering suggestion that it might be appropriate to assume money illusion in agents' behaviour; it afforded experience of high nominal interest rates via 'Fisher effects' of inflation upon interest rates[4]; it brought home the importance of front-end loading; and it established the importance of forward-looking expectations in economic behaviour.

The worldwide increase in savings in the late 1970s came as a surprise to prevailing economic opinion which held that, if it significantly affected savings behaviour at all, inflation would reduce savings and raise current consumption as consumers sought to anticipate future higher prices by buying more today. As the opposite appeared to happen, economists emphasized the role of wealth effects in the consumption function: as prices rose, consumers would seek to save more as a means of restoring the ratio of wealth (held in nominally denominated assets) to income, an effect anticipated by Mundell (1963a). The experience, simultaneously, of low rates of investment was harder to pin down to specifically monetary causes since the generally uncertain outlook for the resumption of economic growth seemed a powerful reason in itself for this performance. Interest rates, though frequently high were often derisory, even negative, in real terms – i.e. after allowing for inflation. The phenomenon of front-end loading, though, might be held to account for some deterrent effect even when the real interest rate was low. Comparing two projects with the same real return, but different inflation assumptions, it is easy to show that payments of interest and repayments of capital are much larger in proportion to cash flow in the earlier years in a high-inflation scenario than they are in a low-inflation case. Risk aversion might therefore lead to the rejection of some projects in the high-inflation case which would be pursued at low rates of inflation.

The inflation experience also exposed the irrationality of money illusion and, first in theories of wage determination and then more widely, emphasized the role of expectations. In turn, experience also exposed the limitations of the assumption of adaptive expectations with the fixed lag implied and paved the way for acceptance of forward-looking schemes and the concept of rational expectations.

Monetary targeting and deregulation

Interest in the monetary aggregates began in the late 1960s under the stimulus not only of monetarist writings but also of an agreement reached with the IMF in 1967 because of Britain's international borrowings. This agreement saw the setting of targets for domestic credit expansion (DCE), which is the increase in M3 arising from domestic sources. The IMF's concern was with the balance of payments. It was assumed that if DCE fell short of the increase in money demanded, then this shortfall would be made up with money from foreign sources, i.e. by way of an increase in international reserves necessarily involving an improvement in the balance of payments (under a fixed exchange rate). Conversely, and this was the major worry, if DCE outstripped the increase in money demand, the excess would result in a balance of payments deficit. The practice of announcing anticipated DCE, later supplemented with a statement of the expected increase in the money supply M3, continued until the reforms of 1971.

Competition and Credit Control was designed around control of monetary aggregates, yet the institution of announcing targets lapsed in 1972. An accelerating rise in the money stock was permitted because it was believed (wrongly it would seem) that the income elasticity of demand for money greatly exceeded unity, which was the finding of the Bank of England's studies of the demand for money function (see Table 4.2). Although confidence in that belief quickly crumbled as demand for money functions began to exhibit marked instability, it was difficult to ascertain to what extent the factors which swelled M3 were matched by equal increases in the demand for money, in the light of the more competitive posture adopted by the banks as a result of the 1971 reforms. As the expansion of the money supply continued into 1973 it became increasingly obvious that monetary growth was 'excessive' under any criteria and that action had to be taken on the supply side to constrain it. The need for this policy was later rationalized on the grounds that changes on the asset side of the banks' balance sheets (especially the surge in bank lending in (1972–3) had forced the growth of bank liabilities away from their usual relationship with nominal incomes and interest rates, as summarized in demand for money functions. On this disequilibrium view of the money market, it was not clear that the resulting money supply increases were demanded, but it was certainly true that they were supplied.

From the end of 1973 attention was refocused upon the behaviour of the monetary aggregates in policy formulation. Initially a target growth rate of M3 was an internal aim of the Bank. Renewed concern about the behaviour of the monetary aggregates led the Chancellor of the Exchequer to declare publicly in July 1976 an M3 target for the financial year 1976–7 of 12 per cent. A ceiling on DCE was later set in December 1976 as a precondition for an IMF loan. Targets for DCE and target ranges for the money supply (now £M3) were set for 1977–8 and 1978–9 and with the change of government, money supply targets were enshrined in the medium-term financial strategy.

In Chapter 3 we considered the possible roles that control of the money supply might play in inflation policy: identifying money as initiating inflation, as accommodating inflation, and as setting the environment for decentralized decision-making in markets. One hope which was entertained at the time was that money supply targets would shape the climate in which wage bargains were struck by exerting a direct impact upon employees' and companies' price and wage expectations, and generally tie down inflation much like the earlier commitment to fixed exchange rates. But when monetary targeting began in earnest at the end of the 1970s the lessons provided confirmed a sceptical view. To start with, it did not appear as though announcements of monetary growth impacted perceptibly on the wage bargaining process, nor even that the interplay of announcement and realization had quite the finely tuned impact on the foreign exchange and gilt-edged markets that was originally supposed. While these markets are highly sensitive to expectations of the future, the perceptions which guide them tend to be of a broader-based nature – what counts is an impression of whether a Chancellor is or is not likely to create or accommodate inflation rather than whether he has or has not fulfilled a given monetary target.

Actual performance in the phase of monetary targeting certainly confirmed the non-triviality of the control problem and emphasized the status of money as an intermediate variable; it was not difficult then to consider alternative intermediate target variables and different operating strategies. Officials at the Bank of England were never wholly persuaded of the importance which the government attached to money supply targeting, and did not radically restructure operating strategies in an attempt to implement them. Since 1844 interest rates have lain at the heart of the Bank's operations, with the instrument being Bank Rate (now its dealing rate) and open market operations in bills. When money supply targets were introduced, control of interest rates remained; but instead interest rates became a step or *operational target* in achieving the money supply (intermediate) target. In effect, with the switch to emphasis upon monetary aggregates, the Bank grafted an additional step into formal operational procedures, thereby retaining continuity with traditional strategies. Thus the policy sequence became

$$I \rightarrow OV \rightarrow IV \rightarrow UV \qquad (5.2)$$

where OV is the operational variable(s) or target. When interest in monetary targeting waned, the Bank merely broadened the intermediate target set beyond the money supply to include other things.

In particular, the targeting of the exchange rate through interest rates came to be seen as a strong rival model, building on the perception that the exchange rate had become the principal channel of effect of monetary policy. But this perception too began to be modified as a result of the deregulation of the financial system and the substantial impact of innovations within it. A significant development was the increase in financial exposure of individuals as the ratio, both of gross financial assets and of gross liabilities to income, rose steeply. Itself interpreted as a stock adjustment response to a new equilibrium, this increase in exposure appeared to support an increased sensitivity of spending decisions to variations in the interest rate, which duly became (see Chapter 7) most heavily relied upon for short-term demand management, while the intermediate variable stage devolved into 'looking at everything'.

A convergence of views

By the end of the 1980s there was probably a good deal more clarity and agreement about the nature of the transmission mechanism of monetary policy than there had been, say, twenty years earlier, and a general view relative to earlier opinions that it was a good deal more important.

The view of the transmission mechanism in a financially sophisticated open economy as in the McKinnon picture (Figure 5.1) stresses the active role of the exchange rate as an asset price like the interest rate and the impact of both on the economy, with the money supply as an endogenous but not purely passive variable. In the transmission process, wealth effects and expectational effects add to the impact of decisions based on variations in interest rates and exchange rates. These effects on the economy in turn feed back onto the determination of asset prices and the stock of money. Jonson (1987) neatly shows these interactions in his picture of the transmission of monetary policy (reproduced as Figure 5.2). This view is a richer and more complex one than the Keynesian schema prevalent in the 1960s and at the same time is considerably more eclectic than 1970s monetarism. Jonson's schema also reflects a central banker's view of the world – Jonson was head of research at the Reserve Bank of Australia – since its starting-point is with market operations and interest rates. In particular, the instruments–operational targets–intermediate targets–ultimate targets sequence can be readily super-imposed.

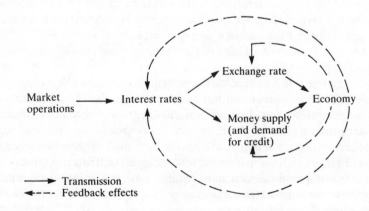

Figure 5.2   The transmission of monetary policy.
Source: Jonson, P. D. 'Monetary Indicators and the Economy', *RBA Bulletin*, December, 1987.

At the same time the view of monetary control as reliably providing a necessary nominal anchor, in the wake of the global resort to floating exchange rates and the failure of incomes policies, has been severely shaken. Commitments to money supply targets foundered on the apparent instability of money demand functions. Britain then had two alternative routes to inflation control: external or internal stabilization. A resort to external stabilization required that Britain go back on the exchange rate decision and peg to a hard currency, the relevant standard for the United Kingdom being provided by the Deutschmark in the guise of the Exchange Rate Mechanism of the European Monetary System. Money supply targets appeared to have ruled themselves out as a means of internal stabilization. An alternative which presented itself was to restore the nominal anchor by commitment to the price level itself, enforced by eclectic use of monetary policy: this is what the government tried to do from 1988 to 1990. In this case, it is not apparent that intermediate target variables are needed. The question of whether they are, and how to choose between them, is addressed below.

5.3 Intermediate target variables

We can distinguish at least two reasons why a target for an intermediate variable might be adopted. Whether that target is a constant one or flexible in some way is an additional question which we explore later.

The two reasons we have in mind are, first, that the variable in question may be a good contemporaneous indicator of a variable of interest (which itself may be an ultimate variable or just another intermediate variable); second, that it may be a good policy summary and *leading* indicator of a variable or variables of interest.

It is helpful to differentiate the first type of intermediate variable target as an 'indicator'. By assumption an indicator variable has no genuine predictive content, but is useful as a contemporaneous indicator or proxy for a variable of interest, information on which takes some time to collect. For example (we are not concerned with the statistical merits of the argument), it is argued that M0 is a good indicator of current 'money GDP',[5] observations on which do not become available for some time after the event. In this particular case the lead is perhaps not so very long. By the end of the 1980s, for example, provisional estimates of the monetary aggregates (including M0) came out about three weeks after the month to which they referred. Provisional estimates of nominal GDP (quarterly) were not available until about eleven weeks after the end of the quarter to which they referred – but the output measure of GDP and some price data (retail and producer prices) were known somewhat earlier than this, making possible quite a good unofficial guess at nominal GDP about seven to eight weeks after the end of the quarter referred to, giving an M0 lead of not much more than a month. Still, having regard to the greater inaccuracy of the early GDP guesstimates, the M0 lead would be valuable if the policy objective is to target money GDP and if the relationship between the two is sufficiently robust.

The second type of intermediate variable target is motivated by different considerations. The variable in question is thought of as a reflection in some degree of policy thrust and as having predictive value. In particular, the classic monetary examples are the money supply and the exchange rate. Their particular rationale is that, with a stable demand for money function in the first case and a stable foreign price level in the second, they provide a forecast for inflation – and variations from target imply deviations from the authorities' commitment to control inflation. Money GDP has also become popular as a target. This can be thought of as a velocity-corrected money supply target.[6] Indeed, a nominal anchor rationale can be seen as underlying all these targets, with the choice between them turning on the criterion of robustness.[7]

Poole's (1970) classic paper dealt with the choice between the interest rate and the money stock in a context where money income was the ultimate target. Later analysis of the choice between monetary and exchange rate targets has followed the path indicated by the stochastic analysis presented in Poole's paper. That is to say, the key test is which of the targets performs best when stochastic shocks are taken into account (see e.g. Artis and Currie, 1981; Aizenman and Frenkel, 1985, p. 188). The general result to be derived from such studies is easy to state: interest rate or exchange rate targeting is to be preferred when the instability is from the demand for money function; monetary targeting is generally preferable when the shocks come from domestic spending or from overseas prices; but there are instances too where the results are inconclusive. Formally, the answer will depend on three things: the distribution of shocks assumed, the model, and the content of the objective function. There is no reason to think that these things stay constant over time or from one political administration to another. In the 1980s the perceived distribution of shocks moved against money supply targeting as evidence of instability in money demand functions cumulated; it moved towards the exchange rate with the rise to prominence of transmission mechanism ideas which stressed the link between the exchange rate and domestic economic developments, and the move was reinforced by the fact that politicians' objective functions included output and employment as well as prices. Thus it is the general principle of robustness which is important rather than specific results.

One of the lessons of robustness analysis is that fixed rules and single-target strategies may be inferior to contingent rules and mixed targets. This touches on an old issue, that of rules versus discretion.

Rules versus discretion

If an intermediate variable is targeted it may be targeted as a constant – as in Friedman's famous (1959) 'expand the money supply at x per cent per annum' rule – or as a contingent variable. The relative merits of the two, or the 'rules versus discretion' debate, is a long-standing issue in the theory of stabilization policy but one which has received increased attention in recent years, reflecting some salutary practical lessons.

It is possible to deny that there is any real substance in the difference alleged between rules on the one hand and discretion on the other. To start with, assuming that discretion means the systematic use of policy instruments to hit targets and not just random behaviour, it appears that discretion can be represented as a rule after all, only a complicated one, for manipulating instruments. On this basis, the comparison is between a rule which is a simple rule and discretion which is a complicated rule. On the other hand, it can be noted that simple rules are never maintained for ever: they are adopted, changed and dropped. The exercise of this choice could be called 'discretion', but we have just pointed out that discretion could be regarded as a rule. If the decisions to adopt, change and drop the simple rule are systematic and not random they could be said to exemplify the operation of a meta-rule.

Progress is best made by considering the substantive issues surrounding the choice of the degree of complexity in a given (lower level, not meta) rule. The strong case for a simple, no feedback or 'open-loop' rule such as Friedman's x per cent rule, where the pre-announced money supply growth rate might be altered secularly over time but not in response to changes in the value of output, is twofold; it avoids the need for fallible forecasting (this was Friedman's own justification), and it avoids the temptation to respond to excessively short-term promptings even if these are not provided by fallible forecasts. The latter is the argument implicit in Kydland and Prescott (1977) and is exemplified clearly in the influential arguments of Barro and Gordon (1981a, b). The suggestion there is that a short-sighted government will always wish to 'trick' the electorate into believing in low inflation because it can then reduce unemployment by a 'surprise' increase in inflation: naturally, over the long run this behaviour will be detected and the electorate will simply come to believe in an inflation rate so high that the authorities, who dislike inflation just as much as private agents, will not wish to add any surprise to it. In these circumstances a constant rule, to which the authorities are (somehow) committed, can certainly produce better results.

On this argument the point of the rule is to bind the hands of the authorities. In this case, of course, the authorities seem unlikely to want to bind themselves and a solution to the problem has to be found by means of adjusting the monetary constitution so that the rule-setting institution is divorced from the democratic prompting that leads governments on this analysis to be too short-sighted. An independent central bank with a constitutional duty to preserve a stable price level is the resultant model, with the German Bundesbank as its most obvious exemplar. (It is for this reason that the option of participating fully in the EMS is sometimes described as one of 'importing the Bundesbank's reputation'.) It can be argued that this analysis is superficial in failing to credit democratically elected governments with any incentive to adopt longer-term horizons in their constitutional recommendations. Short-lived governments come from political parties which have much longer lives; such governments will have an interest in long-run results and will be sensitive to the value of building a reputation for themselves. Nevertheless, for all its shortcomings, the Barro–Gordon model serves the important purpose of illustrating the significance of precommitment and reputation for economic policy.

A countervailing consideration stems from the prevalence of stochastic shocks and structural change. These are endemic in the real world, and mean that the policy-maker is confronted by what appear to be new situations in which the old rules seem to be in need of some modification. In these circumstances a precommitment to a simple rule made in an earlier period will turn out, sooner or later, to be inappropriate; moreover, it will be seen to be inappropriate; and it will eventually be changed. Rational people will understand this from the outset. From this point of view the ideal rule could be a quite complicated innovation-contingent rule; a basic version of such a rule would specify in advance circumstances in which one simple rule should be exchanged for another – e.g. an exchange rate rule may replace a monetary rule if the consequences of following the latter in the new and unforeseen circumstances threaten to drive the exchange rate to an unacceptable level. A more complicated rule allows more flexibility to cope with unforeseen circumstances. There are changes in structure which might make any such rule inappropriate, too: to cope with this one could imagine a 'statement trigger' rule which would specify in advance the circumstances in which the authorities should announce an analysis of the economic situation together with the change in rule which the analysis indicates to be appropriate.

These considerations, taken together, indicate an awkward tension between the simple rule which responds to the problem of avoiding short-sighted policies and the complex rule which responds to the problem posed by unforeseen change. The argument for the simple rule suggests that sticking to the commitment is of the essence; and that simplicity is warranted because it makes it easy to monitor the authorities' success in maintaining their commitment. The danger is that the authorities will be led to take a ride on a tiger's back, defending the simple rule for the sake of their reputation in circumstances in which the rule is hopelessly inappropriate. On the other hand, while the innovation-contingent rule attempts to cover the problem of the unforeseen event, it is likely to be complex, difficult to monitor and liable to lead to situations where flexibility is mistaken for chicanery (or, worse still, the reverse).

The central bank's reputation is an important conditioning variable here. When a central bank is endeavouring to establish credibility for its anti-inflationary policies a simple rule, readily announced and understood, may be needed. Once credibility exists, more complex strategies can be followed. In effect, adherence to a simple rule is an instrument for achieving credibility, and when the necessary reputation has been established, it takes the place of the rule. Experience in the 1980s illustrates some of these themes.

Rules and targets in the 1980s

The 1980s opened in the United Kingdom, as elsewhere, with the case for monetary targeting in the ascendant. The rhetoric of the times and the formal rationale for the shift to monetary targeting policies were that the 1979 OPEC oil shock crucially reinforced the need to take strong counter-inflationary measures and that monetary targeting would build on the connection between money and prices so that the adoption of monetary targets would reduce the cost of bringing inflation down. Monetary targets would provide the critical nominal anchor for the system.

The policy seemed to be well grounded in standard general equilibrium theory in which it was well established that market forces in any economy are capable of determining *relative* prices but not the *absolute* price level. To determine absolute prices, some fixed point is needed to tie down nominal magnitudes in the system. Previously, with a fixed exchange rate, it was the price of domestic money in terms of international money (with the quantity of money adjusting to guarantee external equilibrium). With flexible exchange rates, the price of domestic money relative to international money varies. Some constraint is needed for domestic price stability. In models such as those of Patinkin (1965) there was a 'quantity of money', controllable by the monetary authorities, which could be used for price control.

Moreover, it was reasoned that in the new environment expectations of inflation might be assumed both to be more volatile and to exert a larger influence upon wage- and price-setting mechanisms. Monetary growth targets thus sought to provide a peg for these expectations, attempting to exert a direct influence upon their formation and substituting in the new environment for the anchor which adherence to fixed exchange rates gave in the old (Lindbeck, 1978).

A number of other reasons can be ascribed to the same event, however, in which the theoretical connections between money and prices and between announcing targets for monetary growth and reducing disinflation costs are not decisive. As we argued in Chapter 3, the existence of such a framework was still fundamental in that it facilitated a shift from a regime in which the avoidance of unemployment was still a significant priority of policy to a regime in which the priority was transferred to the reduction of inflation (see also Fforde, 1983). A declared adherence to monetary targets gave cover for this break, diverted attention from the issue of the costs of the change to other issues and in so doing made the shift politically feasible. It is not too difficult to agree with the contention that had the public known what the unemployment consequences would be, the shift of priority would not have been electorally popular: if so, a mere shift of priority for demand management policy from employment to prices might not have taken place. A shift to monetary targets, with the same substantive consequences, could occur.

Many observers, certainly, saw the introduction of monetary targets as a means of forcing governments to reduce their own involvement in the economy, both in the interests of reducing inflation and for other more broadly ideological reasons. Dow (in Dow and Saville, 1988) records a further reason for welcoming the change: 'that, in the face of an evident tendency by the Bank simply to accommodate to events, it would lead the monetary authorities to define their aims and thus have a policy' (p. v). Probably, for the majority, the acceptance of monetary targets was a pragmatic shift, not strongly theory-based, a shift seen as a useful signal to private-sector agents that policy would henceforth be non-accommodating and a potential constraint on the government to make it so.

The course of monetary targets in the United Kingdom, their succession by the use of interest rates to target the price level directly and the flirtation with and final adoption of exchange rate targeting are the substance of the following three chapters. In brief, it appears in retrospect that the monetary control problem was underestimated and that the demand for money did not have the required stability. While this led to the abandonment of monetary targets, inflation was nevertheless substantially reduced. Attention then switched to exchange rate targeting but the authorities held back for some years from the formal adoption of an exchange rate target regime, which for the United Kingdom could have been obtained at any time during the 1980s by full membership of the EMS. Instead, and in view of the unreliability of the broader monetary aggregates, targets for money GDP and as proxy M0 were maintained; yet short-run policy appeared increasingly through 1988–90 to involve the use of interest rates to target inflation directly. In this sense, while the policy priority of reducing and then maintaining a low level of inflation shows continuity, the surrounding framework has been changed quite radically. The policies being pursued at the turn of the decade were oddly reminiscent of the fine-tuning demand management of the 1960s and 1970s, only the goal was simpler and the role of fiscal policy much smaller; this similarity seems likely to be sustained as defence of the EMS exchange rate parity becomes the proximate goal of policy.

Notes

1. It *may* be germane that whereas the Bank of England has always undertaken to meet the excess demand for base money 'at a price', Federal Reserve practice has included that of rationing would-be borrowers of base money – see Chapter 7 and Artis and Lewis (1990).
2. See Parkin (1975). Simple univariate relationships fail to allow for the influence of coincident events and the regime change undoubtedly occasioned by this period marking the transition to floating exchange rates. If we think of monetary changes as embodying an 'anticipated' and a 'surprise' component, the 'surprise' element may have been large and not indicative of the potential for money supply changes to generate monetary disequilibria on future occasions.
3. Investigations of the efficiency of foreign exchange markets do not seem to provide a resoundingly favourable verdict (see e.g. Levich (1989) for a review), and it seems clear that these markets may play host to bubble phenomena (e.g. Blanchard and Watson (1982)). Such bubbles may involve 'rational' investors profiting from the speculative activities of others – see Frankel and Froot (1986).
4. Irving Fisher (1930) argued that *in equilibrium* the nominal rate of interest (i) exceeds the real rate of interest (r) by the expected rate of change of prices, i.e. the expected inflation rate (π), to cover the expected erosion of purchasing power from lending out funds in money terms. Fisher's formula was $i = r + r\pi + \pi$ which, in discrete time, allows for the erosion of purchasing power of both principal (π) and interest payments ($r\pi$).
5. The supporting argument might be that when people spend income they use cash, so that an increase in cash holdings (98 per cent of M0) signals what is happening to money income.

6. In this sense the target is popular with monetarists chastened by the experience of unstable money demand functions. It is also popular with Keynesians since the target is broad enough to be capable of being made a target for fiscal policy (as, for example, it is in Meade, 1984).
7. Conditional on information lags. Information on money GDP is available later than information on exchange rates or money supplies and this must be allowed for (Bean, 1983), perhaps in practice by using M0 as a proxy for money GDP until firm information becomes available.

6

Controlling the monetary aggregates

The medium-term financial strategy (MTFS) unveiled in 1980 set out for the first time a path of monetary deceleration over the medium term – previous monetary growth targets had been set only for the year immediately ahead – and accompanied this by a parallel projection for the PSBR as a proportion of GDP. The target money stock definition was £M3; the choice of this broad definition of the money supply was made on the basis that it had more predictive content than the narrower monetary magnitudes and was 'more exogenous' with respect to current nominal income than the narrow magnitudes. Nevertheless, experience in controlling £M3 was devastating; a substantial and apparently non-inflationary increase in demand was discerned, rendering the target inappropriate, and the implications for the exchange rate of restraining the growth of £M3 were found unacceptable. The targets were extended, first to both the narrower M1 and the still broader monetary magnitude PSL2 (now known as M5), then to the wide monetary base, with the £M3 target being dropped altogether from the 1987 restatement of the MTFS. Table 6.1 summarizes the target ranges set and records the out-turn year by year.

Figure 6.1, adapted from the Bank of England's *Quarterly Bulletin*, sets out the relationship between the various monetary magnitudes as they were labelled in May 1987, at which time PSL1 and PSL2 were renamed M4 and M5 respectively – while £M3 itself has in subsequent presentations been relabelled as, simply, M3. What the figure brings out is that £M3, the original central money stock magnitude in the MTFS, is essentially the sum of cash (notes and coins) in the hands of the private sector together with private sector deposits at banks, excluding foreign currency denominated deposits. Thus, in discussing the control of £M3

Table 6.1 Monetary targets, indicative ranges and out-turns for the MTFS

	1980/1	1981/2	1982/3	1983/4	1984/5	1985/6	1986/7	1987/8	1988/9	1989/90
Targets for £M3										
March 1980	7–11[1]	(6–10)	(5–9)	(4–8)						
March 1981		6–10[1]	(5–9)	(4–8)						
March 1982			8–12[1]	(7–11)	(6–10)					
March 1983				7–11[1]	(6–10)	(5–9)	(4–8)			
March 1984					6–10[1]	(5–9)	(4–8)			
March 1985						5–9[2]	(4–8)	(3–7)	(2–6)	
March 1986							11–15[2]	(3–7)	(2–6)	
Out-turn	*18½*	*13*	*11½*	*10*	*12*	*15*	*20*			
Targets for M1, PSL2										
March 1982			8–12[1]	(7–11)						
March 1983				7–10[1]	(6–10)	(5–9)				
Out-turn, M1			*11*	*11*	*14½*	*22½*				
Out-turn, PSL2			*9*	*12¼*	*15½*	*14½*				
Targets for M0										
March 1984					4–8[1]	(3–7)	(2–6)			
March 1985						3–7[2]	(2–6)			
March 1986							2–6[2]	(2–6)	(1–5)	
March 1987								2–6[2]	(1–5)	
March 1988									1–5[2]	(1–5)
March 1989										1–5[2]
Out-turn, M0					*5½*	*3½*	*2*	*5*	*7*	

Notes:
1. Target for 14 months to mid-April at annual rate.
2. Target for 12 months to mid-February at annual rate.

Source:
Dow and Saville (1988); *Financial Statement and Budget Reports.*

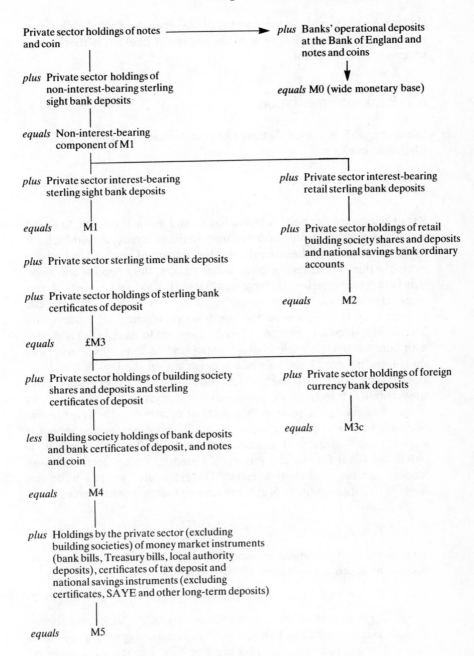

Figure 6.1   Relationships among monetary aggregates and their components. *Source*: adapted from Bank of England *Quarterly Bulletin*, May 1987.

(M3), we are discussing the control of the growth of the liabilities of banking institutions. A review of the theory of banking is therefore a necessary starting-point.

6.1 Bank intermediation

We distinguish two hypothetical forms of banking activity – retail and wholesale banking.

Retail banking

Retail banks are financial intermediaries and as such intermediate the flow of funds from surplus to deficit units in the economy. As banks, their liabilities (or some of them) can be used as a means of payment as well as a store of value. Participating in the retail market, their deposit and loans structure is characterized by large numbers of individual accounts. These three characteristics deserve spelling out. The role of a financial intermediary is to reconcile the portfolio preferences of lenders and borrowers, which are divergent. Borrowers want to issue long-term debt with comparatively simple characteristics and to have quick access to short-term finance. Lenders place a premium on the liquidity of their assets; they want securities which have less default risk and more convertibility, transferability, divisibility and reversibility than they can obtain by holding the primary liabilities of borrowers. The intermediation task is thus to produce from the liabilities of borrowers assets for lenders which meet their demand for liquidity. This value added is purchased (paid for) by the interest differential which in combination lenders sacrifice and borrowers pay. In aggregate, we can write the lenders' (i) supply of funds F_i as an increasing function of interest return r_i and liquidity L_i:

$$F_i = F_i\,(r_i, L_i), \qquad F_{ir}, F_{iL} > 0 \tag{6.1}$$

The borrowers' (j) demand for funds (F_j) can be written reciprocally as a decreasing function of interest payments and liquidity:

$$F_j = F_j\,(r_j, L_j), \qquad F_{jr}, F_{jL} < 0 \tag{6.2}$$

Ignoring transactions costs, banking results in a difference between lenders and borrowers in liquidity – lenders make liquid deposits with banks, borrowers borrow at long term or with implicit guarantees on rollover from banks. We can denote the difference as L_p:

$$L_p = L_i - L_j > 0 \tag{6.3}$$

The system produces this liquidity by hiring real resources (labour, capital, intermediate inputs) to pool claims on ultimate borrowers and to make them indirectly transferable. For simplicity, assume that the costs (C_p) of producing liquidity depend simply on the amount produced:

$$C_p = p\,(L_p) \qquad p' > 0 \tag{6.4}$$

Under competition banking services will be expanded until the marginal cost of liquidity production is equal to marginal revenue, the difference between the interest earned from lending and spent on lending. Thus

$$C'_p = r_j - r_i \tag{6.5}$$

where $r_j - r_i$ is the interest differential.

The manner in which individual banking firms produce liquidity has been treated in two ways in the literature. Both accounts accept that banks must hold cash (currency and bankers' balances at the central bank) since they provide deposit (and loan) facilities which have uncertain maturities, and cash is also needed for interbank settlements (transferability) and to enable convertibility into currency. Some writers treat this demand for cash (or base money or high-powered money) as a reserve constraint. An ordinary productive firm maximizes profits subject to a balance sheet constraint and a technical production function relating the scale of operations to inputs of capital, labour and materials. These constraints also face the bank firm, but the peculiarity is an additional reserve constraint, part of which consists of base money. Other writers treat base money as a direct input into banks' production function. Banks are visualized to purchase primary assets, pool them to eliminate risks and combine them with high-powered money, capital, labour and materials to create a claim which has special characteristics. Among the characteristics desired are convertibility into cash and transferability in the settlement of debts, both of which require inputs of high-powered money.

In both cases, reserves held are a fraction of deposits. Not that the principle of fractional reserves is peculiar to banks, for it is employed by any business which borrows against future income and converts what is borrowed into another form. What is different about retail banks (and other retail intermediaries) is that insurance principles can be used to determine the size of reserve holdings needed to insure against the risks of deposit withdrawals. By using the law of large numbers, retail banks can balance the marginal returns from additional investments against the costs of running out of reserves. An extensive literature exists to describe how an individual bank balances these factors and determines its asset portfolio (Lewis and Davis, 1987). In a sophisticated money market with an efficient interbank market and many cash substitutes, holdings of base money may be very low. But, according to the theory, there is a determinate reserve demand which limits acquisition of non-reserve assets. It is this lever which would be used under a system of monetary base control to restrain the banks' credit creation.

So far we have treated (retail) banks like any other retail intermediary (e.g. building societies, savings institutions), ignoring their involvement in the payments mechanism and any differences which come from acceptance of their liabilities as money. One implication of this acceptance is their use as the principal means of payment and reserve asset of other retail intermediaries. Hence, in Britain, non-bank intermediaries (and non-clearing banks) typically hold bank deposits as primary reserves, while clearing banks hold base money. It is this difference which gives rise to the conception of a pyramid of credit. A transfer of deposits to other intermediaries can have as its *immediate* consequence a change in the ownership of deposits, not in their total. Depending upon acquisitions of public sector debt by the other intermediaries, an indirect extinction process is then substituted for what would otherwise be, and is for other intermediaries, a direct loss of deposits (Llewellyn, 1979). The more significant difference comes from the distinction between acceptance and demand. Bank liabilities are accepted, but may not be demanded except as a 'temporary abode of purchasing power' between transactions, because they can be used later for buying goods and making other payments. Deposits can come into existence without the receiving banks having to offer higher inducements and commit the resources and reserves needed to service them. For banks as a whole, there is a short-run divergence between the costs of having increments to deposits accepted and the costs of retaining them, for they constitute 'money on the wing', not 'money sitting', to use Robertson's (1928) happy terminology.

Thus the differences between bank and non-bank intermediation come from the short-run disequilibrium processes which characterize the market for money and underlie the supply-side analysis of money creation. Neither individually nor collectively do banks gain from this in the long run, since it is a feature only of short-run disequilibrium. But the difference is often seen to give the banking sector a special significance in transmitting monetary disturbances to the real sector, and may influence the choice of monetary control technique.

Wholesale banking

By *wholesale banking*[1] we refer to financial intermediaries classed as banks for which a distinguishing characteristic is the comparatively large size of the units in which business is transacted. Several other characteristics follow from this. Wholesale bankers typically have a small number of large customers, whereas retail banks in a branch banking system number theirs in the hundreds of thousands or even millions. It follows that wholesale banks cannot utilize the law of large numbers to determine optimal holdings of reserves. What is the basis of their intermediation?

One theory is that wholesale banks provide services which are quite different from those of retail banks; they spread liquidity but do not produce it. An absence of maturity transformation is assumed, banks (and lenders and borrowers) dealing in securities of the same type and term to maturity. In doing so, wholesale banks follow the principle of matching their liabilities and assets, in the sense that all loans of a particular maturity are financed by deposits of the same maturity (Revell, 1968). In this way, they obviate the need for reserves. Liquidity distribution could take place off-balance sheet by financial firms engaged in distributive techniques which match up borrowers and lenders. But it is the on-balance sheet business upon which we focus.

According to this theory, transactions costs (widely defined) are the basis of banks' existence. In the retail model, we ignored transactions costs but allowed for differences in liquidity. Here we assume $L_i = L_j$ and focus on transactions costs. The supply of funds from lenders is now

$$F_i = F_i(r_i) \tag{6.6}$$

where r_i is the interest return, net of transactions costs. Borrowers' demand for funds depends on the total cost of loans; that is, interest plus transactions costs, namely

$$F_j = F_j(r_j) \tag{6.7}$$

In the absence of banks, firms would solicit loans from each other incurring various transactions costs in so doing, as indeed do appear in the commercial paper market. Common to borrower and lender are brokerage fees, search costs, communication costs, and costs of recording and administering accounts. Lenders face the additional cost of obtaining information about borrowers and assessing their creditworthiness. These costs drive a wedge between the net interest return to lenders and the total cost paid by borrowers, even though the transacted interest rate is the same for both. Denoting the market clearing rate as r, the net interest return on the last loan transacted is

$$r_i = r - t_i \tag{6.8}$$

where t_i are the marginal transactions costs of lenders, and the cost to borrowers of the last loan concluded is

$$r_j = r + t_j \tag{6.9}$$

where t_j are the marginal transactions costs incurred by borrowers. Thus

$$r_j - r_i = t_j + t_i \qquad (6.10)$$

In equilibrium, the interest rate differential between the cost to the borrower and the return to the lender reflects the sum of their marginal transactions costs.

If financial intermediaries in general and wholesale banks in particular possess a comparative advantage in processing loan transactions, acquiring information about borrowers and monitoring bills of exchange and such market instruments, they are able to enter the market so long as their transactions costs are less than the sum of t_j and t_i (this ignores any costs of dealing with banks). With increased competition, such as seems likely to have occurred in the 1980s with the freeing up of bank lending, r_j would tend to fall and r_i to rise as funds are channelled from lenders to borrowers at lower cost and thus more efficiently when routed through the banks. From (6.6) and (6.7) we should expect the entry of banks to be accompanied over time by an expansion of borrowings and lendings even if the overall (average) level of interest rates is unaltered.

In this model, the *raison d'être* of banks lies in their ability to distribute funds more cheaply than in direct financing. By assumption, the banks balance the maturity of their liabilities and assets. They exchange securities without really changing their basic characteristics. Because they do not create liquidity, they have no need for reserves or holdings of base money.

While matching is an important facet of wholesale banking, the margins to be had now from straight brokerage or rerouting operations are not large, and a bank that was perfectly matched would soon go out of business. Banks can get wider margins by 'riding the yield curve' and taking advantage of interest rate differentials in the term structure of interest rates. If it is the case that $r_j^S < r_j^L$ and $r_i^S < r_i^L$ so that $r_i^S < r_j^S < r_i^L < r_j^L$, where the superscripts s and l denote short-term and long-term securities respectively, then banks can obtain the largest interest differential by combining r_j^L with r_i^S, and undertaking lending which is of somewhat longer maturity than their borrowings.

In this second theory of wholesale banking, banking behaviour is linked with theories of the term structure of interest rates, for it relies upon factors outside the banking system influencing the yield to maturity pattern. If expectations about future short-term rates are the dominant influence, a bank expecting to profit from mismatching pits its judgement of interest rate movements against those of the other transactors – undertaking positive maturity transformation if, in its view, the long-term rate exceeds compounded present and future short-term rates, negative maturity transformation if it is less. Either could occur, but in fact positive maturity transformation prevails. As it seems unlikely that bankers' views would consistently deviate in one direction from the market's view, we must ask why there is a premium upon short-term funds (or a discount upon long-term funds). Uncertainty about interest rates is one factor. Prices of 'longs' fluctuate more than prices of 'shorts' when there is an equal change in yields, so that holdings of longs offer the possibility of greater gain but risk of greater loss. If banks are less averse to risk than the market or are less uncertain about the direction of interest rates, they can profit from others' uncertainty and risk aversion. They balance the expected gains from mismatching, in the form of a wider interest differential (net of transactions costs), against the risks from interest rate variability which arise from an open position. This open position can be covered by holdings in marketable securities since matching is still the rule, and banks are mismatched only to the extent necessary to profit from interest rates; there is no need for holdings of cash.

If this and the previous model are valid descriptions of wholesale banking, then Revell's question as to whether these deposits should be included in the definition of money seems appropriate. Liabilities seem likely to be only a little more liquid than assets and only a little more interesting than the intercompany-type activities they replace. But while this form of intermediation is an important facet of wholesale banking, it is far from a complete picture; our contention will be that wholesale banks do in fact now undertake considerable maturity transformation.

Some idea of the extent of the maturity transformation can be gained from Tables 6.2 and 6.3, which present the sterling and foreign currency business of various categories of British banks, classified according to the remaining period to maturity. Several features stand out. First, both tables show, even for the total balance sheet, an excess of liabilities over assets at the short end of the scale; conversely, at the long end the balance sheets are not matched. When interbank claims are netted out to reveal the banks' business with the non-bank sector, a much greater extent of maturity transformation is evident. Second, there is a strong similarity in the degree of mismatching between foreign currency and sterling business. We may be entitled to speak of characteristics of wholesale intermediation, whether carried out in Eurocurrencies or in domestic currencies. Third, among the various categories of wholesale banks, in both sterling and foreign currency business, the extent and similarity of the mismatching of wholesale balance sheet categories are notable. The major differences come when we compare the wholesale banks and the retail banks. The retail banks have an even more mismatched balance sheet (both in total and with non-bank customers) than the wholesale bankers.

Based on these samples, nearly half of the sterling assets of wholesale

Table 6.2 Maturity analysis of British non-retail banks in sterling and foreign currencies by class of business, as at February 1980 (%)

	Sterling business						Foreign currency business					
	Total		Bank		Non-bank		Total		Bank		Non-bank	
	A	L	A	L	A	L	A	L	A	L	A	L
Sight	17.67	24.38	28.74	16.83	10.52	30.76	18.28	22.50	22.25	18.37	10.88	39.84
1–7 days	9.61	21.61	14.14	10.96	6.68	30.62						
8 days–1 month	12.39	19.35	19.67	21.36	7.68	17.65	12.41	19.31	16.38	19.26	5.25	19.51
1–3 months	14.04	20.55	18.69	32.82	11.04	10.17	18.24	29.92	24.22	31.87	7.10	21.73
3–6 months	7.81	6.94	9.92	10.71	6.45	3.74	11.55	19.33	15.12	21.23	4.89	11.34
6 months–1 year	7.33	3.71	6.39	5.16	7.94	2.48	7.53	6.28	8.07	6.82	6.53	4.51
1–3 years	10.50	2.13	1.96	1.79	16.00	2.43	1.94	1.58	5.86	1.61	17.54	1.45
3–5 years	8.56	1.09	0.37	0.32	13.84	1.73	21.97	1.08	8.10	0.84	47.80	1.62
5 years +	12.09	0.25	0.10	0.05	19.83	0.41						
Total	100.00	100.00	100.00	100.00	100.00	100.00	100.00	100.00	100.00	100.00	100.00	100.00

Notes:
A Assets
L Liabilities

Source: Lewis and Davis (1987), p. 96.

Table 6.3 Maturity analysis of sterling and foreign currency business with non-bank customers of retail and wholesale banks in Britain, as at end-January, 1987 (%)

	Sterling business						Foreign currency business			
	Retail banks		British non-retail banks		Overseas banks		All banks		British banks	
	A	L	A	L	A	L	A	L	A	L
0–7 days	3.54	83.51	13.98	52.83	12.64	41.29	11.96	38.15	11.11	47.95
8 days–1 month	3.49	7.89	3.09	18.74	12.75	21.97	11.00	23.97	8.20	20.70
1–3 months	6.18	6.28	6.27	15.61	15.35	20.88	13.71	18.15	10.21	17.19
3–6 months	5.01	1.00	6.19	4.36	5.69	5.16	9.33	6.87	7.86	6.71
6 months–1 year	5.91	0.67	10.42	4.70	7.20	4.03	6.09	2.68	6.61	2.29
1–3 years	10.21	0.24	18.11	1.83	12.65	2.37	13.11	2.02	15.20	1.74
3 years +	65.68	0.41	41.94	1.93	33.72	4.30	34.80	8.16	40.81	3.42
Total	100.00	100.00	100.00	100.00	100.00	100.00	100.00	100.00	100.00	100.00

Notes:
A Assets
L Liabilities

Source: Lewis and Davis (1987), p. 97.

banking business consists of loans. About half of the loans are nominally for terms in excess of one year, some in excess of five years which are negotiated (rolled over) on a three- or six-monthly basis at variable interest rates. These loans are financed by a succession of short-term borrowings. With these provisions, the interest rate risk (via flexi-rates) and the liquidity risk (via optional renewals) are ostensibly shifted to the borrower. Indeed, it has been argued that they are really six-month loans in a relatively matched balance sheet (Niehans and Hewson, 1976).

In practice, almost all rollover loans are renewed, and a bank which regularly refused to do so 'would soon go out of business', to quote one banker. It is the expectation of renewal which induces the borrower to pay a premium (spread) over six-month money. What otherwise determines the term structure of interest rates under flexi-rates? Any tendency for yields to rise with maturity in the normal course of events cannot be attributed to capital gains and losses on fixed nominal rate securities. Our argument is in terms of transactions costs, with borrowers paying a premium to have guaranteed renewals and to avoid the costs inherent in financing medium-term loans themselves by a succession of short-term instruments. On this interpretation, banks in wholesale markets are undertaking maturity transformation, although probably to a lesser extent than in retail banking. But the major contrast with retail banking is not the extent of the transformation, but the manner in which it is performed. While retail deposits can be withdrawn upon demand or at short notice, in practice they are not all withdrawn at once. The same stochastic principles cannot be applied to wholesale deposits. Matching of maturities and currencies is the rule, but how are loans of three or more years to non-banks matched with deposits of very short-term maturities?

Our contention is that the interbank market performs a 'fiction' which aids liquidity creation in wholesale banking. It may do so in two ways:

1. Wholesale Bank A receives a large deposit. It seeks out some non-bank customers, and lends the rest to the Bank B via the interbank market. Bank B in turn loans out some to non-bank customers and the rest to Bank C, etc. This method of sharing out the transformation can be done in this informal way or formalized in the consortia principle and in syndicated loans.
2. Wholesale Bank C is approached for a loan by a non-bank customer on a six-month rollover basis and bids for three-month interbank funds (liability management). Bank B supplies a three-month interbank loan, itself accepting one-month money from Bank A which has received a call deposit.

The first transaction can be seen as a form of informal risk-bearing. Given the normal maturity of deposits, Bank A is subject to the risk that the deposit may be withdrawn at short notice. In this case the risk is spread across a number of banks, as in this circumstance Bank A will call upon the other banks for repayment of the interbank funds. In the second example another type of informal risk-sharing is illustrated: that of loan risks. The interbank claims held by Banks A and B are backed up by the rollover loan which Bank C has made to its customer. A further dimension to the interbank market is also illustrated in the second example. This is the market's possible role in maturity transformation. The difference in maturity between a customer's deposit at one end and a loan of several years may be broken up into several steps carried out by different banks. In retail banking, one bank will have the demand deposit and the three-year loan.

In one or both of these ways each bank is mismatched, but not to any great extent, so that no one bank is left with a large share of the transformation process. In retail operations the transformation is undertaken fully by the bank which accepts the deposits. In wholesale markets, liquidity and lending risks are to a degree shared out in the banking system as a whole.

A number of implications follow from this third theory of wholesale banking. If banks in wholesale markets were large enough relative to the customers they could conceivably utilize stochastic principles, in which larger banks are always better off than smaller banks. Second, unlike in retail banking where deposits are backed by holdings of reserves, the backing for wholesale deposits consists of command over the ability to obtain funds from the interbank and wholesale funding markets, which at times (such as in the Continental Illinois crisis of 1984) have been volatile. Third, and reinforcing this in so far as the clearing banks are concerned in Britain, banks which operate in both retail and wholesale markets should possess advantages over those specializing in either area. They can rely upon a stable retail deposits base for much wholesale lending, limiting their use of funds bought in wholesale deposits for topping up. By a judicious mix of business, either risks can be lowered or returns increased.

Banking business in the United Kingdom

The categories of retail and wholesale banking are analytical categories devised to facilitate discussion of the theory of banking. They are not supposed to imply that any actual bank should be thought of as a representative solely of one type or another of banking activity. In practice, banks partake in both types of banking, and they also provide a range of other services, in mixes which differ from one bank to another, that are parasitic on the banking function (some of these are new developments which will be dealt with in Chapter 9). In fact, there are no purely retail banks in the United Kingdom. The Bank of England uses the term 'retail' to embrace the clearing banks, the TSB, Abbey National, the Northern Ireland and some other small banks, but over a quarter of the assets of these banks in aggregate are in Eurocurrencies and all have a wholesale book. Even the building societies now take in wholesale funds. There are, by way of comparison, many more retail banks in the United States, essentially consumer and small business banks, and this is one important difference between the US and British financial systems – a point to which we shall return later.

Despite the fact that banking business in the United Kingdom is now inextricably mixed, it bears pointing out that before 1971 there was a much sharper segregation between the two types of business. Retail business, conducted by the clearing banks, dealt with households and small firms and came under the traditional set of controls; this business also was highly centralized, with the control system and the market structure in symbiotic relationship. On the other hand, there was a second tier of wholesale banks dealing in large denomination deposits and loans and operating in both sterling and foreign currency markets. In this sphere, there was a competitive environment and rather little official control for policy purposes. Part of the purpose of the 1971 reform was to sweep away this division between the two tiers of banking and to unify the control system. Some pertinent differences between types of business in the main banking groups operating in the United Kingdom are still evident, however. For example, the data in Table 6.4, which pertains to 1980, exemplify some important differences between the clearing banks and the other groups in the proportion of sight deposits in the total and the fraction of loan business conducted on an overdraft basis. There is probably less dispersion in these fractions across the various groups today than there was in 1980, though the same qualitative difference still persists.

6.2   Direct methods of monetary control

Given the objective of controlling a large monetary aggregate like £M3, various techniques for reaching it have been proposed. We consider first the role of direct controls and the potential for monetary base control. However, neither of these techniques was used in the United Kingdom in the 1980s, when the main weight of attempts to control the money stock

Table 6.4 Various aspects of sterling business of UK banks, February 1980

	London clearing banks	LCB subsidiaries	Accepting houses	Other British banks	UK registered overseas banks	Foreign banks	Consortium banks
A. Sight deposits as per cent of total deposits	44.09	14.14	27.35	13.50	24.12	18.99	22.13
B. Per cent of A which are current deposits	88.12	16.44	14.32	27.78	n.a.	n.a.	13.83
C. Current deposits as per cent of total deposits	38.85	2.32	3.92	3.75	n.a.	n.a.	3.06
D. Deposits with maturity >7 days as per cent of total deposits	24.45		46.66	66.33	60.82	n.a.	68.39
E. Overdrafts as per cent of total advances	60.68	5.49	11.77	10.41	14.06	n.a.	1.30

Source: Item A is from *Bank of England Quarterly Bulletin*; items B to E are based on a sampling of British banks.

fell upon fiscal policy, funding policy and interest rates. We deal with these alternatives at the end of the chapter.

The abolition of exchange control in 1979 led to the abandonment of the most effective direct control on banking, the special supplementary deposit or corset. This development is in line with the view that a principal effect of such controls is to act as a tax on onshore banking, the imposition of which would lead to a shift in business to offshore banks. However, under the post-1980 regime the ordinary special deposit – which, unlike the supplementary special deposit, pays interest at a market rate – was retained. Clearly, it is not just the tax effect, the consequence of a lack of compensation for interest loss, which is at issue. We examine below how the controls work in order to illustrate the point.

Variations in reserve requirements or calls to special deposits, just like the normal method of open market sales of Treasury bills, have the immediate effect of draining funds from the money market. They can differ from such open market operations in two main respects: first, they seem likely to produce different consequences for the structure of interest rates; second, they can 'tax' intermediation. Open market operations are implemented by changes in the supply of government interest-bearing debt relative to private sector debt. Alterations to reserve requirements are implemented via banks' demand for government and private sector debt. There is no reason to expect the time sequence and pattern of interest rates which result to be the same. In general, one might expect open market operations to exert more of an impact upon government interest rates, and changes in reserve requirements to have a larger relative impact upon private sector interest rates.

Different consequences could follow for output and prices. Any differences here may exist even if the tax effect of a reserve requirement is absent.[2] The tax effect comes about because the constraint upon banks' acquisition of non-reserve assets inherent in a reserve requirement can impose pecuniary costs which influence the scale of intermediation that it is profitable for them to undertake.

Consider an intermediary which is maximizing expected short-run profits under competitive conditions, without controls. Intermediation is assumed to expand until zero expected profits are earnt on the 'last' funds transformed. The anticipated net yield on loans is obtained by adjusting the loan rate (i_L) for expected default, i.e. as $(i_L - b)$ where b is the difference between posted and effective interest rates due to default risks. Included in the asset portfolio on prudential grounds is a proportion (α) of reserve assets earning the interest rate i_A. Costs include not only the interest rate on marginal deposits (i_D) but also the costs of labour, capital and materials absorbed in administering the deposit, denoted a.

Each firm seeks a level of operations which equates (short-run) marginal revenue (r) and marginal cost (c): that is, where

$$c = r \qquad (6.11)$$

where $c = i_D + a$ and $r = (1 - \alpha)(i_L - b) + \alpha(i_A)$

As with any other firm in the economy, monetary policy can impinge upon the operations of the financial intermediary in two basic ways (although we examine later whether monetary base control offers a third mechanism). One is by purchasing or selling stocks of commodities and so bringing about changes in relative prices generally which alter the marginal-revenue/marginal-cost conditions facing the intermediary. This is the basis of the interest rate control mechanism, implemented via open market operations, considered later. The other is by taxation. Consider a call to special deposits. The intermediary must place a fraction (s) of its asset portfolio (assumed equal to total deposits) into a special account at the Bank of England at the rate (i_s); the remainder $(1 - s)$ is then invested in the other assets (including the reserve assets) with a net yield (r) at the margin. Hence the new equilibrium is

$$c = (1 - s)r + s(i_s) = r - s(r - i_s) \qquad (6.12)$$

So long as r (and c) exceeds i_s, the call widens the gap between the cost of marginal funds and the net yield which is sufficient to ensure that the marginal funds can earn profit. In the second expression, the first term on the right-hand side is the net expected marginal return from liability incurrence when there is no call to special deposits, while the second term $s(r - i_s)$ indicates the marginal opportunity cost imposed upon the incurring of liabilities due to the call. (We assume that the intermediary's own demand for reserve assets does not contract by an amount equivalent to the special deposits call.)

It follows that we can view the imposition of cash reserve ratios as special deposits as a tax upon intermediation, the tax base being eligible liabilities and the tax rate equal to $s(r - i_s)$. When the tax is effective, some contraction of the scale of the intermediary's balance sheet from that in (6.12) is required to raise r (or lower c). Note that the reduction implied is once-for-all as banks' eligible liabilities contract to the new lower level. This result is not necessarily inconsistent with the view that such controls result in a continuing shift from the taxed institutions. The contraction of bank intermediation in turn forces actual and would-be borrowers to use more costly and more inconvenient finance from untaxed non-bank intermediaries and from a reversion to direct financing (disintermediation). If the tax persists, these alternatives become less costly and less inconvenient; usage makes them better substitutes. Thus over time direct controls promote the development of alternative untaxed sources of finance, and reduce the relative market share of the taxed intermediaries.[3]

At present British banks are subject to two direct controls: ordinary special deposits (but unused in the 1980s) and a 0.45 per cent cash ratio. The cash ratio is not varied directly, and the Bank of England stresses that the purpose of this imposition is to provide it with an income, not to act as a control mechanism. To emphasize the point the requirement is calculated as a fixed sum revised every six months.

Application of the corset (Supplementary Special Deposits) was a different matter. It introduced an additional differential between a bank's marginal loan and deposit rate. Furthermore, the differential rose sharply as a bank moved beyond the allowable growth of interest-bearing eligible liabilities (IBELs) from a base date. Under the arrangements introduced in June 1978, for example, supplementary deposits became payable if an institution's average IBELs for the three months August–October 1978 grew by more than 4 per cent over the average for the six months November 1977–April 1978. The rate of deposit was progressive in three tranches, according to the extent of the excess. We denote each tranche by

$\gamma_0 = 0$ (Corset off)
$\gamma_1 = 0.05$ (First tranche, less than 3 per cent excess)
$\gamma_2 = 0.25$ (Second tranche, 3–5 per cent excess)
$\gamma_3 = 0.50$ (Third tranche, over 5 per cent excess)

Moreover, unlike ordinary special deposits, the supplementary deposits earned the banks *no* interest. Consequently, the equilibrium becomes

$$c = (1 - s - \gamma)r + si_s = r - s(r - i_s) - \gamma r \qquad \textbf{(6.13)}$$

Comparing (6.13) with (6.12) we can see that a bank forced into the third tranche would then have to more than double its asking rate on a marginal loan for it to be profitable to bid for an additional interest-bearing deposit. Despite the fact that a substantial inelasticity of credit demand to interest rates may often prevail, the banks did not raise their loan rates to pay for the SSD calls. Instead, they rationed credit demands. The rationing, though no doubt inconvenient to some frustrated borrowers, was seen as causing less rupture to long-term customer relationships than the alternative.

A form of control like the corset is likely to impinge more upon wholesale banking activities than upon retail banking for several reasons: margins are finer, there is a greater reliance upon interest-bearing deposits, and large corporate customers have a greater ability to bypass the banking system. This is not surprising; the corset was specifically introduced in December 1973 (and continued to February 1975) to make it costly for banks to bid for wholesale deposits. After that, the scheme was used from November 1976 to August 1977 and again from June 1978 to June 1980. By the last occasion the distortions it induced had become obvious. Two practices reduced its effectiveness (Griffiths, 1979). First, banks engaged in window-dressing transactions in anticipation of the imposition of the corset. This involved expanding their IBELs much faster than £M3 in order to start off in the corset with an artificially large base of IBELs, which would then be run down. Just prior to June 1978, IBELs were increasing at an annual rate of 25 per cent, whereas £M3 was increasing at 15 per cent per annum. This was in spite of a warning from the Bank that the corset would be backdated and they would not gain (Pepper, 1979). In the event, the corset was backdated but perhaps by not enough to discourage similar pre-emptive transactions if there was to be a next time round.

These anticipatory actions enabled many banks to sustain their lending and thus their contribution to £M3 during 1978–9 without coming within the corset provisions. By 1979–80 this buffer had gone but the bank acceptance leak grew as banks helped customers to shift their borrowings to the money markets in the form of commercial bills; disintermediation occurred. In the words of the Green Paper (Monetary Control, 1980), 'to the holder, such bills are no less liquid than a certificate of deposit of comparable term, and to the borrower they are a very close substitute for direct bank credit' (p. 5). It was the potential for such disintermediation, as well as the possible Eurosterling leak (marginal banking operations being shifted offshore), which led the Bank of England to abandon the corset as a means of credit control once the exchange control regulations, which inhibited arbitrage between onshore and offshore markets, were removed.

The case against direct controls should not be overstated. If bank acceptances are as good as bank lending, why did reintermediation occur in July 1980 when the corset was lifted? Similarly, the idea that bills are as good as bank deposits ignores the fact that 30 per cent of wholesale deposits are at call and 90 per cent are of maturities of less than three months; although bills can be sold at any time, their price and thus their liquidity is not assured. Because of the extent of maturity transformation now undertaken by the banks in both wholesale and retail business, reintermediation like that in July 1980 is not without effect. Furthermore, some disintermediation is almost inevitable in any policy which restricts the growth of banks' balance sheets, as borrowers are forced to resort to more expensive non-bank finance. This process is one way in which restrictive policy is transmitted from the banking system to other financial markets. So long as interest rates restrain expenditure, the credit restriction remains. Direct controls encourage more disintermediation to occur, depending upon the time horizon over which they apply. Whether this is good or bad needs to be judged against how well other control techniques work. In any case, it can always be argued that even when the effect of the control is largely cosmetic, appearances are sufficiently important in monetary affairs that such an effect should not be altogether despised.

6.3 Money supply identity approaches

Money supply theories are concerned with the processes governing supply conditions in countries with extensive financial intermediation. Three groups are involved in these processes, and the links between the three groups depend upon the institutions, regulations and financial technology which prevail in individual countries. The monetary authorities issue fiat money and determine the conditions under which the financial intermediaries operate. The public allocates its money holdings between fiat money and the claims of financial intermediaries. Financial intermediaries acquire securities issued by the public and the authorities and supply their own liabilities in return.

Two basic approaches have been developed to analyze the interrelationships. Both are based on identities, yet are shaped by implicit hypotheses about the behaviour of the three participating groups. Those identities used in the United States, although they can be applied in any country with a fractional reserve banking system, are based around the quantity of base money and a money multiplier. In other countries, notably the United Kingdom, Australia, France and Italy, it has been more usual to classify the sources of money supply change into credit counterparts by means of the flow of funds.

Monetary base multiplier approach

The idea that the money supply can be controlled by controlling the monetary base comes readily out of the retail banking model. Viewing base money held as bank reserves, R, in the form of deposits at the Bank of England, and till cash as a determinate input requirement of banking business and with the stock of base money held by the public (notes and coin), C, equally related to the volume of bank deposits D, the high-powered money multiplier quantifies the relationship between the supply of money, M, and the monetary base (high-powered money), H. Thus,

$$H = C + R \qquad\qquad (6.14)$$

The money supply is defined as

$$M = D + C \qquad\qquad (6.15)$$

By denoting the ratios C/D and R/D as d and r respectively, one can derive

$$M = \frac{(1+d)}{(d+r)} H = mH \qquad\qquad (6.16)$$

which links the money supply to high-powered money. The ratio $m = (1+d)/(d+r)$ is referred to as the *money multiplier*, and under a system of fractional reserve banking (when $r < 1$) must be greater than 1.

In the simple model the critical ratios are constants; in practice these are ratios determined by choice, perhaps constrained by minimum reserve requirements in the case of r, but in any case in principle amenable to estimation and prediction. The spirit of the model and its control implication is unimpaired provided that the functions governing d and r are stable under the control regime in contemplation. This spirit is one in which the monetary authorities provide a particular quantity of base money, from which the banks must meet reserve requirements and obtain their desired holdings of excess reserves and from which the public acquires its currency holdings. Thus the two groups are in competition for a limited amount of base money, with the entire quantity always claimed. Changes in the quantity of the monetary base will create discrepancies between desired and actual reserves of banks, leading to alterations in the banks' acquisition of earning assets and thus their deposits.

Support for these interpretations of a process running from the quantity of reserves or high-powered money via a relatively constant money multiplier to the quantity of money is offered from studies of the monetary system in the United States (Brunner, 1987). Evidence for the United Kingdom is different. Capie and Rodrick-Bali (1986) show a remarkable change in the multiplier; after having fluctuated within a narrow band in the 100 years from 1871 to 1971, it soared in the 10 years after that (from around 4 to nearly 10), the combination of a sharply declining ratio of currency to deposits and a greatly reduced reserve ratio. Much of the latter can be attributed to the ending, under Competition and Credit Control in 1971, of the conventional minimum 8 per cent cash ratio which the clearing banks maintained by agreement with the Bank of England. But the years since 1971 have seen a rapid growth of, and

British banks' participation in, wholesale banking and liability management (the idea that banks can seek out lending opportunities secure in the knowledge that they can buy in reserves to support their loan book). Such developments suggest the desirability of a money stock formation approach which focuses upon bank lending and its contribution to the quantity of money. The alternative credit counterparts approach does so.

Credit counterparts approach

This approach, also involving identities, is derived from the national flow-of-funds accounts. Table 6.5 is a simplified four-sector version in which the central bank and the government are aggregated into an official sector, along with the foreign sector, private and non-financial sector and the financial sector (comprising in this case only the banks). Columns (i) and (ii) give the income and expenditure items, showing, for each of the four sectors, how funds have been derived through the earning of revenue and used for expenditures, with any difference constituting the particular sector's net borrowing or net lending (along with unidentified items). The remaining columns (iii)–(viii) show how the net borrowings or lending give rise to changes in financial assets and liabilities.

The requirement that total income equals total expenditure is simply the familiar national income identity:

$$S + T = I + G + (X - Z) \tag{6.17}$$

This can be rearranged to give the parallel financing requirement, for the flow of funds provides the financial counterparts of the income and expenditure items which appear in the national accounts:

$$S - I = (X - Z) + (G - T) \tag{6.18}$$

In this form the identity says that borrowing by the overseas sector to finance an excess of home exports (X) over home imports (Z), together with borrowing by the government sector to finance an excess of its expenditure (G) over its revenue (T), must be matched by net lending by the non-financial private sector of the economy arising from its surplus savings (S) over capital formation (I).[4] The financial sector is assumed to have no net saving.

Net lending by the non-financial private sector results in its acquiring more financial assets than it issues by incurring liabilities, corresponding to its increase in net financial wealth. The assets may be acquired directly from the overseas and official sectors in the form of capital outflow $(-K)$ or additional holdings of official debt issued as cash or bonds $(\Delta C + \Delta GS_p)$. Alternatively, the acquisition may occur indirectly via the

Table 6.5 A simplified flow-of-funds account

	(i) Income	(ii) Expenditure	(iii) Deposits	(iv) Non-deposit liabilities	(v) High-powered money	(vi) Govt securities	(vii) Domestic lending	(viii) Foreign lending
1. Official	T	G			$-\Delta H$	$-\Delta GS$		ΔRes
2. Foreign	Z	X						$K - \Delta Res$
3. Private non-financial	S	I	ΔD	ΔNDL	ΔC	ΔGS_p	$-\Delta A$	$-K$
4. Financial			$-\Delta D$	$-\Delta NDL$	ΔR	ΔGS_B	ΔA	
Total	$S+Z+T$	$I+X+G$	0	0	0	0	0	0

banks (the private financial sector) by savers adding to deposits (ΔD) and net non-deposit liabilities (ΔNDL) in excess of the loans obtained by investors (ΔA). From row 3 of Table 6.5 we see how the net surplus is allocated across the portfolio, i.e.

$$S - I = \Delta D + \Delta NDL + \Delta C + \Delta GS_p - K - \Delta A \qquad (6.19)$$

By equating Equations (6.18) and (6.19) and rearranging, we obtain

$$\Delta D + \Delta C = (G - T) - \Delta GS_p + \Delta A + (X - Z + K)$$
$$- \Delta NDL \qquad (6.20)$$

The left-hand side is simply the increase in money supply (sterling M3). The first term on the right-hand side corresponds to the public sector borrowing requirement (or budget deficit). The second is the net sale of government interest-bearing debt to the non-bank private sector. The third term is bank lending to the private sector. The fourth term is the amount of net external flows from the balance of payments identity, as given in row 2 (which includes changes in the official reserves along with various short-term bank flows, e.g. non-resident transactions in sterling deposits and assets and the banks' switched position between sterling and foreign currency). Finally, the last term is the increase in net non-deposit liabilities (bank share capital and internal funds less non-financial assets such as bank premises along with any errors and omissions). In shorthand notation:

> PSBR
> − Gilt sales
> + Increase in bank lending *equals* DCE
> + Net external flows
> − Increase in non-deposit liabilities *equals* Increase in M3.

Comparing the two approaches

Both approaches are based on identities, and in that sense are equally correct.[5] Why, then, is the money multiplier identity favoured in the United States and the credit counterparts identity preferred in the United Kingdom? A possible explanation runs in terms of long-standing institutional differences between the countries.

An implicit hypothesis underlying the money multiplier approach is that banks' acquisition of non-cash assets is governed by the availability of cash reserves. In short, a supply mechanism determines changes in banks' earning assets. However suitable this assumption is for the United States, it is less applicable for the case of bank lending in the United

Kingdom, where widespread use of the overdraft system means that the usage made of lending limits is largely at the customers' volition. An analysis based on the demand for credit rather than the supply of reserves makes more sense, and behavioural relationships about the demand for advances can be slotted readily into a framework such as (6.20). In addition, bank lending has long been a special focus of monetary policy in the United Kingdom, and this is a second reason why the counterparts framework is preferred. Third, the counterparts framework can be readily applied to aggregates which embrace the whole of the banking sector (e.g. sterling M3), but is less readily applicable to the M1 aggregate preferred in the United States. Finally, the money multiplier has the advantage of isolating the impact of reserve requirements on the money supply. Since required reserves do not play a role as a policy tool in its monetary policy formulation, this feature is unimportant for the UK system.

Many of these long-established institutional differences between the United States and the United Kingdom have been eroded. M1 is no longer the dominant aggregate in the United States, and the broader aggregates are now accorded greater emphasis. Paradoxically, this has coincided with a move in the opposite direction, away from broad to narrow aggregates, in the United Kingdom. Likewise, less lending in the United Kingdom is now by means of overdraft than was formerly the case, while more lending in the United States is under loan commitments, both formal and informal. And in terms of the adoption of base money (termed M0)[6] as one of the targeted monetary aggregates, the United Kingdom would seem to have moved closer to US practice.

One difference that remains is the relationship of the Bank of England to the government and the Treasury. Unlike the position in the United States, the central bank is not an independent authority but rather one component of a coordinated centralized policy-making machinery, and the credit counterparts identity has proved useful to those arguing the need for coordination of the various arms of economic policy-making for monetary control.

Fiscal policy, interest rates and funding

The chief means by which the authorities sought to control the wider monetary aggregate £M3 combined fiscal policy, interest rates and funding policy. The fundamental identity (6.20) both informed this approach and has proved a powerful means of suggesting to government that controlling the growth of the money supply is not simply a function of monetary policy, but also requires supportive fiscal policy and a funding policy which facilitates the placing of government debt in safe hands, as well as an active policy for interest rates.

It is clear from this identity how fiscal policy is thought to have a role. The PSBR is simply the budget deficit reduced by any privatization proceeds. Thus the MTFS projections for the money supply have been accompanied from the start by a projection for the PSBR; and the fact that the authorities have resisted suggestions that the PSBR is a poor indicator of fiscal policy and should be replaced by more sophisticated (inflation-adjusted, cycle-normalized) measures can be rationalized in terms of an approach which stresses its role in money supply formation, as in the identity. It can also be understood that funding policy, directed at increasing gilt sales, has a ready rationale, as has a policy of adjusting short-term interest rates to curb bank lending. The authorities have sought to plead that restrictive fiscal policy (reducing the PSBR) can help reduce the interest cost of realizing a given target or the growth of £M3. In terms of the identity, this seems obvious; if individual items can be manipulated independently then it follows that a cut in the PSBR takes the weight off policies to curb bank lending.

Nevertheless, arithmetic is not economics. There appears to have been no reliable link from the PSBR to the growth of the money supply, which has remained high even with negative values of the PSBR (Jackson, 1990). Table 6.6 summarizes the relative contributions of the various factors distinguished to the growth of £M3 over the whole period to mid 1989[7] while Figure 6.2 graphs the PSBR, bank lending and the increase in £M3. In terms of proximate determinants the driving force behind £M3 increases has, most of the time, been bank lending.

In the early part of the 1980s, bank lending displayed considerable inelasticity with respect to interest rates. Why is bank lending so unresponsive to interest rates? At least four factors seem relevant. First, most bank lending is to industrial companies. Studies (e.g. Moore and Threadgold, 1980) of these companies' borrowing from banks indicate that it is significantly determined by the costs that the firms face. Wages, bills, import costs and tax payments all seem to swell bank borrowing and render the money supply partly endogenous to the inflationary process. Circumstances in which the authorities are seeking to restrain monetary growth are typically those in which firms need more finance to meet higher wage bills and imports of oil and other commodities. In short, the attempt to move up the demand curve for loans by higher interest rates is swamped by the rightward shift of the curve. Some would say that this slippage is not undesirable. It ensures that high interest rates do not bankrupt firms facing cost increases over which they have little control. But the demand for funds could reflect other things.

Table 6.6 Counterparts to the increase in £M3, 1979–89, £ million

Year	PSBR	Less sales of govt debt to non-bank residents	Plus increases in bank lending	Plus increases in non-deposit liabilities	Less foreign financing
1979	12 551	10 959	8 585	−768	2890
1980	11 786	9 435	10 025	−1169	644
1981	10 507	11 325	11 405	−1211	153
1982	4 880	10 589	17 556	−1460	2915
1983	11 605	10 817	12 903	−1952	2287
1984	10 281	11 145	16 759	−2182	3604
1985	7 474	7 789	21 218	−3013	2642
1986	2 418	3 568	30 449	−3767	2466
1987	−1 464	2 023	38 692	−4662	−3282
1988	−11 600	−4 419	57 283	−6061	6765
1989 (1st half)	−5 491	−10 218	26 975	−3789	4469

Note: Figures do not add exactly.

Source: CSO *Economic Trends* Annual Supplement, 1989; *Financial Statistics*, August 1989.

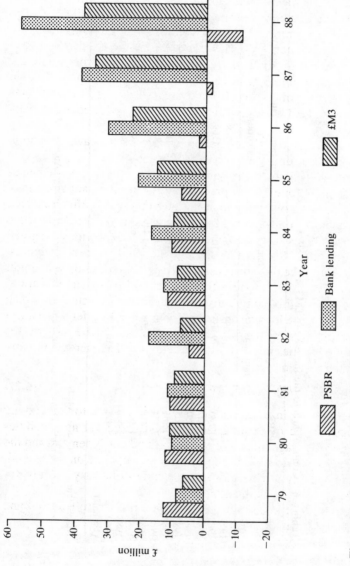

Figure 6.2   Increases in £M3, bank lending and the PSBR, 1979–88.
Source: CSO. *Economic Trends*, Annual Supplement, 1989.

Among these other things we note, second, that many firms apparently use bank borrowings as a more or less permanent source of funds, representing a much higher proportion of external funds than in the 1960s. They borrow from banks because the equity market with its ups and downs cannot always be relied upon, while the debenture market has suffered with inflation uncertainties because of firms' unwillingness to go into debt at fixed interest rates. By contrast, bank lending rates are flexible, adjusted in line with market trends. Firms may see that they have little alternative but to stay with the banks and take the rough with the smooth. In any case, interest rates may prove to be only temporarily high. Clearly the practice of 'Duke of York' tactics in the gilts market (see Chapter 7) may lead to the wrong climate of expectations for bank borrowers.

Third, much of the time when nominal interest rates have been high, real rates (adjusted for inflation) have not been.

Fourth, the behaviour of the banks cannot be ignored, especially as companies may accept loans for precautionary reasons in anticipation of greater difficulties in obtaining loans at later dates. It is often said that banks are unable to control their advances portfolio in times of restrictive monetary policy because customers draw down previously agreed borrowing facilities. Short of cancelling the rights under customers' noses, banks can make the advances more costly, but the usage remains at the customers' volition. In fact this is a considerable simplification, especially in the highly competitive British financial system in which banks compete for the lending business of companies by offering facilities and open credit lines. We can write advances as $A = F(A/F)$ where A is advances, F is facilities and A/F is the usage rate. The increase in bank lending can be written as

$$\Delta A \approx F \, \Delta(A/F) + (A/F) \, \Delta F \qquad (6.21)$$

That is, the increase in advances can be broken down into that coming from changed usage of existing facilities and that from new facilities granted at normal usage rates. We cannot say that one is demand and the other supply, but obviously any supply influences operate on the second, which is proximately attributed to new facilities and may account for much of the increase in bank lending.

The question must be asked, then, whether policies to control bank lending are aimed at the correct target. Without the corset and the reserve assets ratio, the banks' participation in the control of lending is virtually limited to raising base rates in line with Bank of England pressures so that interest rates can operate upon the public's demand for credit. Advocates of monetary base control would argue that under their preferred control mechanism banks would face a different set of circumstances and a different constraint.

6.4 The monetary base debate revisited

The frustrations encountered in the initial attempt to control the money supply (£M3) by the authorities' preferred means of adjusting fiscal policy and interest rates led to the publication of a Green Paper in 1980 which discussed the possible adoption of monetary base control as a superior technique. What ensued was the 1981 package of reforms, but the changes in technique which were implemented fell short of adopting monetary base control (this is discussed in detail in Chapter 7). Runaway growth of the monetary aggregates (and inflation) in the latter part of the 1980s has seen attempts to reopen this debate (for example Pepper, 1990).

There are three sources of base money available at any time so far as banks are concerned: the non-bank private sector, the overseas sector and the authorities themselves. In addition, economies in the requirement for base money on the part of the banks can reduce their resort to any of the three sources.

Extracting base money from the non-bank private sector could be effected by adjusting interest rates on current accounts and offering other inducements for economizing on cash; as a result, currency demand relationships might alter under an effective monetary base control regime. Banks could access base money holdings by borrowing overseas and exchanging the funds for sterling; but this could only relieve an aggregate shortage if the incipient rise in the exchange rate tempted the intervention of the authorities, as it might; otherwise the purchase would be of a sterling deposit with another bank. Thus the authorities are the last resort source of supply of monetary base.

Under the system introduced in 1980, onerous reserve requirements for base money were eschewed, so that the emergent demand should be an unconstrained cost-minimizing one; at the same time the authorities sought to lower the profile of their interest rate setting, putting the ball back in the market's court. These reforms set the scene for a phase of monetary base control which never eventuated: under it, the authorities would, presumably, have coordinated actions to affect the day-to-day money base shortage with a policy of relieving the shortage at a market clearing price. The money base would have been the target and the interest rates emerging from the residual act of clearing the market the consequence. The method, given lags in information, would not hit the target spot-on day by day or even week by week but it could come close to doing so. The control issue can be seen as one of more certain quantity control with more variable interest rates as against less variable interest rates with less certain quantity control. In the long run, the average quantity or the average interest rate could – either one – be set at a level implying the other, if the long-run demand function is invariant to the control regime. In this sense monetary base control and interest rate control are policy duals, and the question arises as to what real differences exist. There are, in our mind, two real differences and they are considerations underlying a dispute which would be difficult to understand if the two options were indeed simply duals of each other.

First, monetary base control can be seen as a way of forcing the authorities to eschew consulting additional criteria in the way that is natural for them to do if interest rate control is pursued. If interest rate control is the regime adopted, it is unlikely that the *only* criterion adopted by the authorities in deciding whether to raise or lower interest rates would be the deviation of the monetary base from target. We have seen this in practice. The fact that the authorities are setting the interest rate inclines them to take into account a variety of additional considerations; and this propensity may be reinforced by pressure groups directly affected by interest rates. In this respect adopting a regime of monetary base control would be like purging the authorities' interest rate reaction function of additional arguments.

Second, the participants in the adjustment process could be expected to behave differently. Under present procedures, the banks have become almost passive intermediaries in the process of monetary control. Their job is to raise loan rates in line with market rates, but if borrowers are not daunted by higher interest rates, the banks bid for deposits and reserves to sustain any expansion of advances. Bank of England officials argue that they have no alternative but to supply banks with the reserves needed to validate deposit growth if stability of the banking system is to be ensured. All they can do is influence the cost at which cash is made available to the system, and even here their effective discretionary power is limited. Considering the margin of excess reserves which banks normally hold in modern-day financial systems, the demand for total reserves is highly inelastic with respect to relevant interest rates. Moreover, now that banks practise liability management, they react to any reserve deficiency by bidding more aggressively for deposits and reserves in the wholesale funding markets to support their lending, rather than disposing of assets. Any failure of reserves to keep pace with deposit expansion will merely see interest rates spiral upwards, seemingly without limit, rather than directly impelling banks to contract their lending.

It is possible to visualize events proceeding differently. Liability management enables banks to 'run but not hide' from system-wide reserve deficiencies, since with flexible exchange rates and funding of the government budget, extra issues of deposits by banks cannot pull in more cash to the system as a whole. Banks usually have the alternative of disposing of earning assets to the non-bank private sector, leaving total deposits unchanged. The idea that there is some new breed of banker who will always eschew asset management for liability management is patently false. If interbank rates are bid up high enough, it would pay some banks to sell bills and bonds to the private sector in order to obtain funds for lending out in the interbank market. Liability management is allowed to succeed because the central bank always provides the reserves needed to validate deposit expansion from bank lending. The deposit increase, in turn, provides the non-bank private sector with funds with which to buy any gilts sold by the monetary authorities. Indeed, firms may even borrow from banks in order to buy the gilts – this being one possible hedging strategy should interest rates be expected to fall.

Behaviour 'next time round' may be influenced. If banks are able to get cash, and at a price not always penal, they are unlikely to rearrange affairs so as to avoid putting themselves into the position of having to seek out cash in the future. Were the consequences of interest rate changes allowed to proceed under alternative arrangements (such as shifting penalty borrowing costs at present borne by the discount houses on to the banks), behaviour next time around might well be different. After being forced to make up reserve shortages at penalty rates, banks would likely exercise much greater care in future when granting overdraft facilities and open credit lines. There would be an incentive for banks individually to refrain from lending and to build up reserves when cash shortages are anticipated. Surges in monetary growth may be less likely to occur.

However, this is perhaps to confuse what could be with what is. Goodhart (1987, p. 50), argues that:

> Central Banks have historically been at some pains to assure the banking system that the institutional structure is such that the system as a whole can *always* obtain access to whatever cash the system may require in order to meet its needs, though at a price of the Central Bank's choosing: and there has been a further, implicit corollary that interest rates will not be varied capriciously. The whole structure of the monetary system has evolved on this latter basis, that is, that the untrammelled force of the monetary base multiplier will *never* be unleashed.

This is perhaps to overstate the point, but the fact remains that two different regimes are being compared: in the one, interest rate variability is higher and the stability of the money base greater than in the other; such characteristics are more than likely to enter the demand function for base money. If they do so in a way which renders that function unstable, then a switch to monetary base control might fail in its first objective[8]; but if they do so in a way which, after an initial transition period, becomes stable, the objective can be attained.

The contrast between the two approaches is a function of the time period for which stability in money base is defined. If only long-period stability is in question then it is pertinent to note that monetary base targets over time are just as likely to be revised as are the additional criteria to enter the authorities' interest rate reaction function. And if only long-run stability is the goal then short-term interest variability should be little affected.

Friedman's analogy

When he was asked to explain the difference between monetary base control and the authorities' conventional approach, Milton Friedman (1980) responded to the House of Commons Select Committee by invoking the retail banking model. He observed:

> Trying to control the money supply through 'fiscal policy and interest rates' [to quote the Green Paper] is trying to control the output of one item (money) through altering the demand for it by manipulating the incomes of its users (that is the role of fiscal policy) or the prices of substitutes for it (that is the role of interest rates). A precise analogy is like trying to control the output of motor cars by altering the incomes of potential purchasers and manipulating rail and air fares. In principle, possible in both cases, but in practice highly inefficient. Far easier to control the output of motor cars by controlling the availability of basic raw materials, say steel, to manufacturers – a precise analogy to controlling the availability of base money to banks and others.

The first point to note is that the authorities' supply-side conception of the contribution of fiscal policy to monetary control via the government financing identity is different from (though not necessarily more correct than) the rationale assigned to it by Friedman in the quotation above, where he supposes fiscal policy to be a regulator of one of the determinants (income) of the demand for money. Friedman's understanding of funding transactions as manipulations of rates of interest, also arguments of the money demand function, is similarly awry as a description of the authorities' view of the role of interest rates.

Friedman's polemic also leads him too far, inasmuch as his treatment of the issue appears to invite the suggestion that he is advocating quotas on the supply of base money and has a 'fixed coefficient' view of the relationship between base money and the money supply, on the lines of the simplest of money multiplier models. There are difficulties in both respects.

A direct quota system for controlling the money supply was in fact proposed by Duck and Sheppard (1978) by means of the issue of special reserve deposits available only to banks which it would be mandatory for them to hold. A simple derivative of this scheme – called negotiable entitlements – was examined in the Green Paper. Such direct controls, equivalent to a marketable quota or ratio of base money, were discounted in the Green Paper as discriminating against the participating onshore banks in favour of offshore banks and domestic non-participants.

But let us return to Friedman's analogy. Admittedly, analogies are never precise, but his is unhelpful in several respects.

First, monetary base control does not directly supply reserves to the banking system, for cash is held by other institutions as well as by individuals and firms. These other holders have a claim to base money and constitute a potential source to the banks in other circumstances. In this respect, as Miller (1980) has observed, the correct analogue would be trying to control motor vehicle production by controlling the supply of steel to *all* industries.

Second, a direct analogy applies at best only to the retail banks which might be expected to react to a threatened constraint on the availability of base money. For a broad aggregate measure of the money supply, like M3, the model is relevant only to a fraction of the banking activity contributing to the total. The wholesale banking activities which govern the rest do not, as we have described them, conform to the model in which money base can be viewed as a production input. Of course wholesale banking activities, like much else, would be affected by the interest rates emerging from the control process, but this is a different story. In this respect, to vary Friedman's analogy, monetary base control might be like trying to control the production of cars made from steel *and* those made from other materials by restricting the input of steel alone. Still, it should be noted that this argument does not logically exclude pursuing monetary base control methods as a complement to other approaches which might exert more leverage over wholesale banking activities.

Third, talk of the physical control of stocks of raw materials is misleading. It is more as if the stocks of materials have to be auctioned off. At the margin the base would need to be kept on course by open market operations and banks would need to restrict loans or bid for cash to reconcile their demands with the limited supply. Changes in interest rates would be involved and this leads us directly to present methods whereby monetary policy is implemented almost entirely by means of interest rates *via* market operations.

In terms of Friedman's analogy, both monetary base control and interest rate control procedures seem a strange approach to the conduct of monetary policy. Suppose that we actually did wish to control the production of a product like motor vehicles because of externalities of one sort or another created by excessive private supply. We would be unlikely to ration inputs of steel – which is monetary base control. It is also unlikely that the government would enter the market, buying up stocks of cars until the price rose enough to choke off private demand – which is the nearest equivalent to interest rate management via open market operations. Rather, variations would be made in the rate of (sales) tax on motor vehicles. Why not do the same with monetary control?

In principle, especially if alternatives do not work, the case for taxation is difficult to deny. We tax alcohol, cigarettes and other commodities not just for their revenue-raising capacities but because excessive consumption has powerful externalities. Given the existence of the externality, such taxation can hardly be called distorting. Indeed, the absence of taxation is distorting. Yet in the case of money the externality of inflation, due to excess supply, is entirely why we would wish to levy a tax to restrict or vary output. Few would deny that inflation is a major distorter in financial and other markets.

At a practical level, taxation may be eschewed because production would not decline but merely be transferred overseas – in this case to Euromarkets – although the offset is unlikely to be complete, especially for retail banking (with the case of Germany offering an illustration). Use of taxation may also be queried because of the availability of close substitutes in the form of non-banking intermediaries and disintermediation to securities markets – in which case plugging up 'tax' loopholes may be the cost of effective monetary control.

But we would argue that the answer is more fundamental, and that Friedman's analogy, in so far as it applies to British monetary policy, is almost certainly predicated on a false premise – that the authorities want to control bank output. Rather, the authorities are aiming interest rates at macroeconomic variables, such as the price level, and alterations to the balance sheets of the banks emerge as a byproduct of that process but not as a necessary precondition.

Central banks were interested in controlling bank output when legal restrictions and regulations made banks and their liabilities 'special'. But in a number of ways, some concomitant with the removal of direct controls and lending directives and others a result of greater competitive forces in financial markets, banks have lost much of their specialness. They have lost their monopoly of credit cards and the payment mechanism. It is the discount houses and not banks which have exclusive access to the discount window of the Bank of England. Under the British deposit insurance system, bank deposits do not have full government backing.[9] In a number of ways the distinctions between banks and other financial institutions are now blurred where once they were sharp, while securitization has eroded many of the barriers which separated market transactions from intermediated ones.

These developments are examined in Chapter 9, which looks at change and innovation in the financial sector. Here we note that a system in which the banking system's responses to monetary policy have become more endogenized has consequences in turn for the use of monetary aggregates as intermediate targets. Benjamin Friedman (1975) and Bean (1983) have demonstrated in general terms the inferiority of using an endogenous variable as an intermediate target. The basic idea is that the information contained in the observations of the endogenous variable can be exploited better by transforming it from an intermediate target into an information variable. All that matters when the money supply becomes such an information variable (i.e. indicator) is whether the observed movements provide information which helps predict future values of the macroeconomic variables such as incomes and prices; the question of whether or not the money supply causes the movements in incomes and prices loses the importance formerly attached to it. Something along these lines seems to have occurred in British policy circles during the 1980s.

Conclusions

There are three principal models governing perceptions of how control of the monetary aggregates might proceed. There is the money demand model, according to which money is endogenous but the authorities can work on the determinants of demand – on incomes via fiscal policy, and on interest rates by monetary and funding policies. This was the rationale offered by Friedman for what the UK authorities were doing. He himself advocated control via control of the monetary base. This involves appeal to the high-powered money multiplier model. One limitation of this model is that it applies at best to retail banking activities, whereas the broad aggregates initially targeted by the authorities encompass wholesale banking activities to which the model seems inapplicable. Another limitation is that the implied endogenization of the interest rate would be unacceptable to the authorities (though it is precisely this kind of reservation which determined advocates of monetary base control seek to override). The authorities themselves seem to have been guided by yet another model, that inspired by the credit counterparts approach. The counterparts approach has an imperialistic tendency, according to which fiscal policy, funding policy and monetary policy (in the sense of short-term interest rate control) are all implicated in the requirement to control the broad aggregate, though not in the ways implied by Friedman.

The original monetary base control controversy melted away as inflation came down without the need to change the basis of control, and the authorities' attention switched from targeting the money supply to the exchange rate. All participants in the controversy had assumed – our rationale of policy suggests incorrectly – that the point of monetary base control was to hit targets for broad money more effectively. It is something of a curiosity therefore that in the later 1980s the authorities, while dropping targets for broad money, adopted them for the wide monetary base (M0) itself. But this was not monetary control for its own sake: rather, movements in M0 were interpreted as indicators of the movement of nominal demand and were an argument in the interest rate reaction function – a leading one, but not the only one.

Interest rate policy was thus involved in all this, but a distinction should be drawn between short-term and long-term interest rates. As explained in the next chapter, the authorities can be considered to treat short-term interest rates as an instrument (despite some qualifications). For long rates, the situation is different. The authorities would sooner not be thought of as treating long rates as an instrument, though funding policy implies effects on long rates and on the yield curve. As attention shifted from control of the money supply, management of short-term interest rates seemed to become more clearly the backbone of monetary policy. This is recounted in the next chapter.

Notes

1. Wholesale or corporate banking was first analyzed by Revell (1968). A detailed analysis of wholesale banking is made by Lewis and Davis (1987, Chapter 4).
2. Funds placed in the reserve requirement could be paid a market rate of return; yet changes in the requirement would still oblige banks to alter their demands for non-reserve assets.
3. We should reiterate that the tax effect is not the only effect of special deposits, for these pre-empt part of the balance sheet, which a fiscal imposition on banking activity or bank deposits would not. Courakis (1987) examines the parallel and the difference between a fiscal imposition and a reserve requirement in detail.
4. This way of expressing the financing identity should not be read as implying that the net flows in the United Kingdom must run in these directions. In the latter part of the 1980s, for example, the government and overseas sectors were net lenders, while the private non-financial sector was correspondingly a net borrower. See Chapter 9, section 5.
5. The link between the two can be made from row 1 of Table 6.5 where

$$\Delta H + \Delta GS = G - T + \Delta Res$$

That is if the official sector is running a deficit and/or adding to international reserves then it must be issuing high-powered money and interest-bearing government securities. The latter can be acquired by either banks or the non-bank private sector so that

$$\Delta H - \Delta GS_B = G - T - \Delta GS_p + \Delta Res$$

Substituting the right-hand side of this expression into (6.20) gives

$$\Delta M = \Delta H + \Delta GS_B + \Delta A - \Delta NDL$$

The last three items on the right-hand side can be described loosely as the net non-cash assets of the banks and, from the balance sheet of the banking sector in row 4,

$$\Delta GS_B + \Delta A - \Delta NDL = \Delta D - \Delta R$$

Using equation (6.16) we can rewrite this as

$$\Delta M = \Delta H + \frac{1-r}{d+r} \cdot \Delta H = \frac{1+d}{d+r} \cdot \Delta H$$

6. MO, the wide monetary base, consists of notes and coin held by the public and banks plus bankers' operational deposits at the Bank of England. It differs from the monetary base (H) defined earlier due to the exclusion of required reserves held by banks at the Bank of England. In principle, a monetarist would see this difference as being of importance, since it is possible to imagine a multiple expansion of bank deposits and the money supply from an expansion of the reserves base which is absorbed fully into required reserves, leaving operational deposits and till money unchanged. On this reasoning, MO is an incorrect aggregate to target. However, as the required cash ratio is in effect a fixed *sum* and special deposits are unused, the distinction between the two base aggregates has no practical significance.

7. With the classification of the Abbey National Building Society as a bank, the £M3 and M3C series were discontinued after June 1989. The presentation underlying Table 6.6 can now be found in official publications redefined for M4 which (cf. Table 6.1) includes *inter alia* building societies.

8. Perhaps not surprisingly, Goodhart suggests that this might well happen – that under an effective monetary base control regime, banks' demand for base money might have a higher mean (to give insurance) and also greater conditional variance.

9. A statutory Deposit Protection Scheme for bank depositors has been in operation since February 1982. Under 1987 amendments to the Banking Act, cover was set at 75 per cent of the first £20,000 of sterling deposits held with authorized institutions, giving a maximum payout per depositor of £15,000. The fund is financed by a levy on all authorized institutions.

7

Control of interest rates

Introduction

The abolition of exchange control in 1979 and the subsequent reforms of the monetary system in 1980–1 appeared to respond to two principal desiderata. One was to set the British banking system on a footing competitive with global banking; this implied most notably the removal of direct controls, the operation of which have a tax-like effect, and accordingly the reserve asset ratio and the corset were abolished.[1] Another, it would seem, was to provide a setting in which the control of the monetary aggregates might be pursued through the techniques of monetary base control. The Bank of England remarked that 'while no decision has been taken to introduce monetary base control, which would represent an important change of policy, the present moves would be consistent with a gradual evolution in that direction.'[2] The Chancellor of the Exchequer amplified this: 'Apart from providing immediate benefits, these changes should help to produce information relevant to assessing the long-term potential of monetary base control.'[3] To this end, steps were taken to lower the profile of interest rate decisions with a view to freeing them from political inhibitions. The accompanying rhetoric spoke of interest rates being 'more determined by the market'. In the event, the ambition to pursue a course of monetary base control withered as inflation fell and emphasis switched from tight control of the money supply to a more eclectic and looser form of monetary targeting, with increasing weight being given to the exchange rate as the proximate policy target (this is described in the next chapter).

The new arrangements, while directed at allowing more flexibility in interest rates – which was seen as one of the requirements of a putative monetary base control – ended up as a framework in which the authorities can exert a powerful influence on interest rates in the pursuit of other objectives. In fact, this might seem an understatement: in the way in which it was used from 1988 onwards, certainly, it seemed that the Bank's influence amounts to a power, in the last resort, to determine interest rates (within limits); if the right set of interest rates does not seem to be thrown up by the market, the Bank can apply an override power to bring them quickly into line. Or it can nudge the market into the posture it desires by less dramatic methods. [4]

The set of interest rates we are discussing here are those lying at the short end of the spectrum, the various money market rates and the Bank's base rate, which is a key rate for the constellation of fixed but adjustable borrowing and lending rates governing the business of the banking system and its competitors. The Bank's influence over longer rates is somewhat weaker and more indirect.

In the discussion which follows we focus first on these key money market rates and the nature of the Bank's influence over them. We then discuss the effects of the Bank's operations on longer-term interest rates. The last part of the chapter examines the place of interest rates in the transmission mechanism.

7.1 The Bank and the money market

Present techniques do not differ all that much from the traditional picture of Bank of England money market operations, as for example found in the Macmillan Report of 1931 or in Richard Sayers (1957) *Central Banking after Bagehot*. In it, the Bank's ability to influence short rates of interest depends ultimately on the fact that the commercial banks in the system have a need for central bank money – reserves at the Bank and currency. Historically, this demand was reinforced by required cash ratios. Given this demand, and a mechanism for redistributing surpluses between individual banks, the focus becomes the banking system's net requirement for central bank money. If the system is short it can, traditionally through the intermediary of the discount houses, go to the Bank of England and borrow from or discount bills with the Bank to meet the shortage. At this point the Bank can enforce a rate of interest (or price) of its own choosing. Since the Bank can anticipate and if necessary create a shortage of central bank money it can put itself in the position of the final arbiter on money market interest rates. An arbitrage mechanism reinforced by learnt reactions ensures that the Bank's control over the rate at which central bank money can be obtained spreads quickly to other related rates. In this way the Bank becomes the price-leader for the banking system: this is the term used by Sayers to describe Bank of England operations after 1825.[5]

The reforms of 1980–1 repeated refrains heard in the Competition and Credit Control reforms of 1971: a desire to put the banking system on a competitive footing and a desire to reduce the Bank's price leadership profile. In the 1971 reforms, the required ratios were reduced – the cash ratio to 1.5 per cent from 8 per cent and the reserve assets ratio (erstwhile liquid assets ratio) from 28 per cent to 12.5 per cent. In 1981 the reserve assets ratio was scrapped and a cash ratio introduced of only 0.5 per cent, subsequently reduced to 0.45 per cent; the reserves held under this requirement are described as non-operational deposits and the declared purpose of the ratio was (and is) to provide the Bank of England with an income (corresponding to the interest that may be earned on it). Besides the non-operational deposits held under this convention, banks were also required to hold a credit balance of operational deposits, for which however no minima were prescribed.

In 1971 Bank rate was 'abolished' and a minimum lending rate (MLR) substituted for it. MLR was to be related directly to a market-determined rate, the Treasury bill rate, standing just 0.5 per cent above it, but this attempt to shift the determination of Bank rate to the market was abandoned and from May 1978, MLR was determined and announced directly by the Bank. In 1981 MLR was in turn abolished; shortages were to be relieved at rates not announced in advance and broadly market-related. But this attempt to play down the intervention of the Bank has also been suspended on some notable occasions, when a post-1978 MLR has in effect been reimposed, but it has not yet been superseded by a permanently different arrangement. Another feature of the continuity is that, throughout, the Bank has continued to deal with the established discount houses; it is with these institutions, rather than with the banks directly, that the Bank prefers to deal in relieving shortages of central bank money.[6] On the other hand, the 1980–1 reforms greatly increased the number of banks for which the 0.5 per cent cash requirement was necessary. At the same time, where the Bank's operations were predominantly conducted in Treasury bills, in the changed conditions of the 1980s and especially up to 1985 the emphasis was shifted to dealings in commercial bills.

How, then, does the current system work? Some helpful descriptions have been offered not only by the Bank itself (*Bank of England Quarterly Bulletin*, August 1988) but also by Llewellyn and Tew (1988), the Bank for International Settlements (Kneeshaw and van den Bergh, 1989),

Wilson (1989), and Llewellyn (1990). The second of these references offers a useful international perspective, illustrating the extent to which the themes underlying the changes in the Bank's procedures are global themes. However, none gets quite to the essence of the Bank's operations.

By way of background, Figure 7.1 depicts the money market under three different regimes: monetary base control and a completely inelastic supply of reserves (S_0); interest rate pegging, and a completely elastic reserves supply (S_1); and where reserves supplied by market operations (R_0), as under monetary base control, can be supplemented by borrowed reserves at above ruling market rates (i.e. a penal rate), giving the supply curve R_0AS_2. This third case corresponds most closely to the pre-1980 system, in which in order to tighten monetary conditions, less of the system's reserves needs were met by open market operations and more came from borrowings as the market intermediaries, the discount houses, were forced 'into Bank', putting upward pressure upon market rates generally. The present system, while seemingly more subtle, effectively works *as if* the pre-1980 system and a curve such as R_0AS_2 were in place. Before examining the workings we look to the institutional features of the money market.

Institutional features of the money market

Three features of the money market are of importance. One concerns the payments system. Payments to and by the government are centralized through the Bank of England, which acts as the main banker to the government and holds its liquid assets. Although the government budget deficit is generally funded fully over the financial year (overfunding was stopped in 1985), there are substantial day-to-day alterations in the cash position. Banks collectively gain cash when the Exchequer has a deficit, and lose cash when it has a surplus. Final settlement of cash each day between the Bank and the banking system, and within the banking system, takes place by transactions on the accounts of the London clearing banks at the Bank of England. These banks hold non-interest-bearing operational balances at the Bank to meet the ebb and flow of transactions. In doing so they have a strong incentive to economize on their holdings by improved information about their prospective cash flows. Estimates are put out each day by the Bank of the budget deficit, flows over the foreign exchanges and gilts markets (which are settled on subsequent days), maturing Treasury bills and discount house lending repaid, and shifts in the public's currency holdings (which have large intra-week fluctuations). But the existence of a facility in London for

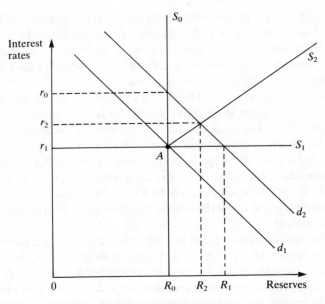

S_0 Monetary base targeting. In the face of an increased demand for reserves, reserves are maintained at the level R_0 consistent with the monetary base target, so that the full impact of a shift in demand falls upon interest rates, which rise from r_1 to r_0.

S_1 Interest rate pegging. In response to an increase in the demand for reserves, reserves of amount $R_1 - R_0$ are supplied by market actions to keep interest rates at the level appropriate for overall policy goals.

S_2 Reserves are supplied by a combination of market operations and borrowing facilities. Extra reserves of $(R_2 - R_0)$ are supplied in response to a shift in demand by allowing institutions to borrow at a penal (above ruling market) rate, forcing market rates up to r_2.

Figure 7.1   Interest rate determination in the money market under different reserves regimes.

settling large cheques on the same day that they are presented means that no participant can know for certain what the net cash position will be at the end of the day. Yet banks are generally expected to keep their operational accounts at the Bank in credit (although the accounts are sometimes overdrawn) and are unable in normal circumstances to borrow reserves through the discount window as in the United States. Instead, two other safety valves come into play, and this is a second feature of the British money market.

One safety valve is inherent in the Bank's transactions. Dealing to maintain the desired cash position occurs twice daily, enabling some intra-day reaction to contrary trends. The other is the borrowing facility held by the discount houses, which are chosen intermediaries between the central bank and the rest of the banking system. 'Tradition' is the best answer to the question of why the discount houses are chosen for this role, for the Bank's market strategies took shape when the most important short-term assets in the financial system were not Treasury bills but those issued by commercial firms. The discount brokers were experts in the assessment and fine-grading of credit risks and they selected, and insured by means of accepting them, bills suitable to be held in their own and others' portfolios. The present relationship between the discount houses and the banks was in place by 1825, although it was not until 1890 that the discount houses were accepted as the main route through which bills came to the Bank for rediscount (with Bank rate being the rate at which the Bank of England would discount first-class bills of exchange; the term was later extended to cover the rate on the Bank's short-term loans to the discount houses).

The discount houses' borrowing facility at the Bank is often described misleadingly as the 'lender of last resort facility'. The day-to-day borrowings from the Bank to meet temporary shortages of cash in the system are more akin to discount window borrowing, as occurs in the US system. One important difference, however, is that while borrowers from the discount window in the United States pay a rate which is usually below the cost of comparable funds in the market, the discount houses almost always pay a rate at or above market rates, so that use of the facility is rationed by price and not by moral suasion, as in the United States. Nevertheless, because the discount houses have such privileged access to assured funds, the UK banks are willing to hold most of their excess reserves in the form of deposits with the discount houses instead of in the form of operational balances at the Bank.

A third institutional feature is the Bank's market operations in the money market, which in recent years have again been conducted principally with eligible bank bills. These are commercial bills drawn to finance a short-term self-liquidating transaction, with an initial maturity of no more than six months, accepted by an eligible bank, and bought from a discount house and therefore carrying at least two 'good' names. Bills can be bought outright or on a sale-and-repurchase basis, but in all cases the obligation to make an offer in respect of price and amount lies with the houses. The Bank then responds and is able to influence short-term rates by its reactions to these offers.

Daily operations

The system works as follows. On a daily basis, forecasts are made of the banking system's requirement for central bank money (cash) and of the surplus or shortage implied. This estimate is circulated electronically early in the day (at present at about 9.45 a.m.) in the form of an overall figure (rounded to the nearest £50 million), with a summary of the main contributory factors including maturing assistance, net Exchequer transactions (which incorporate transactions in the gilts and foreign exchange markets), the increase or decrease in note issue, and any divergence of clearing banks' operational balances from their target level the previous evening; an update of the overall estimate (but not the contributing factors) is released in the same way as the day progresses. In the event of a forecast cash shortage, the discount houses may then receive an invitation to offer eligible bills to the Bank for purchase, indicating when doing so the price at which they wish to sell. The Bank then normally buys bills at the cheapest price (down to its stop rate) up to the amount of the shortage.[7] The results of its purchases are communicated to the market, which thus knows the discount rates the Bank has accepted. Later in the day, after the bill operations have been completed, discount houses may approach the Bank to borrow from it, at rates determined by the Bank. Finally, there is override: 'On particular occasions. . .the Bank may choose to alter its arrangements, for example to deal with exceptional money flows or to give a signal to the market about interest rates' (Bank of England, 1988a, pp. 391–401).

The normal working of the system thus has the Bank agreeing to relieve the shortage, if there is one (which is the usual case), at rates apparently of the discount houses' own choosing; in this sense, the rates are determined by the market. But the Bank has the power to influence the size of the shortage by appropriate operations in other markets (including sales of Treasury bills), and has general override powers. These have been used on occasions (see the observations denoted 'lending rate' in Figure 7.2) when the Bank has refused to relieve the whole shortage at rates determined by the discount houses' offer, and the normal procedures have been overridden by an announcement that discount houses wishing to borrow are invited to do so at 2.30 p.m. On the occasion of these '2.30 arrangements' the interest rate used by the Bank has normally been published; in 1985 the Bank went further and simply announced the MLR it would be using for a short period ahead in its discount house lending. This use of override suggests that the Bank is willing and able, when the need arises, to jolt interest rates into a different range from the one the market was expecting.

The use of override has become more determined over time, reflecting the evolution of policy to more explicit management of interest rates and the consequential realities of market operations. One result of this development must be that the prices at which the discount houses offer bills will more than ever embody a view about the price the Bank wants to

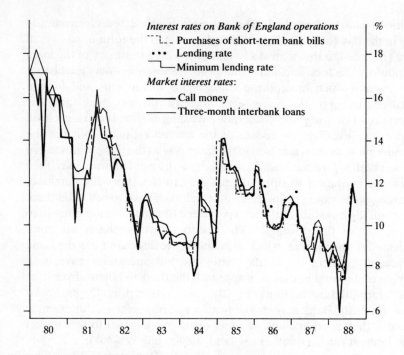

Figure 7.2   United Kingdom: money market interest rates.
Source: Kneeshaw and van den Bergh (1989).

see. In these circumstances the supposition that these prices represent a market view independent of the market's evaluation of the authorities' intentions becomes a fiction. The authorities cannot escape from their own responsibility for interest rate setting.

The Bank's position in the money markets clearly affords it decisive influence on the very short-term rates determined there. However, its object is frequently to influence interest rates slightly further along the maturity spectrum and to influence banks' base rate – itself one of the key measures of the current impact of monetary policy. This is particularly the case when the management of the exchange rate is paramount, or in circumstances of excess demand (as in 1988) when the Chancellor is determined not to make interim adjustments to fiscal policy and so requires the burden of adjustment to fall on interest rate policy, with particular reference to three-month rates, base rate and thus the building societies' rates.

The structure of interest rates

Part of the explanation for the fact that the Bank is able to influence rates up to three months very closely is simply that it can – and does – extend its money market dealings readily across the spectrum. Indeed for operational purposes the Bank divides the bills it is prepared to deal in into four maturity classes or bands; the top, or longest maturity, band is 64–91 days and by varying the amount of paper in this band in which it deals the Bank can influence Treasury bill rate closely. The earliest aspirations for the new policy were, essentially, that the Bank should direct its operations to the lower (shortest maturity) bands, but two factors seem to have frustrated this desire. First, as we have already noted, broad policy objectives developed in such a way that the Bank wanted to influence the higher band rates – though this was an influence chiefly from 1985 on. Before that, for a different reason, the Bank felt obliged to move into the higher bands: the policy of overfunding (described below) produced a situation in which the Bank accumulated a large volume of commercial bills. The redemption of these alone provided immediate cash pressures which the Bank sought to force forward in term by buying more higher band paper – with the result that the need for a conscious policy about these rates was forced upon it.

Another part of the explanation of the fact that by operating in the money market the Bank can influence a nexus of rates important to it is provided by the forces of arbitrage and speculation. At the short end of the market there is a mix of market-clearing, highly flexible, interest rates and administered, fixed-but-adjustable rates. On the one hand there are the bill rates, rates on overnight money and other interbank rates of maturities through to three months, rates on certificates of deposit and so on; on the other, there is the Bank of England's stop rate and MLR, banks' base rates and building society borrowing and mortgage rates. Adjustments in the administered rate are nowadays less inhibited by the costs of change than used to be claimed, while the opportunities for arbitrage tend to force prompt adjustment in highly integrated markets. Usually (although there have been exceptional occasions), a given change in banks' base rates is likely to be communicated to building societies' deposit and share rates and hence to mortgage rates quite promptly. A failure to adjust fairly quickly will be penalized by loss of market share or by marginal loss-making on surplus funds. Competition disciplines the margin between deposit and lending rates both for banks and building societies. The arbitrage process may none the less still be inhibited by political factors and by banks' and building societies' regard for customer relations.

As in goods markets, there is an element of 'custom market pricing'

(Okun, 1981) in banking markets in which the interests of a long-run customer relationship indicate stabilizing the rate set on loans and refraining from the exploitation of the last penny of short-run profit maximizing. More simply, the banks are not politically popular, especially in recessions when base rates lag falls in market rates: in 1981, an excess profits tax was levied; in 1991, adverse press came from small business customers. The presence of fixed-but-adjustable rates stimulates speculation as well as arbitrage. When base rates are thought likely to change (say, to rise), speculative position-taking involving a matched transaction in a market asset will be stimulated (for example, if base rates are thought likely to rise it may pay to borrow in the long end of the market and lend to the banks). An established equilibrium relationship will change if perceptions of the future alter, and in this case either the administered rates will in due course change in line or perceptions will change again and market rates will fall back into their previous relationship with the administered rates. Generally, allowing for differences in perceived risk (Treasury bills are more secure than commercial bills, which are more secure than CDs for the same term) and liquidity (resaleability), arbitrage opportunities can be expected to be swiftly eliminated.

The adequacy of market operations

Dow and Saville (1988) consider there to be an element of paradox in the fact that with so small a quantitative impact in the markets the Bank can exert such widespread effects on interest rates – with many adjustments, e.g. in base rate, happening 'automatically'. They assign a major responsibility for this to the fact that because market rates are indeterminate within a range of their fundamental values, the intervention of the authorities falls on especially receptive ground. The steer given by the authorities thus becomes decisive. A closely analogous piece of reasoning may be applied to the intervention by central banks in foreign exchange markets. Here intervention is often trivial in relation to daily turnover but may provide a signal that the market craves. Still, in the domestic money markets the Bank really is potentially much bigger than it is in the foreign exchange market. What seems to be a pure bootstrap effect may be viewed alternatively as the conclusion of a process of learning in which the driving force is the belief that the Bank could, if it wished, persist in operations which will force the interest rate changes that take place automatically to take place by arbitrage. Participants in the market are well aware that the Bank could make effective its views by altering the form and cost at which reserves are supplied, forcing the system up a curve such as S_2 in Figure 7.1. Because the market knows that this can happen, there is no need for it actually to take place. When all is said and done, the key is that the Bank controls the issue of central bank money in the face of demand which is relatively insensitive to interest rates.

Stated alternatively, the reason why the central bank's transactions are so important is that they are conducted with cash or central bank money. This can be produced by the government at virtually zero cost and in unlimited amounts for the purpose of market purchases. For market sales, the government is limited by the amount of securities it is willing to sell. Accordingly, the authorities' power as a market transactor hinges on two factors. One is their monopoly of the manufacture of cash. The second is the continued acceptability of cash in transactions.

Taking this line of argument one step further, there is the question of whether, at an abstract level, market actions are sufficient for monetary stabilization. As we noted in Chapter 2, the workings of a fiat money system have been extensively studied by Patinkin and others. Patinkin (1961) established the minimum prescriptions which must be set in order to assure the determinacy of the price level. In a general equilibrium framework, some important nominal magnitude needs to be tied down or made in inelastic supply, and since with N assets only $N-1$ rates of return are independent, some rate of return must be exogenously determined. Usually, in monetary theory, the nominal quantity is conceived of as the fiat issue of 'money', used as the means of payment, and the interest rate exogenously set is the zero return on money. As the money supply is cash plus bank deposits, banks are grouped with the central bank as part of the control core in this conception and their deposit rate is assumed to be fixed (at zero). This is a not unrealistic description of how many national monetary systems used to look, but in the last chapter we argued that this grouping is no longer a good description of the way in which the monetary system in the United Kingdom (and other countries) is evolving. With deregulation, banks can no longer be considered part of the core, but must instead be grouped with the other endogenously determined parts of the economy. Thus the area of policy control shrinks, at least at this simplified conceptual level, to the central bank's own balance sheet. The fixed rate of interest then becomes that on central bank money (base money, cash) effectively set at zero. The important nominal quantity which must be fixed is not the quantity of money but the amount of cash, determined by open market operations.

While standard macroeconomic theory thus gives the monetary authorities the power to control macroeconomic variables of importance, the more pertinent question perhaps is whether they should have the power. Proponents of private money see such fiat money as an entirely artificial creation, conceived in sin and likely to remain sinful. They would like the government's monopoly of money creation removed so that private money issuers could be given the opportunity to introduce a more stable money, presumably commodity-based and invulnerable to debasement. It must also be remembered that internal stabilization is not the only route to price stability; external stabilization can be sought by exchange rate management.

But this is to run ahead of the argument, for these issues are the subject matter of later chapters. In the remainder of this chapter we review the workings of interest rate management.

7.2 Funding and overfunding

The money supply formation tables can be arranged to show that, as a matter of arithmetic, sales of debt to the non-bank public reduce the positive impact of the PSBR on the money supply (see p. 158). In the 1980s this relationship, given the emphasis at first laid on the achievement of monetary targets, produced the phenomenon known as overfunding – sales of gilts to the public in excess of the PSBR itself.

Managing the debt so as to achieve, or help achieve, short-term targets for monetary growth is formally different from earlier objectives; yet there is a strong link between the objectives of earlier times and the monetary control objective. With a large national debt/GDP ratio after World War II, there was an apprehension in policy-making circles in the United Kingdom that prudence required the debt to be held at a high average maturity so as to render tractable the problem of renewing maturing debt and to avoid the danger of the effective monetization of the debt with the inflationary consequences that would imply. 'Funding the national debt' was a phrase then used to describe a policy of maintaining and if possible increasing the average maturity of the outstanding stock of debt. Financing the PSBR and the maturing debt was viewed by the authorities in Tew's graphic phrase (Tew, 1978) as dealing with the 'flooding problem'. Even at the end of the 1960s the ratio of the UK national debt to GDP was still high and seen to be considerably higher than in other developed countries.[8] The authorities felt they were engaged in a perpetual struggle to pump out the floodwaters.

The struggle was seen as requiring the development of a wide and receptive market for gilt-edged securities; and this in turn suggested to the authorities that they should refrain from indulging a conscious policy towards interest rates on longer-dated stocks since to do so would impugn the acceptability of the bonds to the public. If the authorities were known to have an active policy towards long rates, 'investors' would apprehend that the value of the bonds they held might be changed at the caprice of the authorities and this apprehension would in itself deter investors from participating in the market. This consideration even inhibited the authorities from employing too obviously the device of cutting prices to stimulate sales; following the logic further, the authorities might be led to *support* bond prices against a fall, the position which emerged by the mid 1960s. While tactics were subsequently changed, with the authorities increasingly less heavily involved, the market has remained captive throughout to the so-called 'Duke of York' sales strategy. The market buys as bond prices rise and desists from buying when bond prices seem certain to slide. The resultant series of erratic investor 'strikes' and the switchback of gilt sales can be seen as a graphic illustration of Keynes' speculative demand for money.[9] They have not disappeared with the changes in the authorities' tactical operations since 1979, the considerable reduction in the ratio of the national debt to GDP or the conversion of the PSBR to a PSDR (Public Sector Debt Repayment).[10]

Overfunding

Overfunding, defined as selling to the non-bank public more than all of the PSBR, though by no means without precedent in earlier years, became a prominent feature of gilt-edged market management in the first half of the 1980s (Figure 7.3). This policy resulted from the conjunction of a continued desire to target the growth of the broad money supply with the realization through experience that the control of short-term interest rates was insufficient to provide the whole solution. (Indeed, it would be fair to observe that the phrasing of the medium-term financial strategy had always referred to the need to avoid 'undue reliance on interest rates'.) Neither were direct controls seen to offer an acceptable alternative (Chapter 6). Finally, in the face of a buoyant demand for bank credit, even a strict fiscal policy – bolstered if necessary by asset sales to produce a low PSBR – could not be relied upon to provide for monetary growth at an acceptable rate. In the circumstances, overfunding the PSBR became the immediate objective of debt management policy. The policy was pursued until mid 1985, when the rapid growth of £M3 was firmly diagnosed as a non-inflationary artefact of financial innovation and the former target for it was effectively suspended.[11]

In the meantime the policy of overfunding turned out to have some uncomfortable effects. In particular, as the sales of long-dated securities successfully pressured the banking system, the authorities encountered correspondingly large offers from the banking sector of commercial bills for sale; the sales were designed to repair the banks' liquidity needs. As the Bank bought in bills in the context of continuing overfunding it not only accumulated a 'bill mountain' but put itself in the position of lending to the private sector short-term while borrowing from it long-term; in

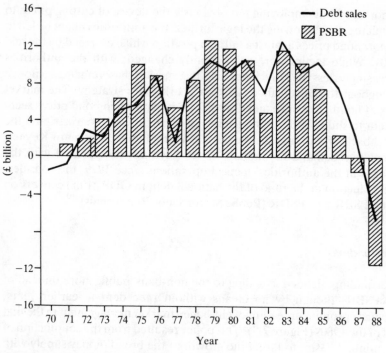

Figure 7.3 Funding the PSBR.

effect, by itself borrowing long and lending short, the Bank was offsetting the intermediation of the banks which were borrowing short and lending long. However, the nationalization of credit implied was embarrassing to the Government and the Bank responded by extending the definition of eligible paper that it was prepared to buy, subsequently purchasing (on repurchase agreement) large quantities of shipbuilding and export credits.

Another source of embarrassment was the likelihood of induced bill arbitrage, since the Bank's policy of purchasing commercial bills was alleged to have produced profitable opportunities not only to switch from borrowing by way of bank advances to borrowing by way of bill finance ('soft' arbitrage), but to borrow by way of bill finance with a view to redepositing with the banking system ('hard' arbitrage). Clearly, while soft arbitrage simply redistributed the form of bank credit, hard arbitrage would lead to a parallel increase in both sides of the banks' balance sheet and could call into question the success of the policy in restraining monetary growth. Careful calculations suggested to the Bank that the scope for hard arbitrage was limited; nevertheless the potential consequences of such a market response were felt to be sufficiently important for the Bank to intervene directly to request the commercial banks involved not to promote this activity (*Bank of England*, 1985, p. 189).

These difficulties were brought to an end with the switch in policy emphasis in mid 1985, and to this extent it seems to have been the policy, rather than any in-built distortion of preferences in the financial system, that was (proximately) accountable for the problem. In so far as such distortions were relevant, however, the motivating influence of inflationary expectations (Bain, 1984) – which may have encouraged long-term lenders and discouraged long-term (private sector) borrowers (with opposing influences at the short end of the market) – itself subsided about this time.

The withdrawal from the policy of overfunding left the Bank essentially dependent on a single instrument of policy – its market operations to exert control over the short-term rate of interest.

Variation in technique

With the removal of the premium on funding policy, fascination with the development of new techniques for selling debt, which reached a high point in the late 1970s, declined.

The authorities' time-honoured approach consists of 'opening the tap' on a stock by announcing the availability of a bond with defined characteristics at a certain price, close to prevailing market prices. The stock is then fed to the market as the market is attracted by it. The system of tap stocks came in for criticism in a context in which greater emphasis was placed on the need to control the monetary aggregates. Rather than leaving gilt sales to the appetite of the market for existing tap stocks with a resultant alternation of feast and famine in gilt sales, the argument became that the necessary amount of gilt sales could be calculated and realized by a corresponding *auction*. By definition, the auction would realize – at some price – the sales required. This suggestion was resisted by the authorities, who argued that despite short-term disturbances in gilt sales the annual record was more reassuring and that the task of forecasting the size and the frequency of the auctions under the alternative system would be far from straightforward.

Beginning in 1987 a series of experimental auctions was held (see Bank of England, 1988c for an account), from which the authorities drew mild encouragement. But in general the authorities have strongly preferred to innovate in improving the attractiveness of gilts and adopting a somewhat more flexible stance in meeting the market's demands. One important innovation was the introduction of index-linked stocks initially restricted in availability to retired persons but subsequently made more generally available. These innovations have combined with other measures to add to a greater range in the authorities' offerings and a greater ability to feed gaps in the structure of available stocks. Together with the conversion of the PSBR to a PSDR, as the government budget swung from deficit to surplus and government securities were redeemed, and with the withdrawal of the overfunding policy, these innovations, together with the auction experiments, have effectively silenced calls that bond auctions should play the predominant role in selling government debt – calls that were loudly voiced at the outset of the decade (see, for example, Griffiths, 1979).[12] Interestingly, with the conversion of the PSBR to a PSDR the auction procedure has been converted on occasions to a 'reverse auction' for bond *purchases* by the Bank!

7.3 The effects of interest rate policy

The authorities' objectives, including that of maximizing the scope for the 'market solution', together with developments in the financial system, have produced a situation in which control of short-term interest rates is in essence the sole effective monetary regulator at the authorities' disposal. Because of arbitrage operations across the maturity spectrum, operations on short-term rates will spill over into longer rates, to an extent which depends on the market's anticipations of the authorities' future policies in the money markets; and 'preferred habitat' considerations may still make the term structure manipulable to changes in the relative quantities of debt offered at various points in the maturity spectrum. To whatever extent these linkages exist, however, it does not appear that the authorities seek to use them in a conscious way. Thus market operations constitute the important policy instrument and the structure of short-term rates is the operational target of policy. Because the authorities in parallel developed the view that fiscal policy should not be adjusted between annual budgets, it in fact appears that short-term interest rates have to bear the entire burden of short-run adjustment policy. Consequently, the mechanisms by which changes in short-term interest rates impact on the economy, the size of the effects created and their timing is a key issue in policy formation and the understanding of policy.

Real and nominal rates

The authorities' proximate control is, of course, over nominal, not real, rates of interest. We say 'proximate' because the Dalton 'cheap money' experiment of 1946–7 convincingly demonstrated that the authorities cannot hold rates at levels well below those which the market regards as appropriate without pumping in liquidity at an inflationary rate.[13] With the nominal rate which the market expects to rule equal to the real rate plus the expected rate of inflation, the authorities can soon find themselves in the position of chasing after an ever-accelerating target, as their market purchases feed inflation expectations and encourage existing holders of gilts to take advantage of the unnaturally high price of gilts on offer.

Standard economic analysis in any case emphasizes that it is real, not nominal, rates that are likely to matter most for spending, for those undertaking expenditure plans are assumed not to suffer from money illusion when they make decisions involving interest as an opportunity cost. In the very short run, the distinction is of little consequence; inertia in the movement of prices (and consequently, inertia in expectations of prices) means that a nominal rate change is a real rate change, not simply on impact but over a significant period of time. In the long run, as stressed by Wicksell and by several authors in the new classical macroeconomics tradition, real interest rates are not even proximately controllable by the authorities and attempts to target a real rate may easily yield unstable solutions (unless they feed back to a nominal quantity anchor). Indeed, difficulties of this kind were cited by the authorities in the 1970s as among the reasons for their non-ideological embrace of monetary targets in a period of high and variable inflation (see Artis and Lewis (1981), pp. 41–2).

The impact of interest rates

The conventional wisdom of earlier decades, at least in the United Kingdom, was that interest rates were a feeble but uncertain tool of monetary policy, having effects as much through induced credit rationing as by any other means. The savings response was seen as theoretically ambiguous and empirically negligible. Investment appeared to be affected by accelerator considerations beyond anything else. Changes in interest rates could induce credit rationing, especially in the case of the building societies: a rise in bank interest rates unmatched to begin with by a rise in building society rates would slow down the inflow of funds into building societies and induce or reinforce the rationing of mortgages. Before the floating of exchange rates and the abolition of exchange control, interest rate variation was seen as an instrument for influencing capital flows to sustain a fixed exchange rate: the rather feeble effects of interest rates on the evolution of the domestic economy would be seen as fortunate in the light of the instability of capital flows. It would be undesirable to have the tail (hot money) wagging the dog (the domestic economy) too much. Uncertainty about the effects of interest rates was attributed to the role of expectations driven by interest rate changes regarded by the market as a signal of the authorities' diagnosis of the situation and the likely severity of future policy actions. Finally, it could of course always be argued that variations in real rates of interest were negligible before the onset of the post-OPEC inflation era. Artis (1978) described this conventional wisdom of an earlier period and the empirical support for it. It is a useful counterpoint to the present conventional wisdom.

Two major changes in the setting of policy have contributed to this change in view. First, the floating of the exchange rate alters the role of the interest rate in regard to external balance and allows the exchange rate to play a role in the transmission mechanism. Second, deregulation, innovation and increased competition in financial markets have transformed the access of individuals to the financial markets and raised their responsiveness to changes in interest rates. This is particularly stressed in a recent study by Dicks (1988), who suggests that in consequence 'the leverage of monetary policy may have been strengthened as a result of deregulation of the financial markets' (p. 2). If this statement seems somewhat paradoxical, it is because in the adjustment to the new financial conditions, consumers have greatly increased their credit/income ratios and this move towards a higher equilibrium ratio has been powerful in stimulating consumption. Interest rate increases would not seem a powerful preventative measure while this adjustment was going on. The argument is instead that at the higher ratios now achieved interest rate variations may have scope for considerable influence. In consequence of these changes, the conventional wisdom now claims a major impact of interest rates on the economy at large.[14]

In most of the measured models of the British economy, the short-term interest rate continues to be treated as the instrument of monetary policy, with money as an output (endogenous) variable. Term structure equations carry some of the effect of changes in the short rate through to longer rates. Changes in the control variable – usually Treasury bill rate – are transmitted to bank base rate and thence to banks' lending and borrowing rates and to building societies' rates. Expenditure on consumer durables and in some cases non-durables is immediately affected as is dwelling investment. The econometric specification is typically driven by some version of the life-cycle hypothesis. Rationing effects do not appear to be very significant. Direct interest rate effects on corporate investment are identified as significant but are not a major part of the story, with second-round accelerator-type influences more important.

The exchange rate is important in the transmission process. A rise in interest rates forces an appreciation of the exchange rate which in turn restrains prices, forces competitiveness down and, *ceteris paribus*, implies a fall in the constant price value of exports and an increase in imports. Wealth effects, with interest rate changes causing revaluations, can be significant in a number of behavioural equations. In the latest crop of estimates (see Wallis *et al.*, 1988) the domestic demand effects dominate in the short to medium run to the extent that the current balance improves, the effect of the fall in domestic demand more than compensating for the decline in competitiveness.

Re-estimation of model equations over a period during which the economic structure is perceived to have been changing, together with the integration of consistent expectations into the models, has made for quite large differences both between models and for a given model across adjoining vintages in the overall effect attributed to variations in interest rates (Wallis *et al.*, 1988). By way of illustration we summarize in Table 7.1 some of the results given in Easton's (1985) study of the importance of interest rates in UK models, and in Table 7.2 the results more recently provided by Wren-Lewis (1988) which reflect the latest re-estimation of the NIESR model and the integration in it of consistent expectations. The figures shown in Table 7.1 are estimates of the effect of a temporary two-point cut in short-term interest rates in the 1985 vintage of three mainstream UK macroeconometric models – those of the National Institute of Economic and Social Research (NIESR), Her Majesty's Treasury (HMT) and the London Business School (LBS). The choice of a *temporary* cut is dictated by the reasoning that, as the models include a version of the interest parity condition a reduction in the differential compared to the base run implies an expectation of appreciation. If the reduction is permanent either a continuous appreciation is in fact realized (under consistent expectations), or expectations are continuously disappointed; neither case is particularly appealing.[15] For purposes of the consistent expectations solution to the LBS model the interest rate cut is assumed to be, on impact, unexpected: otherwise there would be effects on economic variables *before* the cut takes place, due to anticipatory behaviour.

The figures shown in the lower half of the table are the difference between the model simulation with a two-year *temporary* cut of two points in short rates with the exchange rate free to adjust and the results of the same simulation with the exchange rate fixed. This difference is a measure of the work done by the exchange rate in the transmission mechanism.

The overall effect, in all three of the models represented in Table 7.1, is for a reduction in interest rates to raise output and prices and to worsen

192 *Control of interest rates*

Table 7.1 Comparative model responses to a temporary 2-point cut in short-term interest rates

End of year	Total effect			Difference from base	
	GDP (%)	EER (%)	Consumer prices (%)	Current balance (£m)	Long rates per cent points
NIESR					
1	0.07	−2.76	0.34	−365	−0.78
2	0.27	−7.22	1.20	−1,211	−0.81
HMT					
1	0.70	−4.40	0.34	−687	−0.59
2	1.21	−5.03	1.39	−576	−0.44
LBS[1]					
1	0.98	−8.40	1.28	−1,600	0.06
2	1.07	−5.07	2.64	−3,150	0.19
Contribution of exchange rate[2]					
NIESR					
1	−0.07	−2.76	0.34	−310	–
2	0.31	−7.22	1.30	−727	–
HMT					
1	0.25	−4.40	0.94	−397	0.03
2	0.34	−5.03	2.08	215	0.15
LBS[1]					
1	0.40	−8.40	1.62	−560	0.02
2	0.35	−5.07	3.06	810	0.10

Notes:
1. Results are those for the 5-year solution period shown in the source.
2. i.e. the difference between the simulation with the exchange rate free and the simulation with the exchange rate fixed.

Source: Easton (1985).

Table 7.2 Effects of a temporary (2-year) interest rate increase (+2 points) in NIESR model 11

End of year	GDP	Effective exchange rate (%)	Difference from base	
			Consumer prices (%)	Current balance (£m)
1	−0.7	2.6	−1.0	222
2	−0.7	0.8	−1.5	166
3	−0.1	0.1	−1.4	59

Source: Wren-Lewis (1988).

the current account of the balance of payments. There are some clear differences between the models. The NIESR model attributes the smallest price and output responses; the LBS model gives very large balance of payments impacts. Long rates in the LBS models go the other way from long rates in the NIESR and HMT models; people know the shock is temporary and expect gilt prices to fall (after an initial rise on impact) back towards the basic level. Expected capital losses are partially offset by an increase in coupons (the interest rate as measured), so that total returns do in fact fall in line with the cut in short rates. The lower half of the table indicates that the behaviour of the exchange rate itself is responsible for a strong price impulse (this is the subject of further examination in Chapter 8 below), and for an immediate worsening but eventual improvement in the current account balance. In the short term, J-curve effects dominate and all the models yield a worsening current payments position. In the second year two out of the three models give rise to an improvement in the current account from this source alone. The output effects are relatively small.

As explained above, recent developments give ample scope for a reassessment of the effects of interest rates. This is strongly exemplified in the more recent NIESR results shown in Table 7.2 (and it is paralleled by developments in other models too, notably including that of the Bank of England; cf. Easton, 1990). Although the results quoted in this table are for an increase in interest rates, a rough symmetry may be assumed to hold so that a comparison with the results quoted in Table 7.1, with sign reversed, is reasonable.[16] It can be seen that the output responses are now very much stronger than before, price responses somewhat stronger, and exchange rate and current balance effects *weaker*.[17] The exchange rate appreciates strongly on impact to validate the subsequent expectation of depreciation. It is important to stress that the more modest estimates of improvement now given of the current account adjustment give way in later years (not shown in the table) to deficits. Initial J-curve effects and then the effects of lower activity yield over the longer term to poorer competitiveness.

Conclusions

The principal weapon of monetary policy, in essence the only one, is now the authorities' control over short-term interest rates. They have assumed this control in rather forthright fashion in recent years, in contrast to an earlier phase when they endeavoured to cede the determination of interest rates to the market. This switch of emphasis has come with a switch away from monetary targets to exchange rate targets, along with a re-emphasis on the control of demand. In default of mid term fiscal correction between budgets, this adjustment burden has been borne by the rate of interest. This change of tack may be bolstered by, if not partly based on, some suggestions from the data that in the new climate of deregulated competition interest rate variations impact more strongly on the economy than was once believed. This evidence, which is by definition new, must be assessed as to some extent uncertain and speculative. An important channel of effect is the exchange rate, and monetary policy had, for some time before the decision to enter the Exchange Rate Mechanism, been concerned with the exchange rate. The reasons for this are explored in the next chapter.

Notes

1. While the supplementary special deposit (corset) was removed, a provision to call to ordinary special deposits remained, but has not been activated.
2. Bank of England, 1981, p. 21.
3. From the Chancellor's statement on economic policy on 24 November, partially reproduced in the *Economic Progress Report*, December 1980 (No. 128).
4. This is perhaps as well for, as the Governor recently noted, 'The instruments of monetary policy are limited; indeed in essence we are dependent upon a single instrument – the short term interest rate' (see the Governor's Seventh Mais Lecture 'The instruments of monetary policy', *Bank of England Quarterly Bulletin*, August 1987).
5. The Bank's price-leadership has taken a number of forms. From 1825 to 1844, the Bank's share of banking business was such that it could determine market rates by altering the rates charged to its own customers (Sayers, pp. 18–19). Following the Bank Charter Act of 1844 the Bank's share of ordinary banking business fell sharply, but Bank rate was not as yet rigidly

linked to other rates, and the Bank had to make its rates effective through open market operations. The Bank borrowed in the market against the collateral of government securities, reducing reserves of the joint-stock banks and bringing the bill rate up against its discount rate (Bank rate). After about 1878 pure Bank rate policy emerged as market rates simply followed periodic declarations of changes in Bank rate. It may be noted that such is the continuity of Bank operations that its market operations last century were through the agency of Mullens and Marshall: the government broker was a partner of Mullens until April 1986 when he and his team moved inside the Bank to its gilt-edged division.

6. From 1988 additional money market dealing counterparties have been invited to participate, but these continue to exclude banks though they may be bank-owned subsidiaries.

7. In the original official description of the Bank's operations under the new regime (Bank of England, 1982), emphasis was laid upon the Bank accepting offers which lay within prespecified, but unpublished, bands. In the latest description available no such reference appears. The paraphernalia of unpublished bands is perhaps futile, since the basic point is that the Bank is always prepared to relieve the whole shortage on terms and by means acceptable to it.

8. Tew (1978) quotes a Bank of England figure for the United Kingdom of 59 per cent, compared with 29 per cent in the United States and Canada, and 15 per cent or less in Italy, Germany and France (p. 230).

9. This description may make it sound as though investors are excessively myopic, even irrational agents; so it should be borne in mind that interest rate rises (bond price falls) often reflect the reaction to bad news (on inflation, the balance of payments or the exchange rate), while declines (rises in bond prices) are often a sign of improving fundamentals.

10. Total net debt of the public sector was 45.6 per cent of GDP in 1980 and had fallen to 38.6 per cent by 1988 (Bank of England, 1988b, p. 531).

11. The retrospective commentary in the Governor's Seventh Mais Lecture is very clear about this (Bank of England, 1987).

12. The authorities did adopt a tender system, with a pre-announced minimum price, as a means of introducing more flexibility into the setting of tap prices but this, as the Bank claimed, is not what the advocates of a full-blown auction system had in mind. (Bank of England, 1979.)

13. Mr Dalton, the Labour Chancellor, sought to force long-term rates down from 3 to 2.5 per cent, and the authorities found themselves buying more and more securities in the attempt. See R. S. Sayers (1951) for an examination of the policy.

14. If the argument is correct, it translates into the familiar IS/LM framework as a more elastic (i.e. horizontal) IS schedule. At the same time, deregulation of bank interest rates can be expected to result in an LM schedule which is less elastic with respect to absolute rates of interest, as the fluctuation of bank interest rates with market yields offsets to some extent the tendency of the demand for money to vary with 'the' rate of interest (Davis and Lewis, 1982). The combined effect of the hypothesized changes would be to render monetary policy more effective for internal stabilization. See Chapter 9, section 4 for a further discussion.

15. If expectations are consistent (as in the LBS model solution quoted in Table 7.1 and the later NIESR model revision quoted in Table 7.2), the effects of a

permanent interest rate change are precisely the reverse of what we might expect from a temporary shock. For example, as Wren-Lewis (1988) notes, a permanent increase in interest rates must imply depreciation and higher inflation 'not normally the aim of a restrictive monetary policy' (p. 43, n. 5).

16. It should be noted that the NIESR model solution values quoted in Table 7.2, unlike those shown for the NIESR and HMT models in Table 7.1, are for a consistent expectations mode. This change in model solution is part of the new appreciation of policy potential.

17. Wallis *et al.* (1988) note that the NIESR model, from exhibiting the most sluggish responses to interest rates in earlier versions, now exerts the more lively ones. See also Easton (1985) and Wren-Lewis (1988).

8

Exchange rate management and the EMS

Introduction

Exchange rate management involves using the instruments of policy, primarily those of foreign exchange market intervention and interest rate manipulation, in order to influence the exchange rate. In a regime of tight management these instruments are dedicated to targeting a relatively precise value of the exchange rate, in the limit a fixed rate; in a loosely managed regime the exchange rate simply appears in the list of intermediate variables in which the authorities have some interest. In order to manage the exchange rate the authorities may vary domestic interest rates and money supplies. They may also conduct market operations, i.e. intervene in the foreign exchange market, buying domestic currency assets when the currency is weak and selling them when it is strong: this can be regarded as monetary policy by another name. The market's perception that the authorities have a policy of some kind (or not, as the case may be) towards the exchange rate itself exerts an important influence and the actions they take, whether covertly or openly, as well as what they say, can be expected to influence the market's views.

The proximate target of exchange rate management is, plainly enough, the exchange rate itself, though there is more than one reason why a country might choose to elevate this particular asset price to a leading place in its list of policy objectives. The argument with which we shall be most concerned here is related to the role of the exchange rate in the transmission mechanism of monetary policy and in particular in the link between monetary policy and inflation. This involves the *nominal* exchange rate, *e*. Another source of concern stems from the role that the

197

real exchange rate ep/p^* (or its inverse, competitiveness or the cost ratio) plays in the determination of employment and growth. In the short run, with prices sticky, variations in *nominal* exchange rates are highly correlated with variations in *real* exchange rates; but in the medium run the inflation priority, which leads to an emphasis on stabilizing the nominal exchange rate, and the competitiveness priority, which leads to an emphasis on stabilizing the real exchange rate, are more than likely to conflict. Thus a country with a rate of inflation which is already high relative to its competitors faces a dilemma: should it stabilize its nominal exchange rate, resulting in a decline in the competitiveness of its trading sector, or should it depreciate the currency to maintain competitiveness, thereby stimulating inflation?

Domestic considerations are not alone in giving significance to the exchange rate as a policy target. Exchange rates are of necessity two-sided variables and international responsibilities are likely to entail some degree of commitment to exchange rate stability in the interests of preserving a broader international policy regime, especially when market failure – speculative bubbles and other manifestations of inappropriate exchange market behaviour – seems likely to create problems.

All these sources of concern, as we shall see, can be thought of as having had an influence on British monetary policy during the 1980s. As the decade progressed the question first of *whether* and then of *when* Britain should join the European Monetary System as a fully participating member came to dominate proceedings; it was one for which the constellation of arguments, pro and con, to some degree evolved with the development of the System itself.

We first discuss the role of the exchange rate in the transmission mechanism of monetary policy before going on to consider the general case for targeting the exchange rate as an intermediate variable in more detail. We then focus upon the workings of the EMS and Britain's seemingly ambivalent attitude to participation in European monetary arrangements.

8.1 The exchange rate in the transmission mechanism

The quantity theory

The combination of the quantity theory and purchasing power parity (PPP) provides a model of the simplest kind which, though far from empirically robust, none the less underlies much thinking in this area.[1] If

PPP holds then relative national currency price levels, at least of traded goods, determine the exchange rate; and if the quantity theory holds, national price levels are tied to the corresponding money supplies. Hence relative money supplies determine relative price levels and exchange rates. This simple picture can easily be adjusted to allow for some necessary complications – for example, that while PPP may hold for traded goods prices, domestic price levels also incorporate non-traded goods prices. With such complications added, the basic proposition is simply that a country's money supply, price level and exchange rate are determined in a package, given the data for other countries. With output fixed, for example, an x per cent money supply increase will be associated with a rise in prices of x per cent and an x per cent depreciation of the exchange rate. This is the truth behind the phrase that 'the exchange rate is the relative price of two moneys.'

This set of relationships may equally well be inverted so as to say that if a country targets its nominal exchange rate, then, subject to any differences in the linkage between non-traded and traded goods prices domestically and overseas, that country's price level will evolve in the same way as prices overseas. This is the essence of a policy of external stabilization of prices. Such an exchange rate targeting policy would of course imply that the money supply would passively adapt to the resultant demand arising from the path of nominal income so brought about. This illustrates the important truth that exchange rate targeting is incompatible with monetary targeting. It also emphasizes that the pursuit of a fixed nominal exchange rate target for inflation control promises control over *relative*, not absolute, inflation: clearly, targeting the Brazilian cruzeiro would not be intelligent counter-inflation strategy, whereas targeting the German Deutschmark is!

The model as discussed so far has omitted any mention of interest rates. It is interesting to see that if the quantity theory is interpreted as a demand for money relationship and the interest rate is admitted as an additional argument with the usual negative effect, an apparently counter-intuitive result must follow. A rise in interest rates, given the money supply and real income at home and all foreign variables, must result in a *rise* in prices to clear the money market and thence a *fall* (depreciation) in the exchange rate. The rise in interest rates would *reduce* the demand for the (given) stock of money, and since income is given could only occur in equilibrium if prices were to rise.

This conflicts with the conventional prediction that a rise in interest rates – unless it is interpreted as a sign of bad economic management – will lead to a rise (appreciation) of the exchange rate. How is this paradox to be explained? One way of doing so is to view the model involved as a set of long-run equilibrium conditions where in contrast the conventional prediction comes out of a short-run disequilibrium analysis. On this interpretation a rise in interest rates is a sign of bad management in the sense that it implicitly stands in for the expectation of higher inflation and, rationally, in terms of the model, is associated with a rise in current prices, a reduction in the demand for money and a fall in the exchange rate. (The point is clarified in the Appendix to this chapter.)

An illustration of a version of this approach is given in Figure 8.1. In this version income is allowed to be flexible in the short run. The model, which is a diagrammatic version of McKinnon (1976), illustrates a world in which fiscal policy is impotent, and in which prices and the exchange rate are determined by the money supply, given supply conditions and overseas prices; alternatively, inverting the model, the money supply and prices can be determined by the exchange rate, given supply conditions and overseas prices. The economy is taken to be a highly open one producing and consuming a single composite tradable good which is available from world sources at a price in foreign currency, p^* (in logs). Transport costs are ignored and the Law of One Price applies, so that the pricing line (or aggregate demand curve) is given as (in logs) $p = p^* + e$ where e is the exchange rate measured as the domestic currency price of foreign currency. Supply is determined, given fixed nominal wages in the short run, by profit-maximizing entrepreneurs to yield the upward-sloping schedule, AS. Then for a given rate of interest (r) and a stock of money, a monetary equilibrium schedule can be drawn as shown (MM), its slope dependent on the real income elasticity of money demand. As argued above, a rise in the interest rate, given the money stock, would shift the schedule to the right; we can think of the rate of interest in static equilibrium as equal to the foreign rate of interest as it would be in a financially open economy in a fully integrated international capital market. The downward-sloping DD schedule is a hypothetical *domestic* demand schedule.

Equilibrium, for p and y, is determined by the intersection of the AS, AD and MM schedules at A. DD is irrelevant except for determining the trade balance (here a surplus) as the distance between domestic absorption B, where DD intersects AD, and the point A. Fiscal policy (changes in which would shift DD) is irrelevant to the determination of output, but obviously is not to the composition of the balance of payments. A monetary expansion will raise prices and output in the short run as the exchange rate falls (from e_0 to e_1, as shown) and real wages drop. In the longer run (when AS is vertical) the monetary expansion can only raise prices and depreciate the exchange rate in proportion.

This illustrates the simple, but powerful, model of global monetarism in which the exchange rate's position in the transmission mechanism of

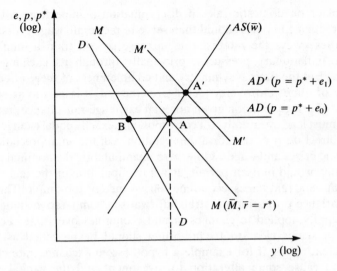

Figure 8.1 The open economy under global monetarism.

monetary policy is critical, unlike closed economy monetarism which treated the exchange rate almost as an addendum (see Chapter 5). We now turn to a more eclectic position on the same subject, following the alternative tradition of starting with the interest rate.

Keynesian models

In the standard short-run Keynesian model the interest rate is taken to be the monetary policy instrument and a flow model of international capital movements is added. Then, a rise in the domestic interest rate, relative to foreign rates, causes the exchange rate to appreciate. The increase in the domestic interest rate has deflationary impacts on domestic demand and, to the extent that this bears down on wage inflation and the ability of firms to mark up over costs, reduces prices. The appreciation of the exchange rate adds several further inflation-moderating influences. First, the domestic prices of imported goods complementary to the production process – raw materials and the like – will fall, leading to a reduction in unit costs. Second, the domestic currency prices of imported competitive goods will fall to some extent, putting pressure on domestic producers to trim their margins and reducing the cost-push pressure on wage-bargainers. Finally, producers providing exportables will be forced to cut their prices in overseas markets and some of the same price-cutting will take place on domestic sales if discrimination is imperfect. All these price-reducing impacts should then serve to moderate wage pressures.

In these ways the interest rate increase sets in train a number of counter-inflationary pressures, principally through its exchange rate impact. But the timing, symmetry and completeness of these effects is a matter of some controversy. As regards the last, it is easy to assert as a matter of principle that a given nominal exchange rate change, taken in itself, must lead eventually to a corresponding exactly equal change in the same direction (i.e. rise for a depreciation, fall for an appreciation) in domestic prices and wages. Otherwise, manipulating the nominal rate of exchange would in itself permit lasting manipulation of the real rate of exchange and real wages: economic policy would be too simple! This kind of invariance proposition is straightforward in comparative statics, but less happily applied to changes in real economies over time. For one thing, it seems clear that equilibrium should be modelled as 'path-dependent'; thus, if for example a hypothesized exchange rate change were to cause some alteration to investment and the capital stock, productivity and long-run real variables would be different in the new equilibrium from what they would otherwise have been.

There are also doubts about the extent to which the effects of exchange rate changes are symmetric, given the well-attested downward rigidity of wages, and how far they are likely to depend on the initial situation of the economy. For example, one suggested reason for the substantial damage caused to the British economy by the large appreciation of sterling in 1979–81 is that it hit British industry at a time when profits were in any case low, so that firms lacked the financial resources to ride out the storm. In Chapter 3 we observed that the data for this period decisively reject the Law of One Price as applied to UK aggregate export price indices: the appreciation of the exchange rate was real as well as nominal. Where rigidities and non-linearities are important features, the effects of exchange rate changes on prices and other variables and their symmetry cannot be so safely inferred as comparative statics results suggest.

8.2 The exchange rate as an intermediate target

It is clear that the exchange rate is an important link in the transmission mechanism of monetary policy. Viewed as a part of a causal sequence

$$m \to e \to p, y, \tag{8.1}$$

a simple but powerful case for treating the exchange rate as an intermediate target variable emerges from two observations: first, that the object of ultimate interest is the variable p or perhaps y (or both);

second, that the first link in the chain between m and e may be loose and unreliable. If so, then the desired effects on the ultimate goals of policy may be more reliably achieved by targeting e directly. Evidently, this is just another way of saying that if the demand for money function is unreliable, a policy of accommodating supply to unforeseen shifts while targeting the exchange rate is a guarantee of counter-inflationary success. Targeting the money supply itself in these circumstances will not do the trick.

In the framework of the monetary approach illustrated earlier, the point can be simply made by reference to Figure 8.2. This uses the same assumptions as the earlier figure. Suppose that the desired price level is p and the overseas price level is p^*. Then the desired result can be achieved, indifferently, by targeting the money supply at M (which underlies the schedule MM) or targeting e at $\bar{e}$, passively supplying the resultant quantity of money demanded. Money and the exchange rate are duals. Suppose, however, that the demand for money is unstable so that the MM schedule corresponding to the supply of money M might shift, as illustrated, between MM' and MM": clearly this would result in corresponding fluctuations in the exchange rate, output and domestic price level. By contrast, however, the price level may be stabilized by targeting the exchange rate $\bar{e}$: MM then becomes a monetary equilibrium schedule in which the money supply automatically accommodates the demand shocks. There is an exact analogy between the way in which stabilizing the

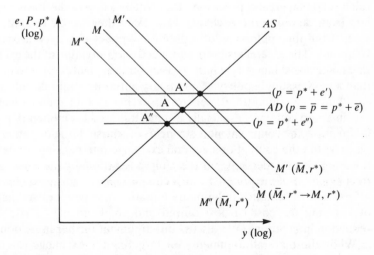

Figure 8.2   Exchange rate and monetary targets.

exchange rate endogenizes the money supply to demand and the way in which, in Poole's celebrated closed economy model (Poole, 1970), targeting the interest rate accomplishes the same automatic accommodation.

This parallel is exploited in Artis and Currie (1981) and other papers which approach policy choice as a matter of selecting the most robust intermediate variable targets. Specifically, money supply targets and exchange rate targets are compared for their stabilizing properties in the face of various random shocks emanating from domestic expenditures, money demand, foreign prices and foreign interest rates. In two of the cases, domestic expenditure shocks and foreign interest rate shocks, the results are inconclusive. Instability in money demand functions undermines monetary targeting; as we have seen, maintenance of exchange rates in this case allows the supply of money to respond to demand. Exchange rate targeting is undermined by instability in the foreign price level. Since exchange rate targeting ties the domestic price level to foreign prices, instability in the latter is transferred to the former. Monetary targeting and exchange rate flexibility allow domestic prices to be disconnected from this link.

Thus one important ground for treating the exchange rate as an intermediate target is that the resultant endogenization of, or loss of independent control over, the money supply is actually desirable when there is instability in the demand for money. There are other reasons, too. An important one is the fact that the exchange rate can be observed day by day, whereas observations of the money supply only become available with a lag. Thus, even if the demand for money function were reliably stable, greater precision of control on a day-to-day basis could be had from targeting the exchange rate. A further, partly related, point stems from the application of reputational policy concepts discussed in Chapter 5. The greater visibility and speed of observation of the exchange rate make an exchange rate policy easier for the private sector to monitor than a money supply policy. A monetary authority might therefore gain credibility by committing itself to an exchange rate target (against a low-inflation country), especially if it has followed lax monetary policies in the past. The commitment is stronger, of course, if the targeting takes place within the context of a general exchange rate-pegging framework, say like that provided now for the United Kingdom by the EMS, rather than as a go-it-alone policy. In such circumstances, the added credibility afforded to the counter-inflationary initiative may pay for itself in terms of lowering the cost (in lost output and employment) of effecting a reduction in inflation. (We discuss this argument further in section 8.4.)

While these are all arguments for targeting the exchange rate in the context of an overall policy priority on lowering inflation, there is also a set of arguments related to international trade and competitiveness. Britain as a major trading nation is dependent on buying from abroad goods which have to be paid for in foreign currency, and on selling overseas local production for which payment must often be accepted in foreign currency. Stability of these exchanges of domestic for foreign currency is thus a special convenience. Large changes in real exchange rates appear to produce substantial economic (and social) costs: as the profitability of the trading sector fluctuates, firms will be forced to make costly exit and entry decisions.[2] Perhaps the critical point is that inertia in consumers' purchasing habits implies that a firm which leaves a market faces substantial reinvestment costs if and when it decides to re-enter that market. Price-setting behaviour reflects this. It is well known that firms set prices which even out the impact of temporary cost shocks; the evidence is particularly strong for international pricing in that relative export price volatility is substantially less than that of relative unit labour costs (even when the latter are normalized for the cycle). The obvious reason for this is that exchange rate changes which can produce sharp variations in relative normalized unit labour costs are partly absorbed in variations in suppliers' profit margins.[3]

Avoidance of substantial exchange rate changes appears to provide a prima-facie case for government intervention. Of course, it can be argued that just because exit and re-entry decisions *are* costly, the market can be expected itself to finance short-run or 'small' departures from equilibrium, as is indeed implied in the pricing behaviour described above. It is for this reason that the case for intervention applies more persuasively to situations where the real exchange rate threatens to depart from equilibrium over a relatively prolonged period of time. While deleterious effects of short-run exchange rate volatility on trade are often alleged they are not by and large widely substantiated,[4] and this does not seem surprising given that the markets provide short-term cover against exchange rate fluctuations. So it is the effects of longer-run departures from equilibrium on investment and production decisions that seem to matter most.

As we noted in the introduction to this chapter, concern of this type about the *real* exchange rate may very well *conflict* with the counter-inflationary purpose of monetary policy and result in an attenuation or attempted limitation of it. Thus Vaubel (1980) has in a graphic phrase noted what he calls the 'implicit emergency clause' of German monetary policy, in which the ambitions of strict monetary policy are set aside when the real rate of exchange appreciates too much.[5]

A final reason for exchange rate targeting, important in recent years, stems from the international spillovers of national policies. An appreciating dollar is a depreciating average rest-of-the-world currency. If the

United States wishes to influence its exchange rate this will, because of the large relative size of US trade in the world total, have important effects on other countries, whose agreement is certainly desirable and may well be necessary to the enterprise.

It may be the case that international agreement which starts by focusing on exchange rates will by the logic of induced events result in greater coordination, internationally, of economic policies; so those who think this end-goal is desirable may also think it appropriate to elevate exchange rates in the hierarchy of policy targets. But this argument is not wholly secure; the results of exchange rate agreements without wider coordination may be worse than the results achieved without agreement; or the exchange rate agreement itself may prove unsustainable without coordination. At the level of theoretical speculation, the question seems open-ended.[6]

The form that an exchange rate target takes can be varied, depending upon the primary purpose of the policy. A tight counter-inflation policy involving a firm commitment against a low-inflation partner is one possible form for the policy (e.g. Austria). The tighter the commitment, the easier it is for households and firms to compute the implied inflation rate targets and to monitor the policy. In this instance bands around the central or target rate of exchange should be rather narrow. On the other hand, if the exchange rate target is an acknowledgement of potential possible problems with the demand for money function, a suitable form in which to enter the exchange rate as a target would be as a conditioning variable on the monetary target; that is, the authorities could make the effective width of the band around the monetary target dependent on the level of the exchange rate. If the problem is an apprehension about the extent to which real exchange rates should be allowed to vary, a natural form for the target to take would be that of adjustable limits with a wide band. If other means to manage speculation are not sufficient, such bands should be soft-edged, i.e. should not involve a provocative commitment by the authorities that promotes the wrecking 'one-way bet'. All these alternatives have been mirrored in recent actual or proposed agreements.

It is usual to think of targets and bands being published, and some of the purposes of exchange rate targeting as we have discussed them benefit from publication. But this is not true of all the objectives of exchange rate targeting and the threat of speculation, especially if the authorities themselves are less than wholly determined, may indicate that it would be better not to publish. Doing so would only encourage speculation and advertise the authorities' disarray when mistakes occur. Perhaps for this reason the exchange rate bands which have been a feature of international policy coordination in recent years have remained unpublished.

A final comment concerns the ability of the authorities to achieve exchange rate goals. Mrs Thatcher's statement 'you can't buck the markets' puts the point clearly enough, and British experience since 1972 offers several illustrations. One of the attractions for Britain of the ERM is the joint intervention obligations placed on member countries, so that parities are defended by the combined reserve assets of the central banks.

8.3 UK exchange rate policies in the 1980s

The transition from the Bretton Woods era of fixed but adjustable exchange rates to the present international regime of managed floating has involved for the United Kingdom, as it has for other countries, some sharp changes in perception of the scope and effectiveness of exchange rate policy.

In particular, the period from the early 1970s has witnessed an increase in the degree of global financial integration and a period of high inflation which served to dispel any lingering illusions about the stability of the price level. The first of these developments, decisively completed from the UK point of view by the abolition of exchange controls in 1979, effectively removed the possibility that the exchange rate could any longer be treated even as a first approximation as a policy instrument in itself – that is, as being capable of being adjusted without reference to other policy instruments, as with sterilized interventions.

In sterilized intervention policies, foreign exchange transactions are offset in their effects on the domestic monetary base, leaving the quantity of domestic money unchanged. Purchases (sales) of foreign currency securities are matched by sales (purchases) of sterling securities, leaving simply a change in the composition of portfolios between domestic and foreign securities. If domestic and foreign securities are relatively close substitutes, so that open market operations in the foreign exchange market differ little in substance from domestic open market operations, the effects on interest or exchange rates may be slight. Sterilized intervention then adds little which cannot already be obtained from domestic instruments; though even so, exercises in sterilized intervention can have some impact as a signal to markets of serious intent. Increasingly, though, exchange rate management and exchange rate policies have come to be seen straightforwardly as the use of monetary policy – unsterilized intervention and interest rate policy – in the pursuit of an intermediate target for the exchange rate.

A second major change in perception of the scope for exchange rate policy emerged over the period with the decline in the belief that it was appropriate to treat a change in the nominal exchange rate as necessarily bringing about some permanent – or even moderately long-lasting – change in the real exchange rate. With a greater emphasis given to the role of real wage resistance in theories of wage inflation, it became obvious that the changes in the terms of trade brought about by a nominal exchange rate change would be mitigated – and in the limit offset completely – by changes in money wages and thence in prices. Ultimately, even if international trade only accounts for a quarter or so of GNP, prices would catch up on the exchange rate change: at the end of the process real wages and the terms of trade would wind up at their original values, and prices would be higher.

The process can be described very simply by appeal to a markup pricing model in which prices depend on unit labour and import costs with a (perhaps variable) profit markup. *Ceteris paribus* (including holding output and capacity utilization constant), the total differential of such a model reduces to

$$\mathrm{d}p = \alpha \frac{\partial w}{\partial p} \, \mathrm{d}p + (1 - \alpha) \, \mathrm{d}pm \qquad (8.2)$$

where α, $1 - \alpha$ are the contributions of wage and import costs in prices, p is the consumer price index, w is wage costs and pm is import prices in domestic currency. With real wage resistance, $\partial w / \partial p = 1$ and so evidently $\mathrm{d}p / \mathrm{d}pm = 1$. The response to a change in the domestic currency value of import prices (which might be brought about by a change in the exchange rate) is complete. Present-day macroeconometric models embody this reasoning by imposing long-run homogeneity on the pricing functions, and their dynamics indicate that this is achieved quite quickly. A comment on Table 8.1, which gives an account of the passthrough from import to domestic prices in the National Institute's Model 11, will help to illustrate what is going on.[7]

In this model wholesale prices are related to wage costs and import prices. Shocking the latter by 10 per cent to correspond to a 10 per cent devaluation while holding wages constant produces the figures shown in the first column – a rise of 2.4 per cent, quickly achieved. Consumer prices in the model depend, *inter alia*, on wholesale prices, wage costs and directly on import prices – the second and third columns of results illustrate the contribution of this equation. The determination of wages in the model depends, *inter alia*, on consumer prices with long-run homogeneity. When the system is solved allowing for the determination of wages and the simultaneous interaction of the equations the result is that the devaluation is offset within four years by a rise in wages and prices, with a mild overshooting of the long-run effect occurring for a short period.

Table 8.1 The exchange rate–price–wage passthrough in NI Model 11[1]: a 10% depreciation

Price/wage variable	Wholesale prices	Consumer prices	Consumer prices	Wholesale prices	Consumer prices	Wages
				Simultaneously determined[2]		
Condition	Wages exog.	Wages, wholesale prices exog.	Wages exog.			
Impact (Q1)	0.5	0.7	0.9	0.7	0.9	0.2
4-quarter (Q4)	1.9	1.7	2.5	3.5	3.5	1.7
8-quarter (Q8)	2.4	1.8	2.8	6.7	6.3	4.6
12-quarter (Q12)	2.4	1.7	2.8	9.1	8.7	7.3
16-quarter (Q16)	2.4	1.7	2.8	10.4	10.1	9.3
20-quarter (Q20)	2.4	1.7	2.8	10.9	10.8	10.4
Peak quarter				11.0 (22)	10.9 (23)	10.9 (26)
Steady state	2.4	1.7	2.8	10.0	10.0	10.0

Notes:
1. The results quoted were obtained by simulating the wholesale, consumer price and wage equations, *ceteris paribus*, the assumption including constant levels of output and capacity utilization.
2. The determination of wages in NI Model 11 involves price expectations, for which the AR(4) process programmed in the model as an alternative to consistent expectations was used here, with a suitable renormalization of the constant term.

Long-run homogeneity of prices in the exchange rate still allows in principle for a real terms of trade advantage to be stolen during the adjustment, but to attempt to hold this over a longer period would require repetitive devaluations and a consequent risk of serious inflation.[8]

These changes in the possibility for, and scope of, exchange rate policy are huge when compared with the position prevailing at the end of the 1960s. At that time it was still regarded as quite sensible to treat the exchange rate as an independent policy instrument, albeit one which it was already recognized required the support of other policies over the medium run to ensure consistent balance of payments outcomes and the support, in the short run, of policies which would limit speculation against the peg. Despite these interdependencies, the force of inertia in wage setting and the claims on the imagination of the declared parity still remained large, as did the effects of intervention in the foreign exchange market.

The United Kingdom was the first developed country to break away from the post-Bretton Woods, realigned Smithsonian System. Where the developed world in general floated from 1973, Britain did so from July 1972. The decision to do this reflected the idea that the fixed exchange rate was a constraint on output, inhibiting the dash for growth which inspired the Maudling–Barber boom. The intention to remove this obstacle was clearly foreshadowed in the budget speech of March 1972 and was duly realized four months later.

The results of the experiment were merged with those of the major monetary reform Competition and Credit Control, the initiation of which predated (and some would say necessitated) the float by some nine months, and they were drowned in the wave of commodity price increases which marked the peak of the world boom in 1973, culminating ultimately in the first oil shock at the end of that year. While the hoped-for growth did not last, this can hardly be reasonably regarded, given the circumstances, as a decisive negative verdict on the decision to float. Nevertheless, the episode was to serve the subsequent perception that the medium-to-long-run real consequences of nominal exchange rate manipulation are nth order rather than central.

During the period of the subsequent Labour Governments (1974–9), the removal of the exchange rate constraint was certainly felt to be of little help, and the view that the exchange rate is a veil was given influential expression during this period by Ball, Burns and Laury (1977). This period saw an interesting episode illustrating the inconsistency of monetary and exchange rate targets. Following the IMF stabilization loan in December 1976 it became clear that the government was following a policy of keeping the real effective exchange rate low. At the same time it had embraced a monetary target. In circumstances where targeting the exchange rate required the use of monetary policy, a conflict between the two targets was latent from the start. By July the conflict was an open one. The swing of sentiment in favour of sterling resulted in upward pressure on the pound which unsterilized intervention could meet only by allowing a corresponding increase in the monetary base. Thus the pressure could be accommodated either by allowing the monetary base and money supply to increase, which would be contrary to the monetary target, or by allowing the exchange rate to appreciate out of line with the exchange rate target. The government chose to uncap sterling in favour of the monetary target. This instructive episode put paid to the concept of an exchange rate target for some time. The Labour Government participated in the decisions leading to the establishment of the European Monetary System (EMS) but declined to join (see below).

Upon assuming office in 1979 the Conservative Government of Mrs Thatcher had the opportunity to reaffirm its opposition to joining the EMS. It went further. In the description of its medium-term financial strategy (MTFS) in the following year the government made a point of relegating the exchange rate to the role of residual (Table 8.2), reasoning (correctly) that the unalloyed attachment to monetary targets broadcast in the MTFS was incompatible – as the episode of 1977 would have reminded them – with adherence to an exchange rate target.

It was not long before practice began to contradict this insouciance towards the exchange rate, however, and only a little longer still before this was publicly acknowledged. The proximate reason for this change of attitude lay in the unprecedented increase in the real exchange rate which ensued on the MTFS through 1980 to 1981. The cumulative loss of competitiveness (measured by the rise in relative unit labour costs) between the fourth quarter of 1976 and the first quarter of 1981 (the peak quarter to quarter loss) was over 80 per cent, more than half of this occurring between the second quarter of 1979 and the first quarter of 1981. Such a drastic and unexpected change to their trading conditions forced many companies to go to the wall. At the same time the targets for £M3 were substantially overrun; although the behaviour of the narrow monetary magnitudes could be interpreted as suggesting that monetary conditions were tight, the behaviour of £M3 suggested otherwise. Since (cf. Chapter 4) the demand for M1 remained relatively stable, and since the supply of M1 must be mainly demand-determined, these observations may simply reflect the fact that (1) there was a deep recession, and (2) the demand for £M3 was not stable and had in fact increased. Whatever the reasons (and the episode still remains a vexed issue) for this turn of events, the government reacted by trimming its reaction to the monetary target overruns, subsequently formalizing and publicizing its policy as

Table 8.2 Design of the MTFS: Extracts from the Financial Statement and Budget Report

---

March 1980
To maintain a progressive reduction in monetary growth . . . it may be necessary to change policies in ways not reflected in the above projections . . .but there would be no question of departing from the money supply policy, which is essential to the success of any anti-inflationary strategy . . . The exchange rate is assumed to be determined by market forces.

March 1982(i)
External or domestic developments that change the relationship between the domestic money supply and the exchange rate may . . . disturb the link between money and prices. Such changes cannot readily be taken into account in setting monetary targets. But they are a reason why the Government considers it appropriate to look at the exchange rate in monitoring domestic monetary conditions and in taking decisions about policy.

March 1982(ii)
Interpretation of monetary conditions will continue to take account of all the available evidence, including the behaviour of the exchange rate . . . and

March 1983
. . . structural changes in financial markets, saving behaviour and the level and structure of interest rates.

March 1985
Equal weight will be given to the performance of M0 and £M3, which will continue to be interpreted in the light of other indicators and of monetary conditions. Significant changes in the exchange rate are also important. It will be necessary to judge the appropriate combination of monetary growth and the exchange rate needed to keep financial policy on track: there is no mechanistic formula.
The Government's overriding aim will be to maintain monetary conditions consistent with a declining growth rate of money GDP and inflation. Short term interest rates will be held at the levels needed to achieve this.

March 1986
Policy will be directed at maintaining monetary conditions that will bring about a gradual reduction in the growth of money GDP over the medium term.
Monetary conditions are assessed in the light of movements in narrow and broad money and the behaviour of other financial indicators, in particular the exchange rate.
There is no mechanical formula for taking the exchange rate into account . . . a balance must be struck between the exchange rate and domestic monetary growth.

March 1987
No target for £M3 'which remains difficult to interpret'.

March 1988
A declining path for money GDP growth requires a reduction in monetary growth over the medium term.
M0 has continued to be a reliable indicator of monetary conditions.
While, as last year, there is no explicit target range for broad money, the assessment of monetary conditions continues to take broad money, or liquidity, into account.
Interest rate decisions are based on a comprehensive assessment of monetary conditions so as to maintain downward pressure on inflation. Increases in domestic costs will not be accommodated either by monetary expansion or by exchange rate depreciation.
Exchange rates play a central role in both domestic monetary decisions and international policy co-operation.
The PSBR is now assumed to be zero over the medium term: a balanced budget. This is a prudent and cautious level and can be maintained over the medium term. It also provides a clear and simple rule with a good historical pedigree.

---

one of conditionalizing the monetary target on the exchange rate (see the second of the selected extracts from successive statements of the MTFS given in Table 8.2).

With the passage of time it became clear that the behaviour of some of the monetary aggregates had become very difficult to explain (cf. the discussion in Chapter 4) and in successive statements of the MTFS the monetary targets were restated, first for a range of aggregates, then for money GDP (with a target for M0 in a supporting role). Finally, in the 1987 budget speech £M3 was explicitly dropped (see Tables 8.2 and 8.3). This was to mark the elevation, for a period, of the exchange rate target to a higher position than it had enjoyed for many years either as a conditioning variable or as an explicit target.

There were three important developments at the time which between them probably accounted for this hardening of the exchange rate target. First, the United Kingdom as one of the G-5 and one of the Summit Seven (G-7) countries was party to the efforts provoked on American initiatives to rekindle international policy coordination in order to effect a soft landing for the dollar following its remarkable appreciation through the year to 1985. In February 1987 this process was renewed in the Louvre Accord in which the G-7 countries pledged to aim to stabilize exchange rates within certain (wide, soft-edged and unpublished) bands. Second, the withdrawal of £M3 from the targeted list of monetary aggregates exposed the MTFS to criticism as an empty shell since the illustrative target ranges for M0 were widely regarded as an insufficient substitute and money GDP could not be continuously monitored. Finally, it appeared that the Chancellor of the Exchequer had become a convert to

Table 8.3   Content of the MTFS

	4-year forward ranges quoted[1]
March 1980	£M3; PSBR
March 1981	£M3; PSBR
March 1982	£M3; M1; PSL2; PSBR
March 1983	£M3; M1; PSL2; PSBR
March 1984	£M3; M0; PSBR
March 1985	£M3; M0; Money GDP[2]; PSBR
March 1986	M0[3]; Money GDP; PSBR; £M3
March 1987	M0[4]; Money GDP; PSBR
March 1988	M0[4]; Money GDP; PSBR (zero)

Notes:
1. Target ranges except as noted below, PSBR as % GDP.
2. 'Broad medium term objective'.
3. 'Illustrative ranges' for 1987/8 on.
4. 'Illustrative ranges' for 1988/9 on.

the idea that the United Kingdom should become a full participant in the EMS, although he was out of step in this with the Prime Minister.

The exchange rate policy which emerged lasted approximately a year. It was not formally announced but informally made known and consistent with the observed facts that the centre of the strategy was a target ceiling of DM3 to the pound. Figure 8.3 displays the policy rather clearly (the bands are drawn on the assumption of a ceiling of DM3 with a central and floor rate at 'EMS intervals' below it).

This policy was abandoned after a year, by which time it had become clear from forecasts of future inflation that some reining back of demand was required. Without a tightening of fiscal instruments, increases in interest rates were necessary, entailing an appreciation of the exchange rate through the DM3 ceiling. In retrospect the market seems to have treated the DM3 value not as a ceiling from which a devaluation should be expected but as a guaranteed rate. Consequently the high interest rates simply exerted upward pressure on the exchange rate rather than protecting it from immediate decline. The problem was one, in a sense, of excess credibility. It would be normal for a currency with a high inflation rate to be expected to depreciate against the low-inflation currency (the DM), the interest rate differential in favour of the high-inflation country offsetting this expectation.

Whatever the explanation, this dramatic end to the episode of exchange rate targeting provided a further illustration of the incompatibility of monetary and exchange rate targets: but does it say that exchange rate pegging against the Deutschmark does *not* guarantee low inflation? The first point to make is that the policy had received insufficient publicity to provide a proper test case. Besides this it should be said that the simple model illustrated in Figures 8.1 and 8.2 is not quite up to the mark. In making the drastic assumption that the economy produces only one tradable good it overlooks the possibility for an economy to generate a demand-led inflation of its own. In the simple model, the excess demand should simply cause a balance of payments deficit; in practice, excess demand appears to be associated with *both* a large deficit *and* rising prices. Allowing for some closed economy effect of this kind, the lesson of the episode seems to be that a policy of pegging to the Deutschmark needs to be accompanied by some flexibility in fiscal policy. If interest rates are the sole weapon available, the authorities sooner or later fall foul of Tinbergen's counting rule: they have two targets – one for the exchange rate and one for inflation – with only one instrument and thus need an additional instrument. In the future this may be less of a problem: as goods market integration grows, the exchange rate and inflation targets effectively merge and the dilemma disappears.

There seems little doubt, however, that the episode was a bad

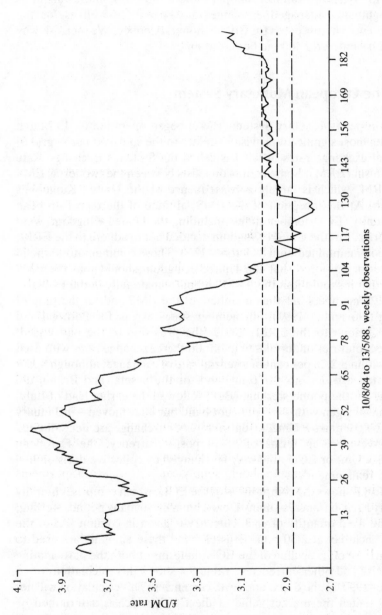

Figure 8.3 The sterling/DM exchange rate.

advertisement for the policy, and put paid to the idea of an early entry to the EMS. We now examine the operation of the EMS, interesting in its own right as a managed exchange rate system, as well as for the consequences it now poses for British monetary policy. We then ask why Britain hesitated for so long before joining.

8.4 The European Monetary System

The European Monetary System (EMS) began operation on 13 March 1979. Its most significant provisions relate to the so-called parity grid of bilateral exchange rates or what is called the System's Exchange Rate Mechanism (ERM). Some confusion exists between the two terms EMS and ERM, which is largely a consequence of the United Kingdom's position. At the inception of the EMS, all nine of the then European Community (EC) member states, including the United Kingdom, were signatories. But the United Kingdom decided not to adhere to the ERM, a position maintained until 8 October 1990. Those commentators who in the interim proposed that the United Kingdom should join the EMS meant that it should join the ERM and participate fully in the EMS.

All EC members are thus members of the EMS and, at the time of writing (November 1990), all member states except for Portugal and Greece belong to the ERM. Under the provision of the parity grid, member countries undertake to maintain their exchange rates with each other within ±2.25 per cent of a central rate of exchange, although Spain negotiated a wider ±6 per cent band for the peseta, and Britain did likewise for the pound sterling. (Both followed the earlier lead of Italy, which also began with a ±6 per cent band but later moved – in January 1990 – to the narrow band.) Central rates of exchange are denominated for convenience in terms of a composite currency, the European Currency Unit or ECU, and may be changed by collective decision in a formal 'realignment'.

Table 8.4 shows the composition of the ECU, which comprises literally so many French francs, so many Deutschmarks, so many pounds sterling, etc. The fixed quantity of each currency is given in column (A) of the table. Each day at 2.30 p.m. Brussels time these amounts are used to calculate the official value of the ECU, in terms of both the participating currencies and other currencies. Table 8.4 shows this calculation for 15 October 1990 for the dollar and EMS currencies. This calculation will not exactly match the market value of the ECU, which is determined by supply and demand. In recent years the ECU has become a major traded 'currency' with quotations for spot, forward, deposit and loan rates, as well as ECU options, swaps and interest rate protection instruments: this

Table 8.4 ECU valuation (EEC calculation) at 15 October 1990

	A Currency amount	B Exchange rate $1=	C $ Value (A/B)	D ECU value (B×*)	E ECU (A/D)	F Central rates (8/10/90)
Deutschmark	0.6242	1.5230	0.409849	2.06141	0.302802	2.05586
French franc	1.332	5.1025	0.261049	6.90632	0.192866	6.89509
Sterling	0.08784	0.5122	0.171508	0.693222	0.126712	0.696904
Italian lira	151.8	1 141.8	0.132948	1 545.44	0.098224	1 538.24
Dutch guilder	0.2198	1.7169	0.128021	2.32385	0.094584	2.31643
Belgian franc	3.301	31.3674	0.105236	42.4564	0.077750	42.4032
Spanish peseta	6.885	95.7496	0.071906	129.599	0.053125	133.631
Danish krone	0.1976	5.8115	0.034001	7.86596	0.025120	7.84195
Irish pound	0.008 552	0.5678	0.015060	0.768563	0.011127	0.767417
Greek drachma	1.44	153.0395	0.009409	207.142	0.006951	205.311
Portuguese escudo	1.393	134.1598	0.010383	181.588	0.007672	178.735
Luxembourg franc	0.13	31.3674	0.004144	42.4564	0.003062	42.4032
			1 ECU = $1.35352		1.000001	

Source: Midland Montagu Research.

is the 'private' ECU market. Column (E) in the table shows the makeup of the ECU on the given date and if these figures are multiplied by 100 this gives the relative percentage weights of the currencies in the basket. These weights are not fixed and will vary according to the current exchange rates of the components. The currency amount values at the ECU central rates are set so as to give relative weights which reflect the importance of members in terms of relative GNP and trade, and are subject to review every five years. The Greek drachma was included in September 1984 and the Spanish peseta and the Portuguese escudo were added on 21 September 1989.

All EMS currencies have an ECU-related central rate; those not participating in the ERM are assigned a notional central rate. These central rates are expressed as a certain quantity of currency per ECU, and are shown in column (F) of Table 8.4; for the pound the central rate is £0.696904 per ECU. By division, cross-central parities are obtained to form the parity grid – the bilateral central rates for each currency participating in the EMS. Around these bilateral central rates, there are the margins of authorized fluctuation. As noted, sterling and the Spanish peseta are not permitted to fluctuate by more than 6 per cent in either direction from the central rates, while the other currencies have bands of ±2.25 per cent. The parity grid as of 8 October 1990 is set out in Table 8.5.

The use of a composite currency in which to denominate the central rate is not strictly necessary to the operation of the parity grid; participants in the ERM could simply have announced their adherence to a consistent set of bilateral central rates and bands. But the use of the ECU has useful symbolic connotations and may be felt to give the System an identity over and above that which would be commanded by a mere agreement to stabilize exchange rates – the identity, in fact, of a potential monetary union. Community transactions are denominated in the ECU (as the official unit of account), as are the debts acquired by central banks intervening to support their currencies in the framework of the EMS – such 'official' ECUs created by the EMCF (European Monetary Cooperation Fund) are not interchangeable with the private ECUs.

Intervention in participating currencies is compulsory when the intervention limits are reached. The central bank of the strong currency is required to purchase the weak currency on its foreign exchange market, while the central bank of the weak currency sells the strong currency (perhaps first borrowing it from the other central bank). However, central banks do not wait until a currency hits its limit against the ECU before acting, and the Nyborg–Basle Agreement of September 1987 provides for intervention before currencies actually reach the extremities of their bands.

For any pair of currencies the effective range of variation is limited by

Table 8.5 Central rates and intervention margins (as of 8 October 1990)

	Germany	France	Italy	Nether.	Belgium	Denmark	Ireland	Spain	UK
Deutschmark (100)	—	343.050 335.386 327.920	76540.0 74821.7 73157.0	115.235 112.673 110.167	2109.50 2062.55 2016.55	390.160 381.443 373.000	38.1825 37.3281 36.4964	6901.70 6500.00 6121.70	35.9970 33.8984 31.9280
French franc (100)	30.4950 29.8164 29.1500	—	22817.0 22309.1 21813.0	34.3600 33.5953 32.8475	628.970 614.977 601.295	116.320 113.732 111.200	11.3830 11.1299 10.8825	2057.80 1938.06 1825.30	10.7320 10.1073 9.5190
Italian lira (1000)	1.36700 1.33651 1.30650	4.58450 4.48247 4.38300	—	1.54000 1.50590 1.42750	28.1930 27.5661 26.9530	5.21400 5.09803 4.98500	0.51024 0.49889 0.48779	92.2400 86.8726 81.8200	0.48105 0.45305 0.42669
Dutch gldr (100)	90.7700 88.7526 86.7800	304.440 297.661 291.040	67912.0 66405.3 64928.0	—	1872.15 1830.54 1789.85	346.240 338.537 331.020	33.8868 33.1293 32.3939	6125.30 5768.83 5433.10	31.9450 30.0850 28.3340
Belgian/Lux franc (100)	4.95900 4.84837 4.74000	16.6310 16.2608 15.8990	3710.20 3627.64 3546.90	5.58700 5.46286 5.34150	—	18.9143 18.4938 18.0831	1.85100 1.80981 1.76950	334.619 315.143 296.802	1.74510 1.64352 1.54790
Danish krone (100)	26.8100 26.2162 25.6300	89.9250 87.9257 85.9700	20062.0 19615.4 19179.0	30.2100 29.5389 28.8825	553.000 540.723 528.700	—	10.0087 9.7860 9.5683	1809.40 1704.05 1604.90	9.43600 8.88687 8.36970
Irish pound (1)	2.74000 2.67894 2.61900	9.18900 8.98480 8.78500	2050.03 2004.43 1959.84	3.08700 3.01848 2.95100	56.5115 55.2545 54.0250	10.4511 10.2186 9.9913	—	184.892 174.131 163.997	0.96424 0.90811 0.85526
Spanish peseta (100)	1.63300 1.53847 1.44900	5.47850 5.15981 4.85950	1222.30 1151.11 1084.10	1.84050 1.73345 1.63250	33.6930 31.7316 29.8850	6.23100 5.86837 5.52600	0.60977 0.57428 0.54085	—	0.55374 0.52151 0.49160
Sterling (1)	3.13200 2.95000 2.77800	10.5055 9.8939 9.3180	2343.62 2207.25 2078.79	3.52950 3.32389 3.13050	64.6050 60.8451 57.3035	11.9479 11.2526 10.5976	1.16920 1.10118 1.03710	203.600 191.750 180.590	—

Upper line = Ceiling; Middle line = Central rate; Lower line = Floor

Source: Midland Montagu Research.

the movement of other currencies. This is because a country's exchange rate cannot be more than 6 per cent below the strongest currency in the system or more than 6 per cent above the weakest. For example, as shown in Table 8.5, with a wide band of ±6 per cent the pound sterling has a 12 per cent theoretical range against the Deutschmark: i.e. around its central rate of DM2.95, from DM2.78 to DM3.13. But should another currency in the system, say the Spanish peseta, be 3.5 per cent above its central rate with the Deutschmark, sterling would reach its lowest permitted level against the peseta well before it hit DM2.78. With that particular juxtaposition of rates, and supposing the Spanish peseta to be the strongest currency in the system, sterling's fall against the Deutschmark would be limited to about (6 − 3.5 = 2.5 per cent), i.e. approximately DM2.87. (This was the position on 22 October 1990, and Figure 8.4 shows the effects in terms of the effective limits on sterling against the Deutschmark implied by the need for sterling to remain within its bilateral limits against all other ERM currencies simultaneously.)

In addition to the parity grid, there is the divergence indicator (DI). The essential role that the DI was designed to perform was that of enforcing timely and symmetrical adjustment. The idea of the indicator was that it should be designed so as to signal when a currency was *becoming out of line with the rest of the System*. Coupled with the injunction that the 'flashing' of the indicator gave a presumption of corrective policy action on behalf of the country whose currency was singled out in this way, the DI would – it was hoped – enforce adjustment equally on a strong-currency country and on a weak-currency country, provided that the currency in question stood out from the pack.

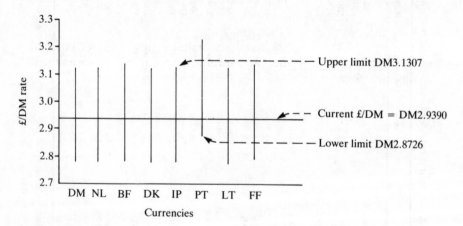

Figure 8.4   Sterling's effective limits in the ERM 22 October 1990.
Source: Bank of England.

Combining this role with that of providing an early warning, the DI was to be triggered when a currency crossed a set threshold. A maximum divergence from its central ECU rate is calculated for each currency. This is not equal to 2.25 per cent or 6 per cent because each currency is part of the ECU and as it fluctuates it alters the value of the ECU.

The divergence indicator[9] is therefore calculated after taking account of the weight of each currency within the ECU based on the central rates. For example, sterling has a weight of 12.6 per cent within the ECU and its maximum allowable movement is therefore 5.24 per cent $(6 \times (1 - 0.126))$. When a currency reaches 75 per cent of this maximum (i.e. for sterling 3.93 per cent), it crosses the threshold of divergence and this results in a presumption that the authorities concerned will correct the situation by adequate measures, as follows:

1. *Diversified intervention*: this means intervention on the foreign exchange market in diverse currencies rather than in the single currency which would deviate most from the currency of the country concerned; diversified intervention should allow a better sharing of the burden of intervention among the various Community currencies.
2. *Measures of domestic monetary policy*: these include, among others, action bearing on interest rates, which can have a direct influence on capital flows.
3. *Change of the central rate*: while the operation of the EMS itself ought to contribute to reducing divergences among participating economies, it cannot prevent real disparities from subsisting and possibly requiring exchange rate adjustments (i.e. realignments of central ECU parity).
4. *Other economic policy measures*: these could include, for instance, measures of fiscal policy or of incomes policy.

Flanking these exchange rate provisions, with the obligation to intervene at the bilateral limits, and the presumption of action created by a triggering of the DI threshold, the EMS also provides for credit mechanisms to enable weak-currency countries to borrow in order to defend their currencies. The principal such mechanism, called the VSTF (very short-term financing facility) provides for the extension of credit from one central bank to another, repayable over a term initially of forty-five days; at the bilateral limits one central bank can call on another for credit in the partner's currency without prospect of a refusal, the amount being repaid under this mechanism. In the most recent extensions to the System negotiated in Nyborg in September 1987, the term of repayment under the VSTF was increased to sixty days and, more importantly, the provision for automatic borrowing for intervention at the limits was extended to cover intervention *within* the limits (so-called intra-marginal intervention). In association with its credit mechanisms the founding of the EMS called for the central banks concerned to pool 20 per cent of their gold and dollar reserves in exchange for ECU in a central fund, the EMCF.

Operation of the system

Our analysis concentrates on the workings of the system prior to British entry in October 1990. The initiative for the establishment of the EMS came not from the European Commission but from the German Chancellor and the French President, Helmut Schmidt and Valéry Giscard d'Estaing. Their decision was in turn guided by a perception that the United States was not capable at the time of exercising a responsible leadership in monetary affairs, and the proximate aim of the EMS was to create a 'zone of monetary stability in Europe'. It was not the first attempt of the EEC members to stabilize their currencies, and the recurrent failures marking these endeavours[10] contributed to the absence of high aspirations to European Monetary Union (EMU) in the stated objectives of the EMS: by contrast, the Werner Committee Report of 1970 had projected the achievement of EMU by 1980! Recent practical experience embodied in the failure of the 'Snake' also contributed to the design of the DI and to a greater degree of self-consciousness about the need for multilateral decision-making on such issues as realignments.

Nevertheless, when it was launched, scepticism was widespread as to whether the System could succeed where its precursors had failed. It was not difficult to greet the inauguration of the EMS as yet further evidence of the triumph of hope over experience. Its survival has belied this early scepticism and there is little dispute that the EMS has so far been something of a success. This accomplishment can be seen as embodied in three principal achievements.

First, despite occasional realignments and fluctuations of currencies within their pre-set bands, it seems that the System has succeeded in its objective of stabilizing exchange rates – not in the absolute sense but in the relevant and realistic sense of bringing about more stability than would have been enjoyed without it. Moreover, this has been done without provoking periodic speculative crises such as marred the demise of the Bretton Woods System.

Second, the claim is made for the EMS that it has provided a framework within which member countries have been able to pursue counter-inflationary policies at a lesser cost in terms of unemployment and lost output than would have been possible otherwise.

Third, while nominal exchange rate stability has been secured it can also be argued that the operation of the System has prevented drastic changes in *real* exchange rates (or competitiveness) from occurring. This is contrasted with the damaging experience in this respect of both the United Kingdom and the United States over the same period.

Finally, although not an immediate objective of the System as such, it is well worth mentioning that in its 'private' form the ECU has become established as a significant currency of denomination of bond issues and other financial instruments, and is actively traded in its own right (including among central banks). This development can be viewed as some testimony to the credibility of the EMS and the successful projection of its identity.

These achievements – all except the last of which we detail and examine below – have not been without some qualifications. One is that the divergence indicator mechanism does not appear to have withstood the test of time. Sceptics would also charge that the counter-inflationary achievements of the EMS in fact amount to little more than a bias against growth and expansion. Finally, the existence until July 1990 of exchange controls in some of the leading countries (notably France and Italy) meant that until then the System had not significantly promoted financial integration and had shielded these countries from the need to con-template the environment for policy-making which was brought about by their removal, as well as by other aspects of the 1992 project for a Single European Market. The System also faces the further challenge of how to integrate the United Kingdom fully into its mechanisms in view of its history of high inflation relative to Germany and other low-inflation countries, and the United Kingdom's apparent reluctance to push on towards monetary cooperation and union. Each of these considerations requires amplification.

Exchange rate stability

As the EMS allows for realignments and for fluctuations of its currencies within the bands, absolute exchange rate stability has not been achieved. Nevertheless, realignments have been few in number, have not always involved the major currencies, have usually been small and have grown less frequent with the passage of time. Table 8.6 details all the realignments that have taken place, from which the support for these contentions is obvious.

A particular feature of the realignment process is that, with some exceptions, it has been free from speculation. When the speculative crises which dogged the end of the Bretton Woods System are recalled, this is a

Table 8.6 ERM parity realignments

	Dates of realignments											
	24/9 1979	30/11 1979	22/3 1981	5/10 1981	22/2 1982	14/6 1982	21/3 1983	21/7 1985	7/4 1986	4/8 1986	12/1 1987	8/1 1990
Belgian franc	0.0	0.0	0.0	0.0	−8.5	0.0	+1.5	+2.0	+1.0	0.0	+2.0	0.0
Danish krone	−2.9	−4.8	0.0	0.0	−3.0	0.0	+2.5	+2.0	+1.0	0.0	0.0	0.0
German mark	+2.0	0.0	0.0	+5.5	0.0	+4.25	+5.5	+2.0	+3.0	0.0	+3.0	0.0
French franc	0.0	0.0	0.0	−3.0	0.0	−5.75	−2.5	+2.0	−3.0	0.0	0.0	0.0
Irish punt	0.0	0.0	0.0	0.0	0.0	0.0	−3.5	+2.0	0.0	−8.0	0.0	0.0
Italian lira	0.0	0.0	−6.0	−3.0	0.0	−2.75	−2.5	−6.0	0.0	0.0	0.0	−3.7*
Dutch guilder	0.0	0.0	0.0	+5.5	0.0	+4.25	+3.5	+2.0	+3.0	0.0	+3.0	0.0

Notes:
A '+' sign indicates the parity has been revalued versus its control rate, a '−' sign that it has been devalued.
*The devaluation of the central rate was combined with the adoption by Italy of the ERM narrow bands. The lower band level remained unaffected by the central rate realignment.

remarkable achievement. An innovation of the EMS in this regard is the practice of carrying out a realignment in such a way that the central rate and bands are changed without disturbing the market rate. This device robs the market of the opportunity to make a 'one-way bet'. The difference is illustrated in Figure 8.5. The one-way bet realignment is sketched in Part (B): the discrete disturbance of the market rate, if correctly anticipated, affords huge gains to speculators. For example, if a currency is allowed to drift to the bottom of its band so that it can only be expected to be devalued by, say, 5 per cent, the gross gains from correctly anticipating the day on which this takes place substantially exceed, in annual interest rate terms, a rate of 1500 per cent (5×365). Speculators could take advantage of this situation by borrowing the weak currency to buy the strong one in anticipation of the devaluation, thereafter redeeming the loan in cheaper currency; clearly, interest rates in the weak-currency country would have to be very high indeed to challenge the huge gains in prospect! The EMS technique of changing the central rate and thus the bands *around* the current market rate in a 'timely' realignment (Part A) robs the speculator of the incentive of such large gains. In practice, EMS realignments have not always been 'timely' – Kenen (1988) estimates the proportion which are timely to be just over 70 per cent – and exchange controls have also played a role in deterring speculation.

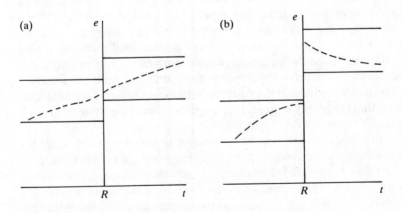

Note:
The figure shows the exchange rate as the dashed line with the bands as solid lines. Time is shown on the horizontal axis; R is the date of a realignment.

Figure 8.5   Exchange rate realignments: (a) a timely realignment; (b) a discrete adjustment.

Given that realignments have taken place and that currencies have fluctuated within the permitted bands, it cannot be assumed that the System has necessarily imparted stability to nominal exchange rates. This question can however be examined statistically. Investigators who have done this have taken to assuming as a counterfactual (or 'antimonde') that in the absence of the EMS, exchange rate stability would have evolved in the same way for the EMS currencies as it did for non-EMS currencies. Thus the examination proceeds by comparing a measure of exchange rate stability for the EMS currencies with a similar measure for non-EMS currencies before, and after, the EMS period itself. By varying the precise measure of the exchange rate used (bilateral or effective), (log) level or (log) change, the data frequency (weekly, monthly, quarterly), and the precise measure of stability employed, this basic counterfactual assumption has supported a variety of estimates. From them, a strong consensus has emerged that the EMS has exerted a stabilizing influence on the bilateral nominal exchange rates of its members.[11]

Inflation control

The successful operation of the System has coincided with the reduction of inflation in member countries and it can be argued that the System offers a framework for reducing inflation at a lower cost in terms of unemployment and output than would be incurred by a go-it-alone counter-inflation policy in a country on a floating exchange rate regime. The model is the Barro–Gordon model of reputational economic policy (cf. Chapter 5), and the argument (which is somewhat elusive empirically) depends upon two propositions: first, that the costs of lowering inflation will be reduced if the counter-inflationary policy is credible and, second, that credibility is greater for a country within the System than it is by going it alone.

On the first, the theory of reputational policies starts with the observation that the credibility of a government's commitment cannot just be taken for granted. For electoral and other reasons a government may be led to renege on commitments it makes; if the apprehension of a weakening is sufficiently widespread the commitment will be distrusted. If a government's announcements about its counter-inflationary intentions and policies are mistrusted, perhaps because of a poor reputation acquired by past behaviour or simply because people consider this to be the way of governments, it will be unable to influence expectations directly. Inflation can then only be brought down by the costly route of demand deflation. But a government may be able to secure greater credibility in various ways: in particular, by committing to policies which are easy to monitor and by raising the visible costs to itself of backsliding. The policies must of course be plausibly related to the goal.

Membership of the EMS offers a number of advantages in these respects for the control of inflation, and this is the second point. Germany is the dominant economy in the System and it has a very secure and well-known record of low inflation. Targeting exchange rates in the EMS involves targeting against the Deutschmark and to the extent that exchange rates reflect relative inflation, a stable Deutschmark exchange rate must imply low, German-like, rates of inflation. An exchange rate commitment is exceptionally easy to monitor; exchange rates are quoted every minute of the day and it is clear what an exchange rate is. Moreover, by committing to the EMS, a government puts its credibility on the line, not only with its own electorate but also with foreign governments; by a government reinforcing its inner resolve with this external link, the commitment is the more credible.[12]

This is the theory. What are the qualifications and what is the evidence? An immediate qualification is that the argument takes for granted that EMS membership puts a heavy premium on exchange rate fixity: yet, as we saw earlier, realignments are a part of the System and were not infrequently used in the early years. How are people to know that the rules have changed from permissiveness to a more disciplined approach and how can they be sure that their government will not go back to the earlier ways of the System? Nor does the evidence really help to give a decisive verdict on the issues. During the 1980s average inflation in the countries that participated in the ERM fell from 12.5 per cent to 4 per cent per annum. Yet these countries are not alone in bringing inflation down from 1970s levels; inflation fell in the United States and the United Kingdom as well. Of course, the claim that the EMS provides a superior counter-inflationary framework does not deny that other countries could bring inflation down – only that the costs for them of doing so are higher when they do not enjoy the anti-inflationary credibility of the Bundesbank, the Bank of Japan or, indeed, the Bank of England under the gold standard.

It must certainly be acknowledged that the EMS has, in fact, been used as a counter-inflationary framework. The Divergence Indicator has been an inevitable casualty of this, for a simple reason. Whereas the DI was designed with the purpose in mind of inducing symmetry of adjustment – and, in particular, of inducing adjustment by Germany – the counter-inflationary policies of the period ran counter to this conception. It was not desirable to induce Germany to raise inflation to the EMS average (even supposing that this could have been done); rather, the point was to bring the average down to the German level.

Competitiveness

The *real* rate of exchange, the nominal rate corrected for relative prices, provides an index of competitiveness. Although the formal provisions of the EMS focus on nominal exchange rates, exchange rate arrangements in a customs union must ensure a degree of stability in real rates of exchange. The reason is that because the real rate of exchange governs an economy's competitiveness, a sharp change – say a large appreciation in the real rate producing a large fall in competitiveness – will arouse protectionist pressures and thus threaten the reversal of the customs union's achievements in removing internal tariff barriers. Other, non-tariff, barriers may be promoted and progress slowed on the removal of these and other obstacles to intra-union trade. Whether reflecting this 'inner logic' or not, the evidence does confirm that whereas the real rates of exchange of both the United Kingdom and the United States have undergone large changes in the 1980s, changes in competitiveness of the EMS economies have been more muted. Thus it appears that among the achievements of the EMS might be included that of reducing the extent of exchange rate misalignment, i.e. deviations of real rates of exchange from equilibrium levels. Figure 8.6 shows measures of competitiveness for the United States, the United Kingdom, Germany, France and Italy.

A qualification must be entered at this stage. It is one thing for the real exchange rate of EMS countries in the mechanism to show less evidence of misalignment than those of some key non-system countries. It is another thing to be sure that the record of the EMS in stabilizing real rates of exchange is adequate. A reason why it might not be adequate is the fact that, as argued above, countries have used the EMS as a counter-infla-tionary framework. Among other things, this has meant that realign-ments, though always changing central rates in the direction indicated by relative inflation, have been deliberately tardy and niggardly in doing so. The object has been to ensure that realignments do not ratify and encourage inflation. A consequence of this is that an economy which persistently inflates above the EMS average rate will undergo prolonged pressure not to adjust its exchange rate to accommodate this and so will gradually lose its competitive edge. Certainly it would seem that the parity changes which have occurred have not fully compensated for inflation rate differentials, bestowing a built-in cost advantage on Germany compared with other countries (Netherlands excepted). Stated alternatively, the Deutschmark has not been sufficiently revalued against the other ERM currencies to offset Germany's lower inflation rate.

Because of the inner logic of real rate stabilization referred to earlier, such a situation could not be regarded as sustainable. The overall success achieved in reducing inflation among the EMS countries, however,

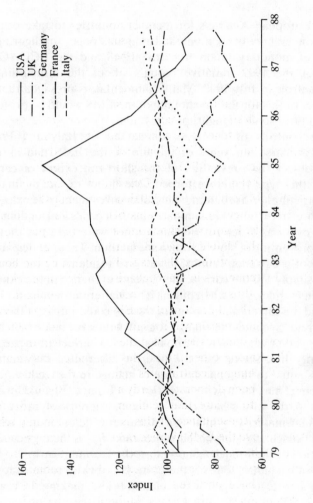

Figure 8.6 Competitiveness 1979–88: normalized unit labour costs.

means that this particular danger is perhaps less acute now than it seemed to be a little earlier.

The challenge of 1992

The Single European Act calls for member countries to take steps to ensure the convergence of economic and monetary policy, prefiguring the emergence of monetary union from the EMS and the ECU. Other provisions of the 1992 initiative brought about the dismantling of exchange controls in July 1990. Many commentators presaged that the consequences of this for the functioning of the EMS would be profound and for its future, some thought, possibly fatal.

Exchange controls of the type maintained by Italy and France throughout the first ten years of the life of the EMS had as their immediate object the prevention of the short-run export of capital. Controls of this type therefore forbade the direct export of financial capital, restricting or forbidding portfolio investment overseas, the holding of foreign currency-denominated bank deposits and lending (and borrowing) overseas. Such restrictions are not watertight but they are effective in preventing or slowing down speculation. Those anticipating a devaluation of a currency cannot, if they are residents of the country concerned, simply sell the currency for foreign exchange in the expectation of making a quick gain when buying it back after the devaluation; nor can they lend the currency to non-residents who could carry out the same speculative raid. Secondly, exchange controls break the link which holds currencies together when there are no obstacles to perfect arbitrage. The interest parity link states that the interest differential between two currencies is equal to the expected rate of change in the exchange rate between them. Thus, taking two countries, say France (F) and Germany (G), interest parity would have $r_F = r_G + d_{F/G}$ where r_F, r_G are interest rates on similar-maturity, similar-risk instruments denominated respectively in the French and German currencies and $d_{F/G}$ is the expected rate of depreciation of the French franc against the German mark.

Removal of exchange controls therefore posed two problems for the EMS. First, a protection against speculation is lost, making the realignment process vulnerable to attack. Second, with the loss of the extra degree of freedom given by the exchange controls it would appear that the position of Germany, the dominant economy of the System, as its 'leader' is reinforced, at least over the longer term. Unless Germany tempers its monetary policy by concern for the economic situation in other countries this could prove to be an unacceptable state of affairs.

These problems were anticipated and various solutions have been proposed. The most complete and the most radical is a rapid push to full European Monetary Union, with a single European currency and a European Central Bank. In such a solution German 'dominance' would be diluted in the collective decision-making of the European Central Bank. This solution, firmly advocated by France and Italy and with strong support from the European Commission, gained striking headway during the course of 1990. It is discussed from an analytical angle in Chapter 10 of this book. Shorter-run solutions to the problem posed by the removal of exchange rate controls (the dismantling of which has been progressive since 1985) include calls for greater monetary policy cooperation, restricting realignments to small adjustments and expanded credit facilities. A widening of the fluctuation bands would be a logical alternative, but this has been felt to be antithetical to the momentum for EMU. In fact, as exchange controls have been removed, the System has operated without any substantive realignments occurring; the expanded credit facilities negotiated in 1987 have been successfully used to protect the System from speculative attack and there has been close following, on occasion, of the Bundesbank's interest rate initiatives (closer monetary cooperation).

Realignments seemed so firmly off the agenda that by 1990 an unforeseen problem (noted earlier) arose in that the strongest currencies in the System appeared to be not the low-inflation Deutschmark and Dutch guilder, but the currencies of the high-inflation countries, Italy and especially Spain. Both countries attempted to maintain high interest rates in order to bear down on inflation, but because the probability of a downward realignment had been marked down by the market in response to its perception of the authorities' policy stance, their high rates tended to force their currencies to the top of the band rather than being seen as compensation for the next devaluation. This problem, reminiscent of that facing the United Kingdom in 1987–8 when the Chancellor shadowed the Deutschmark, meant that interest rate leadership no longer rested unequivocally with Germany, and its solution clearly implies the need for coordination of measures of monetary policy to allow some room for manoeuvre among EMS currencies: in particular, it was apparent by late 1990 that some easing of Spanish interest rates would facilitate a cut in British interest rates. Also, more active fiscal policy in the high-inflation countries, perhaps a temporary use of controls to deter capital *inflows*, or a deflation of the market's exchange rate expectations could ease the position to some extent.

That the problem arose at all might be seen as an index of the success of the System in adapting to an environment free of exchange controls. Certainly, predictions of the early demise of the System were, once again, disappointed.

8.5　The United Kingdom and the EMS

The United Kingdom declined to participate fully in the operation of the EMS, to begin with, out of a belief that the System would be operated in a rigid way which would threaten the United Kingdom, with its high propensity to inflate, with a decline in its competitiveness, especially *vis-à-vis* Germany. Opposition to full membership of the EMS was voiced on these grounds by the Callaghan Labour Government; however, opposition on different grounds was voiced by the incoming Conservative administration. The Thatcher Government wished to run an experiment in monetary policy in order to bring inflation down and reasoned, correctly, that if the instruments of monetary policy (principally, interest rates) are to be directed at reducing the rate of growth of money supply, they cannot simultaneously be used to target the exchange rate. Technically, this dilemma could have been avoided by maintaining a suitably strong set of exchange controls; such controls allow a government some freedom to maintain two different targets for monetary policy. However, the Thatcher Government was keen to remove these controls in any case and did so not long after taking office.

Events were to turn out in a somewhat paradoxical way. In the first phase of the Conservative Government's monetary experiment, the UK inflation rate declined more rapidly than in Italy, France and other high-inflation members of the ERM, but this achievement was associated with a very marked *appreciation* of the exchange rate. Competitiveness (see Figure 8.6) would have been better preserved inside the EMS, and the deep recession that soon set in was attributed by many observers to this cause. The view took root that, although the Thatcher Government was correct to say that membership of the EMS was incompatible with pursuit of an independent monetary policy and would involve a loss of sovereignty in this respect, better results would nevertheless be attained by adhering to the System. In particular, the exchange rate would be steadier and competitiveness more assured while inflation would be dragged – albeit more slowly (and some would add, more surely) – towards the modest German level (we have already described the claims made for the EMS as a counter-inflationary framework).

The view gained momentum as official British policy towards the exchange rate as a target changed and as it became clear that monetary policy was no longer aimed in single-minded fashion solely at controlling the supply of money. In fact, with practice preceding the public statement, the Chancellor of the Exchequer made this very clear in his 1983 budget speech. A House of Lords Report on the question of entry into the EMS, published a little later in the same year, favoured 'early, though not necessarily immediate' entry into the System.

The Report referred to four problems that the United Kingdom had had in relation to the EMS and noted that in each case events had moved in a favourable fashion. The first problem was the apprehension that the System would prove rigid and inflexible: the Committee noted that the System had in fact allowed a number of realignments. The second problem was that the United Kingdom had wanted to put the control of the money supply ahead of the goal of stabilizing the exchange rate: as described, policy had already retreated somewhat on this issue. The third problem arose from sterling's still persistent role as a vehicle currency, i.e. one widely held by agents other than those solely concerned with UK trade. The Committee acknowledged that this might mean that it would not be easy to stabilize sterling in the ERM. The fourth problem was related to the UK position as an oil exporter, with sterling subject to quite a different response than the other EMS currencies to oil price shocks.

There were historical precedents for apprehension on the last count: the failure of the Snake (the precursor of the EMS) in the 1970s followed the disruption created by the first oil shock in 1973–4, in the aftermath of which countries followed different adjustment policies incompatible with maintaining fixed exchange rates between themselves. Yet, the inception of the EMS in March 1979 coincided with the second oil shock. Following a meeting in December 1978, the OPEC countries raised oil prices in several stages through 1979 by some 130 per cent. On the face of it, such a shock coming so soon after the founding of the System might have been supposed to expose it to similar strains and ensure its early demise. In fact, the System not only survived the shock but, in the eyes of some observers, proved to have some added advantages in providing for its members a framework within which to prosecute efficient counter-inflationary policies.

The first advantage that the EMS proved to have over the Snake was the provision for realignment. As Table 8.6 showed, the realignments at the beginning were quite frequent. It was important for the System's survival that it should have been able to allow exchange rate realignments at this stage and still continue as a System. This contrasted with the Snake, where countries changing their exchange rates were deemed to leave the Snake. In the early period, then, as countries adjusted to the inflationary shock of the oil price rise in different ways, the EMS displayed sufficient flexibility to survive.

When the House of Lords Report was written, its authors saw the problems posed by sterling's possible status as a 'petro-currency' as less of an issue as the oil market had become less disturbed. It is ironic that Britain should eventually decide to join the ERM in the middle of the third oil price shock, which resulted from the hostilities in the Gulf in 1990, and which saw sterling rise relative to other EMS currencies –

although no doubt this event was one factor conditioning the decision to adopt the wider ±6 per cent band for sterling upon entry.

The viewpoint of the House of Lords Report appears to have been representative of a wide range of opinion. Although the later report of a subcommittee of the House of Commons Select Committee on the Treasury and Civil Service revived some of the earlier arguments against entry, the general climate of opinion had changed markedly in a favourable direction by the early 1980s. With the passage of time the lingering reservations over the exposure of sterling to oil shocks and over the problem of speculation diminished still further. Meanwhile the case for exchange rate management became more widely and firmly accepted. The initiative launched by the United States in 1985 to secure the coordinated actions of its major partners to bring the dollar down substantially reinforced the latter process.

In September 1986, at the meeting of the International Monetary Fund, the Chancellor of the Exchequer advertised the non-speculative realignment process of the EMS and not long afterwards followed this up with a policy of shadowing the EMS by way of keeping the sterling exchange rate closely in line with the Deutschmark. As we have seen, this policy initiative lasted for just over a year; by the end of February 1988, following a well-publicized exchange of views between the Chancellor and the Prime Minister, sterling was uncapped. Higher interest rates, invoked as a means of dampening monetary growth and inflation, caused the exchange rate to appreciate through its previous working ceiling.

The resurgence of inflation from 1988 raised anew the inflation differential obstacle to UK entry and this was expanded into a number of conditions which had to be met before Britain would join:

1. First, British inflation must be substantially reduced and brought more in line with inflation elsewhere in the EC.
2. At the same time, France and Italy must abandon all remaining restrictions on capital movements.
3. In addition, the EMS must be seen to be functioning well following the total liberalization of capital movements from July 1990.
4. Finally, real progress must be made in the area of completing the internal market.

To these was added in 1989 a fifth condition, for the British Government wanted to see the influence of German unification on exchange rates before joining. As it transpired, Britain joined before all of these conditions – and especially that concerning inflation – were attained, with the Chancellor neatly removing the inflation reduction requirement by redefining the convergence to be one of prospective rather than actual inflation rates.[13]

But it is fair to say that the main sticking-point always was that adherence to the ERM involves a loss of sovereignty, whether conceived of as a loss of the ability to use monetary policy to influence the exchange rate without the constraints involved in collective decision-making or as the loss – in a system free of exchange controls – of the ability to pursue a monetary policy independent of the need to target the exchange rate within the bands established. The question is whether it is worth forgoing these losses. Those who seek a framework for stabilizing the exchange rate, real or nominal, argue that the added credibility given to an exchange rate target by pursuing it within the EMS makes the loss of sovereignty involved in joining the System quite nominal. By the same token, it can be argued that the loss of monetary policy independence by Britain is likely to be high only if Community monetary policy is at variance with that *desired* by Britain. In the light of the benefit to be gained from 'importing the Bundesbank's reputation', the loss might appear purely notional, the gains of substance. Much of the impetus for what might be seen as a change of heart by the British Government was that joining the mechanism was, in the end and with an election looming, the easiest way of restoring quickly the anti-inflationary credibility which had been so hard won in the first half of the 1980s and lost so quickly in the second.

With the European 'financial common market' commencing in January 1993 there was added urgency to the decision. As 1993 got closer, the potential losses from staying outside would have mounted up, for that would have meant having exchange rate risk continue to divide British from other intra-European trade and financial transactions.

Nevertheless, the issue of sovereignty has not gone away, for the EMS that Britain joined is different from that which the then Chancellor of the Exchequer, Mr Nigel Lawson, wanted to join five years earlier in October 1985. Where entry in earlier years would not have compromised an ability to realign relatively freely and would have implied no commitment to full-blown EMU, the recent evolution of the System heavily qualifies both these features. The Report of the Delors Committee (Delors Report, 1989) identifies membership of the ERM with participation in Stage One of an evolution towards EMU, while the concept of a quite rapid movement towards full EMU occupies centre stage in discussions of the operation of the System and contributes to its realignment-free comportment. Yet the UK Government has set its face firmly against EMU or at least against any rapid transition to EMU and has provided its own proposal for a parallel currency (the 'hard ECU') as a counterweight. We take up these matters in Chapter 10.

Conclusions

British monetary policy has flirted with various forms of exchange rate management in recent years. The debacle of the early years of the MTFS gave way to a period in which the exchange rate was used as a conditioning factor in the implementation of (adherence to) monetary targets. Theory indicates that such a policy may be highly appropriate when the demand for money is unreliable. In this case, both those whose primary concern was with the real exchange rate and those who saw exchange rate targeting as a step on the way to efficient inflation control could regard the policy development as favourable to their interest. The subsequent hardening of policy, stimulated partly by world events and partly by an interest in the EMS option itself, ended in a series of somersaults – when the experiment in shadowing the Deutschmark was cancelled, Britain returned to eclectic domestic monetarism, seemingly raised additonal obstacles to EMS entry, and then entered without having cleared the principal hurdle of a convergence of British inflation to EC levels.

The problem of Britain's inflation, and the transition from EMS to EMU, is taken up again in Chapter 10. This is preceded by an analysis of some effects of increased financial and economic integration.

Appendix

In the text, the PPP-quantity theory monetary approach to the exchange rate is outlined. With all variables (except for the interest rate and inflation) in logs, the model outlined there can be written as

$$m = p + ay + br \qquad a > 0; b < 0 \tag{1}$$

and for the 'rest of the world'

$$m^* = p^* + a^*y^* = b^*r^* \qquad a^* > 0; b^* < 0 \tag{2}$$

where (1) and (2) are demand for money equations in obvious notation. Equation (3) is the PPP equation, with e measured as the exchange rate in units of domestic currency (so a rise is a depreciation)

$$p_T = p^*_T + e \tag{3}$$

where the subscript T refers to traded goods, and Equations (4) and (5) express a relationship between overall and traded goods prices as

$$p = p_T + k \tag{4}$$

$$p^* = p^*_T + k^* \tag{5}$$

Substitution then gives

$$e = (m - ay - br) - (m^* - a^*y^* - b^*r^*) + (k - k^*) \tag{6}$$

In stationary equilibrium, with perfect capital mobility, $r = r^*$ and if (for simplicity) the coefficients are the same in both countries and $a = a^* = 1$ (income elasticity of money demand is unity), then

$$e = (m - y) - (m^* - y^*) = (m - m^*) - (y - y^*) \tag{7}$$

To study inflationary equilibrium, assume for additional simplicity that the two countries are of equal size (so the income terms drop out). However, in the domestic country there is inflation; the interest rate incorporates this inflation premium π so $r = r^* + \pi$. Perfect capital mobility requires in equilibrium

$$de = r - r^* \tag{8}$$

Equation (7) under these restrictions will read

$$e = (m - m^*) - (b\pi) \tag{7'}$$

As b is negative, rising prices cause, *ceteris paribus*, a devaluation of the exchange rate.
Since the PPP equation (with $k = k^* = 0$) can be inverted to yield the *price* equation

$$p = p^* + e \tag{9}$$

it is clear that the price level is higher in the inflationary equilibrium than it is in the stationary equilibrium.
To check this, note that (1) also may be inverted to give

$$p = m - ay - br \tag{10}$$

so that the fall in money demand associated with the higher nominal interest rate calls for a higher price level when the money stock and real income are given.

Notes

1. A large volume of empirical work on exchange rate determination is reviewed in MacDonald and Taylor (1989).
2. Williamson (1985) has been particularly eloquent in pressing these arguments.
3. Another way of putting this would be to say that firms use – as far as they can – a notion of the 'normal' or 'permanent' exchange rate in their pricing decisions.
4. See e.g. Bank of England (1984).

5. At the analytical level, analyses like those by Dornbusch (1976) and Buiter and Miller (1981) suggest that the real exchange rate will be an immediate casualty of programmes of monetary restraint.

6. See Kenen (1988) and Laskar (1986) for analyses favourable to the idea of exchange rate agreement as approaching coordination, and Holtham *et al.* (1989) for an empirical model-based and negative verdict.

7. There is a high degree of consensus among the principal models on this issue. For an interesting account of the position at an earlier date, when the consensus was emerging, readers are encouraged to refer to Posner (1978a,b).

8. In some models (e.g. HM Treasury, 1987), *dynamic* as well as static homogeneity is imposed, ruling out this possibility.

9. Formally, the indicator is calculated as follows:

    1. First by calculating the premium (*P*) or discount (*D*) shown by the market rate of the ECU in terms of that currency against its ECU-related central rate:

    $$P \text{ or } D = \frac{ECU \; market - ECU \; central}{ECU \; central} \times 100$$

    2. And then by comparing the result obtained with the maximum divergence spread (MDS), calculated as above, p. 221.

    $$DI = \frac{P \text{ or } D}{MDS} \times 100$$

    In order to permit a comparison of movements in the divergence indicators for each of the currencies participating in the EMS, the maximum divergence spread for each currency is assigned an index of 100. The indicator will therefore be expressed by a figure ranging between 1 and 100. A currency reaches its divergence threshold when the indicator displays the figure of 75. (See Ypersele and Koeune, 1984.)

10. The reader should refer to Swann (1988) for a useful summary and to Kruse (1980) for a detailed account of these past endeavours.

11. A recent example of this kind of approach is provided in a study for the IMF by Ungerer *et al.* (1986). A confirmatory study employing different techniques is Artis and Taylor (1988).

12. The title of the paper by Giavazzi and Pagano (1988) on this issue, 'The advantage of tying one's hands: EMS discipline and central bank credibility', is indicative of the issues at stake.

13. By choosing an ECU central parity which resulted in a Deutschmark central rate of DM2.95 = £1, close to the market rate at the time (around 2.93), the realignment (of actual relative to notional parity) was a 'timely one' which minimized disruptions to domestic policy settings.

9

Change in the financial sector

Introduction

As noted in Chapter 1, change in the financial sector is not a wholly new phenomenon. Yet the pace of change appears to have gathered force dramatically in the decade from the mid 1970s. It affects not only banking but financial institutions and capital markets more generally, as exemplified in the United Kingdom by the 1986 Big Bang which transformed the basis of stock exchange dealing in London and provoked the competitive deregulation of Paris and other continental European bourses. Naturally such changes also implicate banking activities – for example, the Big Bang reforms have led a number of banks to become engaged as stock exchange operators, and generally hastened the trend to universal banking. However, change in the markets is not a seamless web; the factors affecting banking activity have been in part specific and in this chapter we concentrate our attention on a selection of those aspects of change in the financial markets which specifically relate to aspects of banking activities, money and monetary policy.

Treatment of financial innovation highlights three major driving forces. First of all, there is technology. The steep decline in the costs of communication and the widespread introduction of computer technology have had major impacts. The radical reduction in transactions costs implied facilitates the routinization of deals previously regarded as too complex for regular implementation – hence currency and interest rate swaps, conceptually always feasible, are made computationally practic-

239

able; it also provides the basis for more efficient monitoring of large volumes of business and provides a ready flow of data for management decisions. At a fundamental level, computerization offers the prospect of instant clearing and in the limit the disappearance of money: if alternative earning assets can be liquidated on the spot to finance an act of expenditure, the need to hold money in advance will disappear.[1] The reduction in communication costs facilitates arbitrage across national boundaries and the integration of the world's capital markets.

Technology is not the only influence. Two others widely cited are the experience of the high and variable inflation period of the 1970s, and the cycle of regulation and deregulation. These interact with what almost might be seen as a separate contributing factor, namely the process of change and innovation emanating from within the industry as a consequence of the ongoing competitive struggle; this in particular seems to be an important element in many of the new instruments and techniques associated with banks' securitized lending.

The 1970s experience exposed the inefficiency in the more variable climate of the period of the practices inherited from more stable times. In consequence fixed rate gave way to variable rate lending. The premium on more flexible ways of doing business, though arising in particular circumstances, none the less left a permanent residue as intermediaries invested in the technology and learnt ways of doing business which preserved an efficiency gain even when a more stable environment had been re-established. Involved in a similar way is the regulatory framework. Exposed to new pressures as times change, a given regulatory framework provokes profit-seeking institutions to find ways round the rules. Not all the discoveries become redundant when the regulation is changed or removed or when the pressures calling for innovation around the rules subside.

While regulation itself provokes innovations, deregulation provokes even more. As the regulators discovered that the earlier frameworks were increasingly ill-adapted to accommodate technological change or were of diminishing utility in the light of avoidance-innovation activity, these frameworks were changed. Like the other factors mentioned so far, this reaction appears to have been global, even if the United States and the United Kingdom are commonly cited as deregulating most and earliest. Indeed, the deregulation process produces its own dynamic as deregulation in one country shifts the locale of financial activity towards it and puts pressure on legislators in other countries to follow suit. This dynamic dominated the 1980s.[2] The deregulation then changes the rules within which the process of intermediation and the financial markets operate, leading to a new wave of 'innovations' or adaptations. In a longer-term perspective a cycle of regulation, deregulation and reregulation (etc.) seems plausible. Regulation is displaced by deregulation as profit-seeking institutions and technical changes cause the regulatory framework to be seen as outmoded and inefficient. Then the performance of the deregulated system results in a crisis, or in persistent strains that invite its reregulation. The new regulations may differ from the old ones, but set in train a repetition of the process.

The main themes we explore below are the globalization of banking activity and the interplay between domestic and international banking; the growth of the securitization of banking (a form of bank-managed disintermediation); the phenomenon of currency substitution and its implications; and finally the implications of some of these trends for the transmission mechanism and for monetary policy. The latter part of the discussion builds on the themes already presented in Chapter 5.

9.1 International banking and financial integration

Until the 1960s, banks conducted international banking from their home bases. With only minor exceptions, the location of banking and currency of denomination were inseparable: banking was a natural monopoly of the banks located in the country issuing the currency used for borrowing and lending. Deposits were taken from foreigners, and lending to foreigners occurred, in the currency of the country in which the main offices of banks were located. Much international bank lending is still carried out in this traditional way. Thus Deutsche Bank, say, lends marks to foreign borrowers from Frankfurt, and Chase Manhattan lends to foreigners in US dollars from New York. However, at September 1989 only 14 per cent of gross international bank lending outstanding was 'booked out' in this traditional fashion (see Table 9.1). Most international lending is instead externalized in the Eurocurrency centres.

By separating the location of the banking from the currency used for borrowing and lending, the Eurocurrency system also separated currency (exchange rate) risk from political risk. A depositor holding dollar balances in a country other than the United States combines the currency risk of holding US dollars with the political risk of the particular country (Britain, Belgium, Singapore, etc.) which is host to the dollar operations. This 'essential feature', as Niehans (1984) calls it, was instrumental in giving rise to Eurocurrency operations. With the advent of the Cold War,

Table 9.1 Measures of international[1] bank lending and the Eurocurrency market as at end of year, 1977–89 ($ billion)

	1977	1980	1983	1986	1989[2]
I External lending in Eurocurrencies by banks in:					
1. European centres	384.9	751.3	903.4	1 383.5	1 867.1
2. Canada	17.8	34.9	39.5	49.6	43.7
3. Japan	18.2	48.7	78.3	207.4	470.6
4. United States[3]		–	172.4	249.4	343.8
5. Other offshore centres	174.1	318.0	501.1	710.2	1,069.8
6. Total external lending in Eurocurrencies	595.0	1 152.9	1 694.7	2 600.1	3 795.0
II Foreign currency lending to residents in:					
7. Europe, Canada and Japan	153.5	319.0	450.6	753.7	1 122.7
8. Gross Eurocurrency market (6+7)	748.5	1 471.9	2 145.3	3 353.8	4 917.7
III Domestic currency lending to foreigners by banks in:					
9. European centres	81.4	151.7	145.8	301.4	385.5
10. Canada	0.4	0.6	2.4	4.2	3.9
11. Japan	3.5	17.0	30.8	137.9	168.0
12. United States	90.2	172.6	216.9	221.5	226.0
13. Gross international bank lending (8 + 9 + 10 + 11 + 12)	924.0	1 813.8	2 541.2	4 018.8	5 701.1
Memo: Net international bank lending (BIS)	435	810	1 240	1 790.0	2 490.0

Notes:
1. All cross-border and cross-currency business of BIS reporting banks.
2. End of September 1989 figures.
3. Mainly IBFs.

Sources:
Lewis and Davis (1987, T8.2); BIS International Banking and Financial Market Developments, November 1989, February 1990.

Russia and other holders of dollars had a desire to conduct dollar banking business in locales where their balances could not be impounded like those of some foreign countries in the United States during World War II by the alien property custodian.

But growth during the 1960s owed more to economic blockages. Since the US dollar was the intervention currency in the Bretton Woods System, there was a worldwide demand to hold dollar balances in the United States to serve as a means of effecting international payments and consequently as a store of value, for future international transactions. Because the US dollar was the preferred medium for deferred payments, there was a demand also to borrow dollars. This demand was normally met by borrowings from banks and securities markets in New York and from other capital flows in the form of official aid and direct foreign investment by US corporations. Measures were then introduced in the mid 1960s by the US authorities, worried about the US balance of payments deficit, to control outflows. At the same time, domestic reserve requirements and ceilings which limited the interest rates the US-based banks could offer on deposits provided a continuing incentive for recipients of dollars to place deposits, still in dollars, with banks operating in Europe, free of these US controls. Banking had also been separated from the economic risk of taxes and duties levied by the country issuing the currency of denomination.

Banking transactions in US dollars outside the United States expanded rapidly. By dealing in dollars, British and other European merchant and international banks were able to put their expertise to work in international trade financing, despite being restricted in lending overseas in their domestic currencies. Banks in Europe were thus able to survive, and may even have encouraged, increased use of the dollar in world trade. In the late 1940s perhaps nearly 50 per cent of world trade was in sterling. Now the position is markedly different. Almost all trade in primary commodities is invoiced in US dollars. The US dollar is also the vehicle currency in foreign exchange trading, used possibly in over 90 per cent of transactions (Kenen, 1983).

Not all the original Eurobanks were European: US banks were prominent in developing branch networks overseas to accept dollar deposits and to make dollar loans. While originally confined to Europe – hence the prefix 'Euro' – Eurocurrency borrowings and lending are now conducted on a large scale in a number of other locations as well.[3] Customers of the banks are located in almost all countries of the world, yet the great bulk – in the order of 70 per cent – of total gross Eurocurrency activity is business of one bank with another. Some Eurocurrency activity is not international at all and occurs within a country's domestic banking market: deposits are taken from residents and loans made to residents denominated in non-local currencies. Although the US dollar is the main currency of denomination, other currencies account for 20 per cent of operations. US banks are no longer the largest national grouping of participants: Japanese banks hold more international loans. But major banks from virtually all countries conduct Eurocurrency business. There are few Eurobanks, as such: most are merely branches, operations being a compartment of an overall banking balance sheet. Nor is there a Euromarket as such. Although it is located in terms of book transactions in various Eurocentres, the worldwide market physically consists of networks of telephones, telexes and monitor screens around the world – communications equipment which might be used for purposes other than Eurocurrency transactions. From an estimated $20 billion in 1964, the gross size of the Eurocurrency market had grown to $4,918 billion at September 1989 (Table 9.1). When we seek to explain the causes of this growth, we clearly have to go beyond enumerating the factors that gave rise to the initiation of the market, as described above, for most of these are no longer operative and in any case could not explain the rise in Eurobanking in currencies of denomination other than US dollars.

Several explanations of the growth of Eurobanking have been put forward by observers.[4] One group has emphasized the offshore element, so that the operations in the Eurocurrency markets are seen to be providing substitutes for domestic intermediation – like the branches of the German banks in Luxembourg. Where the transactions are between banks, Eurocurrency operations act as an alternative interbank market. Others have concentrated on the currency aspect, looking upon the Eurobanks as adjuncts to the wholesale foreign exchange markets. Yet other have focused upon the cross-border characteristics, seeing the banks' operations as part of a global funds market. There is also the role of some offshore centres as tax havens to be taken into account, for 23 per cent of assets and liabilities are inter-office transactions, some of which may be transfer-pricing activities undertaken by multinational banks to reduce taxation and evade regulations. All these activities can be seen as parts of an even larger whole, in which the Eurobanks are also involved as wholesale intermediaries in the cross-border, cross-currency production of liquidity services.

A common thread running through the various explanations which we review below is the absence of regulation of various kinds. In the Eurocurrency compartment of their balance sheet, banks are normally free of reserve requirements and deposit insurance premiums, and usually have greater freedom to determine the holding of bank capital and to select the quality of their loan and investment portfolio. A bank is to a large extent an accounting arrangement which can be reorganized and restructured readily, and modern communications facilities enable a divergence between the legal and actual location of banking activities. For these reasons a certain amount of Eurocurrency activity, in terms of its location, is associated with tax havens.

The banks are, as a result, able to transact more cheaply than from their home bases. International traders are thus able to hold balances of the major currencies used in international trade, and to cover forward foreign exchange commitments, more cheaply and more effectively than by means of traditional foreign banking. Clearly, this particular competitive advantage of Eurocurrency business would be lost if the domestic rules and regulations were removed.[5] In this respect the markets are a classic example of a regulation product.

But Eurobanks, like all banks, act as financial intermediaries. They activate balances which would otherwise have been idle and put them to use financing projects which might otherwise not have taken place. As compared with domestic banking, the funds are collected across national boundaries. Much of the Eurocurrency banking activity may therefore transcend what banks would carry out in traditional banking. Central to the global funds market theory, interbank markets in centres such as London are seen as efficient allocators of funds on a worldwide basis. The Eurocurrency markets might conceivably retain this advantage even if the cost advantage of the regulatory environment were removed by deregulation in domestic markets.

We argued in Chapter 6 that wholesale banks do more than just distribute liquidity and that interbank markets in wholesale intermediation do more than just rearrange funds. It is our contention that the same holds for Eurocurrency banking: that banks undertake considerable liquidity production in Eurobanking and that the interbank markets (the syndicated loans market and interbank funding markets), like the reinsurance markets in international insurance business, play a major role in sharing among groups of banks the risks of international lending operations.

Because of the freedom from regulation, the view of the Eurodeposit banking multiplier as essentially limitless has been popular. Friedman (1969b) first drew attention to the banking system's ability in principle to create deposits and thereby liberated analysts from the belief, then current, that the size of the Eurodollar market was limited by the US balance of payments deficit. Friedman's point was that reserves for Eurobanks (then predominantly Eurodollar banks) were deposits with US commercial banks; in the absence of formal reserve requirements and a direct means of payment obligation, however, reserve holding was small and the conventional multiplier would appear correspondingly huge. If q is the banks' own reserve ratio and p is the redeposit ratio, the multiplier is $1/[1-p(1-q)]$. If p is thought of as large (an assumption of unity is conventional for a retail banking system) and q as small, then the multiplier obviously assumes large values. Friedman himself and other writers offered several caveats, most of which boil down to suggesting that p is in fact quite low – for example, Lewis and Davis (1987) suggest $p = 0.2$, $q = 0$, giving a multiplier of only 1.25 (p. 283). The growth of the system is thus not due to high multiplier effects [6] but rather to parallel increases in deposits and reserves resulting from portfolio preferences.

Whatever the category of Eurobank under consideration, it is important to remind ourselves that there is not a separate Eurocurrency banking system 'which is segmented from the several domestic banking systems in the same way that the dollar banking system is segmented from the sterling banking system' (Aliber, 1980). Friedman argued that Eurodollars are a segment of the dollar banking system. By similar reasoning, Euromarks are part of the Deutschmark banking system and so on. Where the Eurodollar banks are branches of US banks there is not even a different currency involved (as is also the case with branches of German banks in Luxembourg). Reserves held by the foreign branches of US banks against Eurodollars are not segmented from those of domestic offices. In the same way, reserves of domestic branches are not separated from those at head or regional offices. Banks pool reserves against domestic and offshore deposits, just as they pool reserves against time, demand and other deposit categories, and thus hold few, if any, additional reserves against offshore deposits. Consequently, efforts to compute a fractional credit multiplier for the offshore system are complicated by the difficulty of distinguishing the reserves of offshore banks (and this factor may account for the wide range of the estimates made).

The determination of interest rates on Eurodeposits and loans affords a critical point of linkage with domestic monetary conditions, in the absence of exchange controls. Arbitrage links offshore and onshore rates together, and at the same time hedging links the quotation of interest rates in different currencies. Thus, we expect to find Eurodollar deposit rates for given term to maturity closely similar to onshore bank deposit interest rates of identical term, while the comparable rate quotation for a deposit in currency X simply reflects the US interest rate and the premium in the forward X/$ exchange rate. Rate quotations are in fact typically generated this way (Johnston, 1979; Taylor, 1987).

The role of the Eurocurrency market in intermediating the oil exporters' surpluses in the 1970s provoked descriptions of the system as a global funds system, serving 'as a medium for world-wide redistribution of short-term funds from surplus units and surplus regions to deficit units and deficit regions' (Thore, 1984). Conditions in the 1980s, however, would seem to fit in less happily with this model. Large payments imbalances have again occurred, but these have not been intermediated through banks' balance sheets to anything like the same extent. In-house banking by multinationals and the trend to securitization (see below) point to a reduction in the costs of transacting between non-bank entities. Indeed, the Cross Report (BIS, 1986) wonders whether banks may be losing their comparative advantage in favour of direct financing through capital markets. The model moreover downgrades the role of liquidity creation (maturity transformation), which we believe to be a significant aspect of its operation; the evidence suggests that the process works in much the same way as for sterling wholesale business, discussed in Chapter 6 above (data on Eurocurrency mismatching appear in Lewis and Davis (1987), pp. 94–104 and 304–8). Also, as we argue in the following section, liquidity creation can occur in off-balance sheet transactions.

In summary, Eurocurrency banking operations are complex, and it is not surprising that attempts to explain the nature of the bank's business are numerous. Some see Eurobanking activities as international in location only, arguing that Eurobanks provide facilities which merely replicate offshore the functions of domestic banks and domestic interbank markets. According to this view, they are essentially externally transplanted non-banking intermediaries and substitutes for the domestic money markets. Others see the Eurobanks as supplanting traditional foreign banking, providing international trade financing and forward foreign exchange cover free of regulations which hamper the domestic production of these services. Another view sees Eurobanks as truly international in their operations, collecting idle funds from one region of the world and channelling them via interbank and intrabank networks to other regions of the world. It is possible to agree with all these views: Eurobanking is multidimensional and serves a number of ends. What appears to be disagreement among economists is mostly no more than a reflection of the passage of time. As the market has grown, so it has taken on more functions and has progressively become more integrated and global.

9.2 Securitization

Securities markets can be seen to be passing through a process of globalization, much as occurred in banking. Banking markets in different countries (and currencies) were once separated by exchange controls, reserve ratios, banking laws and regulations, and interest rate controls. These differences created opportunities for banks in the Euromarkets. A near perfect market was established between the various Eurocurrencies, and the diversion of domestic business to the Euromarkets led eventually to pressures for domestic financial liberalization. In the process, there has been created effectively one international short-term money market.

Barriers separating securities markets can be thought of as two types: natural and man-made. Natural barriers arise from all the costs of effecting financial transactions, the different information which parties possess and their risk and liquidity preferences. They have long been supplemented by man-made ones. National authorities have sought to control access by foreign borrowers to the longer-term domestic capital markets through documentation rules, queues, notification procedures, controls on the conversion of domestic into foreign currencies, ownership restrictions on equity holdings, withholding taxes on interest income, inability to issue bearer securities and so on. These have encouraged the growth of Eurobonds, issued largely free of these restrictions. The decline of foreign bond issues in favour of Eurobonds has seen removal of many of the restrictions, paralleling what happened in banking markets.

Nevertheless, this process is far from complete, leaving arbitrage opportunities which can be exploited by banks and other institutions. In conjunction with the other forces for change noted at the beginning of this chapter, deregulation of banking and financial markets seems likely to speed up the international integration of capital markets, if only because of the larger number of institutions participating in international finance.

What is intriguing is the innovative way in which the regulatory structures are being pierced and the natural barriers lowered. One method is that of surrogate borrowing through cross-currency swaps. In a cross-currency swap, the counterparties exchange interest payments in one currency for interest payments in another currency. Such exchanges work on the principle of the 'gains from trade'. Each party raises funds on the market where it has a comparative advantage, and then trades with the assistance of an intermediary. For instance, a US firm wanting Deutschmark funding, but unknown in the German capital market, and a German firm seeking US dollar borrowings, but little known in the United States, can each borrow in their home currency and swap the interest and principal at an agreed exchange rate. Or a German bank may act as a surrogate borrower for an Australian firm in Australian dollars on the Eurobond market, creating by means of the swap an offshore corporate debenture market in Australian dollars (Lewis and Polasek, 1990). Construction of a synthetic market can serve as a substitute for an actual market or, if an onshore market exists, ensure that any controls imposed on it are arbitraged away.

These examples of financial engineering are one part of the trend towards the securitization of bank activities in world and domestic markets which is seeing a merging of traditional commercial banking and investment banking (Lewis, 1990). Securitization refers both to the switch away from bank intermediation to direct financing via capital markets and to the transformation of previously illiquid assets like loans into marketable instruments (Gardener, 1986). With banks still retaining an interest in and profit from the borrowing and lending activity involved, to this extent the phenomenon amounts to a bank-managed disinter-mediation of credit. Curiously, some of the instruments involved in the off-balance sheet activities such as commercial bills of exchange, acceptances and the like are simply rediscoveries of older financing methods, not new in themselves.

The trend appears to go against the traditional perception of the advantages of bank intermediation. When using securities markets for their financing, borrowers and lenders face certain information costs. Lenders must ascertain borrowers' attributes, monitor their performance and possibly devise work out solutions. Borrowers face the costs of providing the information which lenders require and of entering into covenants which ensure compliance with the contract. Lenders also have credit risks and liquidity needs. Assets backing an issue of securities may prove to be worthless or decline markedly in value, while borrowers may be tardy in repaying loans or may default. Spending opportunities and consumption needs may present themselves which lead the lender to want to sell off all or part of the funds lent out. Borrowers are generally unable to provide the risk diversification sought after by lenders; nor, generally, are they well placed to meet lenders' liquidity needs.

Banks and other financial intermediaries specialize in obtaining and using information about credit risks. They acquire proprietary information because firms can thereby avoid having to make business information available through market releases. As providers of transactions services, banks have access to sources of information which enable them to select better loans and monitor their performance at lower costs than would otherwise be the case, or if they sought to use credit rating agencies. These information services are provided when lenders hold claims against financial intermediaries and delegate to them decisions about the allocation of savings to various ends. Banks and other intermediaries offer a flexibility which markets do not provide. They allow depositors to withdraw balances on demand or at short notice, and moreover at full face value. Yet they themselves hold large portfolios of securities with limited saleability and which individually have risk. Banks are able to offer customers these assurances in part because information advantages enable them to select assets which have low individual default risks and in part because their portfolio size enables maturities of assets to be staggered to match anticipated deposit withdrawals. They also offer a risk-pooling service, exploiting the law of large numbers and the regularities which emerge when large numbers of withdrawal options and loan risks are combined. Some of this pooling takes place within the banking institution, as is the case in retail banking. With wholesale banking most of the pooling occurs across institutions, with loan risks spread by participations and syndicates, and liquidity needs shared out among the group of banks which make use of interbank funding markets and correspondent links. Customers could break lots themselves by spreading deposits and writing loans with a number of banks, but the syndication procedures developed by banks and the established interbank markets enable this process to be carried out at less cost. By straddling the retail and wholesale sectors of the capital market, banks perform a size intermediation function and tailor-make financial packages to customers' needs.

Hence traditional on-balance sheet borrowing and lending operations of banks can be seen to be packages of information and risk-sharing (or insurance) services.

We are used to thinking of banks as a collection of assets and liabilities making up a balance sheet. The conception which underlies Figure 9.1 is of a bank as a collection of contracts, only some of which at any given time make their appearance 'on' the balance sheet – the others are off-balance sheet. These contracts define the information and risk-sharing services provided by banks to their customers. The upper portion of the figure shows the services which are embodied in the traditional on-balance sheet deposit and loan contracts offered by banks. In offering these services, banks attenuate the financial risks which their customers face by taking on part of the risk. For this, they receive remuneration in the form of service charges and interest rate spreads, when lenders are prepared to forgo interest income to obtain the bank guarantee.

Off-balance sheet activities are also vehicles for information and risk-sharing services. As such, they attenuate financial risks incurred by bank customers and impose risks on banks. The establishment of a credit line earns a bank a commitment fee and affords the customer protection against liquidity needs, but exposes the bank to offsetting liquidity risk which it is better able to bear. Banks also protect customers against, and themselves incur, asset risk through activities such as bill acceptances and standby letters of credit. In both cases, banks essentially guarantee payment of a customer's liability to a holder of its debt should the customer default. Fees charged to the customer reflect the benefits of the lower interest rate required by the market on the customer's paper once a bank guarantee of payment is attached. Although the initial incidence of the fee is on the bank's customers (the borrower), the ultimate effect of the lower yield is equivalent to the holder of risky (higher-yielding) paper

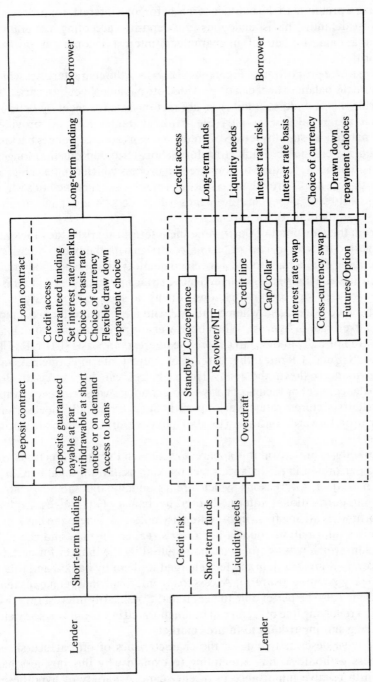

Figure 9.1 Comparison of on- and off-balance sheet banking.
Source: Lewis (1988).

paying a premium to the bank, in terms of forgone interest, for protection against default. This is analogous to a depositor accepting a guarantee from a bank in lieu of unguaranteed interest income on primary securities.

The lower proportion of Figure 9.1 shows how the characteristics which feature on-balance sheet can be provided off-balance sheet by a variety of instruments. Lenders' credit risks are met on-balance sheet by deposits which are repayable at par; the bank guarantee can be provided alternatively by standby letters of credit and bankers acceptances backing the borrowers' name. Banks transform short-term deposits into longer-term guaranteed funding to borrowers, a process which can be achieved off-balance sheet by revolving credit lines or note issuance facilities which put short-term paper in the hands of lenders while guaranteeing long-term funding to borrowers.

From the viewpoint of borrowers, the interest rate risks they face can be averted by writing 'cap' or 'collar' contracts with the bank. A cap is a put option[7] (i.e. a right to sell a specified quantity at a prespecified price) which acts as a hedge to the buyer against rising interest rates. A floor is a series of call options (obligations to buy a specified quantity at a prespecified price), and when combined with a cap in a collar acts much like a fixed rate of interest. When borrowers negotiate a syndicated loan they are normally allowed to choose the interest rate basis (LIBOR, CD rate, US prime, CP rate), the currency of interest rate and principal, and when to draw down the loan. These choices can be exercised also off-balance sheet by means of basis swaps, coupon swaps, currency swaps (for altering interest rates), back-up credit lines (for liquidity needs), and futures or forward contracts (to alter effective drawdown or maturity dates).

From this comparison it is apparent that much the same functions are being performed in off-balance sheet banking as in traditional banking, and moreover for reasons which are essentially the same as those explaining traditional intermediation by banks. Guarantees exploit opportunities arising from information asymmetries, where the bank has access to information about a borrower's real credit risk, and the risk premium which would otherwise be required by the market for certain borrowers is greater than the fees charged to them by banks (and other financial guarantee insurers). Access to the interbank market means that banks may also be better able to bear liquidity risk. Any interest rate risk under a revolving line of credit can be ameliorated in various ways as well, including shifting risk on to futures markets.

We have described some of the characteristics of off-balance sheet business without, so far, attempting to explain why this business has grown in relative importance in recent years. A variety of hypotheses have been advanced, three among these appearing most prominent.[8] They are the *regulatory tax hypothesis*, which views the growth of off-balance sheet activity as a response to regulations (reserve requirements and the like) which have a tax-like effect upon on-balance sheet activity, the *moral hazard hypothesis* and the *bank failure hypothesis*. All three, it is important to stress, should be viewed in the context provided by the kind of technological advance which facilitates the offer of (e.g.) interest rate or currency swaps at attractively low cost. More generally, the critical technological input can be seen as the ability, due to computerization, to unbundle and if necessary recombine financial assets cheaply. According to the moral hazard hypothesis the expansion of off-balance sheet activity has been undertaken by banks on the assumption that customers are protected by implicit insurance from the regulatory agencies, while the bank failure hypothesis explains that customers value the bank guarantee and so prefer to hold bank-acceptance commercial paper rather than to hold the direct claim without any guarantee.[9]

The development of banking activity in this way fits the regulation cycle view. Having produced off-balance sheet activity which is exempt from the regulations falling on regular banking business, banks now find that the regulators are anxious to assess the risk involved to the system. Current provisions for prudential supervision attempt to take into account the contingent liabilities and exposure associated with at least some aspects of the new development.

Growth of markets for futures, options and swaps and the rise of financial technology must also be viewed in the context of the more volatile financial environment occasioned by the switch to floating exchange rates. It has created a demand among the customers of banks for the hedging of exchange rate risks on a routine basis. Currency substitution is another manifestation.

9.3 Currency substitution and policy coordination

The widespread abolition of exchange controls and the introduction of computerized systems make currency substitution possible on a scale not previously feasible. The technology is important because it allows instant quotation of foreign currency-denominated deposit rates and exchange rates at minimal cost. By currency substitution we refer to the holding of foreign moneys in a resident's portfolio or demand-side currency substitution. This stands in distinction from the supply-side substitution which occurs under fixed exchange rate regimes when central banks stand ready to exchange currencies at rates of exchange which are fixed and known in advance.

The motivations suggested for diversifying money holdings across currencies of denomination are transactions-cum-precautionary and (depending on the definition of money in question) speculative. A transactor who buys goods invoiced in a range of currencies will have a corresponding need at the point of purchase for currency of the right denomination. Costs of exchange suggest, as do costs of liquidating an alternative asset in the standard theory of money demand, that a mixed portfolio of moneys may be optimal in this case. Not all these needs can necessarily be programmed in advance, though a perception that they may arise gives substance to a precautionary demand for foreign currency-denominated money. The second motive is precautionary-cum-speculative: holding money in foreign denomination hedges the risk of an exchange rate change if expenditures on foreign goods are planned in any case; it also affords a means of speculating on exchange rate changes which may dominate alternative vehicles such as (say) Treasury bills when costs and ease of acquisition and liquidation are taken into account.

When exchange rates are flexible, individual transactors have an incentive to hold foreign currencies which is not present with perfect supply-side currency substitution, as is the case in a monetary union, and may not be present in the case of a 'usually-fixed-sometimes-adjustable' exchange rate regime. Instead of governments or central banks holding such reserves of foreign exchange as they require in order to finance their exchange guarantee, there will be some compensating increase in private sector demand.[10]

That a high degree of currency substitution has potentially significant effects is not in doubt. Figure 9.2 depicts a decision-tree approach. In part (a) the case of direct currency substitution is depicted. Transactors choose how to divide wealth between money and bonds at the first level and then decide how to divide their holdings of each by currency denomination. Without currency substitution, only one money would be relevant – as is in fact the standard assumption of open economy monetary analysis. With two moneys (in the example of Figure 9.2, the US dollar and sterling) it is clear that, if the two are highly substitutable in people's portfolios, quantitative control of either one, or of both independently, is meaningless and can result only in a volatile exchange rate between the two when people attempt to change the composition of their holdings. An analogy would be attempting to hold constant the stock of pears and of apples separately when the relevant variable is the sum of apples and pears. Seemingly capricious switches from apples to pears occasioned by the appearance (say) of minor blemishes in the appearance

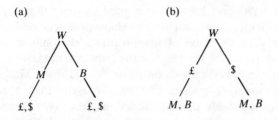

Note:
W is financial wealth, *M* and *B* stand for money and bonds, respectively, while £ and $ indicate alternative currencies of denomination.

Figure 9.2   Models of currency substitution: (a) direct currency substitution; (b) indirect currency substitution.

of one or the other will – because the two are by hypothesis highly substitutable – occasion wild swings in the relative price of pears to apples.

Part (b) of Figure 9.2 depicts the case termed by McKinnon (1984a) 'indirect currency substitution'. In it, the first-level decision is made between the currency of denomination of asset-holding; after that the money–bonds composition is chosen. It can be objected that indirect currency substitution may be a completely misleading label for a situation of good old-fashioned bond substitution; that is, the decision-tree of part (b) is quite compatible with the complete absence of asset trade in moneys as such. At the same time, the prediction of part (a) that exchange rates will prove volatile if moneys are highly substitutable applies as well to part (b) if bonds are highly substitutable. The objection is not wrong and serves to show that exchange rate volatility *per se* is not necessarily evidence of the presence of currency substitution. But it is fair to note that *if* currency substitution is added to bond substitution in part (b) it raises the substitutability of assets of different currency of denomination and, empirically, could be expected to increase the volatility of exchange rates.

In the absence of an understanding of currency substitution, authorities may easily follow inappropriate monetary policies. What appears to be an expansionary stance of policy in the light of a rapid expansion of the domestic money supply may turn out to be an unchanged stance of policy because of strong international demands to hold the local currency. Reacting to the false signal by domestic policies to restrain what seems to be the 'excessive' monetary growth could lead to excessive exchange rate instability.

McKinnon (e.g. 1981 and 1984a) has argued strongly that currency substitution is sufficiently important in fact to have produced undesirable exchange instability in the face of inappropriate national monetary targeting programmes; in (1981) he vigorously criticized the UK policy of the early 1980s as exemplifying such an error.[11] In (1984b) McKinnon advocated world monetary cooperation on the basis that observed instability of national money demand functions (that is, demand for domestically denominated money) was due to currency substitution, still leaving the global money demand function a reliably stable function. His policy conclusion thus favoured global, as opposed to national, monetary targeting or (equivalently) a combination of pre-agreed domestic credit and exchange rate targets.

Empirical evidence in favour of currency substitution is, however, mixed. There is plenty of evidence of asymmetrical currency substitution, notably in some less developed countries (LDCs), where residents use the US dollar widely, but for currency substitution among the industrial countries which might in principle be more symmetrical, the evidence is elusive. Some of the earlier positive studies (e.g. Brittain (1981) and Miles (1978)) have been effectively criticized, e.g. by Cuddington (1983), and a number of negative findings reported, e.g. Bordo and Choudhuri (1982). Melvin (1985) provides a more recent paper embodying positive findings for currency substitution in Western Europe. Dornbusch (1984) has suggested that international asset trade is dominated by trade in bonds, not moneys. In addition, it has become apparent that there is more wrong with money demand functions than can be laid at the door of currency substitution. McKinnon's policy suggestions must be reordered accordingly. The anticipation of widespread currency substitution effects thus appears to have been incorrect; yet, with the globalization of financial markets, the warning is possibly simply premature rather than misleading. We draw attention to Figure 9.3, which depicts the ratio of M3-style deposits in foreign currency (held by residents) to total M3. While some of the wobbles in the ratio can be traced to exchange rate variations, the strong upward trend in the ratio, especially in the period following the removal of exchange control in 1979, is notable, the ratio approximately doubling.[12]

Let us now return to McKinnon's 'rule' that exchange rates should be held constant and that the leading countries (United States, Japan and Germany) should coordinate their domestic credit expansion so as to stabilize world money supply growth. In the new economic and financial environment, exchange rate variability has proved a double-edged sword: on the one hand, the exchange rate plays an important role in the transmission mechanism of monetary policy. On the other hand, excessive variability appears costly and strong negative externalities

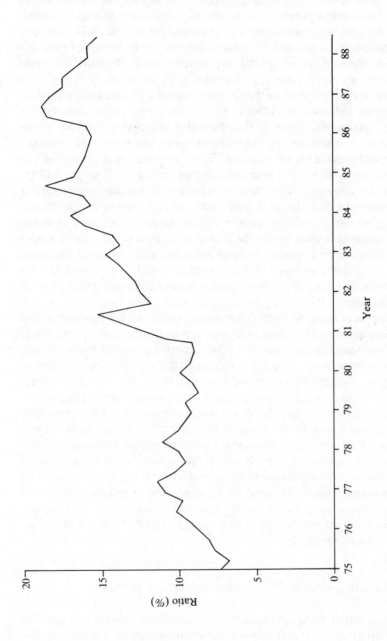

Figure 9.3 Ratio of foreign currency deposits held by residents to M3, 1975 Q1 – 1988 Q3.

attach to monetary policies working actively through the exchange rate simply because one currency's appreciation is another's depreciation. As in other cases, the optimal response to externalities is to internalize them. In this context, internalization requires world (or at least G-3) monetary cooperation. If the global demand for money is stable, then the solution is for joint agreement on global supply (the sum of domestic credit expansion in every country), together with nominal exchange rate targeting by each country: this is the essence of McKinnon's original suggestions (McKinnon, 1984b). But what if the global demand for money is unstable? What if the instability of money demand at the national level is due, as appears to be the case, to factors other than (or additional to) currency substitution? Then a solution is to 'globalize' the model towards which the monetary authorities in the European Community and elsewhere have been moving, specifying the interest rate as the instrument and the exchange rate and/or inflation as the target, omitting the intermediate money supply target. The corresponding global solution is then to set the global *average* interest rate to target world inflation and *relative* interest rates to target nominal exchange rates. In his later writings McKinnon (e.g. 1988) moved towards this suggestion, incurring the obloquy in doing so of advocating 'monetarism without money'.[13]

The general sense of these suggestions is that, while innovations and deregulation may have made the aggregates untrustworthy and imply some constraints on the form that policy may take, central banks can still control interest rates. When they do so, their actions are effective in influencing the real economy and the price level. The policy spillovers that occur in an integrated world suggest that there are efficiency gains to be had from cooperation. In McKinnon's original model such cooperation in effect embodied the transfer of monetarism from a national to a global setting, whereas in the revised version suggested we have 'global monetarism without money' in which the central banks of the United States, Japan and Germany (the major currency blocs) would set interest rates and target world inflation directly. In broader policy frameworks (Artis, 1989), fiscal policy is involved as is some concern for real targets: but the focus on central bank control over interest rates and on the external dimension is the same.

9.4 Banking, deregulation and monetary policy

The argument in the last paragraph follows on from our earlier suggestion (see Chapters 6 and 7) that with deregulation and innovation the effective control core of monetary policy may have shrunk to the central banks' own balance sheet as banks' behaviour is made more endogenous. One area in which banks' responses have become more endogenized is with respect to interest rate variations.

Monetary analysis has long assumed that monetary assets bear no interest and with this assumption, 'the' rate of interest represents both the level of market interest rates and the difference between the interest return on money and non-money assets. The analysis begins with an account of how banks create money, and uses balance sheet identities like those in Chapter 6 to show how banks stand relative to the monetary authorities and the general public. With the money supply embracing cash and bank deposits, this means that banks are effectively grouped with the monetary authorities as part of the control core. Bank money is equated with fiat (central bank) money, and both are assumed to bear interest rates set exogenously at zero. In this way the institution of money is inextricably tied to the institution of banking.

This accurately describes many national monetary systems before deregulation, and the structure can itself be traced to a succession of financial innovations in the nineteenth century which transformed banks in Europe from small regional country partnerships into major national, international and multinational institutions. These developments can be seen themselves as the culmination of a process which began in previous centuries with the sovereign or government encouraging the growth of banks as a way of enhancing the State's credit (and reducing the interest cost of state borrowing), and ended with the government sharing its money-creating powers with the banking system (Hicks, 1969). The banks' form of intermediation and their relationships with borrowers made them central to the finance of industrial growth, and government borrowing from the banking system both widened the government's access to credit and enabled it to extend its control over new sources of money creation. As debt money assumed greater significance and more money came to be created as a byproduct of the lending activities of banks, interest rates and the availability of bank credit came to be seen as the cornerstone of monetary policy, so that monetary policy became indistinguishable from credit policy.

That is no longer the case but it is still unclear in the present transitional stage how much of the textbook analysis will survive the wave of innovation. Our analysis retains the standard framework to focus on the response of bank interest rates to monetary policy.

When some part of monetary assets (i.e. bank deposits) bears interest, it is the differential between the interest return on money and non-money assets which must adjust to restore asset market equilibrium following a change in market conditions. If bank interest rates are regulated, relative interest rates between bank deposits and other assets can be readily altered merely by changes in market rates of interest. With deregulation, it becomes a matter of how bank deposit rates are determined.

Payment of interest on bank deposits is possible due to the intermediation activities of banks whereby bank deposits are used to finance holding of other assets. These other assets are themselves substitutes for bank deposits in the portfolios of the non-bank sector. Consider the following representation of the market for bank deposits,

$$D (r_D, r_A, r_K) W = D^S \tag{9.1}$$

in which D^S is the supply of deposits, and in which the demand for deposits, as a proportion of private sector wealth, W, depends on r_D, the banks' deposit rate, r_A, the yield on securities, and r_K, the yield on capital assets. The demand for bank deposits, then, will depend upon the yield on deposits (r_D) and these other assets (r_A, r_K), while competition among banks will ensure that the deposit yield offered will depend upon the yields available on the assets held in the banks' portfolios.

A process of restrictive monetary policy under deregulation will see banks free to match the market offerings by raising their own rates. This is because the return on banks' asset portfolios will increase with market rates and, under competitive conditions, the higher return will be passed on to depositors. For example, if banks' portfolios are confined to securities, then the course of the deposit rate is given by

$$r_D = (1 - e) r_A - c \tag{9.2}$$

where c is the constant marginal resource cost of deposits and e is the desired reserve ratio of banks. With r_D responding in this way to variations in r_A, achieving a particular change in relative yields, necessary for portfolio equilibrium, will require a larger change in the absolute level of interest rates.[14]

This argument translates into the familiar IS/LM analysis as an LM schedule which is less elastic with respect to absolute rates of interest, since the fluctuation of bank interest rates with market yields offsets to some extent the tendency of the demand for money to vary with 'the' rate of interest. An increase in the market orientation of banks will have other impacts, too, upon the demand for money and the LM curve. In total, four principal effects may be noted:

1. A reintermediation into bank deposit intermediation seems likely to the extent that bank deposit returns were not previously effectively market-determined by the payment of 'implicit' interest. Shifts into now higher-yielding financial instruments which form part of the conventional money supply will increase the demand for money.
2. Transactions balances can be expected to fall, and the interest

elasticity of the supply of deposits will increase, as yields become positive in real terms.

3. The interest sensitivity of money demanded, in the longer term, is likely to decrease as bank deposit rates become more responsive to market rates of interest.

4. The income elasticity of the demand for (narrow) money is, however, likely to fall also, as deposits will be held as interest-bearing liquid assets, rather than simply to facilitate transactions.

The first two of these impacts seem likely to produce trends in broad and narrow money and erratic movements of the LM schedule in the transition. The third, as noted, suggests a steepening of the LM curve while the fourth offsets to some degree the change in interest rate elasticity on the LM schedule.

At the same time, conditions in the real sector cannot be expected to remain unchanged in the face of these developments. Deregulation promotes competition and the decline in computation costs makes interest rate variation much cheaper: together, these developments reduce the incidence of credit rationing. In the United Kingdom such effects, where not officially inspired, were promoted by inertia in the interest rate adjustments in the building society sector, resulting in significant credit rationing effects on the determination of dwelling investment. These effects, if not completely absent, are no longer obvious.[15]

In combination with some other developments, the following effects are suggested in terms of the IS curve:

1. The spread of flexi-rate loan contracts and the development of private hedge markets for interest rate futures make it likely that it is the 'permanent' interest rate expected to rule over the life of the loan contract which is relevant for investment decisions. Consequently, the IS curve may exhibit a reduced elasticity with respect to current interest rate movements, in so far as new expenditures are concerned.

2. Under the system of non-price credit rationing, the flow of credit to some sectors was restricted, while others were sheltered from various interest rate or price changes. Interest rate changes will now affect most sectors directly.

3. Under the old system the impact of rationing and interest rate increases fell heavily upon those borrowers seeking new accommodation from the banks. As flexi-rate loan contracts have become commonplace, all borrowers – existing and new – feel the brunt of monetary changes. For existing borrowers, the effect of higher

interest rates operates much like a tax in squeezing discretionary income and depressing expenditures.

4. The removal of interest rate ceilings will lead to a higher average level of interest rates. Interest costs will therefore form a larger proportion of total expenditure, and changes in the rate of interest could have a greater impact on expenditure and budgets.

5. Inflexibilities in other markets could increase interest rate sensitivity. Borrowers are likely to be more sensitive to changes in interest rates if prices in product markets move more slowly.

The last four factors suggest a flattening of the IS, while the first suggests some possible offset. Overall these considerations, together with the greatly increased financial exposure of the personal sector during the 1980s, suggest that for the time being the transmission mechanism will bear more heavily on the personal sector than the corporate; but this is clearly not a long-run position. The personal sector may reduce its exposure and increasingly take advantage of hedging instruments and swapped contracts, especially if the policy-makers exploit the current position.[16]

For the future, one of the consequences of financial change of the kind now in train is that the dividing line between banks and non-banks is becoming progressively more blurred, depending increasingly upon contingent legislation. The change in status of the Abbey National Building Society from building society to bank in 1989 is a case in point. Not a bank in name and in consequence restricted in its field of action, the passage from one status to the next was none the less easy to effect in the sense that in essentials the organization already performed like a bank. This development was anticipated and analyzed by Fama (1980) and foreshadowed by Tobin (1963) and Gurley and Shaw (1960). As banks come to resemble other financial intermediaries (and vice-versa), and even – as in the case of securitization – come to resemble simply a bundle of contracts in a disintermediated capital market, the broader monetary magnitudes, originally consisting predominantly of 'bank' deposits, not unnaturally lose any substantive distinctive interpretation. One might as well look to still broader magnitudes, as now confirmed by the renaming of PSL1 and PSL2 (public sector liquidity 1 and 2) as M4 and M5 – or, in line with our interpretation of developments, to a narrower one which is not a bank creation at all (M0).

Part of the blurring of the dividing lines has been the reduction of the monopoly over money-transmission services once enjoyed by 'banks'. Technology is changing here, too. Increasing use of credit cards reduces the demand for money to hold before settlement dates; newer developments promise instant debiting of bank accounts reducing clearing times effectively to zero. These changes affect the demand for money in the traditional transactions sense and seem all too likely to impart instability to the demand for monetary base (M0) in consequence. The extreme of the 'moneyless' society, on the other hand, appears a distinctly unlikely prospect: fortunately, for if monetary policy does not require a stable demand for M0 it does require *some* demand for M0 – otherwise (cf. Chapter 7) the central bank's ability to influence ('control') the rate of interest would be absent.[17]

9.5 Monetary policy and the balance of payments

The increased integration of world banking and capital markets places additional constraints on monetary policy. Because of the threat of offshore banking, monetary policy mechanisms which involve a tax effect are of limited use. Currency substitution may yet restrict further the utility of domestic monetary targeting. Policy-makers may also find themselves in the unfamiliar position of having the capital account drive the current account, rather than the reverse causation implied in old Keynesian models, and this can lead to policy confusion – as we suggest later in this section.

Control over the short-term rate of interest now appears to be the principal 'sure thing' in central bank armouries. But at what should this be aimed? Conventional macroeconomic policy, following Tinbergen's approach to economic policy, specifies targets derived from the community's and policy-makers' preferences, and instruments such as monetary and fiscal policy which can be adjusted to achieve policy aims. This framework reflects the presumption that the authorities are not exclusively concerned with the inflation rate but have aims relating to unemployment and the balance of payments position. With the onset of floating exchange rates in 1973, the current account largely replaced the overall balance of payments as an indicator of the need for adjustment in a country's macroeconomic policies.[18] Our point is that in the new environment of financially integrated markets the long-accepted dichotomy between internal balance and external balance as the appropriate policy framework may no longer be useful: the latter balance, however defined, can no longer usefully or indeed reliably be targeted by traditional instruments as monetary policy.[19] A lack of utility in current account targeting is implicit in the modern intertemporal theory of the balance of payments, as expressed for example by Sachs (1981) and by Frenkel and Razin (1987). The process of global financial integration makes the essential assumptions of that theory more nearly realistic and the policy conclusion succinctly put by Cooper (1981) more relevant: 'In the context of overall savings – investment analysis, countries should not take any particular view of their current account positions at all. Some will draw savings from the rest of the world, others will invest in the rest of the world. Nothing is wrong with this. It is as it should be' (p. 269).

A convenient starting-point is the simplified flow-of-funds account set out in Table 6.5 in Chapter 6. Three equivalent definitions can be provided for a current account deficit (CAD):

$$\text{CAD} = Z - X = K - \Delta Res \qquad (9.3)$$
$$= (C + I + G) - Y \qquad (9.4)$$
$$= (I - S) - (T - G) \qquad (9.5)$$

The first is obtained from the balance of payments identity and defines the current account deficit as the private capital inflow and borrowings from overseas (K) net of the authorities' addition to international reserves (ΔRes). The second expression relates the deficit to the excess of absorption, $A = C + I + G$, over domestic income (Y). In the third equality, the current account deficit is presented as equal to the excess of private sector investment (I) over private sector savings (S) and the government budget surplus $(T - G)$.

During the first half of the 1980s, Britain's current account balance was consistently in surplus. From 1986, the current account swung sharply into deficit, reaching record levels in 1988 and 1989. Policy discussion has emphasized the need for overseas borrowings to finance the adverse growth of imports relative to exports, and the inability of domestic production to absorb the fast expansion of British consumption and investment spending. Table 9.2 shows for 1989 the counterparts of the deficit in terms of the sectoral imbalances, with net borrowings from overseas to finance the excess of household and corporate investment over domestic sources of savings. Our argument is that these developments – the deficits for the household sector in 1988 and 1989, for

Table 9.2 Private and government sector imbalances and the current account, 1989 (£ millions)

	Savings	Investment	Surplus (+)/Deficit (−)
Public sector	20 404	14 427	+5 977
Financial sector	16 005	14 384	+1 621
Company sector	31 735	53 972	−22 237
Personal sector	22 551	27 639	−5 088
Overseas sector			+19 624
Balancing item			+103

example, are unprecedented – must be seen against the backdrop of the removal of exchange controls, deregulation of credit in the banking and financial system, and increased financial integration.

For any open economy operating in a milieu of floating exchange rates, financial deregulation and high capital mobility, the current account balance can be understood fully only within the framework of a general equilibrium involving the spending and saving decisions of nationals of many countries. The deficits which the United Kingdom incurs on the current account of the balance of payments must be matched by surpluses on the part of countries with which it has trading and financial relationships. In the new international financial *laissez-faire* environment these individual national relationships should be seen as part of an overall pattern of global saving and investment.

If we accept this as a reasonable approximation of reality and if, at the same time, there are national differences in intertemporal time preferences and the marginal efficiency of capital, those areas with low savings propensities and/or high investment propensities will export financial assets and attract an inflow of capital carried, in effect, by an inflow of goods. Interaction of investors in search of the highest rate of return with the behaviour of savers seeking to maximize intertemporal utility determines the efficient worldwide distribution of savings and investment with its counterpart national current account imbalances.

It then follows that if the comparative advantages in present and future goods differ widely across countries (as it has been suggested that they do between Japan and Germany *vis-à-vis* the United States and the United Kingdom), then even large current payments imbalances among countries can persist, contrary to the conventional view that focuses only on the current transactions section of the balance of payments. Viewed in this global setting, the use of macro and micro policies *purely* to reduce the size of the current account deficit to some tolerable level does not appear to be desirable.

From the viewpoint of macroeconomic policy, the implication is that the current account surplus or deficit simply reflects, in the aggregate, individual saving and investment decisions and thus individual lending and borrowing decisions. In the context of international financial *laissez-faire*, these decisions are made by 'consenting adults' who, we suppose, must know what they are doing. Consequently, if a case for assigning policy priority to the current account is to be made it must rest on identifying externalities in the borrowing process. When global capital markets are undeveloped and imperfect, liquidity constraints provide an example of such externalities and it may be desirable to limit national resort to borrowing from the rest of the world (i.e. to limit the current account deficit); with global capital market integration this becomes a less persuasive argument (see Artis and Bayoumi, 1989). One of us[20] has argued why, in a country like Australia, policy-makers should indeed be concerned with such externalities; but the arguments carry less force in the case of the United Kingdom.

In the absence of a case for market failure in the savings and investment process, the conclusion is that the authorities should confine themselves to the task of monitoring the internal balance, leaving the current account imbalance and the level of private debt to adjust to their policy setting. It is in this strict policy sense that the current account 'does not matter', though of course it will matter in other important respects, such as those influencing the overall structure of the economy in the longer term.

Whether or not a case can be made for policy directed at the current account, it also seems that in current conditions such a policy direction is less feasible than formerly appeared to be the case. Figure 9.4 illustrates the point.[21] In it, PP is drawn to define internal balance in terms of an iso-inflation rate line. If the exchange rate depreciates a higher interest rate is needed to exert an offsetting deflationary pressure. FF by contrast is a foreign exchange market schedule indicating market reactions to the interest rate – which is the policy instrument. The slope of FF indicates the pulling power of higher interest rates in attracting capital inflows, with foreign interest rates unchanged. A country with a current account deficit is by necessity borrowing from abroad. The third line DD assumes that foreign capital adjusts more through the interest rate than through the exchange rate. Overseas borrowings/lendings respond to differentials between domestic and overseas interest rates, and the level of DD indicates the interest rate which corresponds to the amount of overseas borrowing (current account deficit) which the government judges to be sustainable or desirable.

From position A, which is a position of excess demand domestically and an excessive current account deficit, suppose that the government has the Bank of England engineer a rise in interest rates towards B to hold down inflation. They may be thinking, in Keynesian terms, that the higher interest rate will also deflate the economy and improve the current account balance, which will eventually lead to less borrowing from overseas. However, in the new financially integrated environment with a rapidly adjusting capital account, the higher interest rate merely pulls in more capital from abroad and the appreciating exchange rate puts pressure on exports to fall and imports to rise. By contrast, lower interest rates would improve the current account but worsen inflation. The policy dilemma is obvious. Vines (1989) saw a position such as A as depicting the box which the British government had seemingly got itself into in the late 1980s.

Looked at in an instruments/targets framework, the reason for the

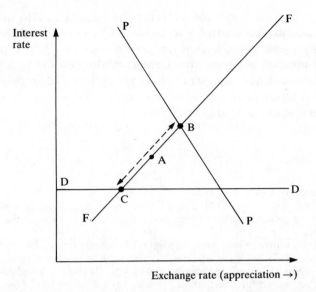

PP   shows what is required in terms of the rate of interest and the exchange rate for the inflation objective to be met.

FF   shows the influence of the interest rate upon the exchange rate.

DD   shows the interest rate which corresponds to the current account imbalance which the authorities are prepared to sustain.

Figure 9.4   Internal and external balance under international financial *laissez-faire*.

policy predicament is obvious: there is one instrument (the interest rate) but two targets (inflation, the current account). Short of discarding a target (the current account), one solution would be to employ an additional instrument. For example, fiscal policy could be tightened: increased taxation, say, would substitute for a higher interest rate in deflating demand, and by shifting the PP line towards C reduce the dilemma surrounding interest rate policy. As another example, incomes policies might be used both to reduce inflation (shifting down PP) and increase competitiveness (shifting FF). Another example would be the imposition of capital controls to free the interest rate for internal balance – although that would be difficult to institute in a European context. In fact, none of these alternatives is readily available in the United Kingdom today. Fiscal policy is far from nimble, being aimed at medium-term objectives, while incomes policies and capital controls are, for different reasons, ruled out.

The case just made out for assigning the interest rate to inflation assumes that inflation control is to be sought by internal stabilization, which was the case in the United Kingdom during the 1980s. If instead control of inflation is sought by external stabilization the policy conclusion is reversed, and interest rates have to be directed to the balance of payments in terms of an exchange rate target – Britain's parity in the EMS. This is made clear in the next chapter.

Notes

1. Cf. Flannery and Jaffee (1973).
2. See Davis and Latter (1989, Table J) for a useful note of the liberalization and deregulation measures conducted in six leading economies during the decade.
3. Davis and Latter (1989) quote BIS figures indicating that in the first half of 1989 about 45 per cent of international bank lending outstanding was associated with European location, of which nearly half was London-based. Japan accounted for a further 20 per cent, the US about 10 per cent.
4. Lewis and Davis (1987) provide a detailed account.
5. The Bank of England (1989a) already detected that an influence on the slowdown in the growth of the Euromarkets in 1988 'may have been deregulation in certain centres which encourage business to go back "on-shore"', (p. 252).
6. The multiplier analysis is now regarded as somewhat *démodé* in any case, since it takes no account of the dependence of the key ratios on their determinants and thus overlooks the probability that they will change over time and may be quite different 'at the margin' than 'on the average'. See Lewis and Davis (1987) for a discussion of the alternative portfolio approach and a reconciliation with the multiplier analysis.
7. Bank of England (1989b) offers instructive examples of the use of options (in its case in the foreign exchange markets).
8. See Chessen (1987), James (1987) and Pavel and Phillis (1987).
9. Lewis (1988), whose analytical perspective on securitization closely informs the above account, amplifies the reasons suggested for the growth in off-balance sheet activity.
10. In the fixed-but-adjustable case the private sector already has some motive for holding foreign money, as the exchange rate guarantee is less than perfect.
11. Note that it would be in principle insufficient defence against this criticism for the authorities to point out that it was £M3 *held by residents* (this is actually how £M3 is defined) which was the subject of the target, not all sterling-denominated broad money, whether held by non-residents or residents. For, in principle, residents operating internationally could express an increase in demand for £M3 by switching from foreign currency-denominated broad money with the same harmful consequences, given the target, as if non-residents were to increase their demand for sterling-denominated broad money. Empirically, however, the scope for the switch by residents cannot have been great: exchange control was abolished only in 1979.

12. In the 1960s the ratio was at even lower levels than in the 1970s, and was still only 3 per cent by the end of 1969.

13. In fact, McKinnon has never entirely relinquished an emphasis on the monetary magnitudes so the characterization, though suggestive, is perhaps not entirely fair. There are of course other blueprints for world economic policy cooperation (for a brief review, see Artis (1989)), more eclectic than McKinnon's, which we have singled out here for its characteristic monetary emphasis.

14. The argument here draws on Davis and Lewis (1982).

15. A degree of credit rationing is endemic in direct lending for the information-asymmetry/adverse-selection reasons outlined in Stiglitz and Weiss (1981).

16. Another example of Goodhart's Law, in the making!

17. Severe instability in demand for M0 could be problematic in making short-run forecasting of the excess demand for central bank money difficult, but if the operational target is a rate of interest, the authorities can in principle still adjust the scale of their operations in M0 to achieve it.

18. See Salop and Spitaller (1980). The current account is a leading variable among the list of indicators for disciplining international policy coordination (see e.g. Crockett and Goldstein, 1987); and current account developments, actual and prospective, are a prominent component in the IMF's conjunctural review and medium-term projections in its *World Economic Outlook*.

19. Artis and Bayoumi (1989); Lewis and Polasek (1990).

20. Lewis and Polasek (1990)

21. The picture is adapted from an oral presentation by Walter Eltis and from Vines (1989) and Fitzgibbon (1989).

10

The future of money in Britain

10.1 Monetary systems and inflation control

Britain was once looked upon as a bastion of monetary stability in the same way that Germany is now. As late as 1963, von Hayek still saw Britain as a model of financial respectability worthy of imitation.[1] Few would do so now. It is a matter of record that in recent decades successive governments of both political persuasions have signally failed to keep inflation under control.

The international monetary system may have made a difference. Britain built its reputation for monetary orthodoxy under the gold standard. And, despite two devaluations (1949 and 1967), Britain was able to hold inflation reasonably in check under the fixed (but adjustable) parities of the Bretton Woods System. Chronic inflation only surfaced in earnest after 1971 when the system of international financial *laissez-faire*, based around inconvertible paper currencies, began and ushered in floating exchange rates. While some other countries have been able to control inflation while adhering to a flexible exchange rate regime, the United Kingdom has not done so. Following on from that observation, pressures developed during the 1980s for a return to fixed parities which for Britain resulted (eventually) in its participation in the Exchange Rate Mechanism (ERM) of the EMS. Some might still hold out hope that the European initiative can be broadened out to a new Bretton Woods.[2]

Monetary regimes

Fixed exchange rates constitute one element of the 'inconsistent quartet' of desirables for international economic relations: namely fixed exchange

270

rates, free trade, full mobility of capital and an independent monetary policy (Wallich, 1972). Policy-makers who simultaneously seek to attain these four objectives will be unsuccessful, for at best only three of the four can be achieved. Under the gold standard, monetary autonomy was sacrificed. Architects of the Bretton Woods System envisaged that official controls over capital flows would reconcile the inconsistency. As world trade expanded and restrictions upon capital were progressively removed in the 1960s, a more complex solution resulted in which all of the four objectives were compromised to some extent and in different ways by member countries. When control over international capital flows effectively passed from national authorities to the markets, and national monetary autonomy was threatened, fixed parities gave way to floating rates.

Experience of floating rates has seen a movement back towards fixed parities, as countries perceived that fluctuations in exchange rates led to uncertainty in international business and upset the development of free trade between countries. At a world level, these perceptions prompted the Plaza and Louvre Accords of the 1980s; these multilateral arrangements echo the Tripartite Agreement of 1936 which marked the return to joint official management of exchange rates by the major blocs. In Europe, the EMS was established in 1979 as a 'zone of monetary stability among European currencies'. Much like the Bretton Woods System, the EMS began with extensive restrictions on capital movements in place in many of the major countries; in both instances the 'leading country' (United States in Bretton Woods, Germany in the EMS) was the major exception. However, in the case of the EMS, with the removal of the capital restrictions it is generally accepted by member states that it is the scope for monetary policy independence which has to go – as it will if the completion of Stage One leads on to monetary union. This is considered below.

Fixed parities are regarded as desirable because it is believed that they expand international trade and capital movements and so offer internationally much the same benefits which come in domestic markets from having a uniform national currency. This is true, up to a point. Money acts as a unit of account, giving a common basis in which to express values; a means of payment, giving a medium by which exchanges can be effected; and as a store of value, allowing transactions to be separated in time and amounts. The relevant considerations when assessing various international systems are transactions costs and exchange rate uncertainty. As we move from floating exchange rates as experienced since 1971 to credibly fixed exchange rates, as under the classical gold standard, both transactions costs and exchange rate uncertainty can be expected to fall considerably.

Ranking of the other actual and potential systems – gold exchange standard, Bretton Woods, EMS and EMU – depends much on their perceived characteristics and workings, and Table 10.1 provides a comparison which underpins our discussion of them. Viewing these systems according to their repercussions on the scope and nature of monetary policy leads to comparisons in terms of exchange rates, reserves, adjustment mechanisms and sovereignty. The exchange rate regime governs the price at which one money is exchanged for another in payments. Any payments system requires that assets later be transferred in settlement of payments imbalances, and the reserves regime defines the assets used in settlements. As imbalances continue, obligations may exist upon participants in the international payments system to correct inflows and outflows, either in terms of understood 'rules of the game' or in terms of market reactions which form the nature of balance of payments adjustments.

Under the classical gold standard there was no essential distinction between domestic and international money. (See the quotation from Keynes on pp. 36–7.) Gold coins circulated freely in the major countries and gold formed the basis, if not the actual means, for the settlement of international transactions. By contrast, under the present 'non-system' there is no recognized international money as such and a variety of different national fiat currencies contribute to the international money supply and serve as the standards for international trade and capital transfers. These are the two polar cases, and the greater the fixity of exchange rates, the more useful internationally each national money becomes and the closer each national money comes to being a common currency.

Monetary autonomy

This leads us to the questions of monetary independence and inflation control under different monetary systems. By autonomy over monetary policy we mean that the choice of the money supply and short-term interest rates is left to the monetary authorities of the various nation states, enabling an individual country to influence its exchange rate and rate of inflation. Under a union, with the ECU replacing national moneys in general circulation, an independent monetary policy would cease to exist, although each country may have some share in the determination of communal monetary policy.

The basic case against joining any sort of fixed exchange rate regime is that while a country retains all of its existing policy targets, it 'loses' the exchange rate as a shock absorber, through variations in which the

Table 10.1 Comparison of different monetary systems

	Gold standard 1879–1914	Gold exchange standard 1925–31	Bretton Woods 1945–68	Dollar standard 1968–71	The 'non-system' 1972–	EMS 1979–	EMU
Exchange rate regime	fixed gold parities	fixed gold parities	fixed gold parities	fixed parities	floating	fixed parities	fixed parities/single currency
Exchange rate variability	within gold export and import points	gold bullion shipping points	±1 per cent	±1 per cent	complete	±2.25 per cent	none
Exchange rate realignments	parities irrevocable		one-sided at discretion of individual country	possible for non-US currencies	complete	require a common decision of all members	none; common currency or irrevocably fixed parities to be determined
Nature of reserves regime	gold institutionalized	gold and gold-backed currencies	US dollar institutionalized	US dollar	national fiat currencies	mixed; ECU official reserves balances; US dollar used most for interventions	
Key currency	sterling	dollars and sterling	US dollar institutionalized as intervention and vehicle currency	US dollar	US dollar as vehicle currency	none institutionalized; evolves to country with strongest currency e.g. DM	ECU
Balance of payments adjustments	symmetric 'rules of game'	asymmetric due to sterilization policies	burdens fall upon deficit countries	burdens fall upon deficit countries	no rules of game	symmetric intervention obligations on all members; but asymmetric sterilization	as in region of country
Inflation control	depends on gold price	link to gold weakened	relied on United States maintaining gold convertibility	relied on United States	depends on individual country	relies upon Germany	depends on ECU issuing authority (ESCB)
Monetary independence	restricted	limited	limited	limited, except for United States, without controls	possible	limited, except for W Germany	none; centralized monetary policy

objectives may be achieved.[3] Put another way, it would seem that adding the exchange rate to the list of policy objectives 'uses up' a policy instrument. Any such 'counting rule' argument needs to be treated with care, since the transition from one regime to another seems likely to alter market mechanisms (the Lucas critique) and may enhance the working of other policy measures.

For example, variations in exchange rates can be seen as a means of effecting changes in competitiveness in the face of shifts in relative demand between countries in circumstances where factors of production are relatively immobile and the change in relative prices that would be required may not be easily brought about by market forces in the absence of exchange rate movements (Mundell, 1961). Exchange rate adjustment does not shelter those in declining regions or activities from reductions in real incomes and loss of spending power. Rather it is a device for achieving flexibility of real wages and debts more conveniently when prices and wages geared to the local currency are sticky. Exchange rate changes quickly lower the real wages and incomes of those with money illusion and contracts in terms of the local currency. So runs the standard argument.

In the particular case of European integration, the Community is moving to increase labour and factor mobility, traditionally identified on this standard argument as a key prerequisite for monetary union,[4] since with a common currency and relatively uniform prices and wages ruling across markets, restoration of factor market equilibrium would rely increasingly upon the migration of labour from low to high employment areas. Regional assistance policies are also in place to aid regions which are hurt by having only one currency.

If it may still be argued (as it clearly can be) that the scope of factor mobility and interregional adjustment assistance is less than that which prevails in the United States, it should be observed that experience with floating rates has weakened the force of the standard argument. And, with more closely integrated markets, 'currency illusion' can be expected to diminish further as transactors become attuned to assessing their position in terms of more than one currency. The result may be that a *nominal* exchange rate change will feed through even more rapidly than at present into home prices, leaving relative prices and the *real* exchange rate unchanged. There are also offsetting gains: loss of the exchange rate instrument makes it easier to finance regional payments imbalances by eliminating or reducing exchange rate risk in financing decisions, since debt in one currency is more nearly a perfect substitute for debt in another member country. In this respect there is a change in regime, as intro-European financing seems likely to prove more efficient than borrowing and lending outside the group. Regime changes may occur in other ways. With firms in uncompetitive regions no longer able to count on exchange rate changes to rescue them from adverse movements in relative prices, prices and wages may have to change directly to bring about the same result. Thus closer economic links within the Community may serve to narrow regional differences in wages and other costs, so that the discrepancies in competitiveness which give rise to trade imbalances may be less likely to occur.

Loss of the exchange rate as a shock absorber may possibly matter more for overall macroeconomic policies. Standard neoclassical analysis however holds that the equilibrium real exchange rate, like the equilibrium rate of employment and the level of output, is invariant to monetary policy and the nominal exchange rate. Thus the floating rate option carries no consequences for real things, but simply allows a country to choose its own inflation rate. The fixed rate option determines inflation as a consequence of the joint monetary policies of all the countries participating in the exchange rate system or, where the system is operating in asymmetrical fashion, as it may in the EMS, upon the policies of the anchor country. It is true that later Keynesian analysis, particularly in the elaboration of the 'hysteresis effect' in labour markets, subverts the dichotomy between the real and monetary sides of the economy on which this argument relies, but in doing so it does not reinstate a traditional Phillips Curve as a menu for policy choice; in any case, since exchange rate behaviour itself does not appear to preserve real exchange rate equilibrium when nominal rates are floating, it is far from clear that the presence of hysteresis effects in labour markets justifies any predilection for floating rate regimes.

Choices for inflation control

For these reasons, the longer-run consequences for inflation have moved to the foreground in the question of the choice of monetary regime. One way of thinking about the issues involved is to note that whether its exchange rate is fixed or floating a country is still responsible for its inflation performance. The choice open to a country seeking price stability is whether to do so by means of internal or external stabilization. *Internal stabilization* of the value of money means keeping the purchasing power of national money reasonably stable in terms of goods and services on domestic markets. It may require disconnecting domestic prices from external developments. Flexible exchange rates equilibrate the balance of payments directly, and this freeing of monetary policy makes each country's inflation rate depend essentially on its own national policy (we ignore here complications posed by currency substitution).[5]

External stabilization involves fixing the value of the domestic monetary unit relative to foreign moneys and thus in terms of foreign goods and services. With a fixed exchange rate, the requirement of balance of payments equilibrium without unlimited reserves means that the quantity of (base) money can no longer be used for inflation control. But this 'sacrifice' of monetary autonomy serves to tie the country's inflation rate to that of the fixed exchange rate system.[6]

This fixing of exchange rates under external stabilization is not in itself sufficient for price stability. It merely fixes relative price relations between countries and allows for only one monetary policy across the exchange rate system. But that policy could be highly inflationary. Some common anchor is needed to ensure that nominal as well as relative price stability results from the common stance of monetary policy. A stable fulcrum could be provided by an outside asset such as gold, a national currency such as the dollar or Deutschmark, a created reserve currency such as the SDR, or a group of national currencies.

Monetary regimes are sometimes characterized in terms of 'hegemons' and 'implicit contracts', where there exists one country which acts as leader and whose monetary policy serves as the anchor.[7] As the provider of the key currency in the Bretton Woods System, the United States had an obligation to sustain nominal price stability by pegging the price of the dollar to gold and by conducting stable policies. Other countries ('satellites') accepted dollar hegemony to gain the benefits of having a stable international money. The system broke down in 1968 when the link to gold came under doubt and convertibility was no longer free. In turn the dollar fiat standard, which effectively grew from it, fragmented when the satellites came to see the United States as generating inflation rather than price stability.

The succeeding non-system can also be interpreted in this vein. Despite having no acknowledged leader, the anchor comes from national policies and especially those of the United States, Germany and Japan which form the major trading blocs. Success of the system required that these countries follow cohesive, stable macroeconomic policies with stability of exchange rates emerging as a byproduct, and this can be looked upon as its implicit contract: real exchange rate stability to underpin the world trading regime and nominal exchange rate stability reflecting joint price stability. When huge trade imbalances and exchange rate fluctuations put the system under strain, pressures developed both for a new implicit contract in terms of the Plaza Agreement and Louvre Accords, and for stability through other mechanisms such as the EMS.

10.2 The external discipline of the EMS

The principal features of the EMS were examined in Chapter 8. Briefly, each member country of the Exchange Rate Mechanism has a central parity rate against the ECU and by division a grid of bilateral central rates of each currency against each other, around which currencies fluctuate within ±2.25 per cent of these parities (more than twice as wide as under Bretton Woods parities), although as of 1990 sterling and the peseta have a wider ±6 per cent band. Rates are kept within these bounds by compulsory intervention by the various central banks, which have an unlimited obligation and open credit lines to purchase weak currencies and sell the strong ones.

British inflation and the EMS

It has always been recognized that countries with greatly different inflation rates cannot adhere to fixed exchange rates. As is apparent from Figure 10.1, upon entry to the ERM in October 1990 Britain's inflation rate was higher and rising faster than in other major EC countries. Suppose that Britain sustained inflation of retail prices of 10 per cent per annum as compared with 3 per cent for the other EC countries. With a fixed parity *vis-à-vis* the ECU and thus with the other member countries of the EMS, British goods would become more expensive causing its exports to fall and imports to increase. While the inflation differential continued, Britain would build up a massive balance of payments deficit with the other EC countries and sterling would likely fall to the bottom of its parity band. Joint intervention by the central banks would see them accumulate pounds, as they met the excess supply of pounds and excess demand for other EC currencies from private sector foreign exchange transactions. Eventually something would have to give: either Britain's parity with the other countries would have to change to allow the pound to depreciate at 7 per cent per annum, or the loss of competitiveness would have to be allowed to work to bring down British inflation.

In the meantime, Britain would be expected to tighten monetary policy by raising interest rates – much the same policy in fact that it would probably want to pursue if it had stayed out of the System. But there is a possible catch which forms the so-called 'Walters critique' of the EMS (Walters, 1986). The scope for Britain to tackle its differential inflation problem through higher interest rates would be limited if its membership of the System was taken to imply a low probability of realignment (as is most likely to be the case), for then interest rates in Britain would have to

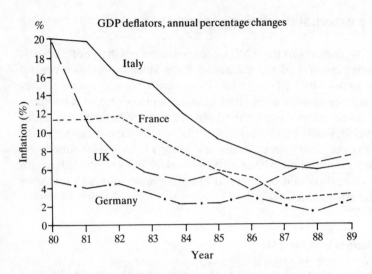

Figure 10.1 Inflation in the UK and the ERM.
Source: IMF International Financial Statistics.

be rather similar to those prevailing elsewhere in the System. In the context of EMU the irrevocably locked exchange rate must of course imply a *complete* absence of any differential between British interest rates and those prevailing elsewhere in the System; risk-free arbitrage would ensure this. Thus an inflationary economy entering the ERM without capital controls will be compelled by financial arbitrage to lower real interest rates, exacerbating inflation. The suggestion that real interest rates in the different countries would be ranked in *reverse* order to the size of their inflation problem is the burden of the critique.

Does this mean, pace Walters, that control over inflation might actually be *weakened* by joining the EMS? To say so would be to ignore two things: the effect of diminishing competitiveness upon profit margins, wages and employment growth if British inflation continues to proceed at a higher rate than that prevailing elsewhere in the System, and the 'Lucas effect'. With the new regime would come a new structure and the decisions of individuals as to consumption, investment and the setting of prices and wages would be shaped by their expectations as to how they think matters will work out. If people were confident that the exchange rate would not fall and that Britain's inflation rate would converge, like that of France, to the Community average, changes could be seen in wage bargaining processes and inflation mechanisms. The credibility of UK adherence to the System would not be confined to the foreign exchange markets. It would affect behaviour of wage and price setters too.

Interestingly, the arguments here bear an uncanny similarity (but with roles reversed!) to those of 1979 when monetarists argued that inflation could be brought down without undue costs in terms of output and employment by having the government declare its unswerving commitment to money supply targets (see Chapter 3). Then it was more the rediscovery of the Phillips Curve with the recession, massive unemployment and corporate shakeouts, and not the new monetary rule book, which squeezed inflation from the system. Those who look to a different scenario in 1991 point to three things: recent econometric evidence[8] suggesting that nowadays UK wages and costs respond more quickly to import prices; the greater credibility of the EMS commitment; and the track record of the System in dragging down Community members' inflation rates.

Community inflation performance

But what governs inflation in the Community? There is a widespread perception that the EMS is a Deutschmark zone, with the Federal Republic of Germany (or its Bundesbank) as the *de facto* leader. The Bundesbank has generally pursued a monetary policy aimed at keeping inflation very low and, by operating more or less independently from the rest of the ERM, it has forced its tight monetary policy on to other members. In this way the EMS is similar to earlier fixed exchange rate systems which also revolved around leaders or hegemons (see discussion in previous section).

Leadership of a system can be institutionalized, as under Bretton Woods, or it can evolve spontaneously via market reactions, and it is only in this latter respect that the EMS can be characterized as a Deutschmark hegemony. Certainly it was not designed as such, but rather as a collaborative and symmetric system and in some important respects it still is, especially in comparison with Bretton Woods. Exchange rate adjustments are not one-sided and no one country or grouping is able to alter central parities unilaterally. All realignments require the common decision of all member states and all must be collectively involved simultaneously.

There are important differences between the role of the Deutschmark in the EMS and that of the dollar under Bretton Woods, for the dollar played five roles. First, with the United States as the sole country with gold convertibility, the dollar was the *key currency*. Second, many other countries pegged their currencies to the dollar either directly or through the pound and the franc, and in this way the dollar was the major *intervention currency*. Third, dollars were held instead of gold by central banks and this made the dollar the main *reserve currency*. Fourth, the dollar was invariably used in trading operations as the 'other' currency, and as the currency of contract became the *vehicle currency*. Finally, the dollar was used in international markets such as that for oil as the currency of quotation, and was the *numéraire currency*. By contrast, in the EMS the Deutschmark performs few, if any, of these roles. Despite EMS statutes specifying use of the ECU for reserve balances, some central banks of EMS member countries do admittedly hold large Deutschmark reserves. ERM members formally peg to the ECU, not to the Deutschmark, although the latter remains the most important bilateral exchange rate. It is revealing that Britain, when entering the ERM, chose to fix the pound sterling to the Deutschmark (working backwards to an ECU central parity). Many EMS central banks use the Deutschmark for foreign exchange interventions, yet the US dollar remains the principal vehicle currency and *numéraire*, even in Community markets.

Treated as a symmetric system, the inflation rate of the members of the ERM ought to depend jointly on the monetary policies of all member countries with the anchor being a basket unit, the ECU, the value of which reflects the (weighted) average of the inflation rates of the member countries. This feature makes the entry of Britain to the mechanism very much a two-edged sword. With a weight of 13 per cent in the basket, and with sterling also a major international currency, it presents rather different problems than, say, the entry of Greece. Under fixed parities, Britain would to a commensurate degree be able to export its inflation to Germany and the other EMS countries within the mechanism.

German leadership

The view that the Bundesbank has acted as leader, making for convergence to the German inflation rate, stems from the asymmetries of the System.[9] These emanate from three aspects of the EMS: the relative sizes of the countries involved; responses of wages and prices in the countries; and different policy behaviour. The first is self-evident. Germany is the most populous country (79 million) and the largest economy (GDP is 28 per cent of the EC total) in the Community, and the Deutschmark is the most important international currency in the System. With the Deutschmark having a weighting of 30 per cent in the ECU, monetary developments in Germany are bound to have a greater impact on any other member country than any single member will have upon Germany. Those countries (e.g. Holland) for which Germany is the largest trading partner treat the Deutschmark link as effectively fixed as a way of reducing the costs of trade. A second difference comes from the behaviour of wages and prices in Germany. These have risen more slowly to improvements in competitiveness than the growth in wages and prices elsewhere in the Community has declined in response to declining competitiveness. The German anchor has held firm, in the words of the Governor of the Bank of England.[10]

Turning now to policy responses, the formal obligatory intervention requirements place equal and opposite pressure upon the weak and strong currency countries. Suppose that the intervention is carried out by the country which reaches its lower intervention point. It will obtain funds for intervention by drawing on the very short-term financing facility of the European Monetary Cooperation Fund (EMCF). These funds consist of base money of the central bank of the strong currency which simultaneously hit its opposite intervention point, and are received by the EMCF from the central bank concerned for on-lending to the weak currency country. Use of the funds for intervention in the foreign exchange market will see the net foreign reserves of the weak currency country decline and reserves of the country with the strong currency rise, with corresponding liquidity effects. Pressures will thus be on the weak country to deflate and the strong country to inflate. In this respect, the System is quite similar in its conception to the 'specie-flow' mechanism of the classical gold standard (see Chapter 2, p. 35).

In practice, intramarginal interventions have far exceeded the obligatory ones, and these have usually been financed with funds held in or borrowed by the weak currency countries in the Euromarkets (until 1987, intramarginal interventions did not qualify for EMCF financing). Instead of a symmetrical response on the part of the central bank with an appreciating currency and the central bank with a depreciating currency, the countries with weak currencies have had to carry the burdens of adjustment. The Bundesbank has generally been unwilling to lower interest rates when the Deutschmark is rising and has avoided intramarginal interventions. It has also sterilized the liquidity effect of its obligatory interventions. As a consequence the monetary base is reduced in the country with a weak currency without there being a matching increase of base money in the strong currency country. As well, the Deutschmark has behaved much like the so-called hard ECU in the British plan for a parallel currency discussed below. Of the twelve realignments within the EMS, not one has resulted in there being a revaluation relative to the Deutschmark (see Table 8.6).

Many regard these asymmetries and thus German leadership as the most important advantage of the ERM arrangement, since Germany lends price stability and anti-inflationary credibility to the others. The Bundesbank, and the checks operating in German product and labour markets, provide the anchors against inflation. The then British Chancellor of the Exchequer, Mr John Major, was quoted approvingly by the President of the Bundesbank as saying: 'Increasingly it [i.e. the ERM] has functioned like a modern gold standard, with the Deutschmark as the anchor' (Pöhl, 1990). Other member countries can then pursue domestic price stability merely by maintaining a stable bilateral exchange rate against the Deutschmark (although as we noted in Chapter 8, strict equality of German and other member country prices holds only for the prices of traded goods).

How much convergence?

Nevertheless, the idea that the ERM is a Deutschmark zone has not gone undisputed. Evidence has been presented to show that German interest rates have not been fully insulated from exchange rate pressures (de Grauwe, 1989). Exchange controls imposed by many weak currency countries may have reduced the dominance of Germany to some extent, allowing both strong and weak currencies to insulate domestic markets – Germany by sterilization, and some others by controls over capital movements. The corollary is that the removal of exchange controls over capital movements in July 1990, under the provisions of the 1992 programme, will have exposed other countries to the rigours of the lead set by German monetary policy more than before.

However, what has been seen as a more or less imposed convergence to the German inflation rate may in fact reflect a common desire on the part of a number of European countries to attack inflation. Spaventa (1989) argues that getting inflation down and keeping it down has become an electoral desideratum and politicians have responded to it by giving central banks a freer rein to pursue anti-inflationary policies. In the process, the external anchor has been strengthened as central parities have been realigned less often and by smaller amounts. Also, external stabilization has been reinforced by internal stabilization as central bankers have competed for rankings in the anti-inflationary stakes. Of relevance here is that to the extent that the system does function around a dominant country and currency, that role is not fixed institutionally as under Bretton Woods, but depends on the continuance of German policies and market responses. Each currency of the EMS, including sterling, could conceivably attain this position – a point sometimes made, not altogether convincingly, in British policy circles. Potential competition in a multicurrency reserve system may act as an important discipline on the leader.

10.3 European Monetary Union

Definitions of monetary union

The nature of monetary union has yet to be determined fully by the members of the European Community. In the Werner Report, four conditions were listed: full convertibility of currencies; no institutional barriers to the free movement of capital; elimination of fluctuation bands for exchange rates; and the irrevocable interlocking of parities. A movement to a single currency was not considered paramount. The Delors Report recognized that it is possible to define a monetary union as an area containing diverse currencies where these are irrevocably locked together on fixed exchange rates: the separate currencies would be as distinctive as nickels are from dimes and dollars (or as pounds are from pence). However, the more customary definition specifies a single currency with no distinctive 'national' components and with a single central bank and monetary policy. The latter definition is easier and more straightforward to work with, especially as the simplicity of a single monetary standard and the absence of exchange calculations (and certainly of costs of conversion) are a main ingredient in the gains from union. Otherwise, intra-community trade and commercial transactions would involve all twelve currencies – indeed, perhaps thirteen, under the British idea that a new hard-ECU should form a parallel currency and for a time compete with the twelve national currencies. A single currency is also what the signatories of the Delors Report appear to have in mind.

There must be doubts on other grounds as to whether the Community can stop short of having a single money; in particular, there is the question of whether exchange rates can be permanently fixed among the European Community countries while each retains the ability to alter the value of its own money. So long as each member nation retains complete political sovereignty over its money supply, there will exist the possibility that differential inflation performance could lead to exchange rate realignments among members. If exchange rates are to be indissolubly locked so that currencies are complete substitutes, a common unit of account, mode of exchange, store of value and denominator for deferred payments is the obvious step and a single central bank and a common monetary policy a corresponding requirement.

Each country could, if it wishes to do so for appearances' sake, continue to issue its own notes so long as each note were to be issued one for one and exchanged at par with the common unit, say one pound equals one ECU, as used to be the case with the Irish punt and still is the case with Scottish notes.[11] We subsume such a 'currency board' idea under the heading of a single currency. In calling the single currency the ECU we follow the Delors Committee. However, it must be different from the present ECU which is a basket of twelve national currencies: the 'new ECU' has to be a currency *sui generis*.

European monetary union consequently can be expected to embrace the following conditions:

1. The removal of all capital controls.
2. Permanently fixed exchange rates leading to a single currency, the new ECU.
3. A uniform monetary policy conducted or coordinated centrally.
4. Creation of a new monetary Community institution, a European central bank, to which national issuing banks will transfer the task of issuing the standard currency and implementing monetary policy.
5. Enactment of a charter for the central bank which defines its goals, degree of independence and accountability both to the twelve constituent national central banks and to the respective governments.
6. A common payments and financial system operating under a uniform set of regulations.
7. A set of parameters for the fiscal budget of the central administration or government. This is to ensure that the Community budgetary stance does not unduly obstruct the monetary policy aims of the European central bank.

In short, the essence of a monetary union is centralized policy-making across the union in which each member country would stand in relation to the central administration much as Northern Ireland, Scotland and Wales do *vis-à-vis* London. These nations consequently lose the ability to have a monetary policy, exchange rate and inflation rate which differ significantly from those ruling in the United Kingdom.

The benefits of union

On this basis the gains from EMU can be briefly summarized as arising from the following:

1. The elimination of exchange (transactions) costs.
2. The elimination of exchange rate uncertainty.

Gains arising under heading (1) are formally similar to the gains arising from tariff reduction or removal, but because there are economies of scale in exchange transactions they are difficult to calculate. The NEDO has, however, suggested a figure of 1–1.5 per cent of GDP as an upper estimate (Eltis, 1989) – though their calculation overlooks the fact that the overwhelming majority of transactions over the foreign exchanges occur on capital, not trade account, and their figure might for this reason more reasonably be read as a central estimate than as an upper estimate.

The larger gains, it is usually assumed, would arise under (2), i.e. in the eradication of the uncertainty that prevails when rates of exchange are flexible. Of course, only one kind of uncertainty is removed by forming an exchange rate union. The fact of monetary union does not eradicate any of the uncertainties that exist about the relative rates of return from investing in, say, Scotland as opposed to England, for example, though it does remove uncertainty about the exchange rate between the Scottish and English pounds. Because the facilities of the foreign exchange markets allow traders to insure themselves against the risk of exchange rate fluctuation over short horizons, it is the reduction of long-period uncertainty and the beneficial effects of this on production location and investment decisions which are usually most emphasized: an improvement in the functioning of the European capital market is implied which would complement the improvements already set in train by the liberalization programmes currently under way. However, using the facilities of the forward markets for short-term transactions is not costless. And the costs are not limited to pecuniary ones: time, trouble and inconvenience are involved as well, so that advantages accruing to intra-union trade from greater stability in exchange rates should not be overlooked. The promotion of trade, in turn, leads to increased competition and greater specialization in areas of comparative advantage, assisting goods market integration. Advocates of monetary union will often suggest the United States as a model of the positive outcomes of monetary union they have in mind, an example which emphasizes that it is to a combination of the large internal market and monetary union to which they are in effect looking; it is quite natural, then, to link the achievement of monetary union to that of the realization of 1992.

The costs of union

There are some attendant potential 'disbenefits' of monetary union, although contemporary analysis suggests that these are not as large as they were once thought. In particular, while it is clear that an EMU must imply the waiver of individual national monetary sovereignty (independent monetary policies), the scope for the beneficial use of such sovereignty is small in any case, limited in the long run to the attainment of a different rate of inflation from other countries – and not even to that if exchange rates are fixed, as they have become in the later stages of EMS. But clearly, it is of critical importance to be sure that the monetary union will itself deliver an acceptable rate of inflation. This is the first important policy problem posed by a move to EMU.

A second question pertains to fiscal sovereignty: if yielding national monetary sovereignty in favour of sharing in a collective European monetary sovereignty can be shown to entail no long-run loss, can the same be said of any related need to yield fiscal sovereignty – indeed, is any such surrender required?

The third issue relates to regional differences in growth, made more pressing by expectations that the Community may be widened to embrace the Scandinavian countries and the Eastern European countries, possibly also Turkey.

A European central bank

Apprehensions about the ability of a European central bank to maintain an acceptable counter-inflationary record are understandable. When countries agree to lock exchange rates they agree to pool monetary policy. Although fiscal policy may be decentralized to some extent, at least in principle, a margin of national sovereignty is resigned in a monetary union in favour of a collective, union-level, sovereignty. This is why a country like France, say, might hope to escape from the domination of Germany within an EMS without exchange control by forming a monetary union in which France would regain, through its input into union-level decisions, a portion of the sovereignty it resigns on agreeing to fix its exchange rate without the protection of exchange control. It is easy (but may not be entirely fair) to construe this as 'softness on inflation' in view of the Bundesbank's counter-inflationary reputation.

The constitutional problem then is how to devise an institution which has an incentive to establish a good counter-inflationary record and which is at the same time representative in some fashion (at a minimum, it should not be the Bundesbank). A European central bank could be accountable to the European parliament or it might report directly to a committee of ministers from national governments: in either case its independence from politicians could be jeopardized, weakening its resolve to fight inflation. (We note that the Bundesbank's charter of safeguarding the currency is not enshrined in the constitution, but is a creation of the German parliament in the form of the Deutsche

Bundesbank Act (Gesetz über die Deutsche Bundesbank) of 1957, which theoretically could vote to change the law.) Alternatively, the European central bank could report to the national central banks or be formed from them, along US lines, where the separately appointed Board of Governors and the twelve regional banks have allotted voting rights in the all-important Federal Open Market Committee – hence the common sobriquet Euro-Fed to suggest that a similar structure could work in Europe. But such arrangements to preserve the central bank's independence would weaken political control, and this is the nub of the present debate.

The Delors Report proposed that monetary policy be vested in a new European System of Central Banks (ESCB), an 'autonomous Community institution' that is 'committed to the objective of price stability'. Still, the Report added that, subject to this objective, the ESCB shall be obliged to support the general economic policy conducted at the Community level. Thus, the matter has yet to be settled thoroughly, and though not incapable of resolution, is one of the cues for the proponents of the hard ECU (see below).

Fiscal sovereignty

The issue of the linkage between fiscal and monetary sovereignty has also not been determined, though the terms for a solution have moved some way from that proposed by the Delors Committee. In the Delors Report, it was suggested that disciplined monetary policy would require limits to be placed on individual countries' budget deficits (as a proportion of GDP) and this view has been reiterated recently by the EC Monetary Committee. Little analysis was adduced in the Delors Report for this suggestion: the implicit argument is that, under flexible exchange rates (or while exchange rates remain adjustable), a country ultimately faces a penalty on 'excessive' fiscal expansion, in the form of a loss of confidence and devaluation of its exchange rate and consequent upward pressure on its inflation rate. If, as in effect under monetary union, the exchange rate is guaranteed, this discipline disappears. Moreover, with exchange rates fixed, the consequences of feckless fiscal policy in one country will spread to other members of the union and inflation will be exported from it to other members of the union.

This view, which implies that fiscal sovereignty is necessarily compromised by the surrender of monetary sovereignty, can be challenged. Indeed, some observers argue that more nimble (responsible, not necessarily more expansionary) fiscal policy is necessitated by the loss of monetary policy and that all that is required is that (a) there should be no bail-out of governments with solvency problems; and (b) there should be some fiscal coordination to ensure that at the level of the Union as a whole fiscal policy decisions do not imply too great (or too small) a call on resources. While the latter forms a constraint on national fiscal sovereignty, it is no more than implied in (admittedly somewhat strengthened) current procedures and is not an outright bar on a country's fiscal decisions.

The logic of these counter-arguments is straightforward. Because the resignation of individual monetary sovereignty removes a policy tool, the authorities will need to have more frequent recourse to alternative (fiscal) tools to deal with country-specific shocks. This makes a case for more flexible fiscal policies so long as idiosyncratic shocks persist. Credible 'no-bail-out' provisions, on the other hand, imply that irresponsible fiscal policy will result in the market discounting that country's government paper as insolvency looms, supplying a necessary discipline and creating incentives to take corrective actions. Finally, the general theory of international policy coordination provides an argument from pure efficiency considerations for the coordinated review and, if necessary, revision of fiscal policy: something of a sort is supposed to happen, after all, at the level of the G-3. As a whole, these arguments seem weighty – though a determined critic might still argue with some plausibility that 'no-bail-out' provisions would have to be tested before their reputation was guaranteed and that a good deal of damage could occur before the results of this test were clear.

Regional policies

As explained in section 10.1, in the short run a flexible exchange rate may represent a useful buffer against disparate real shocks. By forgoing an ability to express national sovereignty directly and by way, if necessary, of a differentiated monetary and exchange rate policy, a country in a monetary union forgoes some potential power to offset disturbances which impact differentially upon it. For this reason, one criterion of an optimum union is that its constituents should be symmetrically, not differentially, open to or affected by disturbances. Failing this, a high degree of intra-union factor mobility can offset the consequences of being unable to fight differentiated shocks with differentiated policy weapons, for in the absence of a policy buffer, such shocks will be absorbed in adjustments in price levels and/or unemployment. Thus different economic disturbances and a degree of wage rigidity do not preclude monetary integration; another criterion (Mundell, 1961) of an optimal currency area is the boundary of labour mobility.

However, the theory of optimal currency areas takes us only so far, for what we are dealing with here is a change in regime, and judgements must be made about how *all* markets are likely to behave in the new post-EMU environment. The economic integration of geographic areas embraces three aspects: the movement of goods, the movement of labour, and the movement of assets (securities). Attention is being given in the Community to the question of labour mobility, but the movement of labour is a relatively inefficient form of economic adjustment since social infrastructure – housing, schools, hospitals – cannot be shifted to where the workers move: wherever possible it is better to take jobs to the unemployed. Financial market convergence will be more complete after the removal of foreign exchange risk, and efficiency gains in banking and capital markets may lead to an improved allocation of capital resources across the Community, attracting inward investment to less well-off regions. At the same time, goods will move in response to regional variations in their prices: this movement will not only keep price differences within the limits set by the cost of transport, but indirectly may help to keep wage costs in line with productivity so limiting cost divergences between regions.

Certainly one factor in the more optimistic appraisal of the benefits of EMU has been an appreciation that the prevalence of country-specific shocks has already declined with the increased convergence (or homogenization) of the European economies. Experience with German Economic and Monetary Union (GEMU) has tempered that judgement to some extent by making apparent the enormous gap in economic performance between the regions, and the political pressures to rectify the disparities. In that case the German government met the social, political and economic strains of merging the rich and poor regions which a different exchange rate might have facilitated to some degree. The lesson for EMU is that if market forces are not given time to work, nationally differentiated policies must be evolved under the collective decision-making of the union; these are, in effect, regional policies.

All these considerations suggest that the political developments required to assist a movement towards monetary union in Europe are considerable. Willingness to cede national monetary sovereignty may have to be matched by a readiness to countenance policies at the union level for dealing with erstwhile national, now regional problems. None of this seems likely to be completed quickly, though the logic of events suggests that a beginning may be made soon.

10.4 From EMS to EMU

Speed of the transition

A fundamental issue in the design of a move towards monetary union is that of its speed. The two basic solutions proposed are those of a 'big leap' towards unification on the one hand, and an evolutionary transition on the other.

EMU could be launched overnight. On 'vesting day', European citizens would wake up to find that they had a unified currency, and a centralized monetary policy operated by a European central bank. As with decimalization, citizens would need to learn prices quoted in new units. Although it is easy to cite objections to this approach (see below), the big leap has one very strong argument in its favour, which is that it minimizes the risk of instability. With no protective exchange controls, the objective of maintaining very stable, nearly constant exchange rates in the transition period seems unlikely to be sustainable for very long. For it to be so, monetary policies have to be so tightly coordinated as to be (essentially) centralized. Any hint of policy inconsistency, let alone any hint that one central bank is contemplating the possibility of a realignment, would be sufficient, the argument goes, to precipitate a speculative raid on the (presumptive) weak currency; in the absence of protective exchange controls, the flow of speculative funds could easily outstrip the resources central banks are prepared to commit. Only if infinite support (foreign exchange intervention) is pledged by the strong currency issuer, or policies are wholly consistent, can the scenario of instability be laid to rest; but these conditions are of course just those that will be satisfied by monetary union.

The case for a more evolutionary approach has several supporting arguments, in particular the following:

1. A steady progression could be used to familiarize citizens with the new money.
2. Further, the new money could be adopted 'naturally' by the market during the transition rather than imposed as under the overnight conversion.
3. An evolutionary path could be used to devise and refine a policy standard, as opposed to the 'leap in the dark' of the rapid changeover.
4. A transitional approach could accommodate the need for the potential member economies to converge further in performance.

These arguments are not as strong as they seem. First, an overnight launch need not be a surprise. Hence there is *some* chance for familiarization to occur – though the imperative to avoid the risk of instability implies abbreviating this period. Second, the suggestion that the transition could be used to allow the emergence of the new common currency through market forces is misleading. A monetary system has aspects of a network implying that individual decisions as to which currency to use are interdependent; the usefulness to one individual of using a currency increases when others use it too. As a consequence, the influence of custom and history is extremely high and currency usage displays strong 'persistence'. Indeed, it is well attested that even in conditions of very high inflation, people continue to use their customary moneys rather than more stable external currencies; only in conditions of hyperinflation or very persistent high inflation does 'currency substitution' appear to occur on any scale.

Third, a fast launch can be adapted for any lack of convergence between member countries by staging the progress to full union, with the most closely aligned economies forming an initial core union, to be joined by other countries as these economies also interlock – the so-called two-speed or, less pejoratively, variable geometry approach.[12]

It can also be questioned just how important is a full convergence. Once inside the union a high inflation country will lose the ability to redress its differential inflation through differential monetary policy (indeed its *real* rate of interest may fall somewhat) but fiscal policy is still available, while the decline in competitiveness will exert its own deflationary pressures. Moreover, the certain prospect that there will be no accommodating exchange rate devaluation seems likely to impact favourably on the context for wage bargaining and price setting: joining the union signals an important regime change. Finally, it must be mentioned that non-convergence is not a problem which can be solved once and for all by the passage of a few more years: the economies of the prospective EMU will remain open to country-specific shocks for some decades to come and these will all pose some problems of adjustment (this is one reason for the earlier suggestion that EMU may require more nimble national fiscal policies). But, if monetary union is worth having, it offers gains which dominate any losses that may be incurred as a result of the loss of monetary sovereignty.

Delors and after

The Delors Committee was set up by the heads of government at the European Council Meeting in Madrid in June 1989 to study and propose concrete steps leading towards monetary union. The desirability of union was taken for granted in the remit, so the Delors Committee was free to set down a timetable for progress.

That timetable envisaged three stages, only the first of which (Stage 1) was given a specific calendar date (1 July 1990). With respect to their monetary implications, the content of these stages may be summarized as follows:

Stage 1   To start no later than 1 July 1990. Exchange controls to be abolished. Realignment of exchange rates still possible. All Community currencies to participate in the ERM on the same terms. Coordination of monetary policy to be intensified. A new Treaty to be ratified to permit the realization of economic union.

Stage 2   To start when the new Treaty comes into force. The basic organs of economic and monetary union to be set up, including the European System of Central Banks (ESCB). Exchange rate realignments allowable 'only in exceptional circumstances'. Margins of fluctuation within the ERM to be narrowed as circumstances permit.

Stage 3   To start with the irrevocable locking of exchange rates and transfer of power to responsible EC organs. The changeover to the single currency would take place during this stage.

This timetable has more of the flavour of a quick launch than of an evolutionary approach. In particular, the Report discusses but rejects the *parallel currency* approach, in which the new money might be introduced while the national moneys still exist, with a view to the new currency crowding out the existing ones.

The momentum of events since the publication of the Delors Report has reinforced this bias towards a rapid transition to EMU. First, although the Greek and Portuguese currencies have not yet been put into the ERM, sterling has (albeit with a wide margin initially), and the wider margin of fluctuation for the Italian lira has been reduced to the ERM norm. Also, the abolition of exchange controls on the part of France and Italy was completed ahead of the deadline for the inception of Stage One. Second, partly because of fears of provoking speculation, realignment has been effectively discountenanced. In this respect, the comportment of the ERM currencies has become more like that advocated for Stage Two than for Stage One, and the system has presented an appearance of calm and of freedom from speculative raids which has encouraged further momentum towards EMU. Third, monetary policies (interest rate policies) have become more tightly coordinated. Moreover, this cooperation in monetary policy extends beyond the EMS. Norway has declared that it intends to operate its monetary policy as if it were a member of the EMS. Like Austria, which has long pegged the schilling to the Deutschmark, Norway and other countries which follow this lead become virtually members of the EMS without formally joining it, so enhancing the benefits from pushing on with the integration programme. Fourth, for extraneous reasons (German unification), the political momentum behind EMU has been strengthened. Finally, earlier opposition from the Bundesbank to EMU appears to have been set as the date for the inception of Stage Two and 1997 has been pencilled in for a review of Stage Two, with an eye to a move to a single currency by the year 2000.

The hard ECU

British proposals for a hard ECU must be seen not just as an attempt to stave off this process but as a suggestion to extract some benefits from union while retaining some nominal and perhaps effective sovereignty. A distinction is drawn in the plan between a common currency and a single currency for Europe, with use of the hard ECU as a parallel currency leaving some potential scope for national authorities to retain responsibility for their respective currencies.

As in the Delors plan, the ECU would change from a basket to a real currency in its own right, and ECU deposits and notes would be issued by a central authority, a new European Monetary Fund (or Hard ECU Bank), in exchange for national currencies. The proposal envisages as the distinctive feature of the hard ECU that *it would never devalue against any (ERM) currency in a realignment*. In this sense it would always be at least as good as the 'best' ERM currency – though the hard ECU guarantee does not imply that it would always be the strongest currency in the ERM at given times. The hard ECU would have the standard ERM fluctuation margins against the other currencies and could move as they can, between the top and bottom of its band. By reason of its construction, the hard ECU has nothing (except the name) in common with the existing 'basket ECU', which is a composite currency of prespecified composition.

But the proposal is not just for a new unit of account. In order to secure the hard ECU's guarantee, the central banks of the issuing currencies would themselves have to be prepared, when called on to do so, to provide (at pre-realignment exchange rates) strong currencies in exchange for hard ECU holdings of their own; and they would have to be required to give such a commitment *ex ante*. If these commitments were not forthcoming or were heavily qualified in some way, the new Fund's ability to make its deposits attractive would be limited, so stultifying the growth of the hard ECU (though the Fund could take the chance of incurring insolvency). For this reason, the contrast the plan appears to afford between, on the one hand, the assured credibility of the hard ECU and, on the other, the perhaps faltering credibility of the pooled twelve central banks in the Delors System, is more apparent than real. Nevertheless, even with somewhat tempered commitments regarding the exchange value of the national currencies held by the Fund, the proposal could in principle, as the asymmetrical EMS did, exert a discipline upon the monetary policies of the central banks issuing 'weak' currencies. In the final analysis, the citizens of a persistently inflating country could simply acquire hard ECU for national currency.

In this respect the British proposal also carries implications for national monetary autonomy if it is to coerce governments with inflationary economic policies to change them. It also has some other features. Currency speculators in particular might find the hard ECU an attractive asset to hold, presenting them with a one-way bet in any future 'untimely' parity realignments in the EMS. If the new ECU was denied status as legal tender in each country, its use would be highly restricted: people could not pay taxes in ECUs; it might be difficult to receive salaries in them; tourists would still have to pay commission and bid-ask spreads when converting national currencies into the ECU; exporters would still face exchange rate risk when converting proceeds into the local currency. Even if the hard ECU were granted legal tender status, it is not clear that it could be expected to displace national currencies in any substantial way purely on the basis of merit. There are huge externalities in the use of a currency which ensure that market forces, unaided, are unlikely to promote the wholesale substitution of a new one for an established traditional currency.

Thus the hard ECU concept avoids the danger that the Delors Report detected in parallel currency proposals – namely that they may themselves add to inflation. (This argument seemed odd in any case since the advocates of parallel currencies have invariably wanted to promote a currency with superior properties which would attract funds away from existing national currencies, not add to them.) But the proposal does not respond to the second criticism of parallel currencies to be found in the Delors Report – namely that an additional currency simply adds to and does not reduce the transactions costs of a multicurrency area.

The EMS was always conceived of as an aid to economic integration within the Community, and as a stepping stone to full economic, monetary and political union. Views about how fully Britain is to participate in Stages Two and Three of the Delors agenda must be shaped by this wider map. It is in this fuller context that Europe presents itself as a fascinating laboratory. Economists have long argued about what characteristics go to make a market. Consider the United States, for example, and suppose for the sake of argument that we consider it to be one market. What makes it so? Is it the absence of customs barriers? Or is it the unrestricted freedom of capital or of labour and other factors of production? Does integration come from the ability to sell and buy and operate business across state lines? Or is it the common political structure? Is it the common currency? Or is it the common language? Because in Europe these elements are being introduced in stages, formation of the 'United States of Europe' offers an invaluable test case.[13]

In Britain's case, the answers which emerge are hardly unimportant ones in view of the parallel development of the single European market for finance. The advantage accruing to London as a financial centre make it a logical focus for the development of a more integrated financial area in Europe following the removal of exchange controls and other regulations on the operation of financial firms and markets. Whether these can emerge if Britain remains in the 'slow-speed' lane is highly questionable.

10.5 Alternative monetary standards?

With the possible exception of the gold standard, all of the arrangements examined so far in this chapter have a common feature – all rest on policies to control inflation which are undertaken at the discretion of individual nations or groupings of nations. In this section we ask whether there are alternatives which offer a more lasting method to anchor nominal values.

Problems of internal and external stabilization

During the 1980s Britain, in concert with other leading countries, followed a policy of internal stabilization, using monetary policy in an attempt to achieve reasonable stability of domestic prices measured by the 'underlying' retail price index: what we described in Chapter 2 as a 'goods standard'. After some experimentation with monetary rules, the policy evolved into one of 'playing it by ear'. When authorities are playing it by ear, onlookers may be agitated by the absence of a score to follow. If they do not know the score they may fail to appreciate fully the performance. If they think they know the score (even though none exists), they may be concerned by deviations from what they expect to hear.[14] Experience in Britain in the second half of the 1980s illustrates such concerns.

Britain switched in 1990 to external stabilization via the EMS. This change does nothing to solve the political character of inflation control, but transfers it – either to an ensemble of nine (or given the effective weightings, six) participating countries (if the ERM works symmetrically) or to the Bundesbank (on the view that the EMS is effectively a Deutschmark bloc) as Britain essentially borrows the Bundesbank's credibility for anti-inflationary policies. In this case history warns that nothing is inviolable – not even a reputation like that of the Bundesbank for anti-inflationary policies. And as Dowd (1988) observes, the Bundesbank's record on inflation is good only when compared with that of other central banks: 2–3 per cent per annum is not the long-run price stability of the gold standard. Some readers may remember the agitation that such 'creeping inflation' caused in the first two decades of the Bretton Woods System.

Inside a fully developed EMU, the problem is simply transferred to the European central bank. At this level the external stabilization route to price stability no longer seems plausible unless there is a new Bretton Woods. But if internal stabilization is the preferred route, the prospect that such a central bank would simply be 'representative' of constituent national interests evokes the prediction that inflation would necessarily increase above the level produced under an asymmetrical EMS by the example of the Bundesbank. This prospect is in fact unacceptable to the Bundesbank. Some opinion (notably that of EC central bank governors) favours the idea of creating the European central bank on the perceived model of the Bundesbank itself: this implies endowing the new central bank with political independence and a duty to stabilize the price level.

Such a prescription is much in line with the advice that stems from the reputational theory of economic policy and from Rogoff's (1987) model of the optimal 'conservative' central banker. The conception is quite subtle in some ways. It is *not* that the electorate's perception of its own welfare is wrong, only that short-sighted governments will succumb to the temptation to allow inflation to rip for the sake of short-run beneficial impacts on unemployment. Everyone would be better off under a regime which systematically excludes the possibility of 'exploiting' inflation in this way; making the central bank independent or appointing a conservative central banker has the right effect. While the reasoning may be somewhat different, there is nothing very new about such proposals, as is betrayed by the following extract from Hugh Gaitskell's evidence in 1959 to the Radcliffe Committee (Gaitskell, 1960):

> There was a time when it was argued that it was desirable to have a central bank independent of the government because it would prevent the government from pursuing inflationary policies. I totally disagree with that attitude. I think

that the government must have complete power and complete responsibility. I think that the democratic processes today are just as likely to produce in the government a fear of inflation as a fear of deflation.

Gaitskell's response is of interest too. He maintains that the electorate is capable of producing the right result unaided and indeed it might be argued that in some not-too-long run this is so: counter-inflationary policies have proven surprisingly popular in recent times.

Monetary rules

Even an independent central bank has discretion, however, and it is the exercise of discretion which is the proximate cause of the problem. A different approach is to adopt a rules-based approach to internal price stability. Monetary authorities like to retain discretion over monetary actions because monetary policy is seen to embrace more than price stability. There is concern for output fluctuations and a desire to insulate the financial system from financial shocks by varying the money stock in line with changes in money demand. When a central bank has a reputation for anti-inflationary policies it is able to engage in stabilization policies and smooth shocks to the financial sector without exciting the expectation that inflation goals will be sacrificed. A 'reputational monetary policy', perhaps paradoxically, gives a central bank concerned the greatest leverage over the economy. None the less, it is a risky game. Reputation is difficult to win, but easy to lose, and often tackling a number of things is a way of achieving none.

Where such reputation does not exist, it may be necessary in order to earn it for the monetary authorities to deliberately forswear certain activities. Much as Ulysses had himself tied to the mast to resist the lure of the Sirens, it may be necessary for the various monetary authorities to enact 'self-binding' arrangements with respect to monetary policy. Monetary targets were originally designed with such a purpose in mind, a clear example being the Humphrey–Hawkins legislation of 1978 in the United States which required the Federal Reserve Board to set and achieve prespecified growth rates of the money supply. This could be taken further, as in the Neal Resolution (H J Res. 409) introduced in 1990, requiring that

> The Federal Open Market Committee of the Federal Reserve System shall adopt and pursue monetary policies to reduce inflation gradually in order to eliminate inflation by not later than 5 years from the date in this enactment of this legislation and shall then adopt and pursue monetary policies to maintain price stability.

Other arrangements are possible. David Friedman, for example, suggests a rule such that money could be printed when the price index gets below some predetermined level and burnt when the price index gets beyond some slightly higher level.[15] These could serve as models for the constitution of the new European central bank.

The difficulty here is that there are no rules laid down which cannot be broken. And perhaps they should be broken. Circumstances change, and the old rules may be in need of modification. But then perhaps they should not. There are those who contend that the present international system, whether rule-based or not, or whether money creation is managed by the Bundesbank or the Fed, is incapable of delivering price stability and that the only way to remove inflation policy from the political arena is to undertake a fundamental reform of the monetary system. Reform might come from a return to some form of commodity money, maybe to gold, or from the innovation of private competitive moneys.

Commodity money

A restoration of the age-old device of ensuring stable prices, namely convertibility into gold, seems unlikely to succeed now that the mystique of gold has been lost – and, once gone, difficult to reconstruct. There has been a loss of innocence. People have learnt that governments can alter parity, tamper with the rules of the game and change the monetary system. That being so, the faults of a gold standard take on greater significance – these being fluctuations in the relative price of gold, the resource costs, and the potential for instability due to the growth of financial intermediation and debt money (see Chapter 2).

Because its supply is highly inelastic, gold does not bring absolute stability. It does not respond readily to shifts in monetary and non-monetary demand. The secular trend in the price of gold is dependent on mineral discoveries, changes in production technique and the depletion policies of the mineral owners. These considerations have led to proposals for other commodity standards, with better price stabilizing properties. Buchanan and others have suggested a *common brick standard*.[16] Bricks can be made anywhere and if in response to altered liquidity (?) preferences it takes too long to bake new ones, existing houses could always be dismantled. It is thus a commodity with a supply curve which is likely to be stable and highly elastic, allowing it to accommodate shifts in the monetary and non-monetary demands without large changes in the value of the commodity and thus the money stock. A bundle of commodities could have the same effect, and there have been a number of proposals for monetary systems based on a basket of primary commodities, for example. If the commodities in the basket are non-durables, there would be substantial resource costs from warehousing and spoilage. Durable commodities could share many of the same problems as gold in terms of their supply response.

In the most recent revival of the idea of commodity-based money, an 'ANCAP standard' of four commodities – ammonium nitrate, copper, aluminium and plywood – has been proposed because a price index of the four commodities combined has tracked the general price index (for the United States) faithfully in the past.[17] The issue of resource costs does not arise since it is a tabular standard and the government would not actually hold the four commodities or issue currency convertible into the commodities. Prices would be defined in terms of a resource unit comprising, say, 50 kg of nitrate + 40 kg of copper + 35 kg of aluminium + 80 sq m of plywood. This resource unit would be the unit of account – a physical construct paralleling the redefinition of the metre in 1960 in atomic mass. Dowd (1988) makes a similar proposal for the United Kingdom. He suggests that the pound sterling simply be redefined as a certain weight of a particular commodity or basket of commodities.

The consequence of such suggestions is to separate the means of payment from the unit of account, and in principle remove 'money' from price determination. Evolution over time of the form of money which was needed under the gold standard to economize on the use of gold and which took place with the growth of the banking system and debt money may be avoided because money as we know it may disappear – an idea borrowed from what is known, perhaps inappropriately, as the 'new monetary economics'. The argument is that much of the present shape of financial intermediation is a reflection of regulation and outmoded technology. Left to themselves, it is said, financial institutions would evolve into unit trusts or mutual funds linked by electronic fund transfer systems.[18] The whole system could operate like a Merrill Lynch cash management account, with instant commands via computer terminals to sell and buy securities, and transfer credits to other accounts in settlements of debts. Even hand-to-hand transactions could be settled by bearer units, with the price in terms of the resource unit of account posted daily in the newspapers in the same way that prices of unit trusts are advertised now. Financial institutions would offer professional portfolio management, risk pooling, brokerage and fund transfer facilities but not asset transformation, for 'deposits' in this new world are just claims to primary securities. Since assets of all kinds would be instantly transferable, the vision is of sophisticated barter, made possible by computer technology and negligible transactions costs. With money eliminated from functioning as unit of account, means of payment and abode of purchasing power, it would no longer matter, in fact no longer exist, and the problems of a monetary economy, inflation and unemployment, would also disappear.

Like the idea of a return to gold, this scenario ignores the lessons of history. The ANCAP standard is likened to physical definitions of length, weight, volume, time, temperature and energy, but unlike those other measures there exist opportunities for profit in supplanting or augmenting the official unit of value. Some institutions might be tempted to offer units, especially bearer ones, with a fixed price in terms of the resource unit of account. Those claims would be greatly valued, for savers could then plan future transactions free from concerns about likely conditions in asset markets, thereby overcoming the uncertainty of barter. There are economies in combining the means of payment and the unit of account. Consequently it might become the practice to state prices in terms of the bearer units, in the same way that contracts written in gold pounds came to be written in paper pounds. The whole process of the erosion of the hoped-for stable standard would be under way again.

A non-political solution?

In our view history teaches that no monetary system can guarantee price stability. Any arrangement will have some potential for inflation and offer some opportunities for inflation control. That is as true of the new 'non-system' of international financial *laissez-faire*, as it is of the gold standard and, we would contend, the new monetary standards proposed. If governments are able to resist inflation under a commodity standard, they are surely capable of resisting inflation under a system of managed money. What is needed is for people to decide upon the basic principles that are to define the workings of the monetary system and then agree to abide by them.

Without this discipline no system can work: a government can jettison a commodity standard if it gets in the way and it can agree to abide by fixed exchange rates but not follow through with the internal discipline which is necessary for external stabilization to work. It follows that hankering after a 'non-political' mode of inflation control is hopelessly naive: adopting a monetary reform is a political act; so is continued adherence, in the face of alternatives, to the rules of a new system.

The present system of managed money is both the best and the worst of monetary systems. With bad monetary policy, price instability can be much worse than is likely to result from any commodity standard, as recent British history has clearly demonstrated. Properly managed with good monetary policy it can, at least in principle, do just as well as any commodity standard in producing internal and external stability.

Preservation of reasonably stable internal policy by the leading countries could yield in turn to reasonably stable economic relations and, thus, exchange rates between them. The present system has two advantages over the other systems considered here. There is no separation of the unit of account function of money from the transactions function and, if it works properly, it is technically more efficient in that there are fewer resource costs involved. It is also an arrangement attuned to the times. Governments will not willingly return to the discipline of gold convertibility and accept a binding set of international rules. Nor will governments, individually or collectively, readily give up the power and seigniorage benefits which come from issuing inconvertible fiat moneys.

Here, in some eyes, lies the heart of the matter. If fiat money is not issued in a proper fashion, and there is much evidence to support that supposition, the true resource cost of the system is much higher as price instability erodes the usefulness of money in its three roles as a unit of account, means of payment and store of value, and spawns a variety of markets, institutions and instruments for hedging price and exchange rate risks. Money market mutual funds, unit-linked insurance, flexi-rate loans and mortgages, markets for futures, options and swaps, and the US savings and loan mess, can all be seen as consequences of inflation and price instability. Rather than have the monetary system adapt in this haphazard way to 'the times', it may be better to change the system. What one group has in mind is for governments to abandon sovereignty over money and the designation of legal tender, allowing individuals to do business in any money they choose to use and encouraging individuals and firms to offer their own private moneys for use.

Competing moneys

Thus Hayek and others[19] contend that the problem of inflation will only be solved by allowing private institutions to issue money in competition with the public sector. Instead of being 'forced' to make deposits convertible at full par value in terms of the national currency and having to hold reserves of that currency, private banks could issue notes and/or deposits denominated in terms of different bases, e.g. there could be gold money, oil money, commodity index money. Such issues might be thought to lead to a proliferation of currencies in use, traded against one another at fluctuating prices, so losing the advantages (in terms of a reduction in costs of calculating and transacting) of having a uniform unit of account. Proponents envisage, however, that the provider who chooses the most appropriate base and controls output in such a way that his or her money maintains value over time would capture market share and come to dominate the market. In effect, Gresham's Law will operate in reverse under free competition, and the good money will drive out the bad.

The paramount question raised by competing moneys is that of whether a standardized money is a public good *par excellence*, and hence inappropriate or inefficient for provision by multiple producers or, in the limit, a private monopoly. The basic objection to a badly managed government fiat money system is the resulting instability of prices which renders money less useful in its functions. Yet this plan has as its central feature the coexistence of several different moneys which would vary in price both within and across countries. Transactions costs and exchange risk would exist in dealing in the various moneys and there would be none of the benefits from having a standard unit of account for the majority of day-to-day transactions. As Kindleberger (1983) has argued:

> A fixed conversion coefficient between metres and yards permits measurement to take place in either. When the relationship between the yard and the metre fluctuates, however, the public good of a standard of measurement is lost (p. 383).

Proponents of competing moneys would retort that this is to confuse standardization with monopoly and that granting the State monopoly rights to issue money may mean that the benefits of standardization are outweighed by the tendency of the issuer to indulge in inflationary policies. Standardization could come about spontaneously by the issuers of money homing in on the same commodity or base for denomination. If all banks made their notes and deposits redeemable in gold, then the various claims should trade at par (with a discount indicating doubts about the ability of the issuer to meet withdrawals). In this way, the desire for standardization and the importance of scale economies in information and transactions costs could be put to the market test. If people value uniformity they would pick and choose among moneys so that a common format emerges, as happened with VHS versus Beta. But the adoption of the QWERTY typewriter keyboard offers a cautionary tale.[20] Here externalities have locked society into the use of a less-than-ideal typewriter keyboard even though everyone is 'free' to adopt a better model. In any case, it may be said that money is rather more important than video recorders (or typewriters) and that people elect governments precisely to take decisions which avoid excessive market turmoil and confusion.

It must also be said that there already exists choice in currency. Admittedly there is at present no competition for the national production of monetary units, but under international financial *laissez-faire* there is competition internationally.[21] A British citizen can hold purchasing power in US dollars or yen, and is able to obtain a home mortgage at low nominal interest rates in Swiss francs or Japanese yen – and some do both. British firms are able to switch from high inflation currencies to low inflation ones. The same choices are now open to citizens of all of the European Community countries, and those choices will continue under monetary union.

Of course, such behaviour falls short of subverting the transactions demand for the traditional domestic currency and the discipline it affords over money creation is correspondingly limited. Freedom from exchange control and the potential for currency substitution are important constraints but are in themselves not enough to permit neglect of the central problem of designing a system which will assist in obtaining relatively stable prices.

Notes

1. Hayek (1976).
2. See Commonwealth Study Group (1983), Meade (1984).
3. Bird (1987) and Chatterji (1989).
4. Mundell (1961), McKinnon (1963) and Laffer (1973).
5. Under floating rates, the more the portfolios of transactors are diversified among highly substitute assets denominated in different currencies (i.e. the greater is currency substitution), the more the price level in any country becomes the result of the joint outcome of the monetary policies of all countries, as under fixed rates.
6. Mundell (1969) argued that the 'true' instruments for the respective regimes are the *price* and the *quantity* of money. The exchange rate, according to Mundell, defines the price of one money in terms of others. Under flexible rates, this price adjusts to bring about equilibrium in the balance of payments, while the quantity of money is used as the instrument for achieving the desired rate of inflation. On the other hand, under a fixed exchange rate regime the price of money is used to tie domestic prices to external prices, while the quantity of money must be varied to keep the balance of payments in equilibrium.
7. Frenkel and Goldstein (1988).
8. Breedon, Murfin and Wright (1990).
9. The symmetries and asymmetries of the system are examined in Ohr (1989) and Bofinger (1989).
10. Bank of England (1990).
11. Giovannini (1989) has suggested that the adoption of a common currency could be accompanied by a currency revaluation in every country so that after the transition ECU notes could be issued with the national currency unit displayed on the reverse side. The revaluation is needed to make the national units simple transformations of the ECU unit, not as would currently be the case, confusing five-figure decimal point equivalents.
12. The pejorative import of the two-speed characterization derives from the

belief that countries outside the initial core will inevitably be disadvantaged in some way. Although it is not clear that this need be the case, it is certain that the politicians react adversely to the prospect of their country being in the slow-speed group.

13. Eichengreen (1990) compares US and European integration.
14. Borrowed from Mason (1963).
15. D. Friedman (1982).
16. Buchanan (1962).
17. Discussed in Fama (1983), Greenfield and Yeager (1983) and Hall (1982). The following comments are based on Lewis (1985).
18. Giddy (1986), Karaken (1986), McCulloch (1986) and Goodhart (1988) developed the ideas.
19. Vaubel (1979), Salin (1984) and Dowd (1988).
20. The argument is that, once adopted, the QWERTY keyboard is very difficult to displace, even though more efficient designs are available. The problem is that training schools and operatives are accustomed to the QWERTY keyboard so that individual employers find it uneconomic to introduce more efficient keyboards – even though starting from scratch a collective decision would favour an alternative configuration. An interesting account of how the QWERTY layout came to be adopted can be found in David (1985). The situation for currencies is not dissimilar in that currency use is dependent on the range of facilities and services offered for that currency, upon customary acceptability and, of course, legal tender laws.
21. International currency competition, we note, kept the great currencies from being debased in the Middle Ages. Coins could always be debased by reissuing them in a base form (with more alloy) to make them go further. But in this case the sovereign ran the risk of losing the mint trade of professional traders and dealers who could always turn to the services of overseas mints. By virtue of the competition in money, the great currencies – the Venetian ducat, the Dutch guilder and the pound sterling – maintained their value for centuries (Cipolla, 1956).

References

Aizenman, J. and Frenkel, J. (1985) 'Optimal wage indexation, foreign exchange intervention and monetary policy', *American Economic Review*, vol. 75, pp. 402–23.

Akerlof, G. A. and Milbourne, D. (1980), 'The short run demand for money', *Economic Journal*, vol. 90, pp. 885–900.

Aliber, R. Z. (1980), 'International banking: a survey', *Journal of Money, Credit and Banking*, vol. 16, pp. 661–78.

Andersen, P. S. (1985), 'The stability of money demand functions: an alternative approach', *BIS Economic Papers*, Basle, no. 14, April.

Artis, M. J. (1978), 'Monetary policy – part II', in Blackaby, F. T. (ed.), *British Economic Policy 1960–1974*, Cambridge University Press: Cambridge, pp. 258–303.

Artis, M. J. (1981), 'Is there a wage equation?', in Courakis, A. S. (ed.), *Inflation, Depression and Economic Policy in the West*, Mansell: London, pp. 65–81.

Artis, M. J. (1989), 'Exchange rate target zones, the Louvre Accord and policy coordination', in Fair, D. E. and de Boissieu, C. (eds.), *The International Adjustment Process, New Perspectives, Recent Experience and Future Challenges for the Financial System*, Dordrecht: Kluwer.

Artis, M. and Bayoumi, T. (1989), 'Saving, Investment, Financial Integration and the Balance of Payments', *International Monetary Fund Working Paper* 89/102, December.

Artis, M. J. and Currie, D. A. (1981), 'Monetary and exchange rate targets: a case for conditionalizing', *Oxford Economic Papers*, (supplement), vol. 33, pp. 176–200.

Artis, M. J. and Lewis, M. K. (1974), 'The demand for money: stable or unstable?', *The Banker*, vol. 124, pp. 239–47.

Artis, M. J. and Lewis, M. K. (1976), 'The demand for money in the UK, 1963–1973', *Manchester School of Economic and Social Studies*, vol. 44, pp. 147–81.

Artis, M. J. and Lewis, M. K. (1981), *Monetary Control in the United Kingdom*, Philip Allan: Oxford.

Artis, M. J. and Lewis, M. K. (1984), 'How unstable is the demand for money in the United Kingdom?', *Economica*, vol. 51, pp. 473–6.

Artis, M. J. and Lewis, M. K. (1990), 'Money demand and supply', in Bandyopadhyay, T. and Ghatak, S. (eds). *Current Issues in Monetary Economics*, Harvester Wheatsheaf: Hemel Hempstead, pp. 1–62.

Artis, M. J. and and Miller, M. H. (1979), 'Inflation, real wages and the terms of trade', in Bowers, J. K. (ed.), *Inflation, Development and Integration*, Leeds University Press.

Artis, M. J. and Nobay, A. R. (1969), 'Two aspects of the monetary debate', *National Institute Economic Review*, vol. 49, pp. 33–51.

Artis, M. J. and Ormerod, P. (1983), 'Wage inflation in Western Europe', Henley Centre for Forecasting, Discussion Paper.

Artis, M. J. and Ostry, S. (1986), *International Economic Policy Coordination*, Chatham House Papers, 30; Routledge & Kegan Paul for Royal Institute of International Affairs.

Artis, M. J. and Taylor, M. P. (1988), 'Exchange rates, interest rates, capital controls and the European Monetary System', Giavazzi, F., Micossi, S. and Miller, M. (eds.), *The European Monetary System*, Cambridge University Press: Cambridge, pp. 185–210.

Atkinson, A. B. (1982), 'Unemployment, wages and government policy', *Economic Journal*, 92, March, pp. 45–55.

Atkinson, P. and Chouraqui, J. C. (1987), 'The formation of monetary policy: a reassessment in the light of recent experience', *Monetary Policy and Financial Systems No.1*, OECD Working Paper no. 32.

Bagehot, W. (1915), *Lombard Street*, John Murray: London.

Bain, A. D. (1984), 'Bank lending, monetary control and lending policy', *paper presented to the Academic Panel of the Bank of England*, London.

Ball, R. J., Burns T. and Laury, J. S. E. (1977), 'The role of exchange rate changes in balance of payments adjustment', *Economic Journal*, vol. 87, pp. 1–29.

Bank of England (1978), 'Reflections on the conduct of monetary policy', *Bank of England Quarterly Bulletin*, vol. 18, pp. 31–7.

Bank of England (1979), 'The gilt-edged market', *Bank of England Quarterly Bulletin*, vol. 19, pp. 137–48.

Bank of England (1981), 'Reporting of economic and financial developments – assessment', *Bank of England Quarterly Bulletin*, vol. 21(1), pp. 18–22.

Bank of England (1982), 'The role of the Bank of England in the money market', *Bank of England Quarterly Bulletin*, vol. 22, pp. 86–94.

Bank of England (1984a), *The Development and Operation of Monetary Policy 1960–1983*, Clarendon Press: Oxford.

Bank of England (1984b) 'The variability of exchange rates: measurement and effects', *Bank of England Quarterly Bulletin*, vol. 24, pp. 346–9.

Bank of England (1985), 'Bill arbitrage', *Bank of England Quarterly Bulletin*, vol. 25, p. 189.

Bank of England (1987), 'The instruments of monetary policy', *Bank of England Quarterly Bulletin*, vol. 27, pp. 365–70.

Bank of England (1988a), 'Bank of England operations in the sterling money market: the extension of the Bank of England's dealing relationship in the sterling money market: draft proposals', *Bank of England Quarterly Bulletin*, vol. 28, pp. 391–401.

Bank of England (1988b), 'The net debt of the public sector: end-March 1988', *Bank of England Quarterly Bulletin*, vol. 28, pp. 530–7.

Bank of England (1988c), 'The experimental series of gilt-edged auctions', *Bank of England Quarterly Bulletin*, vol. 28(2), pp. 194–7.

Bank of England (1989a), 'Developments in international banking capital markets in 1988', *Bank of England Quarterly Bulletin*, vol. 29, pp. 252–63.

Bank of England (1989b), 'The market in currency options', *Bank of England Quarterly Bulletin*, vol. 29, pp. 235–42.

Bank of England (1990), 'The single market and its implications for Europe's monetary arrangements', *Bank of England Quarterly Bulletin*, vol. 30, pp. 62–7.

Barro, R. J. and Gordon, D. F. (1981a), 'A positive theory of monetary policy in a natural rate model', *Journal of Political Economy*, vol. 91, pp. 589–610.

Barro, R. J. and Gordon, D. F. (1981b), 'Rules, discretion and reputation in a model of monetary policy', *Journal of Monetary Economics*, vol. 12, pp. 101–21.

Batts, J. and Dowling, M. J. (1984), 'The stability of the demand-for-money function in the United Kingdom: 1880–1975', *Quarterly Review of Economics and Business*, vol. 24, pp. 37–48.

Baumol, W. J. (1952), 'The transactions demand for cash: an inventory theoretic approach', *Quarterly Journal of Economics*, vol. 66, pp. 545–56.

Bayoumi, T. (1990), 'Saving-investment correlations: immobile capital, government policy or endogenous behaviour?', *IMF Staff Papers*, vol. 37, pp. 360–87.

Bean, C. (1983), 'Targeting nominal income: an appraisal', *Economic Journal*, vol. 93, pp. 806–19.

Beckerman, W. and Jenkinson, T. (1987), 'What stopped the inflation? Unemployment or commodity prices?', *Economic Journal*, March pp. 39–54.

Bird, G. (1987), *International Macroeconomics*, Macmillan: London.

Blanchard, O. J. and Watson, M. W. (1982), 'Bubbles, rational expectations and financial markets', in Wachtel, E. (ed.), *Crisis in Economic and Financial Structure*, Lexington Books: Lexington, Mass, pp. 295–315.

Bofinger, P. (1989), 'The Role of Monetary Policy in the Process of Economic Reform in Eastern Europe, *Centre for Economic Policy Research, Discussion Paper* no. 457.

Bordo, M. D. and Choudhuri, E. (1982), 'Currency substitution and the demand for money', *Journal of Money, Credit and Banking*, vol. 14, pp. 48–57.

Boughton, J. M. (1979), 'Demand for money in major OECD countries', *OECD Economic Outlook*, Occasional Studies, January.

Breedon, F. J., Murfin, A. J. and Wright, S. H. (1990), 'Bank of England model 1989: recent developments and simulation properties', *Bank of England Technical paper*, no. 29, May.

Brittain, B. (1981), 'International currency substitution and the apparent instability of velocity in some Western European economies and the US', *Journal of Money, Credit and Banking*, vol. 13, pp. 135–55.

Brown, R. N., Enoch, C. A. and Mortimer-Lee, P. D. (1980), 'The interrelationships between costs and prices in the United Kingdom', Bank of England Discussion Paper, No. 8, March.

Brunner, K. (1987), 'Money supply' in Eatwell, J., Milgate, M. and Newman, P. (eds.) *New Palgrave Dictionary of Economics*, Macmillan: London, pp. 527–9.

Buchanan, J. M. (1962), 'Predictability: the criterion of monetary constitutions', in L. B. Yeager (ed.), *In Search of a Monetary Constitution*, Harvard University Press: Cambridge, Mass, pp. 155–83.

Buiter, W. and Miller, M. H. (1981), 'Monetary policy and international competitiveness: the problems of adjustment', *Oxford Economic Papers*, (supplement), vol. 33, pp. 143–75.

Burstein, M. L. (1963), *Money*, Schenkman Publishing Co: Cambridge, Mass.

Capie, F. and Rodrick-Bali, G. (1986), 'The behaviour of the money multiplier and its components since 1870', *Economic Briefing*, City University Business School, pp. 38–42.

Carr, J. and Darby, M. R. (1981), 'The role of money supply shocks in the short-run demand for money', *Journal of Monetary Economics*, vol. 8, pp. 183–99.

Chatterji, M. (1989), 'Themes in public policy', *Inaugural Lecture, University of Dundee*, 8 November.

Chessen, J. (1987), 'Feeling the heat of risk-based capital: the case of off-balance sheet activity', *Regulatory Review*, Federal Deposit Insurance Corporation, August, pp. 1–18.

Chow, G. C. (1966), 'On the long-run and short-run demand for money', *Journal of Political Economy*, April, pp. 111–31.

Cipolla, C. M. (1956), *Money, Prices and Civilization in the Mediterranean World: Fifth to Seventeenth Century*, Princeton University Press: Princeton, N.J.

Clower, R. W. (1967), 'A reconsideration of the microfoundations of monetary theory', *Western Economic Journal*, vol. 6, pp. 1–9.

Cobham, D. (1984), 'Convergence, divergence and realignment in British macroeconomics', *Banca Nazionale del Lavoro Quarterly Review*, vol. 37, pp. 159–76.

Coe, D. T., Durand, M. and Stiehler, U. (1988), 'The disinflation of the 1980s', *OECD Economic Studies*, Autumn, pp. 89–101.

Coe, D. T. and Gagliardi, F. (1986), 'Nominal wage determination in 10 OECD economies', *Working Paper no. 19*, Economics and Statistics Department, OECD.

Coghlan, R. T. (1978), 'A transactions demand for money', *Bank of England Quarterly Bulletin*, vol. 18, pp. 48–60.

Coghlan, R. T. (1979), 'A small monetary model of the UK economy', *Bank of England Discussion Paper* no. 3.

Commonwealth Study Group (1983), *Towards a New Bretton Woods*, Longman: Harlow, Essex.

Cooper, R. N. (1981), 'Comment on Sachs', *Brookings Papers in Economic Activity*, 1, pp. 269–82.

Cooper, R. N. (1982), 'The gold standard: historical facts and future prospects', *Brookings Papers on Economic Activity*, vol. 1, pp. 1–45.

Cordon, W. M. (1983), 'The logic of the international monetary non-system', in Machlup, F., Fels, G. and Miller-Groeling, H. (eds.), *Reflections on a Troubled World Economy*, Macmillan: London, pp. 59–74.

Courakis, A. S. (1987), 'In what sense do compulsory ratios reduce the volume of deposits?', in Goodhart, C. A. E., Currie, D. A. and Llewellyn, D. T. (eds.), *The Operation and Regulation of Financial Markets*, Macmillan, pp. 150–88.

Coutts, K., Godley, N. and Nordhaus, W. (1978), *Industrial Pricing in the United Kingdom*, Cambridge University Press: London.

Crockett, A. and Goldstein, M. (1987), 'Strengthening the international monetary system: exchange rates, surveillance and objective indicators', International Monetary Fund: Washington.

Cross Report, (1986), *Recent Innovations in International Banking*, Bank for International Settlements (BIS), April.

Cuddington, J. (1983), 'Currency substitution, capital mobility and money demand', *Journal of International Money and Finance*, vol. 2, pp. 111–33.

Currie, D. A. (1984), 'Monetary overshooting and the exchange rate', *Manchester School of Economic and Social Studies*, LII, pp. 28–48.

Cuthbertson, K. C. (1985), *The Demand and Supply of Money*, Basil Blackwell: Oxford.

Cuthbertson, K. C. (1991), 'Modelling the demand for money', in Green, C. J. and Llewellyn, D. (eds.), *Monetary Theory and Monetary Policy*, (Basil Blackwell: Oxford, forthcoming).

Cutherbertson, K. C. and Taylor, M. P. (1987), 'Buffer stock money: an appraisal', in Currie, D. A., Goodhart, C. A. E. and Llewellyn, D. L. (eds.), *The Operation and Regulation of Financial Markets*, Macmillan: London.

Cuthbertson, K. C. and Taylor, M. P. (1989), 'Anticipated and unanticipated variables in the demand for M1 in the UK', *Manchester School of Economic and Social Studies*, December, pp. 319–39.

David, P. (1985), 'CLIO and the economics of QWERTY', *American Economic Association, Papers and Proceedings*, vol. 75, pp. 332–7.

Davidson, J. (1987), 'Disequilibrium money: some further results with a monetary model in the UK', in Currie, D. A., Goodhart, C. A. E. and Llewellyn, D. L. (eds.), *The Operation and Regulation of Financial Markets*, Macmillan: London.

Davidson, J. and Ireland, J. (1985), 'Buffer Stock Money and Money Demand equations', *National Institute of Economic and Social Research, Discussion Paper* no. 150.

Davis, E. P. and Latter, A. R. (1989), 'London as a financial centre', *Bank of England Quarterly Bulletin*, November, pp. 516–28.

Davis, K. T. and Lewis, M. K. (1982), 'Can monetary policy work in a deregulated capital market?', *Australian Economic Review*, 1st Quarter, pp. 9–21.

Davis, K. T. and Lewis, M. K. (1988), 'The new Australian monetary policy', in *Monetary Policy in Pacific Basin Countries: Paper presented at a conference sponsored by the Federal Reserve Bank of San Francisco*, Heng-Sheng Cheng (ed.), Kluwer Academic Publishers: Boston, pp. 247–77.

Delors Report (1989), Committee for the Study of Economic and Monetary Union (chaired by Jacques Delors), *Report on Economic and Monetary Union in the European Community*, Commission of the European Communities: Luxembourg.

Dicks, M. J. (1988), 'The interest elasticity of consumers' expenditure', *Bank of England Discussion Papers, Technical Series*, no. 20, December.

Dornbusch, R. (1976), 'Expectations and exchange rate dynamics', *Journal of Political Economy*, vol. 84, pp. 1161–76.

Dornbusch, R. (1984), 'Flexible exchange rates and interdependence', *IMF Staff Papers*, vol. 30, pp. 2–38.

Dow, J. C. R. (1958), 'The economic effect of monetary policy 1945–57', *Committee on the Working of the Monetary System*, Principal Memoranda of Evidence, vol. 3, HMSO, 1960, pp. 76–105.

Dow, J. C. R. and Saville, I. D. (1988), *A Critique of Monetary Policy*, Oxford University Press: Oxford.

Dowd, K. (1988), 'Private money': the path to monetary stability', *Hobart Paper 112*, Institute of Economic Affairs: London.

Driffill, J., Mizon, G. and Ulph, A.(1990), 'The costs of inflation', in Hahn, F. H. and Friedman B. (eds.) *Handbook of Monetary Economics*, North Holland: Amsterdam.

Duck, N. W. and Sheppard, D. K. (1978), 'A proposal for the control of the UK money supply', *Economic Journal*, vol. 88, pp.1–17.

Easton, W. W. (1985), 'The importance of interest rates in the five macroeconomic models', *Bank of England Discussion Papers*, no. 24, October.

Easton, W. W. (1990), 'The interest rate transmission mechanism in the United Kingdom and overseas', *Bank of England Quarterly Bulletin*, vol. 30, pp. 198–214.

Edgeworth, F. Y. (1895), 'Thoughts on monetary reform', *Economic Journal*, vol. 5, pp. 434–51.

Eichengreen, B. (ed.) (1985), *The Gold Standard in Theory and History*, Methuen: New York.

Eichengreen, B. (1990), 'One money for Europe? Lessons from the US Currency Union', *University of California, Berkeley, Working Paper no. 90–132*, January.

Eltis, W. A. (1989), 'The obstacles to European Monetary Union', NEDO, *mimeo*.

Engle, R. F. and Granger, C. J. W. (1987), 'Co-integration and error correction: representation, estimation and testing', *Econometrica*, vol. 55, pp. 271–6.

Eshag, E. (1963), *From Marshall to Keynes: An essay on the monetary theory of the Cambridge School*, Basil Blackwell: Oxford.

Fama, E. F. (1980), 'Banking in the theory of finance', *Journal of Monetary Economics*, vol. 6, pp. 39–57.

Fama, E. F. (1983), 'Financial intermediation and price level control', *Journal of Monetary Economics*, vol. 12, pp. 7–28.

Feige, E. (1967), 'Expectations and adjustments in the monetary sector', *American Economic Review*, vol. 57, pp. 462–74.

Fetter, F. W. (1965), *Development of British Monetary Orthodoxy*, 1797–1875, Harvard University Press: Cambridge, Mass.

Fforde, J. S. (1983), 'Setting monetary objectives', *Bank of England Quarterly Bulletin*, vol. 23, pp. 200–8.

Fischer, S. (1986), 'Monetary rules and commodity money schemes under uncertainty', *Journal of Monetary Economics*, vol. 17, pp. 21–35.

Fisher, D. (1968), 'The demand for money in Britain: quarterly results 1951–1967', *Manchester School*, December, pp. 329–44.

Fisher, I. (1920), *Stabilizing the Dollar*, Macmillan: New York.

Fisher, I. (1930), *The Theory of Interest,* Macmillan: New York.

Fisher, I. (1934), *Stable Money, A history of the movement*, Adelphi: New York.

Fitzgibbon, A. (1989) 'Interest rates and overseas debt', *Occasional Papers in Economics*, no. 1, Griffith University: Brisbane.

Flannery, M. J. and Jaffee, D. M. (1973), *The Economic Implications of an Electronic Monetary Transfer System*, Lexington Books, D. C. Heath & Co.

Flemming, J. S. (1988), 'Interest rates and macroeconomic policy', in Eltis, W. A. (ed.), *Keynes and Economic Policy*, Macmillan, pp. 235–45.

Frenkel, J. A. and Froot, K. (1986), 'A tale of fundamentalists and chartists', *NBER Working Report*, no. 1854.

Frenkel, J. A. and Goldstein, M. (1988), 'The international monetary system: developments and prospects', *National Bureau of Economic Research Working Paper no. 2648*.

Frenkel, J. A. and Razin, A. (1987), *Fiscal Policies and the World Economy*, MIT Press, Cambridge, Mass.

Friedman, B. M., (1975), 'Targets, instruments and indicators of monetary policy', *Journal of Monetary Economics*, vol. 1, October, pp. 443–73.

Friedman, D. (1982), 'Gold, paper, or. . . . : is there a better money?', *CATO Institute of Policy Analysis*, September, 23.

Friedman, M. (1953), 'The case for flexible exchange rates', in *Essays in Positive Economics*, University of Chicago Press: Chicago.

Friedman, M. (1956), 'The quantity theory of money – a restatement', in Friedman, M. (ed.), *Studies in the Quantity Theory of Money*, University of Chicago Press: Chicago, pp. 3–21.

Friedman, M. (1959a), *A Program for Monetary Stability*, Fordham University Press: New York.

Friedman, M. (1959b), 'The demand for money – some theoretical and empirical results', *Journal of Political Economy*, vol. 67, pp. 327–51.

Friedman, M. (1969a), *The Optimum Quantity of Money and Other Essays*, Aldine Publishing Company: Chicago.

Friedman, M. (1969b), 'The Eurodollar market: some first principles' *Morgan Guaranty Survey*, October, pp. 4–14.

Friedman, M. (1970), 'A theoretical framework for monetary analysis', *Journal of Political Economy*, vol. 78, pp. 193–238.

Friedman, M. (1977), 'Inflation and unemployment' (Nobel Lecture), *Journal of Political Economy*, vol. 85, pp. 451–72.

Friedman, M. (1980), 'Memorandum on monetary policy in Treasury and Civil Service Committee', *Memoranda on Monetary Policy*, Series 1979–80, HMSO.

Friedman, M. (1986), 'The resource cost of irredeemable paper money', *Journal of Political Economy*, vol. 94, pp.642–7.

Friedman, M. (1987), 'Quantity theory of money', in Eatwell, J., Milgate, M. and Newman P., (eds.) *The New Palgrave Dictionary of Economics*, Macmillan: London.

Friedman, M. (1988), 'Money and the stock market', *Journal of Political Economy*, vol. 96, pp. 221–45.

Friedman, M. and Schwartz, A. J. (1963), 'Money and business cycles', *Review of Economics and Statistics*, vol. 45, pp. 32–64.

Friedman, M. and Schwartz, A. (1970), *Monetary Statistics of the United States*, National Bureau of Economic Research. Princeton, N.J.

Friedman, M. and Schwartz, A. (1982), *Monetary Trends in the United States and the United Kingdom: Their relation to income, prices and interest rates, 1867–1975*, University of Chicago Press: Chicago.

Friedman, M. and Schwartz, A. (1991), 'Alternative approaches to analyzing economic data', *American Economic Review*, vol. 81, pp. 39–49.

Gaitskell, H. (1960), Evidence. *Committee on the Working of the Monetary System*, Principal Memoranda of Evidence, HMSO: London.

Gallarotti, G. M. (1989), 'The classical gold standard as a spontaneous order', *The Cato Institute Seventh Annual Monetary Conference*, Washington, February.

Gardener, E. P. M. (1986), 'Securitization and the banking firm', *Research Papers in Banking and Finance*, 86/15, Institute of European Finance, Bangor.

Giavazzi, F. and Giovannini, A. (1988), 'The role of the exchange rate regime in a disinflation: empirical evidence of the European Monetary System', in Giavazzi, F., Micossi, S. and Miller, M. (eds.), *The European Monetary System*, Cambridge University Press, Cambridge, pp. 85–111.

Giavazzi, F., Micossi, S. and Miller, M. (eds.) (1988), *The European Monetary System*, Cambridge University Press: Cambridge.

Giavazzi, F. and Pagano, M. (1988), 'The advantage of tying one's hands: EMS discipline and central bank credibility', *European Economic Review*, vol. 32, pp. 1055–82.

Giddy, I. H. (1986), 'Assetless banking' in Savona, P. and Sutija, G. *Strategic Planning in International Banking*, Macmillan: London.

Giovannini, A. (1989), *The Transition to Monetary Union*, CEPR Occasional Paper no. 2.

Godley, W. and Norhaus, W. D. (1972), 'Pricing in the trade cycle', *Economic Journal*, vol. 82, pp. 853–82.

Goldfeld, S. M. (1973), 'The demand for money revisited', *Brookings Papers on Economic Activity*, no. 3, pp. 577–638.

Goldfeld, S. M. (1976), 'The case of the missing money', *Brookings Papers on Economic Activity*, no. 3, pp. 683–730.

Goodhart, C. A. E. (1984a), *Monetary Theory and Practice: The UK experience*, Macmillan: London.

Goodhart, C. A. E. (1984b) 'Alternative monetary regimes', *Discussion Paper no. 37*, Department of Economics, University of Hong Kong.

Goodhart, C. A. E. (1987), 'Monetary base', in Eatwell, J., Milgate, M. and Newman, P. (eds.), *The New Palgrave: A dictionary of economics*, Macmillan, pp. 500–2.

Goodhart, C. A. E. (1988), *The Evolution of Central Banks*, MIT Press: Cambridge, Mass.

Goodhart, C. A. E. (1989), *Money, Information and Uncertainty*, (2nd edn), Macmillan Press: London.

Goodhart, C. A. E. and Crockett, A. D. (1970), 'The importance of money', *Bank of England Quarterly Bulletin*, vol. 10, pp. 159–98.

Grauwe, P. De (1989), 'Is the European Monetary System a DM-Zone?', *CEPR Discussion Paper no. 297*.

Graves, P. E. (1980), 'The velocity of money: evidence for the UK, 1911–1966', *Economic Inquiry*, vol. XVIII, pp. 631–9.

Green, C. (1984), 'Preliminary results from a five-sector flow of funds model of the United Kingdom, 1972–77', *Economic Modelling*, July, pp. 304–26.

Greenfield, R. L. and Yeager, L. B. (1983), 'A laissez-faire approach to monetary stability', *Journal of Money, Credit and Banking*, August, pp. 302–15.

Gregory, T. E. (1933), 'Money', *Encyclopaedia of the Social Sciences*, vol. 10, Macmillan: New York, pp. 601–13.

Grice, J. and Bennett, A. (1984), 'Wealth and the demand for £M3 in the United Kingdom, 1963–1978', *Manchester School of Economic and Social Studies*, 3, September, pp. 239–71.

Griffiths, B. (1979), 'The reform of monetary control in the United Kingdom', *Annual Monetary Review*, no. 1, pp. 29–41.

Gurley, J. G. and Shaw, E. S. (1960), *Money in a Theory of Finance*, Brookings Institute: Washington.

Hacche, G. J. (1974), 'The demand for money in the United Kingdom: experience since 1971', *Bank of England Quarterly Bulletin*, vol. 14, pp. 284–305.

Hahn, F. H. (1982), *Money and Inflation*, Basil Blackwell: Oxford.

Hall, R. E. (1982), *Inflation: Causes and effects*, University of Chicago Press for the National Bureau of Economic Research.

Hall, S. G., Hendry, S. G. B. and Wilcox, O. (1989), 'The determinants of the UK monetary aggregates', *Bank of England Discussion Papers*, no. 41.

Hamburger, M. J. (1977), 'The demand for money in an open economy: Germany and the United Kingdom', *Journal of Monetary Economics*, vol. 3, pp. 25–40.

Harrod, R. (1965), *Reforming the World's Money*, Macmillan: London.

Harrod, R. (1969), *Money*, Macmillan: London.

Hawtrey, Sir R. (1938), *A Century of Bank Rate*, Longmans, Green & Co. Ltd: London.

Hawtrey, Sir R. (1947), *The Gold Standard in Theory and Practice*, (5th edn), Longmans, Green & Co. Ltd: London.

Hayek, F. A. (1976), 'Choice in currency – a way to stop inflation', *Occasional Paper 48*, The Institute of Economic Affairs: London.

Heller, H. R. (1985), 'The demand for money: the evidence from the short-run data', *Quarterly Journal of Economics*, May.

Hendry, D. F. (1979), 'Predictive failure and econometric modelling in macroecomomics: the transactions demand for money', in Ormerod, P. (ed.), *Economic Modelling*, Heinemann: London, pp. 217–42.

Hendry, D. F. and Ericsson, N. R. (1983), 'Assertion without empirical basis: an econometric appraisal of "Monetary Trends in . . . The United Kingdom" by Milton Friedman and Anna Schwartz', in *Monetary Trends in the United Kingdom*, Bank of England Panel of Academic Consultants, Paper no. 22, pp. 45–101 (with additional references).

Hendry, D. F. and Ericsson, N. R. (1987), 'Assertion without empirical basis: an econometric appraisal of *Monetary Trends. . .In The United Kingdom*;, University of Oxford Applied Economics Discussion Paper no. 25, March.

Hendry, D. F. and Ericsson, N. R. (1991), 'An econometric analysis of UK money demand', *American Economic Review*, vol. 81, pp. 8–38.

Hendry, D. F. and Mizon, G. (1978), 'Serial correlation as a convenient simplification, not a nuisance – a comment on a study of the demand for money by the Bank of England', *Economic Journal*, vol. 88, pp. 549–64.

Hicks, J. R. (1955), 'Economic Foundations of Wage Policy', *Economic Journal*, vol. 65, pp. 389–404.

Hicks, J. R. (1969), *A Theory of Economic History*, Clarendon Press: Oxford.

Hicks, J. R. (1977), *Economic Perspectives*, Oxford University Press: Oxford.

Hicks, Sir J. (1986), 'Managing without money', *Discussion Paper no. 65*, Department of Economics, University of Hong Kong.

HM Treasury (1981), 'Background to the government's economic policy', Third Report of the House of Commons Treasury and Civil Service Committee, *Monetary Policy*, vol. III, Appendices, HMSO: London.

HM Treasury (1987), *Macroeconomic Model Manual*.

Holtham, G., Hughes-Hallet, A. and Hutson, G. J. (1989), 'Exchange rate targeting as surrogate international cooperation', in Miller, M. H., Eichengreen, B. and Portes, R. (eds.), *Blueprints for Exchange Rate Management*, Academic Press: New York, pp. 239–80.

House of Commons (1985), Report of the Sub-Committee of the Select Committee of the Treasury and Civil Service on the European Monetary System, HMSO: London.

House of Lords (1983), Report of the Committee on the European Communities on the European Monetary System, HMSO: London.

Houthakker, H. S. (1977), 'The breakdown of Bretton Woods', *Discussion Paper no. 543*, Harvard Institute of Economic Research.

Hume, D. (1752), 'Of the balance of trade', reprinted in Cooper, R. N. (ed.), *International Finance*, Penguin: London, 1969, pp. 25–37.

Jackson, P. (1990), 'Public sector deficits and the money supply', in Bandyopadhyay, T. and Ghatak, S. (eds.), *Current Issues in Monetary Economics*, Harvester Wheatsheaf: Hemel Hempstead, pp. 113–41.

James, C. (1987), 'Off-balance sheet banking', *Economic Review*, Federal Reserve Bank of San Francisco, Fall, pp. 21–36.

Johnson, H. G. (1958), 'The Balance of Payments', *Pakistan Economic Journal*, June. Reprinted as Chapter 1 of H. G. Johnson, *Money, Trade and Economic Growth*, Unwin University Books, London, 1962.

Johnson, H. G. (1969), 'The case for flexible exchange rates, 1969', *Federal Reserve Bank of St Louis Review*, vol. 51, pp. 12–24, reprinted in *Further Essays in Monetary Economics*, Harvard University Press: Cambridge, Mass.

Johnston, R. B. (1979), 'Some aspects of the determination of Eurocurrency interest rates', *Bank of England Quarterly Bulletin*, vol. 19, pp. 35–46.

Jonson, P. D. (1987), 'Monetary indicators and the economy', *Bulletin of the Reserve Bank of Australia*, December, pp. 5–15.

Jonson, P. D., Moses, E. R. and Wymer, C. R. (1977), 'A minimal model of the Australian economy', *Reserve Bank of Australia*, Research Discussion Paper 7601, reprinted in Norton, W. E. (ed.), *Conference in Applied Economic Research*, Reserve Bank of Australia, Sydney.

Kareken, J. H. (1986), 'Federal bank regulatory policy: a description and some observations', *The Journal of Business*, vol. 59, pp. 3–48.

Kavanagh, M. J. and Walters, A. A. (1966), 'The demand for money in the United Kingdom: 1877–1961', *Bulletin of the Oxford University Institute of Economics and Statistics*, vol. 28, pp. 93–116.

Keeler, T. E. (1984), 'Theories of regulation and the deregulation movement', *Public Choice*, no. 44, pp. 103–45.

Kenen, P. B. (1983), 'The role of the dollar as an international currency', *Occasional Papers*, no. 13, Group of Thirty, November.

Kenen, P. B. (1988), *Exchange Rate Management*, Routledge & Kegan Paul.

Kent, R. J. (1985), 'The demand for the services of money', *Applied Economics*, no. 17, pp. 817–26.

Kent, R. P. (1956), *Money and Banking* (3rd edn), Rinehart & Co. Inc.: New York.

Kenway, P. (1989), 'UK macroeconomic models: a survey', *University of Reading Discussion Papers in Economics*, vol. 22, July.

Keynes, J. M. (1919), *The Economic Consequences of the Peace*, Macmillan: London.

Keynes, J. M. (1923), *A Tract on Monetary Reform*, Macmillan: London.

Keynes, J. M. (1930), *A Treatise of Money*, vol. 1, Macmillan: London.

Kindleberger, C. P. (1983), 'Standards as public, collective and private goods', *Institute for International Economic Studies, University of Stockholm, Reprint Series* no. 217.

Klein, B. J. (1977), 'The demand for quality-adjusted cash balances: price uncertainty in the U.S. demand for money function', *Journal of Political Economy*, vol. 85, pp. 691–715.

Klein, L. R. and Ball, R. J. (1961), *An Econometric Model of the United Kingdom*, Basil Blackwell: Oxford.

Kneeshaw, J. T. and van den Bergh, P. (1989), 'Changes in central bank money market operating procedures in the 1980s', *BIS Economic Papers*, no. 23, January, Bank for International Settlements.

Knoester, A. (1984), 'Theoretical principles of the buffer stock mechanism monetary quasi-equilibrium and its spillover effects', *Kredit und Kapital*, vol. 17, pp. 243–60.

Kruse, D. C. (1980), *Monetary Integration in Western Europe: EMU, EMS and Beyond*, Butterworth: London.

Kydland, F. E. and Prescott, E. C. (1977), 'Rules rather than discretion: the inconsistency of optimal plans', *Journal of Political Economy*, vol. 85, pp. 473–92.

Laffer, A. (1973), 'Two arguments for fixed rates', in Johnson, H. G. and Swoboda, A. K. (eds.), *The Economics of Common Currencies*, Allen & Unwin, London, pp. 25–34.

Laidler, D. (1986), 'Some evidence on the demand for money', *Journal of Political Economy*, vol. 74, pp. 55–68.

Laidler, D. E. W. (1971), 'The influence of money on economic activity: a survey of some current problems', in Clayton, G., Gilbert, J. C. and Sedgwick, R. (eds.), *Monetary Theory and Policy in the 1970s*, Oxford University Press: London, pp. 73–135.

Laidler, D. E. W. (1982), *Monetary Perspectives*, Philip Allan: Oxford.

Laidler, D. E. W. (1984), 'The buffer stock notion in monetary economics', *Economic Journal*, vol. 94, pp. 17–34.

Laidler, D. E. W. and Bentley, B. (1983), 'A small macro-model of the post-war United States', *Manchester School*, vol. 51, 317–40.

Laidler, D. E. W. and Parkin, J. M. (1970), 'The demand for money in the United Kingdom, 1955–1967: preliminary estimates', *Manchester School*, vol. 38, pp. 187–208.

Laskar, D. (1986), 'International cooperation and exchange rate stabilization', *Journal of International Economics*, vol. 21, pp. 151–64.

Levich, R. M. (1989), 'Is the foreign exchange market efficient?' *Oxford Review of Economic Policy*, vol. 5, pp. 40–60.

Lewis, M. K. (1985), 'Money and the control of inflation of the UK', *Midland Bank Review*, Summer, pp. 17–23.

Lewis, M. K. (1988), 'Off-Balance Sheet Activities and Financial Innovation in Banking', *Banca Nazionale del Lavoro Quarterly Review*, no. 167, December, pp. 387–410.

Lewis, M. K. (1990), 'Banking, securities and commerce: a European perspective', *Cato Journal*, vol. 10(2), pp. 347–56.

Lewis, M. K. and Davis, K. T. (1987), *Domestic and International Banking*, Philip Allan: Oxford and MIT Press: Cambridge, Mass.

Lewis, M. K. and Polasek, M. (1990), 'Whither the balance of payments?', *Australian Economic Review*, 3rd Quarter, pp. 5–16.

Lindbeck, A. (1978), *Economic Dependence and Interdependence in the Industrialized World*, OECD, Paris.

Llewellyn, D. T. (1979), 'Do building societies take deposits away from banks?', *Lloyds Bank Review*, no. 131, pp. 21–34.

Llewellyn, D. T. (1985), 'The evolution of the British banking system', *Gilbart Lectures on Banking*, Institute of Bankers: London.

Llewellyn, D. (1990), 'Money market operations of the Bank of England and the determination of interest rates', in Bandyopadhyay, T. and Ghatak, S. (eds.), *Current Issues of Monetary Economics*, Harvester Wheatsheaf: Hemel Hempstead, pp. 63–91.

Llewellyn, D. and Tew, B. (1988), 'The sterling money market and the determination of interest rates', *National Westminster Bank Quarterly Review*, May, pp. 25–37.

Longbottom, A. and Holly, S. (1985), 'Econometric methodology and monetarism: Professor Friedman and Professor Hendry on the demand for money', *Discussion Paper no. 131*, London Business School.

Lucas, R. E. (1976), 'Econometric policy evaluation – a critique', in Brunner, K. and Meltzer, A. (eds.), *The Phillips Curve and Labour Markets*, supplement to the *Journal of Monetary Economics*, vol. 2, pp. 19–46.

McCulloch, J. H. (1986), 'Bank regulation and deposit insurance', *The Journal of Business*, vol. 59, pp. 79–85.

MacDonald, R. and Taylor, M. P. (1989), 'Exchange rate economics: an expository survey' in MacDonald, R and Taylor, M. P. (eds.), *Exchange Rates and Open Economy Macroeconomics*, Basil Blackwell: Oxford.

McKinnon, R. (1963), 'Optimum currency areas', *American Economic Review*, vol. 53, pp. 717–25.

McKinnon, R. (1976), 'The limited role of fiscal policy in an open economy', *Banca Nazionale del Lavoro Quarterly Review*, June, pp. 95–119.

McKinnon, R. I. (1981), 'The exchange rate and macroeconomic policy: changing post-war perceptives', *Journal of Economic Literature*, vol. xix, pp. 531–57.

McKinnon, R. I. (1984a), 'Why floating exchange rates fail', *Discussion Paper, Banca d'Italia*, no. 72.

McKinnon, R. I. (1984b), *An International Standard for Monetary Stabilization*, Institute for International Economics: Washington, D.C.

McKinnon, R. I. (1988), 'Monetary and exchange rate policies for international financial stability', *Journal of Economic Perspectives*, vol. 2, pp. 83–103.

McMahon, C. W. (1984), 'The business of financial supervision', *Bank of England Quarterly Bulletin*, vol. 24, pp. 46–50.

McMahon, Sir K. (1988), 'The international monetary system over the next twenty-five years', in *The International Monetary System. The Next Twenty-Five Years*, Symposium at Basle University, 12 June, pp. 5–15.

Macmillan Report (1931), Report of the Committee on Finance and Industry, Cmd. 3897, HMSO: London.

Markowitz, H. (1959), *Portfolio Selection: Efficient diversification of investments*, Cowles Foundation: Yale.

Marshall, A. (1887), 'Remedies for fluctuations of general prices', reprinted in Pigou, A. C. (ed.), *Memorials of Alfred Marshall*, Macmillan: London, 1925.

Mason, W. E. (1963), *Clarification of the Monetary Standard*, The Pennsylvania State University Press: Philadelphia.

Meade, J. E. (1951), *The Theory of International Economic Policy*, vol. 1, *The Balance of Payments*, Oxford University Press: London.

Meade, J. E. (1955), 'The case for variable exchange rates', *Three Banks Review*, September, pp. 3–27.

Meade, J. (1984), 'A new Keynesian Bretton Woods', *Three Banks Review*, no. 142, June, pp. 8–25.

Melvin, M. (1985), 'Currency substitution and Western European monetary unification', *Economica*, vol. 52, pp. 79–91.

Miles, A. A. (1978), 'Currency substitution, flexible exchange rates and monetary independence', *American Economic Review*, vol. 68, pp. 428–36.

Mill, J. S. (1940), in Ashley, J. W. (ed.), *Principles of Political Economy*, (8th edn) Longmans, Green & Co: London.

Miller, M. H. (1980), 'Monetary control in the United Kingdom', *Cambridge Journal of Economics*, vol. 5, pp. 71–9.

Miller, M. H. and Orr, D. (1966), 'A model of the demand for money by firms', *Quarterly Journal of Economics*, vol. 80, August, pp. 413–35.

Minford, P. (1981), 'Labour market equilibrium in an open economy', *SSRC-University of Liverpool Research Project on the International Transmission of Fluctuations in Economic Activity, Secular Growth and Inflation*, Working Paper, no. 8103.

Monetary Control. A Consultation Paper by HM Treasury and the Bank of England, (1980), HMSO Cmnd 7858, March.

Moore, B. J. and Threadgold, A. R. (1980), 'Bank lending and the money supply', *Bank of England Discussion Papers*, no. 10.

Mundell, R. (1961), 'A theory of optimum currency areas', *American Economic Review*, vol. 51, pp. 657–65.

Mundell, R. A. (1962), 'Appropriate use of monetary and fiscal policy for internal and external stability', *International Monetary Fund Staff Papers*, March, pp. 70–9.

Mundell, R. A. (1963a) 'Inflation and real interest', *Journal of Political Economy*, vol. 71, pp. 280–3.

Mundell, R. A. (1963b), 'Capital mobility and stabilization policy under fixed and flexible exchange rates', *Canadian Journal of Economics and Political Science*, November, pp. 475–85.

Mundell, R. (1969), 'Toward a Better International Monetary System', *Journal of Money, Credit and Banking*, vol. 1, pp. 625–48.

National Board for Prices and Incomes (1967), *Bank Charges*, Report, no. 34, May, HMSO.

National Institute of Economic and Social Research (1988), National Institute Model 11, *Manual*, December.

Neild, R. R. (1963), *Pricing and Employment in the Trade Cycle*, National Institute of Economic and Social Research, no. 21 Cambridge University Press: Cambridge.

Nickell, S. (1982), 'Wages and unemployment – a general framework', *Economic Journal*, vol. 92, 1–12.

Niehans, J. (1978), *The Theory of Money*, The Johns Hopkins University Press: Baltimore.

Niehans, J. (1984), *International Monetary Economics*, The Johns Hopkins University Press: Baltimore.

Niehans, J. and Hewson, J. (1976), 'The Euro-dollar market and monetary theory', *Journal of Money, Credit and Banking*, February, pp. 1–28.

Ohr, R. (1989), 'A better game than Bretton Woods', *Universität Hohenheim, Discussion Paper* no. 49/1989.

Okun, A. M. (1981), *Prices and Quantities: A Macroeconomic Analysis*, Basil Blackwell: Oxford.

Paish, F. W. (1958), 'The future of British monetary policy', *Committee on the Working of the Monetary System*, Principal Memoranda of Evidence, vol. 3, HMSO, 1960, pp. 182–8.

Paish, F. W. (1959), 'Gilt-edged and the money supply', *The Banker*, vol. 109, pp. 17–25.

Parkin, M. (1975), 'Where is Britain's inflation going?' *Lloyds Bank Review*, No. 117, July, pp. 1–13.

Parkin, M., Sumner, M. and Ward, R. (1976), 'The effects of excess demand, generalised expectations and wage–price controls on wage inflation in the UK: 1956–71', Carnegie-Rochester Conference Series on Public Policy, *The Economics of Price and Wage Controls*.

Patinkin, D. (1961), 'Financial intermediaries and the logical structure of a monetary economy', *American Economic Review*, vol. 51, 95–116.

Patinkin, D. (1965), *Money, Interest and Prices*, (2nd edn), Harper & Row: New York.

Patinkin, D. (1976), *Keynes' Monetary Thought: A study in its development*, Duke University Press: Durham.

Patterson, K. D. (1987), 'The specification and stability of the demand for money in the United Kingdom', *Economica*, vol. 54, pp. 41–55.

Pavel, C. and Phillis, D. (1987), 'Why commercial banks sell loans: an empirical analysis', *Economic Perspectives*, Federal Reserve Bank of Chicago, May/June, pp. 3–14.

Peltzman, S. (1976), 'Toward a more general theory of regulation', *Journal of Law and Economics*, vol. 19, pp. 211–40.

Pepper, G. (1990), *Money, Credit and Inflation*, Research Monograph 44, Institute of Economic Affairs, London.

Pöhl, K. O. (1990), 'Prospects of the European Monetary Union' *Conference on 'Britain and EMU'*, November, London School of Economics.

Polasek, M. and Lewis, M. K. (1985), 'Australia's transition from crawling peg to floating exchange rate', *Banca Nazionale del Lavoro Quarterly Review*, vol. 153, pp. 187–203.

Poole, W. (1970), 'Optimal choice of monetary policy instruments in a simple stochastic macro model', *Quarterly Journal of Economics*, vol. 84, pp. 197–216.

Posner, M. (1978a), 'The search for common ground', Ch. 12 in Posner, M. (ed.), *Demand Management*, Heinemann.

Posner, M. (1978b), 'Wages, prices and the exchange rate', in Artis, M. J. and Nobay, A. R. (eds.), *Contemporary Economic Analysis*, Croom Helm, pp. 43–64.

Posner, R. A. (1974), 'Theories of economic regulation', *Bell Journal of Economic and Management Science*, vol. 5, pp. 335–58.

Price, L. D. D. (1972), 'The demand for money in the United Kingdom: a further investigation', *Bank of England Quarterly Bulletin*, March, pp. 43–55.

Radaelli, G. (1988), 'Is there a NAIRU? An empirical analysis of the US and the UK', *mimeo*.

Redish, A. (1988), 'The evolution of the gold standard in England', *Discussion Paper no. 88–36*, University of British Columbia, Department of Economics: Vancouver, December.

Revell, J. R. S. (1968), 'Changes in British Banking', *Hill Samuel Occasional Paper*, no. 3.

Richardson, P. (1981), 'The link between money and prices in the Treasury model', Annex B to Appendix 3, memorandum submitted by HM Treasury, Third Report of the House of Commons Treasury and Civil Service Committee, 'Monetary policy', vol. III.

Robertson, D. H. (1928), *Money*, Cambridge University Press: Cambridge.

Robertson, D. (1948), *Money* (4th edn), Cambridge University Press: Cambridge.

Robinson, J. (1946), 'Obstacles to full employment', *Nationalokonomisk Tidsskrift*, reprinted in *Collected Economic Papers*, vol. 1, Basil Blackwell: Oxford.

Rogoff, K. (1987), 'Reputational constraints on monetary policy', *Carnegie–Rochester Conference Series*, vol. 26, pp. 141–82.

Rowlatt, P. (1988), 'Analysis of the recent path of UK inflation', *Oxford Bulletin of Economics and Statistics*, vol. 50, pp. 335–60.

Sachs, J. (1981), 'The current account and macroeconomic adjustment in the 1970s', *Brookings Papers in Economic Activity*, vol. 1, pp. 201–68.

Salin, P. (ed.) (1984), *Currency Competition and Monetary Union*, Martinus Nijhoff: The Hague.
Salop, J. and Spitaller, E. (1980), 'Why does the current account matter?', *IMF Staff Papers*, March, pp. 101–34.
Sandler, T. and Tschirhart, J. T. (1980), 'An economic theory of clubs: an evaluate survey', *Journal of Economic Literature*, vol. XVIII, pp. 1481–521.
Savage, D. (1978), 'The channels of monetary influence: a survey of the empirical evidence', *National Institute Economic Review*, no. 83, February, pp. 73–89.
Sawyer, M. (1982), 'The non-Keynesian nature of the Phillips Curve', *mimeo*.
Sayers, R. S. (1951), *Modern Banking* (3rd edn), Clarendon Press: Oxford.
Sayers, R. S. (1957), *Central Banking after Bagehot*, Clarendon Press: Oxford.
Sayers, R. S. (1967), *Modern Banking* (7th edn), Clarendon Press: Oxford.
Smith, G. W. (1982), 'The normal cost hypothesis: a reappraisal', in Artis, M. J. *et al.* (eds.) *Demand Management, Supply Constraints and Inflation*, Manchester University Press.
Smith, P. R. (1979), 'A reconsideration of Keynes' finance motive', *Economic Record*, vol. 55, pp. 236–47.
Smith, R. G. and Goodhart, C. A. E. (1985), 'The relationship between exchange rate movements and monetary surprises: results for the United Kingdom and the United States compared and contrasted', *Manchester School of Economic and Social Studies*, vol. 53, March, pp. 2–22.
Spaventa, L. (1989), 'The new EMS: symmetry without coordination?', in *The EMS in Transition*, Centre for Economic Policy Research: London.
Stein, J. R. (1982), *Monetarist, Keynesian and New Classical Economics*, Basil Blackwell: Oxford.
Steindl, F. G. (1973), 'Price expectations and interest rates', *Journal of Money, Credit and Banking*, November.
Stiglitz, J. E. and Weiss, A. (1981), 'Credit rationing in markets with imperfect information', *American Economic Review*, vol. 71, pp. 393–410.
Sumner, M. T. (1978), 'Wage determination', in Parkin, M. and Sumner, M. T. (eds.), *Inflation in the United Kingdom*, Manchester University Press and Toronto University Press, pp. 75–92.
Swann, D. (1988), *The Economics of the Common Market*, (6th edn), Penguin: Harmondsworth.
Swan, T. W. (1955), 'Longer-run problems of the balance of payments', reprinted as Ch. 24 in Arndt, H. W. and Corden, W. M. (eds.), *The Australian Economy*, Cheshire: Melbourne,1963.
Taylor, M. P. (1987a), 'Covered interest parity: a high frequency, high quality data study', *Economica*, vol. 54, pp. 429–38.
Taylor, M. P. (1987b), 'Financial innovation, inflation and the stability of the demand for broad money in the United Kingdom', *Bulletin of Economic Research*, vol. 39, pp. 225–34.
Tew, B. (1978), 'Monetary policy – part I', in Blackaby, F. T. (ed.), *British Economic Policy 1960–1974*, Cambridge, University Press: Cambridge pp. 218–57.
Thore, S. (1984), 'Spatial models of the Euro-dollar market', *Journal of Banking and Finance*, pp. 621–31.
Thornton, D. L. (1985), 'Money demand dynamics: some new evidence', *The Federal Reserve Bank of St. Louis Review*, vol. 67, pp. 14–35.
Tinbergen, J. (1956), *Economic Policy: Principles and design*, North Holland: Amsterdam.

Tobin, J. (1956), 'The interest-elasticity of the transactions demand for cash', *Review of Economics and Statistics*, vol. 38, pp. 241–7.

Tobin, J. (1958), 'Liquidity preference as behaviour towards risk', *Review of Economic Studies*, vol. 25, pp. 65–8.

Tobin, J. (1963), 'Commercial banks as creators of money', in Carson, D. (ed.), *Banking and Monetary Studies*, pp. 408–79, reprinted in Tobin, J., *Essays in Economics, vol. I, Macroeconomics*, North Holland: Amsterdam, 1971.

Tobin, J. (1969), 'A general equilibrium approach to monetary theory', *Journal of Money, Credit and Banking*, vol. 1, pp. 15–29.

Tobin, J. (1978), 'Monetary policies and the economy: the transmission mechanism', *Southern Economic Journal*, vol. 44, pp. 421–31.

Tobin, J. (1989), 'On the theory of macroeconomic policy', (Tinbergen Lecture), The Hague, reprinted as *Cowles Foundation Discussion Paper 931*.

Tobin, J. and Brainard, W. C. (1968), 'Pitfalls in financial model building', *American Economic Review*, May, pp. 99–123, reprinted in Tobin, J. *Essays in Economics*, (1971), vol. 1, Markham: Chicago.

Topping, S. L. and Bishop, S. L. (1989), 'Breaks in monetary series', *Bank of England Discussion Papers, Technical Series*, February, no. 23.

Toynbee, A. J. (1954), *A Study of History*, vol. VII, Oxford University Press: London.

Triffin, R. (1960), *Gold and the Dollar Crisis*, Yale University Press: New Haven.

Triffin, R. (1968), *Our International Monetary System: Yesterday, today and tomorrow*, Random House: New York.

Ungerer, H. O., Evans, T., Mayer, T. and Young, P. (1986), 'The European Monetary System: recent developments', *IMF Occasional Papers*, no. 48, December.

Vaubel, R. (1979), 'Free currency competition', *Weltwirtschaftliches Archiv*, vol. 113, p. 435.

Vaubel, R. (1980), 'International shifts in the demand for money, their effects on exchange rates and price levels and their implications for the pre-announcement of monetary expansion', *Weltwirtschaftliches Archiv*, vol. 116, pp. 1–44.

Wallace, N. (1990), 'Why markets in foreign exchange are different from other markets', *Federal Reserve Bank of Minneapolis Quarterly Review*, Winter, pp. 12–18.

Wallich, H. C. (1972), *The Monetary Crisis of 1971 – The Lessons to be Learned*, The Per Jacobsson Lectures, Bank for International Settlements.

Wallis, K. F. *et al.* (1988), 'Comparative properties of models of the UK economy', *National Institute Economic Review*, no. 127, November, pp. 69–87.

Walters, A. A. (1986), *Britain's Economic Renaissance*, Oxford University Press, Oxford.

Weale, M. (1986), 'The structure of personal sector short-term asset holdings', *Manchester School*, June, pp. 14–161.

Williams, D., Goodhart, C. A. E. and Gowland, D. (1976), 'Money, income and causality, the UK experience', *American Economic Review,*' vol. 66, pp. 417–23.

Williamson, J. (1965), 'The crawling peg', *Princeton Essays in International Finance no. 50*.

Williamson, J. (1976), 'The Benefits and Costs of an International Monetary Non-system' in M. Bernstein *et al.*, *Reflections on Jamaica*, Essays in International Finance no. 15 (International Finance Section of Princeton University, April).

Williamson, J. (1985), *The Exchange Rate System*, Institute for International Economics, Washington.

Wilson, J. S. G. (1989), *The London Money Markets*, SUERF: Tilburg.

Wren-Lewis, S. (1981), 'The role of money in determining prices: a reduced form approach; in HM Treasury (1981), *op. cit.*

Wren-Lewis, S. (1985), 'Private sector earnings and excess demand from 1966 to 1980', *Oxford Bulletin of Economics and Statistics*, vol. 47, pp. 1–18.

Wren-Lewis, S. (1988), 'Supply, liquidity and credit: a new version of the National Institute's domestic econometric macro-model', *National Institute Economic Review*, no. 126, August, pp. 32–43.

Ypersele, J. van and Koeune, J.-C. (1984), *The European Monetary System*, The European Perspectives Series, Brussels.

Subject index

adjustments in the monetary sector, 105–
8, 113–14, 116–22, 181–3, 258–63
see also transmission mechanism of
monetary policy
advances requests, *see* direct controls
arbitrage
between bank and market rates, 16,
182, 186–7
between Eurosterling and domestic
market, 17–18, 153, 246
in London money market, 174, 181–2,
188
Australia, 4, 26, 42, 43, 53, 77, 126, 154,
248, 266
Austria, 206, 293
autonomy, *see* national monetary
independence

balance of payments
capital account, 42, 156, 264–7
see also capital flows
current account, 191, 193, 194, 264,
265, 266, 269
and monetary policy, 120–4, 263–8
balance of payments standard, 25, 40
balance sheets of British banks, 7–8, 11,
14, 16, 124, 143
bank lending
contribution to money supply, 156, 158,
159, 160, 161, 163
interest elasticity of, 117, 160, 163
Bank of England, 1, 6, 10, 63, 115, 119,
124, 125, 132, 165, 169, 193, 194, 266,
281
and funding policies, 159, 184–8

money market operations, 11, 18, 20,
174–84, 263
prudential supervision, 11, 20–1, 253
Bank rate, 36, 37, 52, 125, 175, 178, 179,
195
bankers' deposits, *see* cash-ratio deposits,
bank's
banking, theories of, 138–48, 241–53
Banking Act 1979, 20
amendment 1987, 20–1
base money, *see* monetary base
base rates, banks', 180, 181, 182, 190
Belgium, 39
Big Bang, 21, 239
'bill mountain', Bank of England, 185–7
bills
commercial, 153, 175, 178, 182, 186
Treasury, 150, 175, 179, 182, 254
bimetallism, 25, 29, 32
bonds, 57, 82, 85, 255
Bretton Woods international monetary
system, 2, 3, 23, 38–44, 270, 271, 272,
276, 279, 296
buffer-stock function of money, 81,
102–11
building societies, 10, 13, 21, 172, 261, 262
Bundesbank
credibility of, 130, 227, 235, 270, 277,
281, 286, 296, 298
European Monetary System, 226–7,
231, 279–82, 296, 298
European Monetary Union, 286–7

Cambridge 'k', 85
see also income velocity

Canada, 4, 42
capital adequacy of banks, 14, 21
capital flows, 35, 36, 37, 39, 40, 189, 190, 231, 266, 271
cash (central bank money), 139, 183
    see also high-powered money; monetary base
'cash-in-advance' constraint, 80
cash-ratio deposits, banks', 15, 17, 152, 175
central banking, 126, 130–1, 154–63, 169, 183–4, 258–9, 296–7
    development of under gold standard, 35–8
    see also Bank of England
City of London, 10, 15, 21, 235, 295
clearing banks, 8, 10, 13, 86, 148
cointegration, 89–90
commodity money, 2, 298–300
    commodity based system, 22, 23, 26, 27, 30, 38
    composite commodity reserve standard, 25, 298–9
competing currencies, 46, 301–3
Competition and Credit Control, 8, 15–7, 86, 93, 101, 104, 118–19, 123, 155, 175, 210
competitiveness (external), 42, 198, 205, 211, 223, 228–30, 232, 274, 277
Conservative Government policies, 17, 18, 211, 232
    see also Thatcher economic policies
consumption, 117, 123, 190, 264
convertibility, commodity, 25, 28, 34, 38
Cooperation Fund, *see* European Monetary Cooperation Fund
Corset, *see* Supplementary Special Deposit scheme
credibility
    in monetary policy, 41, 49, 204, 226–7, 235, 238, 296, 297
    of Bank of England, 227, 270, 278, 296
    see Bundesbank
credit
    counterparts approach, money supply, 156–9, 161, 167, 184
    creation, 138–47, 154–6, 245–6
    policy, 14, 259
    rationing, 152, 189, 190, 261, 269
currency substitution, 253–8, 276, 294, 303
    direct, 254
    indirect, 255

Dalton 'cheap money' experiment, 188–9, 195

deflation, 51, 57
    under gold standard, 30–2
Delors Report, 235, 283, 284, 287, 291–3, 294
    see also European Monetary Union (EMU)
demand for money, 78–111
    estimation of, 83–90, 108
    income elasticity of, 96, 98, 261
    interest elasticity of, 96, 97, 124
    long run, 87, 90–3
    precautionary motive, 80, 254
    price elasticity of, 83, 85, 88–9, 90
    short run, 87, 93–6
    speculative motive, 82
    stable (stability of), 90, 93, 96–102, 110–11, 256, 260–1, 269
    theories of, 79–83
    transactions motive, 79, 254, 263
    wealth effects, 83
demand-for-money functions, 15, 72, 73, 83, 93, 99, 106, 109, 110, 134, 203, 256
deposit banks, 7, 11
Deposit Protection Scheme, 169, 172
deposit rates, 11, 13, 101, 259–60
deposits, bankers', *see* cash-ratio deposits, banks'; operational deposits (ODs)
deregulation, 14, 183, 240–1, 265, 268
    effect on demand for money, 260–1
    implications for monetary policy, 182–4, 190, 258–63
    theories of, 12–13
Deutschmark role in European Monetary System, 39, 127, 199, 220, 228, 231, 276, 279–82
direct controls, 10, 11, 12, 13, 15, 16, 18, 99, 148–54, 168, 173
discount houses, 10, 13, 36, 166, 174, 176, 178, 179
discount rate, *see* Bank rate
discount window, 169, 177, 178
disinflation, 52–8
    effect on demand for money, 102
    see also deflation
disintermediation, 16, 17, 151, 153, 169
Domestic credit expansion (DCE), 123, 124, 158, 173, 256
'Duke of York' gilts strategy, 163, 185

earnings standard, 25, 26
economic growth, 42
economic policy, theory of, 53–4, 112–16, 214, 263
ECU, *see* European Currency Unit
EEC Banking Directive, 20
Eligible liabilities (ELs), 151, 152

EMS, *see* European Monetary System
error correction model (ECM), 77, 84, 88,
    89, 90, 93
Eurobonds, 248
Eurocurrency banking system, 143, 148,
    241, 243, 244, 246, 247
Eurodollars, 241, 243, 245–6
Euromarkets, role in deregulation, 12, 15,
    247–8
Europe 1992, *see* Single European Act
European central bank, *see* European
    Monetary Union (EMU)
European Community, 1, 21, 216, 258,
    274, 283, 303
European currency 'Snake', 222, 233
European Currency Unit (ECU), 221,
    272, 280, 283, 284
    hard ECU, 235, 281, 283, 293–5
    official unit, 216–18
    private market, 217–18, 223
    role in monetary union, 218, 272–3,
        283–4, 303
European Monetary Cooperation Fund,
    218, 222, 281
European Monetary System (EMS), 4,
    20, 39, 204, 216–31, 271, 272
    asymmetries of system, 227, 281–2
    effect on competitiveness, 228
    exchange rate stability, 222, 223–6
    German leadership, 271, 279–82, 286
    inflation control, 222, 226–7, 277–82
    inflation convergence, 5, 230, 234, 236,
        278, 282
    symmetries of system, 4, 220, 227, 280,
        281, 296, 303
    UK attitudes towards, 198, 204, 211,
        232–7
    see also Exchange Rate Mechanism
        (ERM); German monetary policy;
        Walters critique
European Monetary Union (EMU), 5, 7,
    222, 231, 272, 303
    benefits of, 283, 284–5
    costs of, 285–6
    defined, 283–4
    European central bank, 5, 231, 284,
        286–7, 296, 298
    fiscal sovereignty, 284, 287–8
    regional policies, 274, 288–9
    transition from EMS to EMU, 271,
        290–5
Eurosterling, 18–19, 153, 246
exchange controls, 38–9, 246–7, 303
    for ERM currencies, 223, 225, 230, 231,
        234, 282, 286, 290, 303
    in Britain, 17, 18, 150, 153, 207, 256,
        265, 268

Exchange Rate Mechanism (ERM), 4, 45,
    127
    British entry, 6, 207, 270
    broad and narrow bands, 4, 216–22, 234
    divergence indicator, 220, 221, 223,
        227, 238
    exchange rate parity realignments, 4,
        221, 223, 231, 233, 235, 277, 279,
        294
    intervention arrangements, 219, 221,
        222, 277, 281
    parity grid, 216, 218, 220, 277
    very short term financing facility
        (VSTF), 221
exchange rate target, 125, 173, 180, 198,
    202–7, 210
    'shadowing the Deutschmark', 214–16,
        231, 234, 236
    transition from money to exchange rate
        targets, 131–3, 202–16, 232–6
exchange rates
    asset theory, 48–9, 120–2
    Bretton Woods system, 38, 40, 41, 207,
        223, 270
    currency basket, 25, 276
    elevation in British monetary policy in
        1980s, 125, 127, 133, 194, 202–16,
        232–6
    expectations, 121, 230, 231
    fixed, 38, 39, 41, 72, 119, 121, 131, 254,
        271, 272, 276, 287, 303
    flexible (floating), 38, 43, 48, 54, 103,
        119–22, 131, 190, 210, 254, 265, 270,
        271, 275, 287, 303
    intervention, 114, 162, 179, 182, 197,
        205, 207, 210, 211
    Keynesian models, 120, 201–2
    monetarist models, 198–201, 236
    nominal vs real, 198, 199, 202, 205,
        207–8, 210, 223, 228, 238, 274
    overshooting, 116, 121–2, 208
    policy, 14, 207–16
    standard, 25, 26, 37
exogenous money, 72, 103–10
expected inflation, 56, 132
external price stabilization, 4, 127, 184,
    199, 268, 295–7

Federal Reserve system, 159, 178, 297
fiat money, 2, 6, 22, 23, 24, 25, 26, 32, 33,
    38, 39, 45, 183, 259, 300–1, 302
fiduciary money, *see* fiat money
financial innovations, 6, 190, 239–69, 299
    effect on demand for money, 101, 185
    role of technology, 1, 11, 239, 253, 299
    sources of, 239–40

financial innovations–*contd.*
under gold standard, 8, 33, 259
see also integration of markets; off-
the-balance-sheet activities
financial market (sector, system)
competition in, 101–2, 190, 240, 260
Financial Services Act 1986, 10, 21
fiscal policy, 159–63
internal–external balance, 41–3, 267
relationship to monetary policy, 18, 42,
54, 159–60, 167, 214, 221
transmission mechanism, 113, 220
flow of funds
balance of payments, 264, 265
money supply determination, 156
fractional reserve banking, 32, 139, 155
France, 39, 45, 154, 223, 228, 230, 231,
232, 234, 292
free banking, 183, 301–2
funding policies, 159–63, 184–5
see also overfunding

G-7 Summit, 52, 213
GDP target for monetary policy, 127–8,
133, 134, 212, 213
German Economic and Monetary Union
(GEMU), 234, 289, 291, 293
German inflation, 4, 45, 223, 227, 228
German monetary policy, 205, 281–2
Germany, 56, 228, 230, 231, 256, 258, 265,
276, 281
gilt(s), *see* gilt-edged securities
gilt-edged securities, 166, 176, 184, 195
auction sales, 187–8
gold reserves, 32, 33
gold standard, 26, 27–38, 270, 271, 295,
298, 299
convertibility, 28
ending of, 44
exchange rates under, 34, 35, 36, 37, 39
gold bullion system, 25
gold exchange system, 25, 272
gold points, 34, 35, 36, 40
gold specie system, 25
interest rate policy, 36–9
limping gold standard, 25, 28
mint parity, 2, 28, 34
price stability, 29, 30
resource costs, 32
'Goodhart's Law', 116, 269
goods standard, 25, 26, 50, 295
'Gresham's Law', 29, 302

hard ECU, 235, 281, 283, 293–5
hedging of risks, 23, 252, 253, 261, 263,
285
high-powered money, 82, 139, 155
see also monetary base

HMT econometric model, 117, 191–3, 238
hysteresis in labour markets, 69, 70, 275

income velocity, 83, 85, 99, 128
incomes policy, 16, 26, 55, 58, 76, 221
indicators of monetary policy, 114–16,
127, 170
inflation, 3, 51–77
costs of, 56–7
desirable goal, 56–8, 296–7
effect on money demand, 86, 102
era of inflation first, 51–8
expected (expectations of), 56, 75, 83,
107, 132
export and import prices, 58, 60, 63, 64,
208
indirect taxes, 62, 77
monetary influences, 47, 72–6
oil price rises, 51, 119, 131, 210, 233,
234
under alternative systems, 270–6, 295–
7, 300–1
wage-price controls, 58, 60, 62–6
wages and price effects, 58–72, 278–9
see also unemployment–inflation
relationship; Phillips curve
information costs
bank intermediation, 141, 142, 249
demand for money, 81, 302
innovations, *see* financial innovations
instruments of monetary policy, 1, 54,
112, 125, 126, 190, 194, 197
'insular economy' modelling, *see*
transmission mechanism of monetary
policy
integration of markets, 241–7, 263, 265,
274
see also currency substitution
interbank market, 8, 147, 245, 250, 252
interbank rates
relation to Bank of England dealing
rate, 180, 181
interbank settlements, 176–7
interest bearing eligible liabilities
(IBELs), 152–3
interest rates
and borrowing (bank lending), 117,
152, 160, 163, 261–2
and supply of money, 15, 106, 123–7
as an intermediate target, 128, 132–3
as an operational target, *see* operation
targets of monetary policy
ceilings, 13, 262
determination, Bank of England, 1, 18,
20, 174–84, 188–9, 263, 266
effect on demand for money, 90–6, 188,
261

long term, 180, 182, 184–8, 189, 190, 193
monetary policy effects on, 105–10, 116–26, 173–94, 258–63
nominal, 30, 86, 122, 133, 163, 188–9
on money (own rate of interest), 83, 86, 98, 101, 259
parity, 230, 246, 278
real, 30, 86, 133, 163, 188–9, 190
short term, 178–82, 188, 190, 191, 194
structure of, 142, 146, 181–2
intermediate targets of monetary policy, 113, 115, 127–33, 170
exchange rate versus monetary targets, 128, 202–7, 210–1, 214
money supply versus interest rates, 128, 189
intermediate variables of monetary policy, 112–15, 125, 126
intermediation, 138–48, 245–7, 249–53, 299–300
internal–external balance, 41–3, 263, 266, 267
internal price stabilization, 4, 127, 184, 268, 275, 295–7
international banking, 8, 241–8
international financial *laissez-faire*, 46, 49, 265, 275, 300, 302
international gold standard, 28, 38
International Monetary Fund (IMF), *see* Bretton Woods international monetary system
international monetary 'non-system', 45–50, 272, 300
intervention, *see* exchange rates; Exchange Rate Mechanism (ERM)
investment, 117, 189, 190, 264, 265, 266, 289
IS, 114, 116, 195, 261, 262
Italy, 110, 154, 216, 223, 228, 230, 231, 232, 234, 292

Japan, 4, 45, 56, 110, 227, 256, 258, 265, 276, 303

Keynesian theory, 114, 201–2
balance of payments, 263, 266
demand for money, 79–81

Labour Government policies, 16, 17, 210, 211, 232
labour standard, 25, 26
law of one price, *see* purchasing power parity
Lawson Chancellorship, 55, 213–4, 231, 235
lender of last resort facilities, 166, 169, 174, 176, 178

liability management, by banks, 156, 165, 166
liquidity
creation, *see* credit creation
preference, *see* demand for money
trap, 57, 188–9
LM, 114, 116, 195, 260, 261
loan rates, *see* base rates
London Business School (LBS) econometric model, 191–3
Louvre agreement, 39, 213, 271, 276

market operations, *see* open market operations
maturity transformation, 33, 141, 143, 144–5, 153
Medium Term Financial Strategy (MTFS), 17, 18, 55, 56, 76, 135, 160, 211, 212, 213
merchant banks, 8
metallic standards, *see* gold standard
Minimum Lending Rate (MLR), *see* Bank rate
monetarism, UK policy, 55–6, 73–6, 131–2, 211–13, 232, 236
monetarist theory, 66, 73, 117, 258
see also Friedman, M. (author index); money multiplier approaches
monetary aggregates, 15, 76, 123, 124, 135–72, 184–8, 211–13, 255–8
monetary authorities, *see* Bank of England
monetary base (cash, central bank money), 115, 139, 159, 164–72, 183
M0 definition (wide monetary base), 137, 172, 263, 269
relation to money supply, 154–6, 158–9, 164–70
see also high-powered money; money multiplier approaches
monetary base control, 18, 140, 148, 163, 164–72, 263
monetary constitution, *see* monetary standard
Monetary Control, 153
monetary disequilibrium, 102–11, 124
monetary hegemony, 273, 276, 279, 282
monetary independence, *see* national monetary independence (autonomy)
monetary instruments, *see* instruments of monetary policy
monetary mechanism, 5–7
monetary objectives, *see* ultimate variables of policy
monetary operational targets, *see* operational targets of monetary policy

monetary policy, 1–21, 35–8, 41–3, 46–50, 52–6, 78, 96, 103–4, 174–84, 188–9, 202–16, 232–6, 255–8, 259–68, 270–303
  and direct controls, *see* direct controls
  German, *see* German monetary policy
  goals variables of, *see* ultimate variable of policy
  instruments, *see* instruments of monetary policy
  intermediate variables of, *see* intermediate variables of monetary policy
  reforms of 1981, 8, 164, 175
  under deregulation, 169–70, 182–4, 190, 258–63
  see also Bank of England; balance of payments; Competition and Credit Control; European Monetary System; European Monetary Union; gold standard; interest rates; monetary targets; transmission mechanism of monetary policy
monetary rules, *see* rules versus discretion
monetary standards, 3, 5, 23, 24, 76, 270–2, 295
monetary systems, 5, 23, 24, 45, 155, 270–6
monetary targets, 16, 18, 55, 73, 76, 128, 131, 132, 173, 211, 297
monetary theory, demand for money, 79–83
money
  as a buffer stock, 80–1, 102–11
  base, *see* monetary base
  broad measures, 268
    M2, 137
    M2, old definition, 91
    M3, 73, 76, 99, 124, 135, 185, 256
    M3c, 137, 172
    £M3, 18, 97, 101, 124, 135, 136, 137, 148, 153, 158, 159, 160, 164, 172, 211, 213, 268
    M4, 135, 137, 262
    M5, 135, 137, 262
  demand determined, 103–4
  high-powered, *see* high-powered money
  narrow measures,
    M0, 76, 127, 133, 134, 136, 137, 159, 171, 172, 213, 262, 263, 269
    M1, 76, 135, 136, 137, 159, 211
  purchasing power of, *see* purchasing power parity (PPP)
  quantity theory of, *see* quantity theory of money

money market, 174–88
  daily operations of Bank of England, 178–80
  institutional features, 176–8
money market operations, Bank of England, *see* money market
money multiplier approaches, 154–6, 167, 268
money supply determination, 102–8, 135–71, 184–8
money supply policy, 14
monometallism, 25, 29
moral suasion, 11, 20
mortgages, 181, 189, 261

National Institute of Economic and Social Research (NIESR) econometric model, 117, 191–3
national monetary independence (autonomy), 232, 235, 271, 272–5, 276, 286, 287–8, 289, 291, 294
natural rate
  of unemployment, 68, 70, 77
  of inflation, 56
Netherlands, 39, 56, 228, 231
new monetary economics, 32, 299
New Zealand, 53
non-bank institutions, 17, 140, 151, 169, 262
Nyborg–Basle Agreement, 218, 221

objectives of policy, *see* ultimate variables of policy
off-the-balance-sheet activities, 141, 250, 252, 268
open market operations, 36, 114, 125, 150, 151, 174–84
  see also Bank of England
operational deposits (ODs), 176, 177
  see also Bank of England
operational targets of monetary policy, 125–7, 188, 269
overdrafts, and monetary policy, 158–9, 163
overfunding, 181, 185–7

parallel markets, 12
payments habits, 79
Phillips curve, 41, 58, 60, 66, 69, 70, 71, 275, 279
Plaza agreement, 39, 271, 276
policy coordination, 206, 213, 231, 234, 238, 256–8, 269, 290, 292
pound sterling, 2, 27, 33, 39, 216, 218, 220, 277, 304
price stability, *see* inflation

private money, *see* competing currencies;
free banking
private sector liquidity measures, PSL1,
PSL2, 76, 135, 136, 213, 262
prudential supervision, *see* Bank of
England
public sector borrowing requirement
(PSBR), 18, 55, 135, 160, 184, 185,
188
public sector debt requirement (PSDR),
185, 188
purchasing power equity (PPP), 34–5, 47,
48, 63, 119, 121, 198–200, 202, 236

quantity theory of money, 47, 48, 82,
198–201
see also Friedman, M. (author index)

Radcliffe Committee, 296
rational expectations, 115–16, 130, 274
reintermediation
effect on money demand, 99–101, 260
reputation, *see* credibility
reserve assets ratio, 15, 17, 163, 173, 175
reserve base control, *see* monetary base
control
retail banking, 138–40, 143, 148, 152, 154,
250
rules versus discretion, 24, 129–31, 295,
297–8, 300–1

savings, personal, 122–3, 156–7, 189, 264–
6
securitization, 169, 240, 247–53, 262, 268
self-regulatory bodies, 10
'shock-absorber' models, 104–5
silver standard, 27–30
Single European Act, 223, 230–1, 235
single European currency, 27, 231, 283
'Snake', *see* European currency 'Snake',
South Africa, 32, 43
sovereignty, *see* national monetary
independence (autonomy)
Soviet Union, 43, 243
Spain, 216, 218, 220, 231, 277
Special Deposits scheme, 12, 14, 15, 16,
17, 151, 152, 194
sterling M3
relation to asset counterparts, 156–63,
167, 184
stock market
reform of, 12, 21
Supplementary Special Deposits system
('corset'), 16, 17, 18, 73, 150, 152,
163, 173, 194
supply of money, *see* money; money
supply determination

swaps
cross-currency and interest rate, 239,
248, 252, 253, 262
Switzerland, 4, 39, 56, 303
symmetallism, 25, 26, 32

tabular standard, 25, 26, 32, 299
'tax' effects of monetary policy, 16, 115,
150–2, 169, 171
technology, *see* financial innovations
Thatcher economic policies, 55, 58, 207,
214, 232
transactions costs, 141, 302
demand for money, 79
financial innovation, 239
transmission mechanism of monetary
policy, 5–7, 107, 112–34, 188–95,
198–207, 258–63
central bank views, 126–7
common funnel theory, 54
insular economy tradition, 119
open economy models, 120, 191, 193,
197, 198–202, 202–4, 256, 263–8
Tripartite Monetary Agreement of 1936,
39, 271

ultimate variables of policy, 53, 112, 113,
203
unemployment–inflation relationship, 55,
68, 69, 70, 71, 226–7, 296
see also Phillips curve
United States of America, 43, 110, 158,
159, 206, 228, 256, 258, 265, 276,
287, 295
United States dollar, 4, 38, 43, 45
Bretton Woods international monetary
system, 39, 43, 243, 271
gold backing, 2, 28, 34, 36, 38, 43–4, 276
present international role, 243, 280
United States monetary policy, 154–5,
158–9, 178

velocity, *see* income velocity

wages
relation to inflation, 66–72, 278–9
Walters critique, 277–8
wealth
demand for money, 85
Werner Committee Report, 283
wholesale banking, 8, 140–7, 148, 152,
153, 156, 171, 247, 250
wide monetary base, *see* monetary base,
M0 definition

yields, *see* interest rates

Author index

Aizenman, J., 128
Akerlof, G.A., 81
Aliber, R.Z., 246
Andersen, P.S., 109
Artis, M.J., 72, 77, 90, 92, 97, 101, 109,
  117, 118, 128, 133, 189, 190, 204, 238,
  258, 266, 269
Atkinson, A.B., 77
Atkinson, P., 102

Bagehot, W., 36
Bain, A.D., 187
Ball, R.J., 62, 210
Bank of England, 1, 15, 21, 100, 135, 137,
  149, 173, 175, 179, 187, 194, 195, 220,
  237, 268, 303
Barro, R.J., 129–30, 226
Batts, J., 91
Baumol, W.J., 79
Bayoumi, T., 36, 266, 269
Bean, C., 134, 170
Beckerman, W., 52, 77
Bennett, A., 97, 101
Bentley, B., 109
Bird, G., 303
Bishop, S.L., 73
Blanchard, O.J., 133
Bofinger, P., 303
Bordo, M.D., 256
Boughton, J.M., 95
Brainard, W.C., 103
Breedon, F.J., 303
Brittain, B., 256
Brown, R.N., 63, 64
Brunner, K., 155

Buchanan, J.M., 50, 298, 304
Buiter, W., 122, 238
Burns, T., 210
Burstein, M.L., 50

Capie, F., 155
Carr, J., 105
Chatterji, M., 303
Chessen, J., 268
Choudhuri, E., 256
Chouraqui, J.C., 102
Chow, G.C., 87
Cipolla, C.M., 304
Clower, R.W., 80
Cobham, D., 119
Coe, D.T., 52, 69
Coglan, R.T., 95, 109
Commonwealth Study Group, 303
Cooper, R.N., 50, 263
Cordon, W.M., 46
Courakis, A.S., 171
Coutts, K., 63
Crockett, A., 88, 97, 269
Cross Report, 246
Cuddington, J., 256
Currie, D.A., 116, 128, 204
Cuthbertson, K.C., 85, 88, 89, 90, 105,
  108, 111

Darby, M.R., 105
David, P., 304
Davidson, J., 106, 109
Davis, E.P., 268
Davis, K.T., 26, 106, 139, 144, 145, 171,
  195, 242, 246, 247, 268, 269

Deane, P., 3
Delors Report, 235, 283, 287, 291–3, 294
Dicks, M.J., 190
Dornbusch, R., 121, 238, 256
Dow, J.C.R., 90, 132, 136, 182
Dowd, K., 296, 299, 304
Dowling, M.J., 91
Driffill, J., 77
Duck, N.W., 167
Durand, M., 52

Easton, W.W., 191, 192, 193, 196
Edgeworth, F.Y., 32
Eichengreen, B., 35, 50, 304
Eltis, W.A., 269, 285
Engle, R.F., 89
Enoch, C.A., 63, 64
Ericsson, N.R., 84, 90, 93
Eshag, E., 79
Evans, T., 238

Fama, E.F., 262, 304
Feige, E., 87
Fetter, F.W., 29
Fforde, J.S., 132
Fischer, S., 27
Fisher, D., 103
Fisher, I., 32, 37, 79, 133
Fitzgibbon, A., 269
Flannery, M.J., 268
Flemming, J.S., 114
Frankel, J.A. 133
Frenkel, J.A., 128, 263, 303
Friedman, B.M., 170
Friedman, D., 298, 304
Friedman, M., 2, 6, 7, 22, 23, 48, 51, 55,
    79, 82, 83, 84, 86, 93, 102, 118,
    119–20, 129, 167, 168–9, 170, 245, 246
Froot, K., 133

Gagliardi, F., 69
Gaitskell, H., 296–7
Gallarotti, G.M., 50
Gardener, E.P.M., 249
Giavazzi, F., 238
Giddy, I.H., 304
Giovannini, A., 303
Godley, W., 63
Goldfeld, S.M., 87, 88
Goldstein, M., 269, 303
Goodhart, C.A.E., 21, 45, 88, 97, 105,
    116, 166, 172, 304
Gordon, D.F., 129–30, 226
Gowland, D., 118
Granger, C.J.W., 89
Grauwe, P. De, 282
Graves, P.E., 91

Green, C., 103
Greenfield, R.L., 304
Gregory, T.E., 22, 23
Grice, J., 97, 101
Griffiths, B., 153, 188
Gurley, J.G., 262

Hacche, G.J., 97, 101
Hahn, F.H., 56
Hall, R.E., 304
Hall, S.G., 90, 101
Hamburger, M.J., 87
Harrod, R., 27, 32, 36, 50
Hawtrey, Sir R., 29, 36
Hayek, F.A., 270, 301, 303
Heller, H.R., 87
Hendry, D.F., 84, 88, 89, 90, 93, 97
Hendry, S.G.B., 90, 101
Hewson, J., 146
Hicks, J.R., 26, 29, 34, 50, 56–7, 259
HM Treasury, 191, 193, 196, 238
Holly, S., 93
Holtham, G., 238
Hopkins, S.V., 3
House of Commons, 234
House of Lords, 232–4
Houthakker, H.S., 41, 43–4
Hughes-Hallet, A., 238
Hume, D., 35
Hutson, G.J., 238

Ireland, J., 109

Jackson, P., 160
Jaffee, D.M., 268
James, C., 268
Jenkinson, T., 52, 77
Johnson, H.G., 41, 48
Johnston, R.B., 246
Jonson, P.D., 109, 126

Kareken, J.H., 304
Kavanagh, M.J., 90
Keeler, T.E., 12
Kenen, P.B., 225, 238, 243
Kent, R.J., 45, 102
Kenway, P., 117
Keynes, J.M., 27, 36–7, 50, 57, 79, 82,
    114, 272
Kindleberger, C.P., 302
Klein, B.J., 102
Klein, L.R., 62
Kneeshaw, J.T., 175, 180
Knoester, A., 105
Koeune, J.C., 238
Kruse, D.C., 238
Kydland, F.E., 129

Laffer, A., 303
Laidler, D.E.W., 87, 90, 105, 109, 110
Laskar, D., 238
Latter, A.R., 268
Laury, J.S.E., 210
Levich, R.M., 133
Lewis, M.K., 26, 50, 90, 92, 97, 101, 106,
    109, 133, 139, 144, 145, 171, 189, 195,
    242, 246, 247, 248, 249, 251, 268, 269,
    304
Lindbeck, A., 132
Llewellyn, D.T., 21, 140, 175, 176
Longbottom, A., 93
Lucas, R.E., 115–16, 274

MacDonald, R., 237
Macmillan Report, 174
Markowitz, H., 82
Marshall, A., 32, 50
Mason, W.E., 45, 50, 304
Mayer, T., 238
McCulloch, J.H., 304
McKinnon, R.I., 46, 119, 120, 126, 200,
    255, 256, 258, 269, 303
McMahon, Sir K. (C.W.), 21, 45, 46
Meade, J.E., 41, 48, 134, 303
Melville, Sir L., 49–50
Melvin, M., 256
Milbourne, D., 81
Miles, A.A., 256
Mill, J.S., 24, 26
Miller, M.H., 72, 80, 122, 168, 238
Minford, P., 69
Mitchell, B.R., 3
Mizon, G., 77, 84, 88, 89
Moore, B.J., 160
Mortimer-Lee, P.D., 63, 64
Moses, E.R., 109
Mundell, R.A., 42, 49, 54, 117, 123, 274,
    289, 303
Murfin, A.J., 303

National Board for Prices and Incomes, 15
National Institute of Economic and Social
    Research, 117, 191, 193, 196, 208
Neild, R.R., 62–3
Nickell, S., 66
Niehans, J., 27, 77, 80, 146, 241
Nobay, A.R., 118
Nordhaus, W.D., 63

Ohr, R., 303
Okun, A.M., 181–2
Orr, D., 80
Ostry, S., 77

Pagano, M., 238

Paish, F.W., 90
Parkin, J.M., 66, 87, 133
Patinkin, D., 22, 79, 132, 183
Patterson, K.D., 90
Pavel, C., 268
Peltzman, S., 21
Pepper, G., 153, 164
Phelps-Brown, E.H., 3
Phillis, D., 268
Pöhl, K.O., 282
Polasek, M., 50, 248, 269
Poole, W., 128, 204
Posner, M., 238
Posner, R.A., 21
Prescott, E.C., 129
Price, L.D.D., 94

Radaelli, G., 77
Razin, A., 263
Redish, A., 28
Revell, J.R.S., 141, 171
Richardson, P., 115
Robertson, D.H., 3, 34–5, 50, 140
Robinson, J., 76
Rodrick-Bali, G., 155
Rogoff, K., 296
Rowlatt, P., 62

Sachs, J., 263
Salin, P., 304
Salop, J., 269
Sandler, T., 21
Savage, D., 117
Saville, J.D., 132, 136, 182
Sawyer, M., 66
Sayers, R.S., 7–8, 174, 175, 194, 195
Schwartz, A.J., 82, 84, 93, 118
Shaw, E.S., 262
Sheppard, D.K., 9, 167
Smith, G.W., 63
Smith, P.R., 111
Smith, R.G., 116
Spaventa, L., 282
Spitaller, E., 269
Stein, J.R., 62
Steindl, F.G., 86
Stiehler, U., 52
Stiglitz, J.E., 269
Sumner, M.T., 66, 68
Swan, T.W., 41, 42
Swann, D., 238

Taylor, M.P., 85, 89, 97, 101, 105, 108,
    237, 238, 246
Tew, B., 175, 184, 195
Thore, S., 246
Thornton, D.L., 97

Threadgold, A.R., 160
Tinbergen, J., 41, 53, 62, 214, 263
Tobin, J., 54, 55, 79, 82, 103, 118, 121, 262
Topping, S.L., 73
Toynbee, A.J., 27
Triffin, R., 43, 52
Tschirhart, J.T., 21

Ulph, A., 77
Ungerer, H.O., 238

van den Bergh, P., 175, 180
Vaubel, R., 205, 304
Vines, D., 266, 269

Wallace, N., 47
Wallich, H.C., 271

Wallis, K.F., 191, 196
Walters, A.A., 90, 277, 278
Ward, R., 66
Watson, M.W., 133
Weale, M., 103
Weiss, A., 269
Wilcox, O., 90, 101
Williams, D., 118
Williamson, J., 45, 46, 50, 237
Wilson, J.S.G., 176
Wren-Lewis, S., 69, 73, 191, 193, 196
Wright, S.H., 303
Wymer, C.R., 109

Yeager, L.B., 304
Young, P., 238
Ypersele, J. van, 238